# C++ Programming

## for the absolute beginner

# C++ Programming

## for the absolute beginner

Premier Press

DIRK HENKEMANS
AND MARK LEE

**Important**: Premier Press cannot provide software support. Please contact the appropriate software manufacturer's technical support line or Web site for assistance.

Premier Press and the author have attempted throughout this book to distinguish proprietary trademarks from descriptive terms by following the capitalization style used by the manufacturer.

Information contained in this book has been obtained by Premier Press from sources believed to be reliable. However, because of the possibility of human or mechanical error by our sources, Premier Press, or others, the Publisher does not guarantee the accuracy, adequacy, or completeness of any information and is not responsible for any errors or omissions or the results obtained from use of such information. Readers should be particularly aware of the fact that the Internet is an ever-changing entity. Some facts may have changed since this book went to press.

ISBN: 1-931841-43-8

Library of Congress Catalog Card Number: 2001091131

Printed in the United States of America

01 02 03 04 BB 10 9 8 7 6 5 4 3 2 1

**Publisher:**
Stacy L. Hiquet

**Associate Marketing Manager:**
Heather Buzzingham

**Managing Editor:**
Sandy Doell

**Series Editor:**
Andy Harris

**Acquisitions Editor:**
Melody Layne

**Developmental Editor and Technical Reviewer:**
Greg Perry

**Project Editor and Copy Editor:**
Melba Hopper

**Interior Layout:**
Shawn Morningstar

**Cover Design:**
Mike Tanamachi

**CD-ROM Producer:**
Arlie Hartman

**Indexer:**
Johnna VanHoose Dinse

**Proofreader:**
Jeannie Smith

**To all the children of the twenty-first century—if you can dream it, you can make it happen.**

# Foreword

The video game industry is unique in that it regularly incorporates every major discipline of computer science. From 3D graphics and artificial intelligence to operating system theory and database design, if you are designing a commercial video game, you will eventually run into problems from each of these fields. Some of these fields mean working with specialized languages, but ultimately the two languages that are as common to the game industry as crunch time, caffeinated beverages, and pizza are C and C++. Despite a few commercial games written in Java (which is very similar to C++), almost every game that you play is written in either C or C++. It doesn't matter whether the game runs on a PC, a game console, or even an arcade machine, chances are that C or C++ routines are at its heart. Even in cases when performance dictates that a routine needs to be written in assembly language to squeeze out more speed, it is common practice to first write the routine in C or C++.

During my years in the industry, I have interviewed over one hundred applicants for programming positions and have read resumes from thousands more. Through all of this, I continually look for three things in a strong candidate. The first is strong problem-solving skills. With constantly changing technologies and fierce competition, game programming is always throwing new problems at us. Consequently, excellent problem-solving skills are not only a luxury, but they are also a requirement. Second, a good candidate has been exposed to the entire spectrum of computer science disciplines. Even when programmers have specialized in one area, the solution to a problem often lies in a field outside their area of expertise. Finally, I look for strong C/C++ skills. C/C++ skills are to a game programmer what paint and brushes are to a painter. They are the tools of the trade and, as such, they need to be finely honed.

Although C++ is widely used as a teaching language, this wasn't always the case. I can still recall my first exposure to C programming. Until that time, all of my programming had been in Basic (my first video game was written in it), Pascal, and Fortran. I had heard of C; according to rumor, it was going to be the language to know. I was looking forward to my next computer science course: "Introduction to Programming Languages." I assumed that the course would teach me how to program in C. I was wrong. The only reference to C in the entire course was,

"Here is your assignment. Write it in C. Hand it in on Wednesday." "Okay," I thought. "At least one of the course textbooks is about C." As it turned out, that textbook was about accessing UNIX operating system information from the C language. That was useful if I was interested in accessing process IDs or using shell commands, but not a great help if I wanted to know how to read a file or write a function.

Somehow I managed to struggle through the assignment and to actually learn something while I did it. It wasn't the best way to learn a new language, but it was better than my first exposure to C++. That was during my first job after graduation. I was working for the university's athletic department writing software for various research projects. One of the projects that I inherited from the previous programmer was only half complete and was written in C++. Once again, I had before me a sink-or-swim proposition. This time, I had access to a function reference that explained only the syntax of the language, not how to use it. I would have killed for the book that you are currently holding in your hands. Well, maybe not killed, but I certainly can't overestimate the importance of learning C++ in such an organized and straightforward manner. As you read this book, please have some sympathy for those of us who didn't have the fine learning tool you have.

**Scott Greig**
Director of Programming
BioWare Corp.

# Acknowledgments

Many fine people are involved in the process of publishing a book, and this book is no exception. Although it is difficult for us to really understand the amount of time and effort that everyone put into this book, we do know that it was considerable.

First and foremost, we thank our parents for putting up with us and for the support they have always given us.

Next, we thank Premier Press, our publisher, for making this book possible. We especially thank Melody Layne, our acquisitions editor, for believing in and supporting our concept. Melody is fully aware that this book is one that we have always wanted to find on a shelf.

We express deep gratitude to Greg Perry, the developmental editor and technical reviewer. Thanks for your excellent feedback, Greg, and for helping to ensure that the code in this book all works exactly as it should.

Melba Hopper, our project editor and copy editor, deserves a whole page of credit. Her hand touched, tweaked, or improved every line in this book. Melba, you put up with us exceptionally well, told us when our manuscript wasn't quite right, and gave us the information and encouragement we needed to move on. Most of all, you made the writing process fun. Thanks!

We extend a special thank-you to everyone else who played a role in preparing this book for publication, including Andy Harris, the *Absolute Beginner* series editor; Arlie Hartman, the CD producer; Shawn Morningstar, the layout artist; the artists at Argosy who turned our art into something legible; Jeannie Smith, the proofreader; and Johnna VanHoose Dinse, the indexer. All of you played a big role in making this book what it is.

We give praise to Scott Greig, the lead programmer at BioWare Corp. and the author of this book's Foreword. Scott, you are our idol. Without you, who could we aspire to be?

Finally, we extend special thanks to Nolan Bard for helping us—at 4:00 a.m.—meet a submission deadline and to Jackie Nagy for his encouragement and for not walking out on Dirk while writing.

# About the Authors

**Dirk Henkemans** has written amateur game development tutorials and has been a contributing writer to the Web site EastCoastGames.com. He is co-founder of FireStorm Studios, an expanding multimedia development company.

**Mark Lee** has been a computer consultant and a co-system operator for a text user network. He is co-founder of FireStorm Studios. He is fluent in the use of C, C++, Java, Visual Basic, assembly language, and database systems.

# Contents at a Glance

# Contents

## CHAPTER 7 Building Namespaces 177



## CHAPTER 8 Introducing Inheritance 193

## CHAPTER 9 Using Templates 227



## CHAPTER 10 Using Streams and Files 269

## CHAPTER 11 Errors and Exception Handling 291

## CHAPTER 12 Programming with Windows 307

## CHAPTER 13 Using DirectX 343

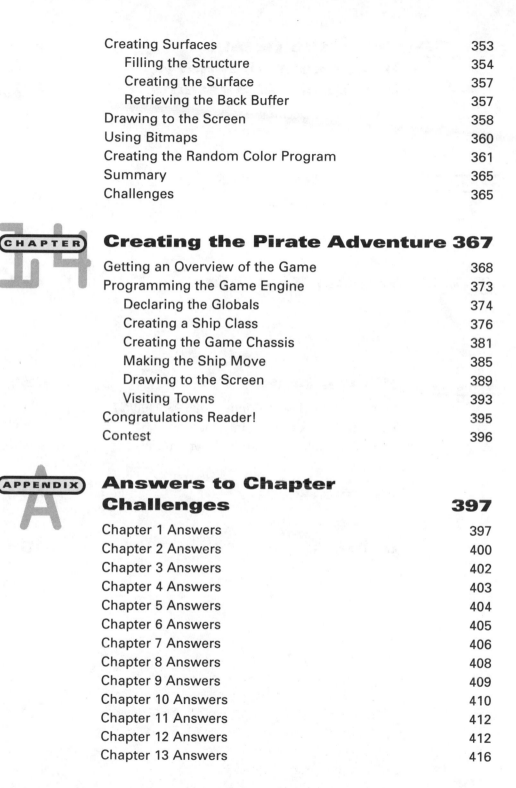

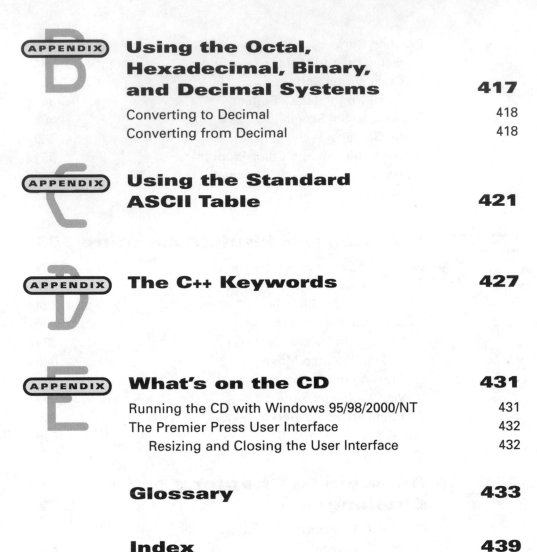

# Introduction

C++ is the most widely used programming language around and is an industry standard for programming applications of all kinds. In addition, C++ is a highly efficient programming language that can conserve resources more effectively than languages such as Visual Basic or Delphi. In fact, because of its functionality and style, in many ways, C++ is the only non–Web-based programming language that you might ever need to know.

We chose to teach you C++ through game programming because initially many people experience computers through playing computer games. More important, computer games are a wonderful way to learn how to program because they teach you how to display an interface on a monitor, how to receive commands from the user, and how to manipulate information. Ultimately, games are a blend of art and science that taps into logical and creative minds, providing stimulating visual, audio, and mental experiences for programmers and users.

Over the course of this book, you will discover many innate programming techniques that apply not only to C++, but also to programming in general. These common programming techniques will make it easier for you to learn how to program in other languages and create applications other than game applications.

## What's in This Book

The book moves from simple text-based programs to more complicated games with actual graphics. If you are an absolute beginner at programming, we suggest that you go through the chapters in their natural order. On the other hand, if you already have some experience in programming, you might want to gloss over the first six chapters, which cover the basics, and jump ahead to more advanced topics.

The book is conceptually, though not physically, organized into four sections. First, Chapter 1, "Starting the Journey," through Chapter 6, "Advanced Data Types," give you the basic knowledge you need to program in C++. Because of the sequence of the topics in these chapters, we suggest going through them in order. For example, you will probably need to work through Chapter 4, "Writing Functions," before turning to Chapter 5, "Fighting with OOP."

The second section of the book (Chapter 7, "Building Namespaces," through Chapter 11, "Errors and Exception Handling") consists of the advanced C++ topics. You can cover these chapters in any order and fully comprehend them.

The third section consists of Chapter 12 through Chapter 14. Here you put together everything you learn in the earlier chapters and apply it to programming, first with Windows (Chapter 12, "Programming with Windows"), then with DirectX (Chapter 13, "Using DirectX"), and finally by developing a rocking pirate game using industry standard techniques (Chapter 14, "Creating the Pirate Adventure").

The fourth section includes appendixes with extra information that you will find helpful, beginning with Appendix A, "Answers to Chapter Challenges," and ending with Appendix E, "What's on the CD."

However you read the book, remember that a big part of learning to program with C++ is hands-on experience. The more you program, the better you will become at problem-solving (an important skill in programming, as you will discover) and detecting errors in your code. Who knows, if you program enough, you might even be able to calculate pi to a million digits . . . in your head (though doing so is not guaranteed by the authors of this book)!

Throughout the chapters, you will find small bits of code that illustrate concepts we present. At the end of each chapter, you will find a complete game that demonstrates the key ideas in the chapter, a summary of the chapter, and a set of challenges that tests your newfound knowledge. We hope that you will try the games and challenges because they will really help you develop the feeling of programming. The solutions to the challenges are in Appendix A, and copies of the complete chapter programs are included on this book's CD-ROM. However, we strongly encourage you to try the challenges before looking at the solutions (even if you need help). They are all fairly short, so you can type them into your compiler (which is, again, a good way to gain experience).

## What You Need to Get Started

Learning to program is an excellent way to take advantage of the power of your computer. However, before you can begin programming, you need to have the following on hand:

- A PC with a 75 MHz or faster processor.
- A DirectX-compatible operating system, such as Microsoft Windows 95 or 98, Windows ME or XP, or Windows 2000.
- At least 16MB of RAM.

- At least 125MB hard drive space.
- A compiler such as CodeWarrior by MetroWerks.
- A CD-ROM drive.
- Knowledge, time, and patience. The information in this book will give you enough knowledge to effectively utilize both C++ and CodeWarrior, or most other compilers.

## Special Features in This Book

Along with the complete games and challenges at the end of the chapters, here are some other special features in this book:

**Hints. Provide a little extra information on hard topics.**

**Traps. Alert you to pitfalls to avoid.**

**Tricks. Flag tips that will make programming easier and more efficient.**

**IN THE REAL WORLD**

**These sidebars relate programming stories and information straight from the programming "front."**

# Starting the Journey

The idea of programming might sound like a daunting task, but don't worry. We designed this chapter so that you can get your feet wet without having to delve into the deeper complexities of programming. The chapter begins with a discussion on *CodeWarrior*, a C++ compiler. The chapter continues with the basics on creating a program. Then you get to play with some strings and numbers. With our help and your ingenuity, you will soon be creating your own programs. Later, we're sure that your programs will become increasingly complex, but everyone must start the journey someplace. Here and now, *your* adventure begins!

The outset of your adventure includes the following:

- How to use CodeWarrior
- How to write code
- How to write your first program
- How the programming development cycle works
- How to use text
- How to use numbers

## Using CodeWarrior

In this section, you find out how to use CodeWarrior to create a program from generated source code. *Source code* is text that represents a specific set of instructions that a computer must follow. Source code is not written in English. It is written in a programming language. Although you can use many different programming languages, in this book, we teach you how to use C++. Later in this chapter, you learn how to create programs by writing your own source code (actually, by editing the code that CodeWarrior provides).

CodeWarrior makes creating a program easy work because it uses an *Integrated Development Environment* (IDE). IDE enables you to use a common graphical interface for your compiler, file browser, settings, and *source code editor* (the window in which you edit and view source code). For example, when we started programming, we used a free C++ compiler that required us to enter all the settings for a program at the DOS prompt. Doing so was time consuming. The IDE takes care of all your project and file settings, which makes programming faster and easier.

**We wrote this book based on the assumption that you are using CodeWarrior Professional 5.0 (by Metrowerks). However, it isn't a big deal if you are not. Most of the information in this chapter and the other chapters will apply regardless of the compiler that you are using.**

It's time to start your quest into the world of programming. As we explain how to create a project with CodeWarrior and present the code, try the information on your computer. Practice makes the unfamiliar seem natural.

### Creating a New Project

The first time you open CodeWarrior, it will appear as shown in Figure 1.1. As you can see, nothing magic is going on (well, maybe just a little). CodeWarrior is simply an application, as are Microsoft Word and Netscape Navigator, except CodeWarrior is an application that you use to create other applications.

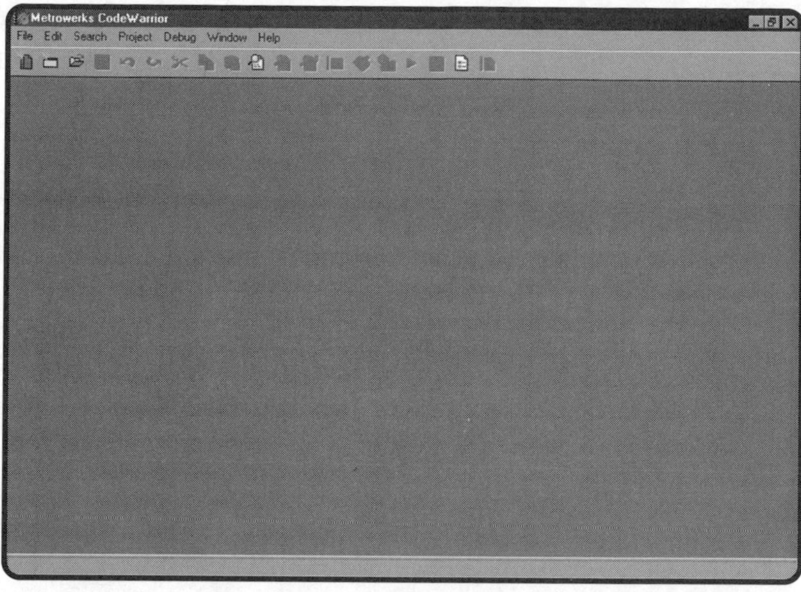


**FIGURE 1.1**

This is what CodeWarrior looks like the first time you open it.

To create a new C++ project, with CodeWarrior running, follow these steps (note that the names of menus, dialog boxes, and other options might be different on your compiler):

1. Go to the CodeWarrior main menu bar and click the File menu.
2. From the drop-down menu that appears, click New. The New dialog box opens (see Figure 1.2). From this dialog box, you can create almost any type of application.
3. Under the Project tab (already selected in Figure 1.2), choose Win32 C/C++ Application Stationery.

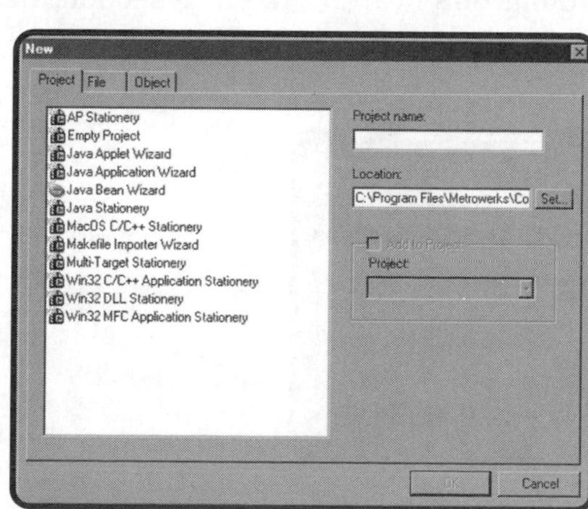


**FIGURE 1.2**

Use the New dialog box to select the kind of project you want to create.

4. In the Project name text box, type **Hello** as the name of your project.
5. Click OK. The New Project dialog box appears (see Figure 1.3).

   The New Project dialog box enables you to select the type of *run-time environment* in which the program will run. The run-time environment consists of the conditions in which the program will execute. Most often these conditions include only the operating system for which you will be compiling. For example, DOS-based programs operate in a DOS environment, whereas Win32 programs require a 32-bit Windows environment. The compiler will optimize the program for a particular environment. The end result is that your file sizes will be smaller and your programs will run faster. C++ Console applications are Windows applications that open a window similar to DOS prompts that are used to display text. They use a version of the DOS environment.
6. Select C++ Console App from the list in the New Project dialog box and click OK.

   After CodeWarrior finishes creating the settings you requested for your project, a new window opens. This window bears the name of your project, hello.mcp. The extension .mcp is CodeWarrior's project file extension. A project file stores all the settings for your project. It also contains a list of all the source files that are part of your project. A *source file* is like a text file, except that it stores source code. A source file has a .cpp extension.
7. Click the + icon beside the folder to open the folder. The folder icon opens revealing the project file, hello.cpp (.cpp is the extension for C ++ source files).
8. Double-click the file to open it. The window shown in Figure 1.4 appears on your screen.

You have made it to the dungeon's heart. In the next section, we explain all the cryptic text shown in Figure 1.4.

**FIGURE 1.3**

The New Project dialog box enables you to optimize your programs.

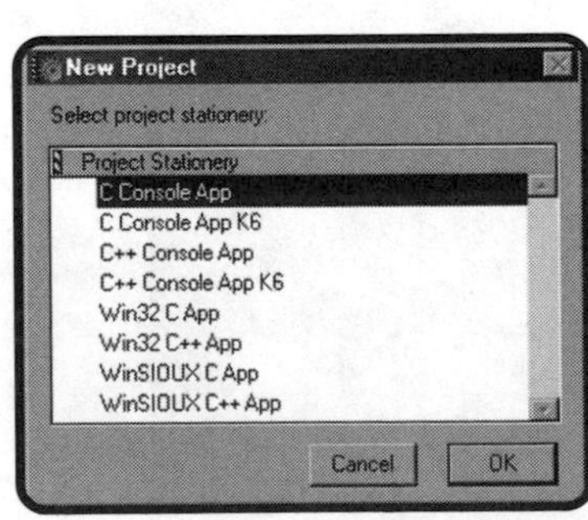

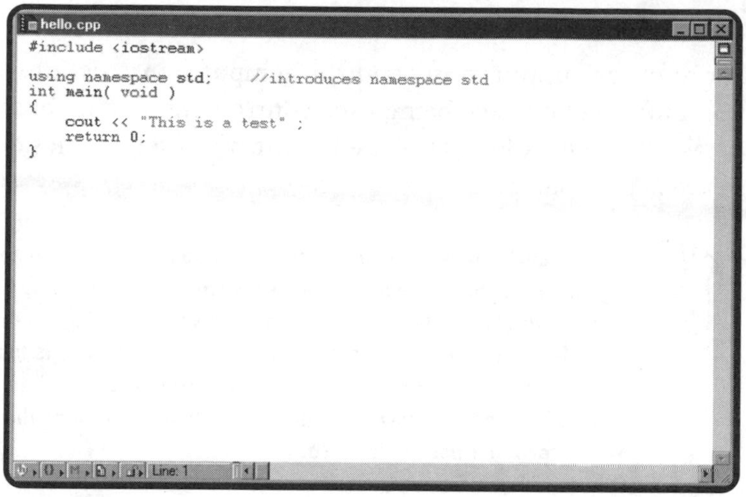

```
#include <iostream>

using namespace std;      //introduces namespace std
int main( void )
{
    cout << "This is a test" ;
    return 0;
}
```

**FIGURE 1.4**

You enter source code in this text editor.

### In the Real World

In early 1980, Bjarne Stroustrup, at AT&T Bell Laboratories, began developing the C++ language. C++ officially received its name at the end of 1983, a name that cleverly acknowledges its predecessor, C. In October 1985, the first commercial release of the language and the first edition of the book, *The C++ Programming Language*, by Bjarne Stroustrup, appeared.

In the 1980s, the C++ language was refined until it became a language with its own personality, which it managed to do practically without any loss of compatibility with C or loss of C's most important characteristics. C++ still maintains C's strong structured programming techniques, but adds the functionality of *object-oriented programming* (or OOP; see Chapter 5, "Fighting with OOP," for more on this topic). C++ owes its origin to other languages as well—BCPL, Simula67, Algol68, Ada, Clu, and ML have all contributed to the C++ language. Luckily, C++ incorporates the advantages of all these languages so that you don't need to learn all of them.

In 1990, an ANSI *(American National Standards Institute)* committee called *X3J16* began to develop a standard for C++. Up to the publication of the standard's final draft in November 1997, C++ went through a great expansion and now is the most widely used language in the development of applications.

## Defining Source Code

In order to program, you must send the computer instructions via source code. The programming language being used controls the syntax for the source code—in this case, the syntax for C++ is used. (*Syntax* is a set of rules determining how a language is put together.)

**Why can't you tell the computer what to do in English? Because English is a very complex language, and a computer would have a hard time figuring out what you are trying to say. C++ is like a simplified version of English that CodeWarrior can understand. In the next section, you learn that even C++ is too complex for a computer to understand directly. CodeWarrior must translate your C++ code into *machine code*. For now, though, you just focus on writing the source code and the specific rules for doing so.**

C++ is very specific about how you write things. For example, punctuation and order are important in C++. Even capitalization matters because C++ is *case sensitive,* which means the compiler can tell the difference between uppercase and lowercase letters (the compiler thinks that *K* is different from *k*).

To create a program, first you enter your source code into a source code editor. Then the compiler converts the source code into a language that your computer can read (machine code). The compiler and the source code editor are both integrated into the CodeWarrior IDE. The compiler is the more important part, so often IDEs and everything in them are called *compilers.*

Each line of code does something different, similar to each ingredient in a recipe. The compiler breaks these lines of code into instructions called *commands.* Each command is a single instruction to the computer.

A bit earlier, we wrote that CodeWarrior is an IDE and, as such, does a lot of work for you. The text that you see in the hello.cpp window is an example of that work. This text is generated code that will serve as the basis for any program you create. Think of the total program as a bridge that you're building; the generated lines of code are supports. Every bridge needs supports, but if the bridge relies only on supports, it is useless.

Take a look at this generated code; it displays `This is a test` onscreen:

```
#include <iostream>
using namespace std;       //introduces namespace std
int main( void )
{
      cout << "This is a test" ;
      return 0;
}
```

These lines are some of the valid instructions that you can send to the computer. You can edit and add to this code (or just erase and start from scratch) if you want to create your own program. However, assume for the moment that this code is a program that you wrote. In this case, you compile and run the generated code to create a working program.

### Compiling

Before you can run a program, you must convert the code that you write (C++) into language that a computer can read. This is where your compiler goes to work. Imagine that you are an elf, and the computer is a dwarf. In order for the computer to understand your instructions, you must overcome a language barrier. You need a translator that can speak both Dwarven and Elven. In the computer world, this translator is a *compiler*. As we mentioned earlier, a compiler turns your language into a language called *machine code* that your computer can read. However, this translation goes only one way. The compiler cannot translate machine code into source code.

Using CodeWarrior to compile, follow these steps:

1. On the main menu, click Project and select Compile from the drop-down menu. A window named Building Hello.mcp appears. (This step sometimes takes a few minutes. Just let the compiler finish its work.)

   When this window is active, it is converting the file into machine code and checking to make sure that you haven't broken any of the rules of the C++ language. If you altered the code that CodeWarrior gave you, an error screen might appear. If you did not change the code (or your changes are error-free), the compiler will close the Building Hello.mcp window when it finishes turning your program into machine code. The program is now ready to be run.
2. Select Run in the Project drop-down menu.

   Now a window appears showing the output of your program (see Figure 1.5). You should see `This is a test` onscreen.
3. Press any key to close the window.

## Writing Your First Program

Wait! Don't turn off that computer yet. It gets more exciting. Next, you write your first program: the HelloWorld application. It displays the message `HelloWorld` onscreen. This project will help you understand the C++ language and how it works. First, however, you need to know what CodeWarrior has already done for you.

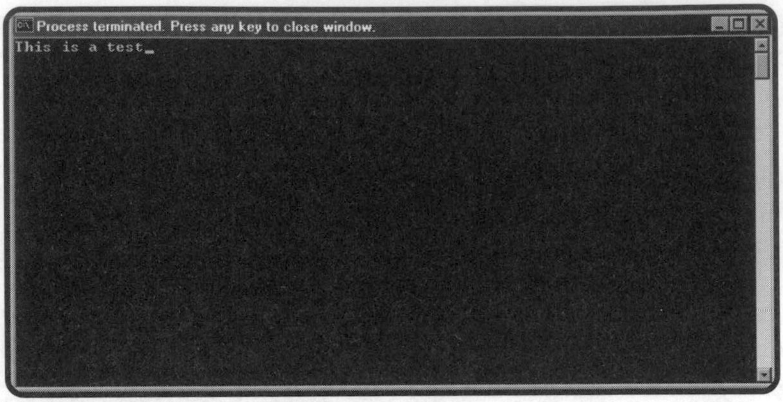

**FIGURE 1.5**

After you compile your program and run it, here is what you will see onscreen.

## Starting Out with the Default Program

When you create a new project, CodeWarrior writes some code for you. This is a basic framework within which you can program. You can delete all or part of it, depending on your needs, but most of the time, generated code helps get you started. This code is called the *default program*. It should look like the following code. Here, we guide you through it line by line:

```
#include <iostream>
using namespace std;      //introduces namespace std
int main( void )
{
      cout << "This is a test" ;
      return 0;
}
```

The first line tells the compiler that you will be using commands from the iostream library. iostream is an existing library that comes with CodeWarrior and all other C++ compilers. It is part of the standard C++ library. Before moving on, we need to explain a few other terms that we will be using:

- **Commands.** This is a generic word for lines of code entered into the source code editor that act as instructions for a computer. (These do not include comments.)
- **include directives.** These are lines of code that begin with `#include`. You use them to incorporate files you or others have created containing source code into your program. After `#include`, you place the name of the file surrounded by < and > (for the standard library files) or quotation marks (for every other file). Strangely enough, the standard library files have no file extension. That is why you include iostream rather than iostream.cpp.

However, most of the other files you include will have a file extension, and you must remember to include it. Normally, include directives are placed near the beginning of a file. (Don't worry too much about how include directives work. For now, all you have to know is that you use them to include other code in your program.)

- **Libraries.** Sets of existing code provided for your convenience as part of C++. (Different libraries are available with different compilers. You can find others by searching the Web. You can find a particularly good resource for free C++ libraries at http://www.cnet.com.) Libraries are a kind of compiled include file. For example, you might generate a random number using the random number generating function `rand` because it is in the cstdlib library (C Standard Library). You then have to put the line `#include <cstdlib>` at the beginning of the program. This opening statement tells the compiler which library you are using. Library files typically have a header file extension (.h file), except for the C++ standard library files, which have no extension.

You use the second line of the preceding code, `using namespace std`, to make the standard libraries work correctly. The details of how this line works and what it does are advanced topics. You learn more about this line in Chapter 7, "Building Namespaces."

The second part of the line `//introduces namespace std` is a *comment.* It has no influence on the way the program runs. Whenever you type two forward slashes (//) together, you are telling the compiler to ignore the rest of that line. The purpose of comments is to help make the code more understandable. Comments can be written in one of two ways. A single-line comment (like the preceding one) consumes only one line. Everything after the // on the line is ignored, as shown here:

```
// I am an army of one
```

Another form of the C++ comment enables you to spread a single but lengthy comment over as many lines as you want:

```
/* dragons rule the world */
```

or

```
/* dragons rule
   the world */
```

Although it is usually confusing, you can place the multiple-line comment into code at almost any point, as illustrated here:

```
using namespace /*introduces namespace std*/ std;
```

However, just because a possibility exists does not mean that you use it. Using comments like this can quickly make your code unreadable. A good rule of thumb is to use comments simply to make your code more understandable. If they aren't helping, take them out.

Again, nothing within a comment affects the code. Use comments only to explain complicated or large parts of the program in plain English. The compiler ignores the comments when it turns the program into machine code.

The next line, `int main( void )`, specifies the beginning of the `main` function. You put most of your code inside the `main` function. In Chapter 4, "Writing Functions," you learn how to put your code in other functions, but for now, almost every line you write will go inside the `main` function. The `main` function begins with `{` and ends with `}`. Within these brackets, you can place almost any line of code. Every program must have a `main` function (and only one).

The next line says that the code of the `main` function starts here with the open bracket (`{` ).

The next line displays the message `This is a test` on the screen. The word `cout` displays text on the screen. Because it is not built into the language but is part of the iostream library, you must include the iostream library in order to use it. We cover the `cout` statement in more detail in the section "Working with Text," later in this chapter. (*Statements* are single thoughts or commands–think of them as equivalent to sentences. They usually end with a semicolon.)

`return 0;` tells the computer that you don't want to do anything more in the `main` function and to exit the function.

The closing bracket (`}`) in the last line tells the compiler that there are no more lines of code within the `main` function. `return 0;` is an executable statement that exits the function, but the closing bracket is there to indicate that no more executable statements are in the function.

Note that all the semicolons *must* be included. Most statements must end with a semicolon. In Chapter 3, "Taking Command with Control Statements," you learn about statements that do not require semicolons, but until then, every statement you encounter must terminate with a semicolon. The exact rule is that every executable statement must end with a semicolon. You use the semicolon to indicate the end of a statement, rather than use the end of the line, which means that you can have more than one statement on a single line.

Now that you have overcome the first challenge, your quest should be looking even easier.

**IN THE REAL WORLD**

**Comments are useful, not only so that others can read your code, but also so that *you* can read your code.**

**Some time ago, we were re-creating an old Nintendo classic called "Iron Tank." Shortly into the project, we had more than 30 pages of code. Then we found it necessary to put the project aside for a while. When we started working on it again, we spent almost a week just trying to remember what all the code was supposed to do. If we had included adequate comments in the code, we might have figured out what the code did in less than one day!**

## Creating Hello World

You are now ready to create your very first program, which we suggest naming "Hello World" (although you could name it anything you want). This program will display the message `Hello World` onscreen. By creating this program, you will learn how to edit source code and become a bit more familiar with how the source code generated by CodeWarrior works. Begin by replacing

```
cout << "this is a test";
```

with

```
cout << "Hello World";
```

Now, when you compile and run the new program, you will see `Hello World` onscreen.

The finished code is shown here. (Note that we added a comment at the beginning of the program to provide the names of the program and the author. Although not necessary, doing so is a good idea.)

```
//1.1 - Hello World - Dirk Henkemans -Premier Press
#include <iostream>
using namespace std;      //introduces namespace std
int main( void )
{
    cout << "Hello World!!!" ;
    return 0;
}
```

Follow the same steps that you used to compile the code generated by CodeWarrior, or you can (with most compilers) just press F5 to compile and execute the program. The program displays the message `Hello World` onscreen.

## The Development Cycle

The *development cycle* describes the process that you must go through in order to create a program. You will eventually find that this process is straightforward and easy. The flowchart in Figure 1.6 illustrates this cycle.

Generally, to create a program, you follow these steps:

1. Type the code in the source code editor (CodeWarrior or some other editor). You did a little bit of this in the earlier section, "Writing Your First Program," and you will do a lot more by the time you finish this book.
2. Compile the code. If there are errors, you must go back to the code to fix them. For step-by-step information on compiling code using CodeWarrior, refer to the earlier section "Compiling."
3. Link the code. *Linking* the code is the process of checking to see whether the code works with all the files that you included in the program. If you get an error, you must return to Step 1 to fix the error. CodeWarrior does

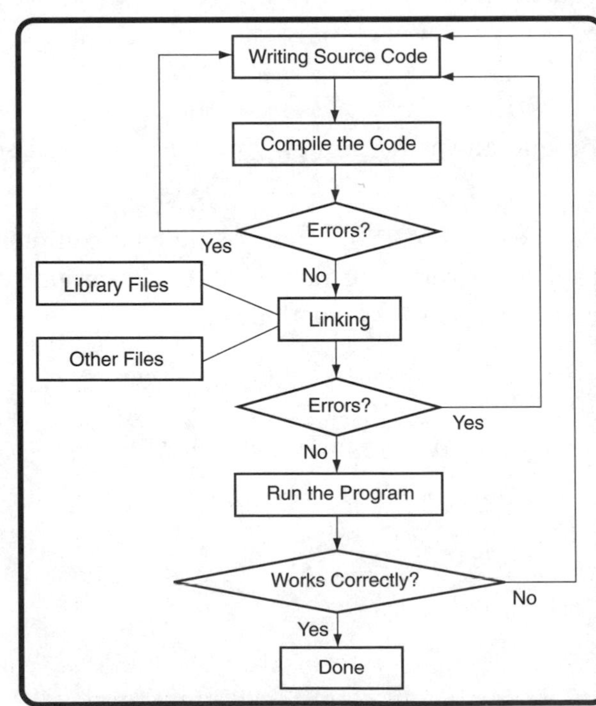


**FIGURE 1.6**

This chart shows the process for creating a working program.

this automatically for you. You don't even have to worry about the linking process unless you get an error.

4. Test the program. You test the program to be sure that it functions properly. In other words, you test it to be sure that that there are no semantic errors. *Semantic errors* are problems with the way your program works. Basically, a semantic error is when your program compiles and runs, but it doesn't do what it is supposed to do. For example, if you write a program to display the word `Hello` on screen but get the word `Good-bye` instead, you have a semantic error that must be fixed. However, the code will still compile with semantic errors.

   If your program makes it through all of these steps successfully, then the development cycle is now complete. Turn to Chapter 5 for more on testing programs and fixing errors.

## Working with Text

Before the advent of graphics, text was the basis of all programs. Text-based adventure games and text-based Bulletin Board Systems were our first programming experiences. Text is still a very important element of programming. In this section, you find out how to assemble and store text.

Text creates the simplest medium for displaying the output of programs. This book starts by using only text because text is sufficient to display the output of most programs. This approach also enables us to delay going into the complexities of graphics until the later chapters.

The technical name for text in the computer world is *string*. For example, in the "Hello World" program, `"Hello World"` is a string.

### Assembling Strings

A *string* is a collection of characters; in general, we think of a *character* as a symbol that you can type from the keyboard, including spaces. The computer interprets strings such as `"For Honor!!!"` as a series of characters, each occupying one letter or space ('F' is the first character, 'o' is the second, and so on). Strings are enclosed within quotation marks, but characters are enclosed within single quotes. For example, `"a"`, `" "` (space), `"4"`, and `"%"` are all strings consisting of one character. However, 'a', ' ', '4' and '%' are all characters. You can use characters almost anywhere that you can use a string.

However, characters are not always what you might expect. You cannot type some characters from the keyboard. There are 256 different kinds of characters.

You can access many other characters by holding down Alt and writing their numeric values. For example, the numeric value of *A* is 65. Appendix C, "Using the Standard ASCII Character Table," provides a reference for the standardized characters and their numeric values.

It is important to realize the distinction between strings and characters. Strings are made up of characters, but are quite different from them. In addition, a character can easily be converted to a string, but a character is not a string.

This might all seem complex, but creating strings is actually easy to do. The following are some examples of strings. As you can see, they are just a little bit of text surrounded by quotation marks.

```
"For Honor!!!"
"Pass me my sword."
"Who put my staff on the wagon?"
```

## Storing Strings

You can store strings in a computer so that you don't have to write them more than once. Specifically, you store strings by putting them in *memory* (we cover memory in detail in Chapter 2, "Descending Deeper . . . into Variables"). The code for strings is held in a library aptly named the *string library*. In order to store strings, you must include the string library. You do this by including the following line at the beginning of your program:

```
#include <string>
```

When you want to store a string, you must provide a name for it so that the computer knows which string you want to access in the future. For example, we will put `"A dragon is coming"` into memory and name the string `yell`.

There is one small complication, though. A computer can store many things in memory, not just strings, and it stores different things differently. For example, a number is stored differently than a string is stored. So, you must also tell the computer what kind of thing it is storing. Here's what you must provide the computer:

- The type of thing that is being stored (in this case, a string)
- The characters that make up the string
- The name of the string

Although C++ does not provide you with the ability to store strings, the standard library does. In order to use it, though, you must include the `<string>` library in your program.

Here is how you store a string, after you include the library:

```
string yell = "A dragon is coming";
```

First comes the type of thing being stored: a string. Second comes the name of the string: `yell`. The equal sign tells the computer that the string, `"A dragon is coming"`, is being stored in `yell`. Last comes the semicolon, which tells the computer that you have finished the command and are moving on to another command.

## Displaying Strings with cout

Now that you know how to write a string, you probably want to display it. In this section, you find out how to display strings in multiple ways.

You display a string with the `cout` command. The `cout` command is a command that comes in the standard C++ library in the file iostream. Here is the `cout` command statement used earlier:

```
cout<< "Hello World";
```

You can display any string using `cout`, for example:

```
cout<< "For Valour!";
```

First, you type **cout**, then the two less-than signs (<<), and then the string that you want to display followed by a semicolon (which, as you probably recall, tells the compiler that the command is finished).

## Displaying Multiple Strings with cout

You can now use the basics of `cout`, but there's much more to learn about `cout` and strings. For example, you can display multiple strings at the same time. Say that you want to display two things, but they are in two different strings. According to the preceding techniques, the code will look something like this:

```
cout<<"Red";
cout<<" Dragon";
```

**Output:**

```
Red Dragon
```

However, there is an easier method. You can display as many strings as you want side-by-side and separated by <<. You can create the previous code fragment like this:

```
cout<<"Red"<<" Dragon";
```

**Output:**

```
Red Dragon
```

The output for both code fragments is identical, yet the second one is a little simpler. Also, because of the way C++ is written, you can split up code over more than one line. For example, the previous code is also equivalent to the following:

```
cout
<<"Red"
<<" Dragon";
```

**Output:**

```
Red Dragon
```

This is actually a trivial example because you can use a single, larger string (`"Red Dragon"`).

Generally, you structure your code so that it is easy to read. You should place a new `cout` at the beginning of each phrase. For example, to display a sentence about dragons and a sentence about elves, everything in the dragon sentence should be after one `cout`, and everything in the `elven` sentence should be after a different `cout`. In this way, your code is more organized and easier to read.

## Working with Escape Characters

You cannot express characters such as quotation marks (") and line breaks literally in a string. If you include a quotation mark as part of a string, the compiler will think that the quotation mark indicates the end of the string. For example, to create a string quoting someone, you might write

```
"He said, "This is a quote"."
```

However, the compiler will interpret this as two separate strings, `"He said, "` and `"."` Because the words `This is a quote` are assumed to be non-strings, you wind up with a syntax error. A similar problem occurs with line breaks. All strings must be contained on a single line, so if you try to place a line break in the middle of a string, you get a syntax error. Fortunately, there is a solution to problems like these.

The solution is to use escape characters. *Escape characters* (or meta-characters) are a set of characters used to represent characters that cannot be expressed literally. To create an escape character, you combine a backslash (\) and the particular character. For example, the escape character for a quotation mark is `\"`. Here's what it looks like in the code:

```
"He said, \"This Is a quote\"."
```

This code produces the desired string. If you were to output this string, `He said, "This is a quote".` would be displayed onscreen. There are many other escape characters as well. Table 1.1 summarizes the important ones.

**Table 1.1 Escape Characters**

| Name | Escape Character |
|---|---|
| newline | \n |
| horizontal tab | \t |
| backspace | \b |
| alert | \a |
| backslash | \\ |
| question mark | \? |
| single quote | \' |
| double quote | \" |

You will want to become familiar with most of these escape characters because they come in handy; in fact, some of them, such as the line break, are essential.

## Displaying Stored Strings

Up to this point, you have displayed only literal strings. Now, you are ready to display stored strings. Using the name of the string in place of the string itself enables you to display stored strings. Here, as a quick reference, is the earlier string example:

```
string yell = "A dragon is coming";
```

To display the string, you use its name, which is `yell`, rather than the actual text:

```
cout<<yell.c_str();
```

The preceding line does the same thing as the following one, which we used earlier in the section "Storing Strings."

```
cout<<"A dragon is coming";
```

Don't worry about the `.c_str()` after the name of the string; it is just "magic" code that causes the string to display properly. We explain this magic code in Chapter 6, "Moving to Advanced Data Types."

## The Town Crier Program

You've learned how to create saved strings and how to display them onscreen using cout. Now, it's time to test that knowledge by creating the "Town Crier Program."

Imagine that a dragon is approaching your village and you have to yell a warning to everyone. If you can yell your warning four times faster than usual, the village will be saved. This is obviously a job for our heroes . . . the saved string and cout—only they can save the village. Your objective, therefore, is to create a program that will display the text of your warning four times in a row.

Following is a code listing that illustrates one way to create this program, but we suggest not looking at it unless you become stuck while creating your own program:

```
//1.2 - Town Crier Program - Dirk Henkemans - Premier Press
#include<iostream>
#include<string>
using namespace std;      //introduces namespace std

string yell = "A dragon is coming, take cover!!!";

int main(void)
{
    cout<< yell.c_str() <<endl
        << yell.c_str() <<endl
        << yell.c_str() <<endl
        << yell.c_str() <<endl;

    return 0;
}
```

**Output:**

```
A dragon is coming, take cover!!!
A dragon is coming, take cover!!!
A dragon is coming, take cover!!!
A dragon is coming, take cover!!!
```

## Using cin

In your programming, you need to set up the capability for users to use and store their input. For example, after typing their names, they should be able to store and then use their names. You need a way to retrieve and use information from the user when the program is running (run-time), rather than when you are writing the program (design-time) because you can't anticipate what users will write. In this section, you find out how to accept user input and store that input so that it can be used later.

## Storing Strings Using cin

You can store strings using `cin` much as you've stored them before, except now you declare the name and assign its value later. When you assign this value, you use the `cin` object. (An *object* is a programming construct that represents an entity or concept. The `cin` object represents the keyboard or some other input device, whereas the `cout` object represents the screen or some other output device. (You learn more about objects in Chapter 5.) Here is an example of storing a user-input string:

```
string name;
cin>>name;
```

Notice that you use `cin` in much the same way that you use `cout`. Notice that the less-than signs are now greater-than signs. These signs indicate that the computer is accepting data rather than printing it.

Here is an example of a complete program using `cin`:

```
//1.3 - Hello Program - Dirk Henkemans - Premier Press
#include <iostream>
#include <string>
using namespace std;      //introduces namespace std
string name = ""; //  "" means empty string
int main( void )
{
    cout<< "What is your name?";
    cin>>name;
    cout <<endl<<  "Hello " << name.c_str() ;
    return 0;
}
```

**Output (bold word is user input):**

```
What is your name?
Jackie
Hello Jackie
```

**With some compilers and situations, Windows closes the window for your program without displaying the last section of the program. Actually, Windows is recognizing that only text is to be displayed; once the text displays, Windows immediately closes the window. To see the end of your program, you can place a `cin` statement at the end of the program (which you will do in the "Pirate Musketeer Game," later in this chapter). Windows will not close the window until after you press Enter at the end of your program.**

In line 5 of the preceding code, `string name` tells the computer that there is space in the computer for a string called `name`. Remember that you must include the string library in order to use strings.

In line 8, `cout<< "What is your name?";` displays a prompt for the user. This prompt asks the computer to write the user's name.

In line 9, `cin<<name;` tells the computer to stop in order for the user to type. When the user presses Enter, the computer assigns everything that the user typed before pressing Enter to the string called `name`.

In line 10, `cout<< endl << "Hello " << name.c_str();` begins by telling the computer to start on the next line. The computer then displays `Hello` onscreen followed by the user's name. For example, if the user types `Joe` or `Jane` for his or her name in line 9, line 10 will display `Hello Joe` or `Hello Jane`. The space between `Hello` and the name is generated because a space is added at the end of the "`Hello` string (before the closing quotation mark).

Although you can learn much more about text, you now have the basic information regarding using text, so we turn your attention to using numbers.

## Working with Numbers

A computer is entirely number-based. Even the text you worked with earlier is made up of numbers (for example, if you add one to *B*, it becomes *C*). Numbers are the foundation for everything that happens on the computer. Having a good grasp on numbers is essential in the computer world. In this section, you find out about basic math, the modulus operator, and how to use integers (see also Chapter 2 for more on integers).

### Introducing Integers

Computers can store information many ways. For now, however, we cover the basics on integers and how to use them. *Integers* are all the whole numbers, including zero and the positive and negative numbers. For example, 5, 0, and −100 are all integers, whereas 0.5 is not an integer. If you try to store a decimal as an integer, the computer will respond by truncating the remaining section; that is, the computer will chop off everything after the decimal.

## Taking Action with Operators

In a general sense, an *operator* is any symbol or double symbol such as <=, and in some cases even terms such as `sizeof()`, that causes the compiler to take an action. The actions of adding, subtracting, multiplying, and dividing use operators. For example, when you ask a computer to add two numbers, you use the addition operator (+), which makes perfect sense, doesn't it? We all know that 2 + 2 = 4. Here's how you do the same thing in code with C++:

```
cout<<2 + 2;
```

This line displays `4` onscreen.

These four basic operators are self-explanatory; they do exactly what you probably think they do, but take a moment to review the symbol for each one:

| | |
|---|---|
| Addition | + |
| Subtraction | - |
| Multiplication | * |
| Division | / |

As in math, these operators do not all execute from left to right. The multiplication and division operators execute before the addition and subtraction operators, for example:

```
1 + 3 * 2
```

`3 * 2` is executed first, and then `1` is added, resulting in the number `7`.

Parentheses increase the order of precedence. If you take the preceding formula and add parentheses, as shown here

```
(1 + 3) * 2
```

`1 + 3` executes first, producing `4`, which is multiplied by `2`, resulting in `8`.

**Add lots of parentheses. Doing so makes debugging much easier. The rule of thumb is as follows: If you think your formula might need parentheses, put them in. This course of action will make your code easy to read and understand.**

### The Modulus Operator

Remember way back to sixth grade when you did long division and your answers always worked out to be whole numbers? Then you began to work with remainders because you couldn't yet deal with decimals. Sometimes, it is especially useful to know the remainder of a number when it is divided. You get this information using the modulus operator. The *modulus operator* is the remainder of x divided by y (`x % y`). To find the remainder of 5 divided by 2, you write the code like this:

```
5 % 2
```

This line returns `1`. Here's another easy example. Imagine that there are five pirates and 16 shiny gold coins. The pirates need to figure out whether the treasure can be divided evenly among themselves or whether they will have to get into a big, drunken brawl, which leads us to the next game. (Mind you, they will probably get into a drunken brawl anyway.)

## Creating the Pirate Musketeer Game

It's now time to test your new-found skills. Although this program is on the CD-ROM at the back of this book, we highly suggest that you try it on your computer. This program will be your first *real* program and will test your knowledge on your use of numbers and text. Happy swashbuckling!

```
//1.4 - Pirate Musketeer Game - Dirk Henkemans - Premier Press
#include <iostream>
#include <string>
using namespace std;       //introduces namespace std

int main( void )
//tells a pirate story
{
     int buddies;
     int afterBattle;
     string exit;

     cout<< "You are a pirate and are walking"
          << " along in the crime filled " << endl
          << "city of Havana (in 1789).  "
          << "How many of your pirate buddies "<<endl
          <<"do you bring along? (lots)"<<endl;
     //records the amount of friends you bring along
     cin>>buddies;
     //calculates the amount of pirates left after the battle.
     afterBattle = 1 + buddies - 10;
```

```
    cout<< "Suddenly 10 musketeers jump out "
          << "from the local tavern and " <<endl
          << "draw their swords. "
          << "10 musketeers and 10 pirates die in the " <<endl
          << "battle.  There are only "
          <<(buddies + 1 - 10)<< " pirates left." <<endl
          <<endl;
  cout<< "They drop 107 gold coins.  That is "
          <<(107 / afterBattle)
           << " gold coins each." <<endl;
    cout<< "There is a big drunken brawl for the last "
          <<(107 % afterBattle)<< " coins.";
    //pauses so you can see the result
    cin>>exit;

    return 0;
}
```

## Summary

The easiest way to write text or numbers to the screen and to set up things so that the user's input to the program can be read is to use the iostream library. You use `cin` to take and process the user's input and `cout` to display to the screen. In order to use `cin` and `cout`, you must include `<iostream>` at the beginning of your program. You can display and store strings and integers in order to use them again and again. You can use this stored data to make your programs shorter and more efficient. Also, remember that you can display many strings and integers at the same time in one `cout` statement, but they must be separated by `<<`. That's all for now; your adventure continues in Chapter 2.

### CHALLENGES

1. **Create a program that displays a picture of a house that looks like the ASCII house in Figure 1.7.**

## CHALLENGES *(CONTINUED)*

2. **What is the output of the following program?**

```
#include <iostream>
using namespace std;        //introduces namespace std
int x = 25;
string str2 = "This is a test";

int main( void )
{
        cout<<"Test"<<1<<2<<"3";
        cout<<25 %7<<endl<<str2.c_str();
        return 0;
}
```

3. **Write a program that asks users for their names, that greets them, and that asks them for two numbers and then provides the sum.**
4. **What happens when you store 10.3 as a integer? What about 0.6? Can you store –101.8 as an integer?**
5. **Write code that will multiply some number by 2 if the number is between 1 and 100 (including 1 or 100) and if it is evenly divisible by 3; otherwise, multiply by 3 if it is between 1 and 100 but not divisible by 3; finally, if it isn't between 1 and 100, multiply the number by the number modulus 100. (Hint: Use the nested `if` statement.)**

# Descending Deeper...into Variables

The rhetoric of variables might sound intimidating to a beginning programmer. However, in this chapter, we sort through the confusion, with the hope that the information here will serve as a torch to guide you through the darkness. By the end of this chapter, you will have a good working knowledge of variables. In this chapter, you learn the following:

- What variables are
- How to store data
- How to declare and assign values to variables
- The fundamental types
- How to determine the size of a variable
- How to use `typedef`
- How to covert hex to decimal
- How to cast from one type to another
- How to use constants

## Understanding Variables

Going back to earlier days, remember when you had a formula such as 3x + 5? *x* could represent any number. Often there would be a limitation saying that *x* was an integer, a whole number, a rational number, and so on. This limitation determined what values *x* could hold. Variables work the same way.

A *variable* is a symbol that represents numerical values, strings (text), and true or false values. You define a variable to be of a certain type (integer, for example), and then that variable can represent any number of that type. For example, if *x* is defined as a whole number, 2 will be a valid value for *x* to hold, but 2.5 will not be a valid value.

Every variable you create from a fundamental type (see the section "Introducing the Fundamental Variable Types," later in this chapter) carries with it three pieces of information: its *identifier,* the name by which programmers refer to it; its *size,* which tells the computer the amount (or size) of data contained; and the *data* itself. You give the variable its name and size according to the kind of variable it is.

In the world of computers, a variable is a certain section of memory on a computer. The data that is associated with a particular variable is stored in this section of memory. Imagine that all kinds of boxes of equal size are lined up in a row. All of them are numbered sequentially (the first is 1, the second is 2, and so on). This is how variables work. Each variable is one or more boxes, and inside the boxes is the data that the variable holds. These boxes are places in a computer's memory. This is where variables store their data. By assigning a name to that data, you can conveniently access it from memory (as illustrated in Figure 2.1).

## Sorting Out the Relationship between Variables and Memory

As you advance, you will realize more and more that much of a programmer's life is spent manipulating or deciding how to manipulate data. Data is at the core of a computer's world. Know how to manipulate data, and you know how to program.

In general, you can refer to data two ways: as literals and as fundamental types. *Literals* are, as the name implies, literal representations of data. For example, the number `2` or the word `Hello` are both literals. In Chapter 1, "Starting the Journey,"

**FIGURE 2.1**

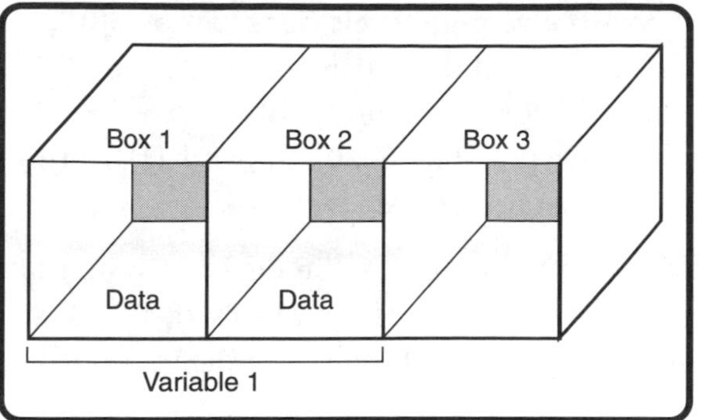


In this diagram, the first two boxes (bytes) are part of the memory containing Variable 1. The third box is still free space because it's not being used to store a variable.

you encounter many literals. `"The dragons are coming!"` is a string literal, and the number `8` is an integer literal. If you refer to data the way a non-programmer does, you are probably using a literal.

*Fundamental types*, on the other hand, are unique to programming. The idea behind a fundamental type is that you can refer to data without using its literal. This approach is advantageous because it provides a level of abstraction between your code and the data it manipulates, meaning that a particular line of code can manipulate different data every time it runs.

Fundamental types fall into four categories, each corresponding to a different kind of data: *boolean type, character types, integer types, and floating-point types*. From these four categories, you can represent any data in a program.

Before going further with variables, however, you need to learn a little bit about what memory is and how it stores data.

A computer has two basic types of memory: *Random-Access Memory* (*RAM*) and *Read-Only Memory* (*ROM*). RAM consists only of RAM chips on a computer motherboard and peripheral cards (video cards, sound cards, and so on). RAM stores data temporarily. This is the memory that applications work within, and it is the kind of memory with which programmers are most concerned. ROM is a *non-volatile* (unchanging) memory that holds the boot and self-test instructions that execute when you turn on your computer. Our discussion is limited to RAM.

**Another kind of memory is *disk storage*. Disk storage consists of hard drives, floppy disks, CD-ROM drives, or any other semi-permanent storage device. Disk storage retains its information when a computer is shut down.**

Computer memory is made up of millions of tiny electrical switches; each switch is called a bit. (A *bit* is the smallest unit of memory on a computer.) Each switch, or bit, can hold two possible voltage levels (for example, 0V and +5V). Therefore, each bit can hold two values—call them 0 and 1 or true and false. A single switch, therefore, holds a single bit (either 0 or 1). When two bits are combined, four combinations, or values, are possible (00, 01, 10, and 11). Here you have the birth of the *binary* numbering system, or base-two.

The most common numbering system is the decimal system. In the decimal, or base-ten, system, each digit has ten possible values (0, 1, 2, 3, 4, 5, 6, 7, 8, 9). Table 2.1 shows the numbers 0–10 in their binary and decimal forms.

Don't be too intimidated by the binary system. All your old, familiar numbers are still there; the binary system just represents them differently. Converting a number from binary to decimal is relatively easy. Take the first digit (the digit on the far right of the binary number, in this case 1) and multiply it by 2^0 (where *x^a* means *x* raised to the power of *a*). Then take the next digit and multiply it by 2^1. Repeat this process until you go through all your binary numbers. For example, if the number is 0110101, the conversion is as follows:

```
 1 x 2^0 =  1
 0 x 2^1 =  0
 1 x 2^2 =  4
 0 x 2^3 =  0
 1 x 2^4 = 16
 1 x 2^5 = 32
+0 x 2^6 =  0
         ----
         = 53
```

Unfortunately, converting from decimal to binary is a little bit more difficult. First, take a number and divide it by 2^(n) where *n* is the column (so 101 would have three columns) with which you are working. Then subtract the resulting remainder in the result from the total number. To find the value of the binary digit in the column, divide the remainder by 2^(n−1). Repeat these steps until the subtraction yields 0. Here are the steps for converting 9 to binary:

**Column number 1:**

9 / 2^1 = 4 Remainder: 1

Binary digit = 1 / 2^0 = 1

Binary number so far: 1

9 − 1 = 8

**Table 2.1 Binary System versus Decimal System**

| Decimal | Binary |
|---|---|
| 0 | 0 |
| 1 | 1 |
| 2 | 10 |
| 3 | 11 |
| 4 | 100 |
| 5 | 101 |
| 6 | 110 |
| 7 | 111 |
| 8 | 1000 |
| 9 | 1001 |
| 10 | 1010 |

**Column number 2:**

8 / 2^2 = 2 Remainder: 0

Binary digit = 0/2^1 = 0

Binary number so far: 01

8 − 0 = 8

**Column number 3:**

8 / 2^3 = 1 Remainder: 0

Binary digit = 0/2^2 = 0

Binary number so far: 001

8 − 0 = 8

**Column number 4:**

8 / 2^4 = 0 Remainder: 8

Binary digit = 8/2^3 = 1

Binary number so far: 1001

8 − 8 = 0

As we mentioned, each electrical switch is called a bit, and a bit can hold two possible values, 0 and 1. Eight bits in a row are called a *byte.* A byte can hold 256 possible values, 0–255. According to the box analogy at the beginning of this chapter, the rows of boxes represent memory. Each box is one byte of memory. One byte is the smallest amount of data with which a computer can work. If more than one byte is needed, the computer uses more than one box. A *kilobyte* (K) is 1024 bytes. Don't forget that a kilobyte is not actually 1000 bytes per kilobyte; it's 1024 bytes. Memory doesn't follow the metric system perfectly. 1024K is a megabyte (MB). 1000MB is a gigabyte (GB). This information is summarized in Table 2.2.

**TABLE 2.2 MEMORY MEASUREMENTS**

| Memory Unit | Number of Bits | Number of Values |
|---|---|---|
| bit | 1 | 2 |
| byte | 8 | 256 |
| kilobyte (K) | 8192 | 2^8192 |
| megabyte (MB) | 8388608 | 2^8388608 |
| gigabyte (GB) | 8589934592 | 2^8589934592 |
| terabyte (TB) | 8.796093022 * 10^12 | 2^(8.796093022 * 10^12) |

Think of memory in a RAM chip as a sequence of bytes. Each byte has a distinct address. An *address* is a number, such as 10345, that tells a computer exactly which byte is being referred to. However, the number that the computer gives you is in a base-16 number system called *hexadecimal.* The numbers on the boxes are memory addresses.

Now that you know a little more about how data is stored and represented by a computer, you are ready to go deeper into variables.

## Describing Variable Identifiers

*Identifiers* are the names that you give to your variables in order to refer to them. For example, a variable that stores user input might be called `input`. The rules for naming variables are as follows:

- The name must start with a letter or underscore (_).
- Every other character can be a letter, underscore, or number.
- Identifiers can be long (more than 200 characters).
- You cannot use keywords as variable names.
- C++ is case-sensitive (*aVariable* is different from *aVARIABLE*).

Some examples of valid identifiers are `_file5G`, `String7F4`, `input`, `__my_variable`, and so on. Some examples of invalid identifiers are `9variable` and `&variable`. It is not a good idea to use identifiers beginning with two underscores because they are often reserved for special system variables. Also, keep in mind that even though an identifier is valid, it might not be useful. An identifier should describe the thing to which it refers so that when you read your code three weeks later, you will have a better idea about what the identifier is referring to.

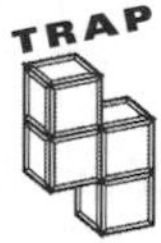


**Don't use keywords as variable names accidentally. (You might recall from Chapter 1 that keywords are the main set of commands and functions you use in programming.) Using keywords in this way can cause unpredictable results and lead to many headaches. For example, `int` is already reserved to represent an integer, so if you try to use `int` as a variable name, the compiler will give you an error when the program is built.**

## Declaring and Assigning Variables

Before you can use a variable, you must declare it. By declaring a variable, you are telling the computer to set aside a certain amount of space to store data and giving that space a name. Different types of variables need different amounts of memory. For example, to declare an `int`, you type the following:

```
int x;
```

The sytax for the `variable` declaration is this:

```
variable_type identifier;
```

Then to assign data to that variable, you use the assignment operator (=). (*Operators* are symbols or words that perform . . . well, *operations.* The operators can represent mathematical, relational, or other types of operators. In this chapter, we cover only the mathematical operators and the assignment operator. The assignment operator puts the values on the right side into the values on the left side. Here's an example:

```
x = 5;
```

Here `x` is now holding the value `5`. The memory that was set aside for `x` is filled with the value `5`. Be sure to distinguish between the equal sign in mathematics and in programming. Here, the data on the right is assigned to the variable on the left. This has nothing to do with testing whether both sides are equal. The single equal sign does *not* mean "is equivalent to." You might take a minute and read this information again; it is an important concept.

Variables can also be on the right side of the assignment operator, as shown here:

```
x = y;
```

This puts the value stored in y into x.

Remember, literal data cannot be on the left side of the assignment operator:

```
5 = x;
```

This is an illegal statement. This statement would put the value stored in x into 5, which does not make sense.

If you want to assign a value to a variable right away, you can do it on the same line:

```
variable_type identifier = value;
```

This is called *initializing the variable* because you are giving it an initial value.

With declaring variables and assigning them values under your belt, you are ready to learn about the different types of variables.

## Introducing the Fundamental Variable Types

Variables come in quite a few types, but we cover only four of them in this chapter. The type of variable you use determines how much memory you need to allocate for it, which determines how large the numbers can become (how much data you can store in one variable). The four types covered in this chapter are a boolean type, character types, integer types, and floating-point types. Table 2.3 summarizes some of the different variable types.

**TABLE 2.3 VARIABLE TYPES**

| Type | Size | Values |
|---|---|---|
| bool | 1 byte | true (1) or false (0) |
| char | 1 byte | 'a' to 'z', 'A' to 'Z', '0' to '9', space, tab, and so on |
| int | 4 bytes | -2,147,483,648 to 2,147,483,647 |
| short | 2 bytes | -32,768 to 32,767 |
| long | 4 bytes | -2,147,483,648 to 2,147,483,647 |
| float | 4 bytes | +-(1.2 x 10^-38 to 3.4 x 10^38) |
| double | 8 bytes | +-(2.3 x 10^-308 to -1.7 x 10^308) |

## The Boolean Type

The *boolean* type is the simplest data type. It is one byte long (the smallest possible amount of data with which a computer can work). It can store two values, `true` and `false`. Use the boolean type when you have only two possibilities. For example, you might have a variable named `end`, which is `false` until the program ends. You can use this variable to find out whether you've reached the end of your program. You declare a boolean variable using the keyword `bool`:

```
bool myBool = true;
```

## The Character Types

A *character* type can hold any one of 256 different characters, which can be any letter or symbol shown in Appendix C, "The Standard ASCII Table."

A *character literal* (a literal representation of data is data that is not represented in a variable form) is surrounded by two single quotes. For example, `'a'`, `'5'`, `'%'`, and `'W'` are all character literals.

You declare a character type using the keyword `char`:

```
char myChar = 'a';
cout<< "the character is" << myChar;
```

## The Integer Types

There are three integer types: `int`, `short int` (or `short`), and `long int` (or `long`).

We introduced the `int` type in Chapter 1. It is 4 bytes long (on most computers). It can store from −2,147,483,648 to 2,147,483,647. This type is the most commonly used data type. The integer types cannot store decimals or fractions (for example, 2.1 or ⅓). You declare it with the `int` keyword:

```
int myInt = -3;
```

A `short` type is half the size of an `int`—that is, 2 bytes. It can store from −32,768 to 32,767. When you have values that are relatively small, this type is very useful. It is twice as efficient because it takes only half the memory. You declare short types with the `short` (or `short int`) keyword.

```
short myShort = -56;
```

You can also display the preceding line as follows:

```
short int myShortInt = -56;
```

Next in this exciting journey through data types is the `long` data type. It is the same length as an `int`, 4 bytes. It can store the values –2,147,483,648 to 2,147,483,647 as well. As you might have guessed, you declare the `long` data type with the `long` (or `long int`) keyword. It is synonymous to an `int`:

```
long myLong = 32056;
```

is exactly the same as

```
long int myLong = 56789;
```

You can put the keyword `unsigned` in front of all the integer types to assign them only positive values. An `unsigned short` has the range of 0 to 65535, and an `unsigned long` or `int` has the range of 0 to 4,294,967,295. Unsigned integers still take up the same amount of memory as normal (`signed`) integers consume. You can also use the keyword `signed` to make sure that negative values can be stored, but this is unnecessary because `signed` is the default.

```
unsigned int anUnsignedInt; // 0 to 4,294,967,295
unsigned short anUnsignedShort; // 0 to 65535
signed long aSignedLong; // -2,147,483,648 to 2,147,483,647
int anInt; // -2,147,483,648 to 2,147,483,647
```

### Integer Wrapping

If an integer exceeds its range, it does a peculiar thing. It starts at the beginning again. For example, if you were to store the value 4,294,967,295 in an unsigned integer (one more than its range), the unsigned integer would store its value as zero (`0`). An unsigned integer starts over at `0`, but a signed integer starts over at its lowest negative value. An example might help clarify this point:

```
//2.1 - Integer Wrapping - Dirk Henkemans and Mark Lee - Premier Press
#include <iostream>
using namespace std;

//displays an example of integer wrapping
int main()
{
      unsigned int unInt = 4294967295;
      signed short aShort = 32767;
      cout << "Unsigned int's value is: " << unInt << endl;
      cout << "Short's value is: " << aShort << endl;
      unInt = unInt + 1;
```

```
        aShort = aShort + 1;
        cout << endl << "Unsigned int's new value is: "
             << unInt << endl;
        cout << "Short's new value is: " << aShort << endl;
        return 0;
}
```

**Output:**

```
Unsigned int's value is: 4294967295
Short's value is: 32767
Unsigned int's new value is: 0
Short's new value is: -32768
```

On lines 8 and 9, respectively, `unInt` and `aShort` are assigned their maximum values. In lines 12 and 13, they are incremented by 1. As you can see, they have wrapped. This is a small issue, but keep it in mind—just in case.

### The Increment Operator

If you want to increase the value stored in an integer by exactly one, you can use the increment operator (++ )to make your code much shorter. The *increment operator* is a kind of mathematical operator that indicates the value of a variable is equal to one more than its current value. (A *mathematical operator* is any operator that is used to perform math.) Instead of writing

```
count = count + 1;
```

you can write

```
count++;
```

You can also use the decrement operator (--) in the same way to decrease an integer's value by one. The decrement operator subtracts one from the value of the number. Instead of using

```
count = count - 1;
```

you can use

```
count--;
```

## The Floating-Point Types

If you want to store decimals or fractions, you need the floating-point data types, `float` and `double`.

The `float` or single-precision floating-point data type is 4 bytes long. It can store the positive or negative decimal or non-decimal values with a maximum and minimum precision of 1.2 x 10^-38 to 3.4 x 10^38. Remember that these can be positive or negative.

Often, programmers express `float` and the other non-integers in *scientific notation*. Scientific notation is a way to express extremely large or small numbers in a relatively small space.

Scientific notation is just a short cut method for writing floating-point numbers that begin to get out of hand, such as 0.0000000000000000002. Here are some numbers written in scientific notation:

```
5.6543e17        -4.02934e5        -17.204e-10      2.0e-19
```

Here's the rule to turn a scientific notational number into a regular format: Move the decimal as many places as the number to the right of the `e` (the number after the `e` is called the *exponent*). To convert 5.6543e17 to a regular number, you do the following:

1. Locate the number to the right of the `e`, the 17.
2. Move the decimal 17 places to the right. You know it's right because the 17 has no negative sign in front of it. Pad the new spaces with zeros.

   You end up with 563430000000000000.0, which is what 5.6543e17 means. This is better than typing 563430000000000000.0.

If the number has a negative exponent such as 5.6543e-17, you just move the decimal to the left 17 places and end up with 0.000000000000000056343.

Whatever number you are storing is converted into scientific notation. Then it is rounded to the nearest 10^−38 place. This is its level of precision. For example, if you store PI (3.14159265358979323846 . . .) with a precision of two decimal places, the number will be rounded to 3.14, the standard PI.

You declare the floating-point using the `float` keyword:

```
float aFloat = 3.156;
float negativeFloat = -678.876;
```

To store a fraction, a computer must convert it from its a/b (fractional) form to a decimal form. When you access the fraction, the `float` will give you the most accurate decimal version that it can store.

The `double` data type is 8 bytes long. It can store 2.2 x 10^−308 to 1.7 x 10^308 for positive values and −2.3 x 10^−308 to −1.7 x 10^308 for negative values. Thus, the `double` is rounded to the nearest 10^−308 place. This is extremely high precision.

Basically, the `double` can handle anything you want to store. You declare a `double` using the `double` keyword. *aex* means *a**10^*x*.

In the following example, 2.2e-308 means the same thing as 2.2 *10^-308:

```
double aDouble = 2.2e-308;
double negDouble = -2.3e-308;
```

You're now familiar with the fundamental data types. Make a habit of using the smallest one possible. Doing so will save memory and make your program more efficient.

## Using the sizeof() Operator

This relatively simple operator is built into the C++ language. Use it on any variable, and it will give the amount of memory, in bytes, that the variable consumes. You use it in the following way:

```
sizeof(identifier);
```

To display a `double`'s size to the screen, you might use this code fragment:

```
double aDouble;
cout << "The size of a double is" << sizeof(aDouble); // is equal to 8
```

Because it represents an integer data type (the *number* of bytes), you can use this operator anywhere that you can use an integer.

You can also use the keyword of the type rather than an identifier, as shown here:

```
cout<< "The size of  2 integers is" << 2 * sizeof(int); // is equal to 4
```

### The Data Type Game

Throughout your adventures, you happen to come across an elven village. You're in luck intrepid adventurer, for this is the perfect chance to try your newly acquired skills. This village is under attack by a horde of dragons! To protect the village, you must summon data type warriors from the mystical forest to come to the elves' rescue.

To save the elven village, you must utilize your recently acquired skills on integers, floating-points, and doubles. Are you ready to accept the challenge? If so, read on:

```
//2.2 - Data Type Game - Dirk Henkemans and Mark Lee - Premier Press
#include <iostream>
using namespace std;   //introduces namespace std
```

```
//plays the data type game
int main( void )
{
     int intWarriors;
     double doubleWarriors;
     float floatWarriors;

     cout << "The village of the elves is being attacked"
          <<" by dragons."<< " In order to save them you";
     cout << "must create each kind of data type warrior to "
          <<"defend the elven city." << endl << endl;
     cout << "How many int warriors do you want to send out?";
     cin >> intWarriors;
     cout << endl << "Luckily, each int warrior has a strength"
          << " of " << sizeof(intWarriors) << ", " << endl
          << "which almost defeats the blue dragons." << endl;

     cout << endl << "Quick! How many double warriors "
           << "should we send?";
     cin >> doubleWarriors;
     cout << endl << doubleWarriors;
      cout << " double warriors attack the last few blue "
            << "dragons" << endl << "They kill "
            << sizeof(doubleWarriors) << " blue dragons."
           << " All of the blue dragons are now dead."
            << endl << endl;

     cout << "How many float warriors do you send out?";
     cin >> floatWarriors;
     cout << endl << "Each of the "<< floatWarriors
            <<" float warriors shoots ";
     cout << sizeof(floatWarriors) << " arrows." << endl;
     cout << "This Is just enough  to kill the green dragons."
             << endl << "Congratulations, you have saved "
            << "the elves!";
}
```

## Making Life Easier with typedef

Sometimes, it becomes very inconvenient to keep using the keywords `unsigned short int` again and again. Using `typedef` enables you to rename a variable's type. You could rename `unsigned short int` to `USHORT` or to something even more convenient. The format for `typedef` is as follows:

```
typedef variable_type new_name;
```

To rename `float` to `f`, do this:

```
typedef float f;
```

Then you can declare a `float` with the newly defined keyword:

```
f radius = 4.7639;
```

**Keep in mind that your new variable type name should not only be convenient, but also meaningful.**

## Casting

You might find it necessary at times to convert from one variable type to another. You accomplish this with casting. (*Casting*, sometimes called *type casting*, is the act of converting data from one type to another, retaining almost the same value.) Sometimes particular data types are required for certain libraries (which is often the case in DirectX programming). Here is the format for casting from one data type to another:

```
float pi = 3.14;
int roundedPi = (int) pi;
```

This snippet of code makes `roundedPi` equal to `3`. The decimal is truncated. Note that the value is not rounded to the nearest one. The decimal is simply removed.

## Using Constants

C++ has two types of constants. You've already seen one of these, the *literal constant*. A literal constant is the same as a literal (refer to the section "Sorting Out the Relationship between Variables and Memory," earlier in this chapter, for more on literals). Examples of literal constants are the number `2` and the string `"Hello"`. These are defined as constants because you cannot change their values.

The second type of constant is the *symbolic constant*. The symbolic constant is like a variable in many ways except that its value cannot be changed. At the top of your program, you might define the word PI to be the constant for 3.14. When the code is compiled, every instance of the identifier PI will be replaced by the number 3.14, which means that as far as the computer is concerned, there is no difference between using a symbolic constant and a literal constant. But before you start wondering about why and when to use symbolic constants, you need to learn how to use them.

You can declare a constant two ways. The first way is to use the #define directive. (A *directive* is a line of code that is executed by the compiler immediately before compiling the rest of the code.) The syntax for this directive is as follows:

```
#define CONSTNAME value
```

CONSTNAME is the identifier that you want the constant to have, and value is the value that you want to assign to it. Notice that there is no semicolon at the end of the line, just as with the #include directive. A directive is not a C++ executable statement, but a precompile directive that the compiler follows. The #define directive tells the compiler to replace all occurrences of CONSTNAME in the program with its value. The compiler, after making the replacement, compiles the code. In your program, you can now use CONSTNAME wherever you would have put the literal constant. For example, you can declare a constant for pi:

```
#define PI 3.14159
```

Now, if your code has something like

```
y = 3.14159 * x;
```

you can use the constant instead:

```
y = PI * x;
```

The advantages of using constants are immediately obvious in terms of readability. If you use the number 3.14159, it is not immediately clear that you mean pi; but if you use a constant and call it PI, what you are referring to is crystal clear.

The second way to define a constant is by using the const keyword. The syntax is almost exactly the same as the syntax for declaring a #define:

```
const constType CONSTNAME value;
```

The key difference here is that with const, you declare the type of your constant, which can be any of the possible variable types. This difference provides an advantage over #define because of type-checking. The compiler can now check to make sure that you are using your constant where use of its type is allowed. For example, if you make a string constant by using

```
const string HELLO "Hello";
```

or by using

```
#define HELLO "Hello"
```

you can use the constant's name in code as a replacement for the string `"Hello"`.

Remember though that `const string HELLO` has type-checking, which means that you can use `const string HELLO` only where you would normally use a string. However, `#define HELLO` will simply try to make it work with some weird results:

```
int x = HELLO;
```

The constant string declared with `const` will have a compile error, but the one declared with `#define` will not. If the compiler picks up your problems, you won't have to try to find the errors yourself. This is incredibly advantageous for large applications.

Using the second method, the `pi` example is as follows:

```
const float PI 3.14159;
```

**Remember to initialize constants when you create them. After that, the value cannot change. If you don't initialize the constant at the time of creation, you will get an error when you attempt to set the constant's value.**

Using constants offers numerous advantages. Suppose that you type a number, such as 3.14, throughout the program every time you need to use the value of pi. Then you realize that your application requires a higher precision; you'll have to change every occurrence of 3.14 to the higher prevision value such as 3.14159. If, instead, you use a directive to define pi as 3.14 and later need to increase the precision, you will only need to change the `#define` directive and recompile the program.

### In the Real World

**Imagine that you are the CEO of a major corporation that has been paying each employee $10.78 per hour, and you give everyone a raise to $11.78 per hour. You don't want to go through the thousands of entries in your payment program. Using a constant to store your employees' wages, you must change the constant in only one place, which saves you, and the corporation, a lot of time and effort.**

If you have a really long number (such as pi to 22 decimal places), typing it every time that you use it will also be annoying—and if you are like us, you might easily make a mistake. Using a constant simplifies this situation considerably.

## The Circle Game

For tomorrow's math assignment, you must calculate the area and circumference of a circle. Well, maybe we can help. In the following program, we do both by using constants. You use a constant to store `PI` (3.141592). Then the user only has to enter the radius into the program, and the program will calculate both the area and the circumference of the circle. Remember that the user's input should be stored as `float` so that the user can enter decimal numbers as a radius. Excellent; now it's time to build the program:

```
//2.3 - The Circle Game - Dirk Henkemans and Mark Lee - Premier Press
#include <iostream>
using namespace std;

//calculates the area and circumference of a circle
int main()
{
      typedef float f;
      const f PI = 3.141592;
      f radius, circumference, area;

      cout << "Welcome to the circle creator!" << endl;
      cout << "What would you like the radius "<<endl
           <<"of the circle to be? ";
      cin >> radius;

      area = PI * radius * radius;
      circumference = PI * (radius * 2);
      cout << "The area of the circle is: " << area << endl;
      cout << "The circumference of the circle is: "
           << circumference << endl;
      cout << "Thank you for playing the circle creation game!"
            << endl;

      return 0;
}
```

## Understanding the Syntax

So far in this book, we have covered many different types of words—keywords, identifiers, directives, and so on—and many types of statements—assignment, include, and so on. In this section, we go through all the C++ syntax covered so far. (*Syntax* refers to the grammatical rules of a language.)

We start with the keywords, the basis of the C++ language. From these words, everything is built. A C++ compiler can understand only these words until it is "taught" more by the programmer.

Table 2.4 lists each of the keywords you've learned so far and gives their function and syntax.

As we indicated, keywords are the heart of the C++ language. They each have a special meaning and purpose. Know these words, and you are well on your way to being a C++ master.

**Table 2.4 C++ Keywords and How to Use Them**

| Keyword | Function | Syntax |
|---|---|---|
| `const` | Used to declare a constant | `const const_type const_name value;` |
| `int` | Used to declare an integer | `int variable_name;` |
| `short` | Used to declare a short | `short variable_name;` |
| `long` | Used to declare a long | `long variable_name;` |
| `float` | Used to declare a float | `float variable_name;` |
| `double` | Used to declare a double | `double variable_name;` |
| `bool` | Used to declare a boolean | `bool variable_name;` |
| `string` | Used to store a string | `string string_name;` |
| `unsigned` | Used to make integers positive | `unsigned int_type variable_name;` |
| `return` | Needed at the end of the `main()` function | `return 0;` |
| `sizeof()` | Returns the size of a variable | `sizeof(variable_type)` |
| `void` | Needed beside the `main()` function | `int main (void)` |
| `main` | Beginning of the main program | `int main (void) { }` |
| `typedef` | Used to rename variable types | `typedef variable_type new_name;` |

Next are identifiers. You now know about three types of identifiers: literal identifiers, constant identifiers, and variable identifiers. Table 2.5 summarizes their uses and how to format them.

**TABLE 2.5 USE AND FORMAT OF IDENTIFIERS**

| Identifier | Use | Format |
|---|---|---|
| Literal | To store literal data (3,2) | No formatting rules (just use value) |
| Variable | To store changing data | Assign the literal value to the variable identifier using the assignment operator (=) |
| Constant | To store constants | Like a variable, but can only be assigned once at the time of creation |

You have no choice about how to name literal identifiers; they are named what they are. Constant identifiers are usually all uppercase, although they don't have to be. Variable identifiers are usually all lowercase, unless they are two words combined (for example, `variableName`). Try to make your identifier names as descriptive as possible. Doing so will improve your code's readability.

We haven't covered preprocessor directives very much yet, but you know two of them. These two are `#include` and `#define`. (As we wrote earlier, directives are messages to the compiler telling it to do something when it compiles.) `#include` tells the compiler to add another file to the current one. For example, in the "Hello World" program

```
#include <iostream>
```

tells the compiler to add the library `iostream` to hello.cpp when you compile. `<iostream>` has a lot of predefined code, such as `cout`.

`#define` tells the compiler to replace every instance of the constant defined with its value at compile time. Preprocessor directive statements do not have semicolons at the end.

As we mentioned earlier, operators are symbols or words that perform operations. You know about nine operators so far: the mathematical operators—addition (+), subtraction (-), multiplication (*), division (/), and modulus (%)—the increment operator (++), the assignment operator (=), the `sizeof()` operator, and the type-casting operator (( )). Table 2.6 summarizes these operators and what they do.

**Table 2.6 Use and Syntax of Operators**

| Operator | Use | Syntax |
|---|---|---|
| Addition (+) | To add two numbers | `number1 + number2` |
| Subtraction (-) | To subtract two numbers | `number1 - number2` |
| Multiplication (*) | To multiply two numbers | `number1 * number2` |
| Division (/) | To divide two numbers | `number1 / number2` |
| Modulus (%) | To modulus two numbers | `number1 % number2` |
| Increment (++) | To increment an integer | `integer++` |
| Assignation (=) | To assign a value | `variable1 = number1` |
| sizeof() | To find the size of a type | `sizeof(identifier)` |
| type casting (( )) | To change one kind of variable to another | `(type)Variable` |

Feeling comfortable with variables? If not, you might want to read through parts of this chapter again and practice the sample code. Practice is the key.

## Creating the Weapon Store Game

While wandering through a dark forest, you come across a mysterious weapon store in the middle of nowhere. You are in luck, worthy traveler, for this is the perfect opportunity to test what you have learned in this chapter, including constants, casting, operators, data types, and so on. You must try to compile and run this program in order to visit the weapon store:

```
//2.4  - The Weapon Store Game - Dirk Henkemans and Mark Lee
//Premier Press
#include <iostream>
#include <string>
using namespace std;

//contains the code for the weapon store game.
int main (void)
{
      string name;
      cout << "Welcome to the weapon store, noble knight."
            << " Come to equip the army again?" <<endl
```

```
          << "What is your name? ";
     cin >> name;
     cout << "Well then, Sir " << name.c_str()
           << ", Let's get shopping!" << endl;

     float gold = 50;
     int silver = 8;
     const float SILVERPERGOLD = 6.7;
     const float BROADSWORDCOST = 3.6;
     unsigned short broadswords;

     cout << "You have " << gold << " gold pieces and "
          << silver << " silver." <<endl<< "That is equal to ";
     gold += silver / SILVERPERGOLD;
     cout << gold << " gold." << endl;

     cout<< "How many broadswords would you like to buy?"
          <<" (3.6 gold each)";
     cin >> broadswords;
     gold = gold - broadswords * BROADSWORDCOST;
     cout << "\nThank you. You have " << gold << " left.";
     silver = (gold - (int)gold) * SILVERPERGOLD;
     gold = (int)(gold);
     cout << "That is equal to " << gold << " gold and "
          << silver << " silver. " << endl
          << "Thank you for shopping at the Weapon Store. "
          << "Have a nice day, Sir " << name.c_str();

     return 0;
}
```

# Summary

You covered a lot of information in this chapter. You learned how a computer stores data in its internal memory, how you can store data temporarily for later use, and about the different types of data. You learned about constants and about `typedef`, `sizeof()`, and the assignment operator. You also reviewed the C++ syntax covered so far.

You have journeyed deep enough now to safely be called a beginning programmer. Be proud; only an elite few make it this far.

In the next chapter, we introduce you to control statements, which are the beginning of true power over your computer. Sit back for a minute and let all this information condense; then suit up, jump in, and fasten your seatbelt—you've got a great journey ahead!

## Challenges

1. What is the correct variable type for storing the following data:

   The number of books in a bookshelf

   The cost of this book

   The number of people in the world

   The word *Hello*

2. Provide meaningful variable names for the variables in the first challenge.
3. Name two reasons to use constants rather than literals.
4. Write a program that calculates and displays the sizes of all the fundamental types.
5. Test what happens if you declare a character as unsigned. Do you get the results you expected? Formulate a reason why or why not.

# Taking Command with Control Statements

In earlier chapters, you create programs that execute from start to finish. Each statement is executed only once, and every statement must be executed. However, this linearity is acceptable only for basic programming. To create advanced, dynamic programs, you must master using *control statements*, which enable programs to jump to a certain piece of code or to execute a section of code more than once. In this chapter, you learn about the following:

- Boolean logic and operators
- Selection statements
- Iteration statements
- Branching statements
- Random numbers

## Using Boolean Operators

In Chapter 2, we noted that the boolean variable can hold one of two possible values: true (1) and false (0), and all conditional statements evaluate to a boolean value. Quite a few operands can determine the boolean value of a condition (whether a condition is true or false); these operands are called *boolean operands.* You can use these operands to form *conditions* (expressions that evaluate to either true or false). In this section, we discuss each of these operands in turn so that you will be able to use any one of them as needed.

### The Equivalence Operator

The simplest boolean operator is the equivalence operator. The equivalence operator (==, or two equal signs) is a *binary operator,* which means that it takes two operands, one on each side. The general syntax for this operator is

*operand1 == operand2*

where `operand1` and `operand2` are the two operands. This operator evaluates to `true` if the values of the two operands (that is, the bit patterns of the data contained within them) are the same. Here is an example to help clarify things. If you have previously declared variables as

```
long elves = 8;
int dwarves = 8;
```

you can use them in a condition like this:

```
if (elves == dwarves)  //true
if (dwarves == 8) //true
if (dwarves == 0) //false
if (dwarves == elves) //true
```

Each of the preceding conditions evaluates to `true`, except the third one. But, wait! You might say that `elves` and `dwarves` are two different data types (integer and long integer), so their bit patterns cannot be the same, which is true, but C++ is smart enough to account for this. During execution time *(run-time),* when the first condition is encountered, the computer converts *(casts)* `dwarves` to the type long (the largest data type involved in the statement) and then compares the values. For example, if a double (8 bytes) and an int (4 bytes) are being compared, the computer will first cast the int to a float and then compare the two. The third condition evaluates to false because the value of dwarves is not 0; it's 8.

The equivalence operator is *left-associative,* which means that if more than one equivalence operator is in a single statement, the operators are evaluated from left to right. For example, if you have a condition like

```
if (dwarves == elves == dragons)
```

dwarves will first be compared to elves. The value that this comparison evaluates to (true or false) will then be compared to the variable dragons. This comparison determines the result for the entire expression.

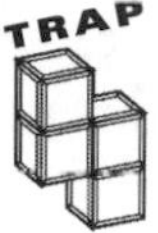


**Don't confuse the equivalence operator (==) with the assignment operator, which is one equal sign (=). The assignment operator makes the value of the variable on the left side of the assignment operator the same as the value on the right. The equivalence operator tests whether two operands are the same, but does not change them. It is common for beginners to mix them up. In other words, don't let what you already know about these symbols get in the way of what you are learning.**

## Introducing the Does-Not-Equal Operator

The opposite of the equivalence operator is the does-not-equal operator (!=). This operator is binary and is left-associative as well. The syntax for the does-not-equal operator is almost the same as for the equivalence operator:

```
expr1 != expr2
```

*expr1* and *expr2* are valid expressions. The expression formed by this operator is a condition. This operator evaluates to true if *expr1* and *expr2* are not equivalent. It evaluates to false if the two expressions are equivalent. For example, if you have two variables declared as

```
int plasmaGun = 50;
int rifle = 10;
```

you can use them with the does-not-equal operator, as shown here:

```
if (plasmaGun != rifle) //true
if (plasmaGun != 50) //false
if (rifle != 0) //true
```

## The Less-Than and Greater-Than Operators

The less-than (<) and greater-than (>) signs do in computers about the same thing they do in fourth-grade math. For example, `3 < 4` evaluates to `true` because 3 is less than 4. The same is the case with the greater-than sign: `4 > 3` is `true` because 4 is greater than 3. Check out the following variables and what they evaluate to:

```
int elves = 4;
int dwarves = 5;

if (elves<dwarves) //true
if (dwarves < elves)  //false
if (dwarves > (2 / 3)) //true
if (elves < (23 *117)) //true
```

The less-than and greater-than operators are both binary operators and are left-associative. For example, the following code might not do what you think:

```
if (0 < x < 99)
```

If you remember your math really well, you might think that this tests whether `x` is between `0` and `99`. However, this is not what happens. First, `x` is compared to `0`. Whatever this comparison evaluates to (`true` or `false`) is then compared to `99`. Because both `true` (1) and `false` (0) are less than `99`, this condition will always evaluate to `true`, regardless of the value of `x`.

## Merging with the Equivalence Operator

You might also recall experience with the less-than-or-equal-to and the greater-than-or-equal-to signs in math. In C++, they are written slightly differently, but they still exist. Instead of a line under the less-than or greater-than sign, you put an equal sign after it. Thus, the greater-than-or-equal-to operator is >=, and the less-than-or-equal-to operator is <=.

These operators work exactly as the less-than and greater-than operators work, except that if the two things being compared are equal, the operator also returns `true`. Here are some examples:

```
if (5 <= 5) //true
if (6 >= 7) //false
if (1 <= 8) //true
```

Just like the less-than and greater-than operators, the greater-than-or-equal-to and less-than-or-equal-to operators are binary and are left associative.

## The Logical or Operator

The logical or operator (||) is a binary operator. It will return `true` if one of the operands evaluates to `true`. Both sides of the or statement must first be evaluated to a boolean form (`true` or `false`) before the or operator can be evaluated.

Table 3.1 shows the first example of a *truth table* (a table in which all the possible values for the operands are listed, along with the resulting value to which the operator evaluates). The first column states the value of the first operand (called A for convenience), the second column states the value of the second operand (called B), and the third column states the value of A||B.

**Table 3.1 Truth Table for the or Operator**

| Value of A | Value of B | Value of A\|\|B |
|---|---|---|
| True | True | True |
| True | False | True |
| False | True | True |
| False | False | False |

Surprisingly, Table 3.1 includes every possible combination of the operand's values. Here are examples of conditions with or statements and what they evaluate to:

```
if (true || false)  //true
if ((2>3) || false) //false
if ((3*5) < 90 || (3<5)) //true
```

The or operator is left-associative as well. However, having more than one or operator in one statement is not always trivial, as it is for the less-than and greater-than operators. If any of the operands are `true`, the entire condition will be `true`.

This means that the computer executing your code can short-circuit. *Short-circuiting* is when a computer realizes that it doesn't have to execute the rest of a statement. For example, if the computer comes across a condition with an or operand in it and the first operand is `true`, the computer does not have to evaluate the second operand. It skips the second one because it knows that the whole condition will evaluate to `true`, regardless of the second operand.

## The and Operator

The and operator is similar to the or operator. It is also a binary operator and left-associative. In order for the and operand to evaluate to `true`, both operands must be `true`. The and operator is represented by two ampersands (`&&`). Table 3.2 shows the truth table for the and operator.

**Table 3.2 Truth Table for the and Operator**

| Value of A | Value of B | Value of A&&B |
|---|---|---|
| True | True | True |
| True | False | False |
| False | True | False |
| False | False | False |

Here are some examples of the and operator:

```
if (true && true) //true
if ((3<4) && (3<5)) //true
if ((99> -32) && (-32>0.11)) //false
```

## The not Operator

The not operator (`!`) changes a boolean value to its reverse boolean value—for example, `true` to `false` and `false` to `true`. It is a *unary operator*, which means that it takes only one operand. Table 3.3 shows the truth table for the not operator.

Here are some examples of the not operator:

```
if ( !true) // false
if ( !(2>3)) //true
if ( !( (2>3) || (3>2) ) ) //false
```

**Table 3.3 Truth Table for the not Operator**

| A | !A |
|---|---|
| True | False |
| False | True |

# Choosing Code with Selection Statements

Often, people base their decisions on certain conditions. For example, a person might go to a doctor if he or she feels sick. The decision, whether to go the doctor, is based on a certain condition: feeling sick. The same is true when using programs. You can design your program so that it selects which code to execute based on certain conditions.

As you have learned, conditions in C++ have two possible values, `true` or `false`. The operators and operands that make up the condition determine a condition's value.

There are two types of selection statements: `if else` statements and `switch` statements.

## Testing Conditions with if Statements

Probably the most important selection statement is the `if` statement. The idea behind the `if` statement is that a special section of code contained within the statement (called the *controlled statement*) will be executed only if a certain condition (called the *controlling condition*, or just the *condition*) holds true. The general syntax for the `if` statement is

```
if (condition)
    controlledStatements
```

Here *`condition`* is the condition being tested, and *`controlledStatements`* is zero or more controlled statements. These controlled statements are executed only if *`condition`* evaluates to `true`. Note that there is no semicolon after *`condition`*. The entire two lines of this general syntax are one statement, so a semicolon is not required. Also, note that *`condition`* is in parentheses to separate it from the rest of the statement. These parentheses are required. If *`controlledStatements`* consists of only one statement, the syntax is this:

```
if (condition)
    theStatement;
```

Here *`theStatement`* is the single statement. Note the semicolon at the end, telling the compiler that this is the entire `if` statement. When *`controlledStatements`* consists of more than one statement, the syntax looks like this:

```
if (condition)
{
```

```
    statementList
}
```

Here *statementList* is zero or more C++ statements, each ending with a semicolon. Note that no semicolon is required at the end of the last curly brace ( } ). You might recall from Chapter 2 that a block of code is any section of code separated by curly braces. Blocks of code can be put anywhere a single statement is allowed. This is one example. Throughout this chapter, you will see quite a few examples of blocks of code. Keep an eye out for them.

It is possible to have zero statements in both forms of the syntax (note the semicolon in the first form and the lack of a semicolon in the second form):

```
if (condition);
```

or

```
if (condition) {}
```

Here is an example:

```
int swords = 9;
if(swords < 8) //the condition
{
    cout<<"The number or sword is less than 8";
}
```

The `cout` statement will never be executed because the condition (the controlling condition), `swords < 8` (is the value of the integer variable `swords` less than 8?), evaluated to `false`. Nine is not less than eight. Because you want it to execute only one line of code, you can display this example in the alternate way—without the braces, as shown here:

```
int swords = 9;
if(swords < 8) //the condition
    cout<<"The number of swords is less than 8";
```

In this example, because the braces are not used, the `if` statement consists of everything up to (and including) the semicolon. You can also create `if` statements without controlled statements, as shown in these two examples:

```
if(swords < 8);
if(swords < 8){}
```

However, there is not a good reason to use an empty `if` statement because the statement doesn't accomplish anything.

As we said earlier, the `if` statement is the most common control statement. When combined with the `else if` statements and `else` statements discussed next, the `if` statement can be one of your most powerful tools.

### Including else if and else Statements

Sometimes you might want to take an alternative course of action if a certain condition does not hold true. Say, for example, that you feel sick. You might go to see a doctor; otherwise, you will stay home. The statement following the word *otherwise* is the alternative course of action. If the condition, feeling sick, is not true, you will take the alternative action, stay home.

In C++, the word *otherwise* is represented with the `else` statement. An `else` statement must always follow an `if` statement. An `else` statement cannot occur by itself. The syntax for an `else` statement is this:

```
else controlledStatements
```

Here *`controlledStatements`* is one or more statements. If you have more than one statement in *`controlledStatements`*, you must use a block, surrounded by curly braces, as shown here:

```
else
{
      statementList
}
```

In the preceding, *`statementList`* consists of zero or more statements, separated by semicolons. If *`controlledStatements`* is zero or one statement, a block is not needed:

```
else theStatement;
```

You connect an `else` statement with an `if` statement by putting the `else` statement right after the `if` statement:

```
if (condition)
      controlledStatements1
else controlledStatements2
```

The keyword `else` must immediately follow the `if` statement; if placed anywhere else, a compile error will occur.

Here's an example:

```
int swords = 9;
if (swords <8)
```

```
    cout << "Swords is less than 8";
else
    cout << "Swords is not less than 8.";
```

Here, the text `Swords is not less than 8` will display onscreen because the `if` statement's condition is false; the `else` statement executes automatically. If the integer variable, `swords`, were initialized to 6, for example, the text `Swords is less than 8` would display, and the entire `else` statement would be skipped.

It is possible for the statements controlled by an `else` statement to be composed of another `if` statement. This is how the infamous `else if` statement is formed. This is how it would look:

```
if (condition1)
    controlledStatements1
else if (condition2)
    controlledStatements2
```

Here *condition1* and *condition2* are two separate conditions, and *controlledStatements1* and *controlledStatements2* are two separate sets of controlled statements. The preceding block of code executes as follows:

- If `condition1` is `true`, *controlledStatements1* is executed and the computer skips the rest of the `if, else if` structure.
- If *condition1* is `false` and *condition2* is `true`, the *controlledStatements2* is executed, and the rest of the `if, else if` structure is skipped.
- If *condition1* and *condition2* are both `false`, neither one of the controlled statements is executed.

Putting one `if` statement inside another `if` statement is called *nesting* `if` statements. See Figure 3.1 for a diagram showing how the `if, else if, else` structure works.

## The Three Tests of Honour Game

You are a brave knight standing in front of a labyrinth full of dark, cruel looking rooms. You must pass a number of tests that an evil wizard has set before you in order to rescue the damsel whom the evil wizard has kidnapped. If you manage to pass all these tests of honor, you and the damsel (in distress) will live happily ever after. The first room is a room full of gold. If you take any of the gold, you fail the test; however, you get to keep the gold you take. The second room is full of diamonds. If you take these, you will prove your greed and will not be able to rescue the damsel. In the last room, you must help rescue a peasant from a dragon. If you pass all three tests, the evil wizard will release the damsel.

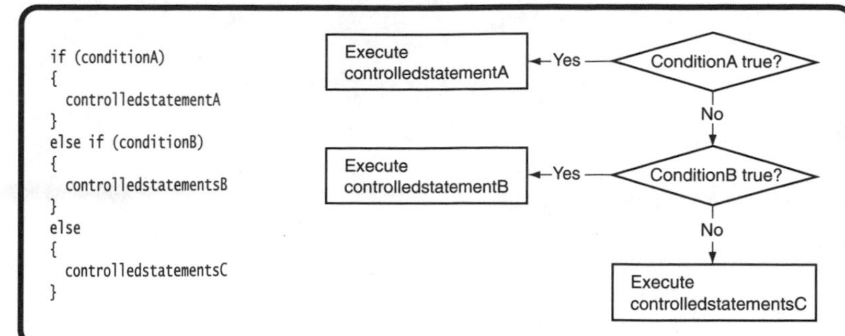


**FIGURE 3.1**

This is how the `if`, `else`, `if else` structure works.

Here is how this example looks using `if` and `else` statements:

```
//3.1 - The Three Tests of Honour -- Mark Lee and Dirk Henkemans
//Premier Press
#include <iostream>
using namespace std;
int main(void)
{
cout << "Welcome to the Three Tests of Honour."
      "\nAn evil wizard has kidnapped a damsel and "
      "it is up to you to rescue her."
      "\nHe says you must pass the three tests of "
      "honour in his Labyrinth of Doom.";
bool goldTaken, diamondsTaken, killedByDragon;
cout << "\n\nYou enter the first room. "
      "\nIt is full of so much gold you can hardly believe it."
      " \nDo you take the gold (1 for yes, 0 for No)? ";
cin >> goldTaken;
if(goldTaken)
      cout << "\nYou keep the gold, "
            "but you have failed the first test. "
            "\nGame Over.\n\n";
else
{
      cout << "Congratulations, "
            "you have passed the first test of honour!"
            "\n\nYou move into the second room."
            " It is full of sparkling diamonds"
            "\nDo you take the diamonds"
            " (1 for yes, 0 for No)? ";
```

```
        cin >> diamondsTaken;
        if(diamondsTaken)
            cout << "You take the diamonds, "
                "but you have failed the second test."
                "\nYou have proven your greed. "
                "\nGame Over.\n\n";
        else
        {
            cout << "Congratulations, you have "
                "passed the first and second test of honour."
                "\n\nYou enter the third room. "
                "\nA poor peasant is being attacked "
                "by a dragon!"
                "\nDo you ignore the peasant and "
                "move on (1 for yes, 0 for No)?";
            cin >> killedByDragon;
            if (killedByDragon)
                cout << "\nAs you sneak by, "
                    "the dragon turns his attention to you."
                    "\nHe burns you to a crisp "
                    "with one breath."
                    " You are dead."
                    "\nGame Over.\n\n";

            else
                cout << "Congratulations, you "
                    "have passed all three tests!\n\n"
                    "You exit the labyrinth and "
                    "confront the evil wizard.\n\n"
                    "He tries to turn you into a frog,"
                    " but you manage to evade.\n"
                    "With one swing of your "
                    "sword it is over.\n\n"
                    "You and the damsel live "
                    "happily ever after.\n\n"
                    "The End.\n\n";
        }
    }
    return 0;
    }
```

As you can see in this example, the main part of the program starts with an `if` statement, which tests to see whether the player has chosen to take the gold or not. If the player takes the gold (by entering the number `1`), the condition inside the parentheses evaluates to `true` (`1` is equivalent to the value `true`), and the player can keep the gold. If the player keeps the gold, however, the player does not move on to the next test (and, therefore, the third test), the second room with the diamonds. In other words, if the first condition evaluates to `true`, the rest of the `if`, `else` structure is skipped.

On the other hand, if the player chooses not to take the gold, he or she passes the first test and moves on to the next room. If the player then chooses to take the diamonds, he or she can keep the diamonds, but in that case, the player will not have a chance to save the peasant or rescue the damsel. If one of the conditions holds `true`, the computer will execute the controlled statements that are controlled by the condition that held `true`. So, in this example, if the player takes the diamonds, the computer will execute the code that lets the player keep the diamonds and then it will skip to the end of the entire structure.

The third `if` statement is similar to the previous two. The player cannot rescue the peasant if he or she has taken the gold or diamonds. The line `if (killedByDragons)` is an example of one `if` statement. Notice that you do not need the braces around the statement. However, if you choose to place braces around the `cout` statement, the program will not change.

Last come the `else` statements. The `else` statements are *default statements,* which means that if the condition of the related `if` statement does not hold `true`, the code inside the `else` statement will be executed. That is, if the player did not take the gold or diamonds and defeated the dragon, the player—the brave knight—may marry the damsel and live happily ever after.

### In the Real World

**Do not underestimate `if` statements. They are one of the most important statements in the C++ language. The `if` statement is the basic structure from which the computer can decide what to do. `if` statements make your code nonlinear. Instead of following a basic start-to-finish path through the code, the computer can change the order in which things are executed to adapt to changing circumstances.**

**You will find many uses for `if` statements as you program. One example of when you can use `if` statements is in the creation of *AI* (artificial intelligence). Another more common example is when you are responding to user input in a computer game. If the user presses the right arrow, the user's character should move to the right.**

### The Conditional Operator

Some conditions are very trivial, yet you still have to write a complete `if` statement for them. Observe the following:

```
if (x>y)
      z=y;
else
      z=x;
```

This code snippet assigns the minimum of `x` and `y` to `z`. Writing a complete `if`, `else` statement for something so short can be tedious. Fortunately, C++ provides an alternative: *the conditional operator*. The preceding example is much more concise when you use this operator:

```
z = (x>y) ? y : x;
```

The general syntax for the conditional operator is as follows:

```
condition ? expr1 : expr2
```

Here *`condition`* is a valid condition, and *`expr1`* and *`expr2`* are valid expressions. If *`condition`* is `true`, the conditional operator evaluates to *`expr1`*; otherwise, it evaluates to *`expr2`*. The conditional operator is an expression and can be used anywhere that other expressions can be used. You can see that this is similar to using an `if` statement. However, keep in mind that *`expr1`* and *`expr2`* are expressions and *not* statements (as are `if` statements). You cannot, for example, do the following:

```
(x>y)? cout << "x is greater than y." : cout << "x isn't greater than y.";
//error
```

Here is an example to illustrate the proper use of the conditional operator:

```
int soldiers = 5;
int tanks = 10;
int max = (b>a) ? b : a;
int min = (b<a) ? b : a;
cout << "The largest value is: " << max << endl;
cout << "The smallest value is : " << min << endl;
```

**Output:**

```
The largest value is: 10
The smallest value is: 5
```

## Using the switch Statement

The second type of selection statement is the `switch` statement. Many programmers try to avoid the `switch` statement, but if used correctly, it can be a powerful tool.

Imagine that you are programming a game that displays a menu with six choices. One way to respond is to use six `if` statements in a row. Even better, use an `if`, `else if`, `else` structure. The `switch` statement is an even simpler solution. It enables you to test one variable against certain values and respond differently to each one. Here is the general syntax for the `switch` statement:

```
switch(expression)
{
case expr1:
      controlledStatements1
      break(opt.);
case expr2:
      controlledStatements2
      break(opt.);
case expr3:
      controlledStatements3
      break(opt.);
...
}
```

Here *expression*, *expr1*, *expr2*, and *expr3* are variables or expressions whose values you want to test. We discuss the `break(opt.)` lines shortly. This syntax is equivalent to an `if`, `else if` structure in meaning:

```
if (expression == expr1)
      controlledStatements1
else if (expression == expr2)
      controlledStatements2
else if (expression == expr3)
      controlledStatements3
...
```

You can see how much more inconvenient an `if`, `else if` structure can be. When the `switch` statement executes, the computer goes through each `case` statement and tests whether *expression* equals *exprN* (where `N` is any number). If they are equal, everything after the `case` statement will be executed until the computer encounters the `break` keyword. If none of the tests evaluate to `true`, the whole `switch` statement does nothing.

The break keyword is new to you. It *exits* (causes the computer to go to the end of) the nearest enclosing switch statement or iteration statement. If the break keyword is not enclosed by a switch statement or iteration statement, a syntax error occurs when you try to compile. The line break(opt.) in the general syntax means that the break keyword is optional there. Shortly, you will learn the implications of leaving this word out, but for now, put it at the end in every case.

Now that you've made it through all the confusing definitions, it's time for an example:

```
int menuChoice = 3;
switch(menuChoice)
{
      case 1:
            cout << "You chose 1!" << endl;
            break;
      case 2:
            cout << "You chose 2!" << endl;
            break;
      case 3:
            cout << "You chose 3!" << endl;
            break;
      case 4:
            cout << "You chose 4!" << endl;
            break;
}
cout << "You are now out of the switch statement!" << endl;
```

**Output:**

```
You chose 3!
You are now out of the switch statement!
```

As you can see from the output, the computer chose the correct case statement and executed it. All the other case statements are ignored.

Note that a break statement isn't required within every case statement (and sometimes it is useful not to have one). Observe the following example:

```
int choice;
cout << "Please enter a number: ";
cin >> choice;
switch (choice)
{
```

```
        case 1:
        case 2:
        case 3:
            cout << "You chose 1, 2, or 3." << endl;
            break;
        case 4:
            cout << "You chose 4!" << endl;
        case 5:
            cout << "You chose 4 or 5." << endl;
            break;
}
```

**Output (when the user enters 1):**

```
Please enter a number: 1
You chose 1, 2, or 3.
```

**Output (when the user enters 4):**

```
Please enter a number: 4
You chose 4!
You chose 4 or 5.
```

### The default Case

You might not always be able to account for all possible values in a `switch` statement or you might sometimes want to perform the same action for many cases. C++ provides an `else` statement, called the `default` statement, that is part of the `switch` statement. The `default` statement is just like the `case` statement except that there is no value to test. The syntax for the `default` statement is as follows:

```
default:
    controlledStatements
    break;
```

If the `default` statement is encountered, *`controlledStatements`* automatically executes. There is not a test for the `default` statement as there is for the `case` statement. You must place the `default` statement at the end of the list of `case` statements. Here is an example:

```
int choice;
cout << "Please enter a number: ";
cin >> choice;
switch (choice)
{
```

```
        default:
                cout << "\nYou chose " << choice << endl;
}
```

**Output:**

```
Please enter a number: 5
You chose 5
```

## Following the Order of Operation

When more than one operator is in a single expression, the computer must determine the order in which to execute them. Fortunately, operators are executed according to a standardized order called the *order of operation*.

You might be familiar with this standard. Does the term BEDMAS sound vaguely familiar? It is the term used in elementary school math to teach the order of operations, as shown here:

Brackets

Exponents

Division/Multiplication

Addition/Subtraction

This list is called an *order of precedence list*. Entries at the top of the list have the highest precedence, and entries at the bottom of the list have the lowest precedence. If two operators are at the same level in the list, they are said to have *equal* precedence. For example, if you have a math expression, such as

(3+7*3)/6-2*2

you can use the order of precedence list to determine how to evaluate the expression. First, all brackets (the operation at the top of the list; actually, they are parentheses, but PEDMAS doesn't sound quite right) are evaluated. This involves evaluating everything inside the brackets. The first thing to evaluate is the expression `3+7*3`. Two operators are in this expression: multiplication and addition. Because multiplication is higher on the list, it is evaluated first and then the addition, giving you `3+21` and then `24`.

The expression remaining is `24/6-2*2`. Next, because division and multiplication are on the same level of precedence, they are evaluated from left to right. The expression then becomes `4-4`. The expression remaining is easy to evaluate. The final answer is `0`.

C++ has a similar order of precedence list as well (see Table 3.4):

**Table 3.4 The Order of Precedence for C++ Operators**

<table>
<tr><th>Operator</th><th>Common Name</th></tr>
<tr><td>::global</td><td>Scope Resolution operator</td></tr>
<tr><td>lvalue++, lvalue--</td><td>Postfix increment, Postfix decrement</td></tr>
<tr><td>sizeof(expr), ++lvalue, --lvalue</td><td>sizeof operator, Prefix increment and decrement</td></tr>
<tr><td>*, /, %</td><td>Multiplication, Division, Modulus</td></tr>
<tr><td>+, -</td><td>Addition, Subtraction</td></tr>
<tr><td><, <=, >, >=</td><td>Less-Than, Less-Than-Or-Equal-To, Greater-Than, Greater-Than-Or-Equal-To</td></tr>
<tr><td>==, !=</td><td>Equivalence, Does not Equal</td></tr>
<tr><td>&&</td><td>Logical and</td></tr>
<tr><td>||</td><td>Logical or</td></tr>
<tr><td>expr ? expr : expr</td><td>Conditional operator</td></tr>
</table>

In Table 3.4, `expr` is any valid C++ expression, *`lvalue`* is any identifier whose value can change, and `global` is any global variable. As you can see, these rules are much more complex than the simple BEDMAS, but in a short amount of time, this list will become second nature to you. Learn to love it, but avoid code that is so complex that it depends on this list.

You can use any and all of the preceding operators together in a conditional statement. You can even make a conditional statement more than one line long. However, doing so is probably not a great idea because the conditional statement can become impossible to read. Instead, if you have a long or multiline conditional statement, try breaking it into more than one statement. For example, the following algorithm calculates whether the integer `k` is between two numbers. The first number is the summative from `1` to `n` (the summative from `1` to `n` is the sum `1 + 2 + 3 + . . . + n`; the formula for this summative is `n * (n + 1) / 2`). The second number is the same summative but from 1 to n + 1 (the summative `1 + 2 + 3 + . . . + (n + 1)`; the formula is `(n + 2) / 2`. To get the formula, just substitute `n + 1` for `n` in the normal formula: `(n + 1) * (n + 2) / 2`:

```
if(n * (n + 1) / 2 >= k && ((n + 1) * (n + 2) / 2 ) <=  k)
//calculates whether or not k is between the
//summatives of n and n + 1
```

```
{
      cout << "k is between  the summatives of n and n+1";
}
```

Although this example is not long, it is intensely mathematical and therefore should probably be broken into more than one line. If you look at the order of precedence list, you can see that `&&` is evaluated last in the preceding condition. This means that the condition can be simplified to the form `A&&B`, where `A = (n * (n + 1) /2) >= k` and `B = ((n + 1)*(n + 2) /2) <= k`. This is a highly effective way to simplify your expression. Here is how this method looks in the code:

```
int a = (n * (n + 1) /2) >= k;
int b = ((n + 1) * (n + 2) /2) <= k;
if (a && b)
{
      cout << "k is between  the summatives of n and n + 1";
}
```

## Continuing with Iteration Statements

*Iteration statements* are control structures that repeat continuously until a certain condition is no longer met. Perhaps we can explain this concept by comparing it to the myth of Hercules. Hercules was assigned nine tasks, and he could not continue with his life until he completed them (that is, the iteration statement would repeat continuously). Once he completed the nine tasks, however, he was free to continue with his life. In programming, these tasks can be written as a loop having to execute nine times, doing a task every time; but once the loop finishes the ninth task, the computer can continue to execute the rest of the program's code.

### The while Loop

You could program the Hercules example with the `while` loop. The `while` loop will continually execute until a particular condition becomes `false`. The syntax for a `while` loop is as follows:

```
while(condition)
      controlledStatements
```

Here *`condition`* will be tested every time the loop executes. When *`condition`* is no longer `true`, the loop will terminate. Remember, if the condition is not `true` to begin with, it is possible that the loop will never execute. Also, keep in mind that you have to make sure that your loops will terminate after a certain amount of time. Avoid *infinite loops* (loops that will never fail their precondition).

You are now ready to program the nine tasks of Hercules (mentioned in the preceding section). The following example shows how you can create the program using a `while` loop. Here you want to limit the `while` loop to a particular condition; you want the task number to be less than or equal to nine.

```
//3.2 - Nine Tasks of Hercules - Dirk Henkemans and Mark Lee
//Premier Press
#include <iostream>
using namespace std;        //introduces namespace std

int main( void )
{
//the variable that stores how many tasks you have completed.
int taskNumber = 0;

    while(taskNumber < 9) //until taskNumber >= 9
    {
        taskNumber++;
        cout<<"Hercules has now completed "
            << taskNumber << " tasks." << endl;
    }
    return 0;
}
```

**Output:**

```
Hercules has now completed 1 tasks.
Hercules has now completed 2 tasks.
Hercules has now completed 3 tasks.
Hercules has now completed 4 tasks.
Hercules has now completed 5 tasks.
Hercules has now completed 6 tasks.
Hercules has now completed 7 tasks.
Hercules has now completed 8 tasks.
Hercules has now completed 9 tasks.
```

Notice that the final value for `taskNumber` is `10`, not `9`. This is because `taskNumber` must become `10` in order to make the condition `false`. Also, notice that `taskNumber` is incremented every time through the loop. This not only keeps track of Hercules' tasks, but also guarantees that the loop will eventually terminate. See Figure 3.2 for a diagram of how the `while` statement works.

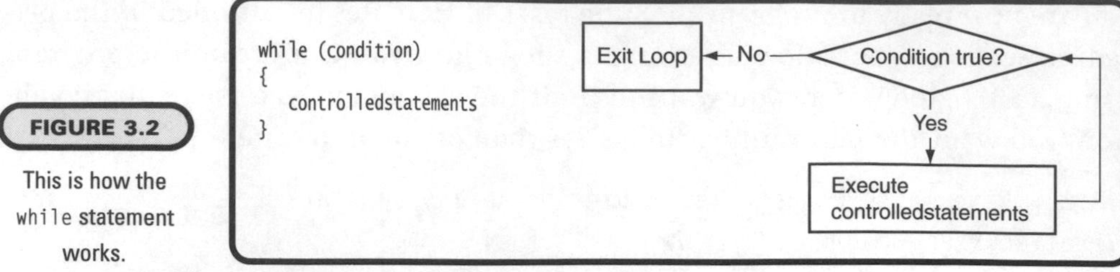


**FIGURE 3.2**

This is how the `while` statement works.

## The Increment and Decrement Operators Revisited

You can make the preceding program more concise by incorporating the ++ operator into the condition. As we discussed before, you can incorporate multiple operators into a condition. The same is true for the condition in the "Nine Tasks of Hercules." First you must learn about postfix and prefix operators. For both the increment and decrement operators, you put the operator before (prefix) or after (postfix) the operand as shown here:

```
operand$$ //post
$$operand //pre
```

Here `$$` represents an operator, and `operand` represents an operand. However, each has a slightly different meaning. As a postfix, the operation is applied to the operand after it is retrieved, but as a prefix, the operation is applied before the value of the operand is retrieved. Here is an example:

```
int x = 5;
int y = 6;
int z = y++; // z = 6, y = 7
z = ++x; // z = 6, x = 6
```

Here is an example of how you might use these operators in the Hercules example:

```
int taskNumber = 0;
while(taskNumber++ < 9)
{
     cout<<"Hercules has now completed "
          <<taskNumber<<" tasks."<<endl;
}
```

**Output:**

```
Hercules has now completed 1 tasks.
Hercules has now completed 2 tasks.
...
```

```
Hercules has now completed 8 tasks.
Hercules has now completed 9 tasks.
```

The question you might ask now is whether C++ will increment `taskNumber` before or after it checks whether `taskNumber` is less than `9`. The answer is simply this: If ++ comes after the variable, the variable will be incremented after the entire expression is computed. If ++ comes before the variable, the variable is incremented first, before anything else is computed.

Here is another example of using the postfix and prefix:

```
//3.3 - ++ Example Program - Dirk Henkemans and Mark Lee
//Premier Press
#include <iostream>
using namespace std;

int main( void )
{
      int var1 = 0, var2 = 0;

      cout << var1++ << endl;
      cout << ++var2;

      return 0;
}
```

**Output:**

```
0
1
```

Although both `var1` and `var2` have a value of `1` after this program runs, you can see that `var1++` will increment `var1` after the value of `var1` is output, whereas `++var2` increments `var2` beforehand.

The -- operator works the same way. Place this operator before the variable to make the -- take precedence over everything else, or place it after the variable so that it is evaluated after the rest of the expression.

## Looping with the do while Loop

The `do while` loop is like the `while` loop, except that the condition is tested after the iteration is finished. In this way, the loop will always execute at least once.

The syntax for the `do while` loop looks like this:

```
do
{
    controlledStatements
}
while(condition);
```

Remember to add the semicolon after *condition* (this is easy to forget). A `do while` loop will execute until its condition evaluates to `false`, just like a `while` loop does. However, a `do while` loop will execute once and then test the condition, so no matter what, a `do while` loop will execute once.

A good example of using the `do while` loop is when programming a game menu, as shown next. You want to display the menu in the loop, but before you ask the user for input. Then, if the user does not enter the correct information, the menu is displayed again and again until the user inputs the correct information. For example, if you number your menu items 1–4, you will want to loop until the user input is between `0` and `5` (a valid menu number). As soon as the user does enter valid input, the loop will exit.

```
//3.4 - A Simple Menu - Dirk Henkemans - Premier Press #include<iostream>
using namespace std;
int main(void)
{
      cout<<"Your party is adventuring "
                  << "through hills outside of Que'll \n"
            <<"when suddenly you are "
                  << "ambushed by rouges!!! \n \n";

      int response = 0;
      do
      {

            cout << "What action would you like to take? \n"
                  << " 1) Attack the evil rouges!!! \n"
                  << " 2) Run from the onslaught  \n"
                  << " 3) Try to talk to the rouges \n";
            cin>>response;
      }
      while (response < 1 || response > 3);
```

```
        if (response == 1)
        {
              cout << "The battle drags into the night "
                    << "and by sunset no one knows \n"
                    << "who is still alive!\n";
        }
        else if (response == 2)
        {
              cout << "You run from the rouges into "
                    << "the trees never to see them again.\n";
        }
        else
        {
              cout<<"You try talking to them "
                    << "but they seem unlikely to listen. \n"
                    <<"They take all your money "
                    << "and depart happy and you poor.\n ";
        }
        return 0;
}
```

This program displays a short introduction and then allows the user to respond to the three choices given in the menu. If an invalid choice is made, the program is displayed again, and this process repeats until a valid choice is made. Each menu item selected displays a different ending.

Menus are the basis for almost everything text-based, and they provide a convenient user interface. In Chapter 4, "Writing Functions," you learn how to create a general menu for a text adventure game that can be used continuously.

## Using the for Statement

The `for` statement is one of the most versatile statements that you will encounter. The `for` statement is an iteration statement that performs its own loop maintenance. The syntax for the `for` statement is shown here:

```
for (initialization; condition; expression)
      controlledStatements
```

Here *initialization* is any valid variable initialization statement or expression, *condition* is any valid condition, and *expression* is any valid expression.

A definition like this one can be overwhelming to a beginner. However, the `for` statement is really a simple device. Take a look at this example:

```
for(int count = 0; count < 10; count++)
{
     cout << count << " ";
}
```

**Output:**

```
0 1 2 3 4 5 6 7 8 9
```

The numbers `0` to `9` are displayed onscreen. Though this program might look complicated, it really isn't. The order in which things are executed in the `for` statement is illustrated here:

1. Execute initialization statement.
2. Test the condition (if `false`, the `for` statement is done).
3. Execute *`controlledStatements`*.
4. Execute *`expression`*.
5. Test *`condition`*. If `true`, go to Step 3.

The `for` statement is done.

The first part of the `for` statement is the *initialization* statement. It is executed as soon as the `for` statement is encountered, but is executed only once (unlike the rest of the loop). `initialization` can be any kind of variable initialization, and there are three main forms. You saw the first one in the previous example (`int count = 0`). This type includes a variable declaration and initialization. The second form occurs when a variable has been previously declared and `initialization` just sets the variable's value (for example, `count = 0`). The third form is to leave `initialization` empty. The following example illustrates these three forms:

```
for (int count = 0; count < 10; count++) //first form
     cout << count << " ";
cout << endl;

int count;
for (count = 0; count < 10; count++) //second form
      cout << count << " ";
cout << endl;

int index = 0;
```

```
for (; index < 10; index++) //third form
      cout << index << " ";
cout << endl;
```

**Output:**

```
0 1 2 3 4 5 6 7 8 9
0 1 2 3 4 5 6 7 8 9
0 1 2 3 4 5 6 7 8 9
```

This example also illustrates another issue. Notice how `count` is declared twice. This is legal here because of where the declarations are located. The second declaration is in the local scope, as you've already seen, so the second `count`'s scope lasts until the end of the function or code block (to the end of this code snippet). However, the first declaration is not local. Variables declared in `initialization` have a restricted scope. These variables' scopes last until the end of the `for` statement, which means that once the `for` statement ends, the variable(s) declared in `initialization` no longer exist. Thus, when the second declaration is encountered, there is no conflict because the first `count` no longer exists.

The second main part of the `for` statement is the condition. The condition is exactly the same as conditions in every other control statement. It is tested right after `initialization` is executed, and then every time through the loop. As soon as the condition evaluates to `false`, the `for` statement terminates.

You can omit the condition, as shown in the following example:

```
for (int index = 0; ; i++)
      cout << index;
```

This code snippet will create an infinite loop. Omitting the condition is equivalent to having a condition that is always `true`.

The third part of the `for` statement is the expression. The expression is executed immediately after *`controlledStatements`*. This means that if *`controlledStatements`* is never executed (the condition fails the first time), the expression is never executed.

The expression can be omitted as in the following example:

```
for (int count = 0; count < 10; )
{
      cout << count;
      count++;
}
```

Note that placing an expression (count++) at the end of *contolledStatements* is equivalent to placing it in the expression.

The most common way to use a for statement is to do some task a certain number of times. To do this, you first declare a variable and initialize it with some value in the initialization statement. In the expression, you either increment or decrement the variable declared in the initialization so that the condition will fail after a certain number of loops. Try to avoid changing the value of this "counter" variable within *controlledStatements*. The most common counter variable names are count or index (sometimes referred to as c and i for short).

## Nesting

As your programs become more and more complex, you will need to nest control structures. *Nesting* involves placing programming structures in other programming structures. For example, you might need to put an if statement in a for statement. Any control statement can legally be placed in any other control statement. Here is an example of a do while loop in an if statement:

```
if (choice == displayMenu)
{
      do
      {
      //displayMenu
      }
      while(!valid Input);
}
```

You could use a multiplication table, which requires two nested for loops. In the following example, the inside for statement loops fully for each loop of the outside for statement. This example illustrates one way to print a multiplication table:

```
//3.5 - A Multiplication Table - Dirk Henkemans
//Premier Press
#include<iostream>
using namespace std;

int main(void)
{
      cout << "A multiplication table:" << endl
```

```
             << "   1\t2\t3\t4\t5\t6\t7\t8\t9" << endl
             << " ---------------------"
             << "------------------------"
             << "--------------" << endl;
        for(int c = 1; c < 10; c++)
        {
             cout << c << "| ";
             for(int i = 1; i < 10; i++)
             {
             cout << i * c << '\t';
             }
             cout << endl;
        }
        return 0;
}
```

**Output:**

```
A multiplication table:
      1        2        3        4        5        6        7        8        9
   -------------------------------------------------------------------------------
1|    1        2        3        4        5        6        7        8        9
2|    2        4        6        8        10       12       14       16       18
3|    3        6        9        12       15       18       21       24       27
4|    4        8        12       16       20       24       28       32       36
5|    5        10       15       20       25       30       35       40       45
6|    6        12       18       24       30       36       42       48       54
7|    7        14       21       28       35       42       49       56       63
8|    8        16       24       32       40       48       56       64       72
9|    9        18       27       36       45       54       63       72       81
```

As you can see, nesting control statements is a very useful tool for many different situations.

## Leaping Around with Branching Statements

Branching statements leap from one area of code to another altering the natural course of execution. Four kinds of branching statements are summarized in Table 3.5.

**Table 3.5 Branching Statements**

| Keyword | Purpose |
|---|---|
| break | Exits the nearest enclosing switch statement or iteration statement. |
| continue | Starts the next loop of the nearest enclosing iteration statement. |
| goto | Jumps to a particular place in your code. |
| return | Ends a function and returns a value (see Chapter 4). |

We have already defined the break statement (see the section "Using the switch Statement," earlier in this chapter). When used in an iteration statement, the break statement provides an alternative way to exit a loop.

We define the return statement in Chapter 4, where that statement is more applicable.

## The continue Statement

The continue statement shifts execution to the beginning of the next loop of an iteration statement. This statement makes programming in C++ more convenient. Sometimes, the only way you can make a section of code work correctly is with a continue statement. Without it, you would have to totally rework a large section of code. Here is an example:

```
int input;
for ( ; ; ) //'forever' - an infinite loop
{
     cout << "/nPlease enter a number between 1 and 10: ";
     cin >> input;
     if (input < 1 || input >9) continue;
     break;
}
```

**Output:**

```
Please enter a number between 1 and 10: 10
Please enter a number between 1 and 10: -50
Please enter a number between 1 and 10: 5
```

In this example, the for statement will continue to loop until the user enters valid input (a number between 1 and 10). The continue statement ensures that the break statement is never reached unless the if statement fails.

## The goto Statement

Many programmers dislike the goto statement. They think it creates complicated code and is just a lazy man's solution. This is often the case, but the goto statement does have its uses.

The goto statement jumps to a specified section in your code, which you specify by labeling the section. A *label* is an identifier followed by a colon. It can be placed at the beginning of any statement (even an empty one). The syntax for a label is

```
label: statement
```

where statement includes the ending semicolon of the statement. The syntax for the goto statement is

```
goto label;
```

The computer will now jump to the line of code with label at the beginning. Here is an example:

```
int i;
int j;
int input;
cout << "Please enter a number: ";
cin >> input;
for (j = 0; j < 10; j++)
     for (i = 0; i < 10; i++)
          if (input == i*j) goto FoundIt;
FoundIt: cout << "\nYou entered " << i*j;
```

**Output:**

```
Please enter a number: 10
You entered 10
```

In this example, as soon as i*j is equal to input, the nested loops will be exited. Although this program is flawed—if you enter a prime number or number more than 81, the program responds as though you entered 100—it serves the current purpose.

Breaking out of nested control structures is one of the most practical uses of the `goto` statement because the `break` statement will exit only from the innermost control structure.

## Creating Random Numbers

Random numbers do not exist in computers; however, you can create pseudo random numbers using complex mathematical formulas. We do not discuss these formulas here because they are way too complex for a beginner, and you do not need to understand them in order to use them.

Random numbers are created from a random seed. (A *random seed* is a number that is used to start the random number generator.) This random seed usually comes from the second hand of the computer system's clock.

This is an ideal choice for a random seed because it is so unpredictable. The chance of a program being used twice in one second is unlikely, so the random number will probably be different every time.

The process for generating random numbers consists of two parts: first, setting the seed; second, generating the random number. In order to gain access to the second hand of the computer's clock, you must include part of the standard C++ library: either `<ctime>` or `<time.h>`:

```
#include <ctime>
```

The random number generator is also part of the standard library, so you must include either `<cstdlib>` or `<stdlib.h>`:

```
#include <cstdlib>
```

In order to seed the random number generator, you use the `srand()` (seed random) function (see Chapter 4 for more on functions). You put the number with which you want to seed the generator within parentheses. This can be any number, but in this case, you are using the `time()` function. The `time()` function gives the number of seconds that have passed since January 1, 1970, which seems bizarre, but it is the standard way of getting the computer's second hand. Here's how you seed the random number generator:

```
srand(time(0));
```

The `(0)` is beyond the scope of what you are learning here, so we don't go into it. Just make sure that this line is executed only once. Don't seed the generator repeatedly; doing so can cause it to lose some randomness (a loop can sometimes take much less than a second).

Now that you have seeded the generator, you are ready to use it. To generate a random number, you use the `rand()` function. This function gives a large random number, such as 2453. Here's what the `rand()` function looks like in code:

```
cout << rand();
```

In order to generate a random number between two other numbers (for example, a random number between `1` and `10`), you use this formula:

```
rand() % (max - min + 1) + min;
```

Here *`max`* is the higher value and *`min`* is the lower value. For example, to generate a number between `10` and `20`, you use a formula like this one:

```
int num = rand() % 11 + 10; // (20 - 10 + 1) = 11
```

This formula works because `rand % 11` evaluates to a number from `0` to `10`. Then adding `10` gives a number somewhere between `10` and `20`.

The `rand()` function is very useful and is an integral part of the following game.

## The Number Guessing Game

Up to this point, you have created games that do not change their behavior based on the user's input. Now is the time to learn how to use random numbers, selection statements, and iteration statements to create dynamic, responsive programs.

Throughout the rest of the book, you will create increasingly difficult games that respond to the user's input. The first of these responsive games is the "Number Guessing Game." This program works by randomly picking a number from one to 100. The user must guess the number, and the program tells the user whether the number is too high, too low, or the right one. When the user guesses the number, the program exits, telling the user how many guesses it took to get the right number.

```
//3.6 - Number Guessing Game - Dirk Henkemans
//Premier Press
#include<iostream>
#include <ctime>
#include <cstdlib>
using namespace std;

int main(void)
{
      cout<<"Welcome to the number guessing game!!! \n";
```

```
    cout<<"I have picked a number between 1 and 100. \n \n";

     srand(time(0));
    //stores the random number
    int numPicked = rand() % 100 + 1;
    int guess = 0; //stores the number the user guessed
    int guessNum;  //stores the number of guesses

    for(guessNum = 0; guess != numPicked; guessNum++)
    {
         cout<<"What would you like to guess? \n";
         cin>>guess;

         if(guess < numPicked)
              cout<<"\nYou guessed too low!!! \n \n";
         else if(guess > numPicked)
              cout<<"\nYou guessed too high!!! \n \n";
    }
    cout<<"\nYou guessed it!!! \n"
         <<"It took you "<<guessNum<<" guesses.";

    return 0;
}
```

**Output:**

```
Welcome to the number guessing game!!!
I have picked a number between 1 and 100.

What would you like to guess?
50
You guessed too low!!!

What would you like to guess?
75
You guessed too high!!!

What would you like to guess?
63
You guessed it!!!
It took you 3 guesses.
```

## Creating the Roman Commander Game

While jumping around in the clouds of code city, you happen to come across the Emperor of Rome. He is desperately in need of a commander to lead an attack against the Germanian Hordes. Will you accept the challenge?

And, of course you, seeing this as an excellent opportunity to work on your new skills, including random numbers, `while` loops, `do while` loops, `if` statements, `switch` statements, and the conditional operator, accept.

Type the following code into your compiler's source code editor and try it out. Think about each of the control statements in the code. Can you read them as though they were in English? If not, you will be able to very soon.

```
//3.7 - The Roman Commander Game - Mark Lee and Dirk Henkemans
//Premier Press
#include <iostream>
#include <string>
#include <ctime>
#include <cstdlib>

using namespace std;      //introduces namespace std
int main( void )
{
      srand(time(0)); //seed the random number generator

      string name; //used to store the player's name
      bool end = false; //used to test if the user chose to quit
      bool lost; //used to test if the user lost the game

      int menu_choice; //stores the user's choice from the menu

      //units that the player starts with
      int archers = 50;
      int catapults = 25;
      int swordsmen = 100;

      //units that the Germanians start with (random)
      // random number between 70 and 20
      int g_archers = rand() % (51) + 20;
      int g_catapults = rand() % (41) + 10; //between 50 and 10
      //between 150 and 50
      int g_swordsmen = rand() % (101) + 50;
```

```
//stores which numbers correspond to which menu choices
int archers_menu, catapults_menu, swordsmen_menu;
int fight_menu;

cout << "Welcome Adventurer, what is your name?\n";
cin >> name;
cout << "Well, " << name
    << " welcome to the Roman Commander Game.\n"
    << "\nYou are the commander of the Roman Army"
    << " attacking Germania.";
while (!end) //main game loop
{
    //variables to store how many units the player sends
    int archers_sent=0, catapults_sent=0;
    int swordsmen_sent=0;
    cout << "\nYou have " << archers
        << " archers, " << catapults
        << " catapults, and "
        << swordsmen << " swordsmen.\n"
        << "\nGermania has " << g_archers
        << " archers, "
        << g_catapults << " catapults, and "
        << g_swordsmen
        << " swordsmen.\n";
    do //pre-battle loop
    {
        //keeps track of which menu numbers
        //are being used
        int i = 1;
        if (archers > 0 &&
            ((archers - archers_sent) != 0))
        {
            archers_menu = i;
            cout << "[" << i << "] Send Archers\n";
            i++;
        }
        else archers_menu = 0;
        if (catapults > 0 &&
            ((catapults - catapults_sent) != 0))
        {
            catapults_menu = i;
            cout << "[" << i << "] Send Catapults\n";
            i++;
```

```
        }
        else catapults_menu = 0;
        if (swordsmen > 0 &&
              ((swordsmen - swordsmen_sent) != 0))
        {
              swordsmen_menu = i;
              cout << "[" << i << "] Send Swordsmen\n";
              i++;
        }
        else swordsmen_menu = 0;
        fight_menu = i;
        cout <<"["<< i <<"] Go Fight\n";

        cin >> menu_choice;
        if (menu_choice == archers_menu)
        {
              do {
                    cout << "How many archers"
                          " would you like to send?\n";
                    cin >> archers_sent;
              }while (!(archers_sent > -1
                    && archers_sent <= archers));
        }
        else if  (menu_choice == catapults_menu)
        {
              do {
                    cout << "How many catapults"
                          " would you like to send?\n";
                    cin >> catapults_sent;
              }while (!(catapults_sent > -1 &&
                    catapults_sent <= catapults));
        }
        else if (menu_choice == swordsmen_menu)
        {
              do {
                    cout << "How many swordsmen"
                          " would you like to send?\n";
                    cin >> swordsmen_sent;
              }
              while (!(swordsmen_sent > -1 &&
                    swordsmen_sent <= swordsmen));
         }
}
```

```
//end pre-battle loop
while (menu_choice != fight_menu);

cout << "\nEntering Battle...\n";

int archers_dead, catapults_dead, swordsmen_dead;
int g_archers_dead, g_catapults_dead;
int g_swordsmen_dead;

//each catapult kills 2 archers
archers_dead = 2 * g_catapults;
//each swordsman kills 1 catapult
catapults_dead = g_swordsmen;
//each archer kills 3 swordsmen
swordsmen_dead = 3 * g_archers;

g_archers_dead = 2 * catapults_sent;
g_catapults_dead = swordsmen_sent;
g_swordsmen_dead = 3 * archers_sent;

//makes sure that the number of
//units does not go below 0.
archers = (archers_dead < archers) ?
     archers - archers_dead : 0;
catapults = (catapults_dead < catapults) ?
     catapults - catapults_dead : 0;
swordsmen = (swordsmen_dead < swordsmen) ?
     swordsmen - swordsmen_dead : 0;

g_archers = (g_archers_dead < g_archers) ?
     g_archers - g_archers_dead : 0;
g_catapults = (g_catapults_dead < g_catapults) ?
     g_catapults - g_catapults_dead : 0;
g_swordsmen = (g_swordsmen_dead < g_swordsmen) ?
     g_swordsmen - g_swordsmen_dead : 0;

cout << "It was a long battle. "
      << archers_dead << " archers died.\n"
      << catapults_dead << " catapults died.\n"
      << swordsmen_dead << " swordsmen died.\n";
//if player's army is dead than they have lost
if ((archers + catapults + swordsmen) == 0)
     end = lost = true;
```

```
        //if germanium army is dead, player has won
        else if ((g_archers + g_catapults
             + g_swordsmen) == 0)
        {
             end = true;
             lost = false;
        }
    } //end of main game loop

    //display appropriate ending message
    if (lost)
    {
        cout << "\nYou lost. Try again next time.\n";
        return 0;
    }
    cout << "\nCongratulations, you won!\n";
    return 0;
}
```

**Output:**

```
Welcome Adventurer, what is your name?
Marcus
Well, Marcus welcome to the Roman Commander Game.

You are the commander of the Roman Army attacking Germania.
You have 50 archers, 25 catapults, and 100 swordsmen.

Germania has 61 archers, 50 catapults, and 52 swordsmen.
[1] Send Archers
[2] Send Catapults
[3] Send Swordsmen
[4] Go Fight
1
How many archers would you like to send?
50
[1] Send Catapults
[2] Send Swordsmen
[3] Go Fight
1
How many catapults would you like to send?
25
[1] Send Swordsmen
[2] Go Fight
```

```
1
How many swordsmen would you like to send?
100
[1] Go Fight
1

Entering Battle...
It was a long battle. 100 archers died.
52 catapults died.
183 swordsmen died.

You lost. Try again next time.
```

## Summary

In this chapter, you learned how to create a program that can make choices and adapt to user input. By learning first about boolean operators and then about selection and iteration statements, you continued your journey into an area never before ventured into. These lessons are an integral part of programming and will increase the functionality of your programs dramatically.

### CHALLENGES

1. **Write a conditional statement (an `if` statement) that will assign x/y to x if y doesn't equal 0.**
2. **Write a `while` loop that calculates the summative of positive integers from 1 to some number *n* (if you want to check this, the formula is n * (n + 1) /2).**
3. **Write a conditional statement that assigns x * y if x is even; otherwise, if x is odd and y doesn't equal 0, assign x to x / y; if neither of the preceding cases is `true`, output to the screen that y is equal to 0.**

# Writing Functions

**If you have been working through this book in its natural sequence, you have progressed far on your journey. Sit for a moment and let all the information sift through your brain; then get a cup of black coffee, settle into your favorite chair, and brace yourself. You've got an exciting trip ahead.**

**In this chapter, you learn about the following:**

- **Writing functions**
- **Using the `void` keyword**
- **Creating default arguments**
- **Differentiating variable scope**
- **The `main` function**
- **Developing macros**

## Divide and Conquer

Imagine that you are the commander of the Roman Empire's army, attacking the barbarian hordes in Germania. As any of your royal strategists will tell you, attacking your opponent's entire army at once is not very strategic. It is much more cunning to splinter the army into sections and attack each section separately. Doing so puts your army at a significant advantage and allows the might of the Roman Empire to grow even further.

The same is true for programming in C++. If you have a massive application to design and are working on a time limit, the easiest way to tackle the problem is to divide it into several programming tasks and then handle each task separately. As any mathematician will tell you—divide the problem into a group of problems that have already been solved, and you are done. This is the idea behind using functions.

*Functions* enable programmers to divide their code into many manageable pieces. Also, using functions, rather than repeating code numerous times, you can write it once and then use it again and again. With functions, instead of having to figure out a solution every time you encounter a problem, you allow a function to do that job for you. Then you can use the solution wherever it is needed.

For example, you might write a function called `getWindowSize` that calculates the size of a certain window. Whenever you need to know the size of a particular window, you just allow that function to calculate the size. Keep in mind that the function and the code asking the function to perform a task must communicate with each other. In the current example, the `getWindowSize` function needs to know which window is in question, and the function has to send the asking code the size of that window.

Before proceeding, here are some definitions we use as we continue through this chapter (you might not understand all of them now, but you will by the time you finish this chapter):

- **Arguments.** Pieces of information (data) that the *calling procedure* sends to functions (see the following bullets on calling procedure and function). This is also sometimes called a *parameter*.
- **Argument list.** A list of arguments that must be passed in order to call a certain function.
- **Block of code (or code block).** Any code enclosed within curly braces.

- **Calling a function.** Asking a function to perform a task.
- **Calling procedure.** Any piece of code that calls a function (that does the asking).
- **Function.** A segment of code that performs a specific task.
- **Return value.** Any value that a function returns to the calling procedure. Note that a given function can have only one return value, as illustrated in Figure 4.1.

## Exploring Function Syntax

In this section, we move from a theoretical to a practical level in which you learn how to write the code required for functions. To do so, you must first learn the art of function syntax. For now, however, you need to be concerned only with three parts of a function. The following three parts will be the foundation for your programs' interactions with functions and for your declaration of functions:

- The function declaration
- The function definition
- The function call

In the following sections, we discuss each of these parts.

### Declaring a Function

A function declaration tells the compiler that a function exists. You tell the compiler the name of the function, what the arguments are, and what the function returns. A function declaration is also called a *prototype* because it is a model of the function. Here is the general syntax for a function declaration:

```
return_type function_name(argument_list);
```

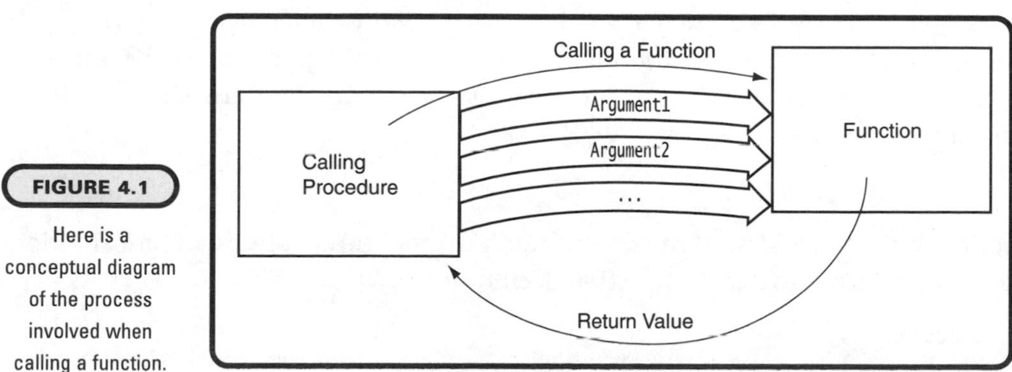


**FIGURE 4.1**

Here is a conceptual diagram of the process involved when calling a function.

Here *return_type* is the type of data that the function returns, *function_name* is the name of the function, and *argument_list* is a list of arguments that the function requires. Don't forget to add a semicolon at the end of the declaration.

*argument_list* can be blank if there are no arguments:

```
return_type function_name();
```

Otherwise, the argument list is a list of variable declarations separated by commas:

```
return_type function_name(arg1_type arg1_name, arg2_type arg2_name, …);
```

Notice that each argument declaration is just a simple variable declaration (you might recognize this syntax from the material in Chapter 2, "Descending Deeper . . . into Variables").

### Example—the add Function

The idea behind the `add` function is relatively straightforward–take two numbers, add them, and return the result. Although we use integers for this example, any numerical data type will work.

To write the function declaration, you need three pieces of information:

- The function name
- The function return type
- The function argument list

The function name can be any valid identifier (refer to Chapter 2 for more on identifiers). However, a concise name that describes the function's purpose makes the most sense. In this case, deciding on a name is relatively easy. It is named `add`.

The function return type needs to be an integer. You use the integer type (`int`) because the function returns a number.

The last piece of information needed is the function argument list. Because the function takes two arguments, you must write two variable declarations, which we arbitrarily refer to as arguments `a` and `b`. Both `a` and `b` must be integers because they represent the two numbers that you will add. Here is the resulting argument list:

```
(int a, int b)
```

Following the general syntax, you can put the three pieces of information together to form the `add()` function declaration:

```
int add(int a, int b);
```

Before you continue creating this function, you need to know how to define a function.

## Defining a Function

The information in this section is the heart and soul of a function. In this section, you write the code that a function contains. A function definition is like a function declaration with two curly braces ({ and }) within which you place the code. Here is the general syntax:

```
return_type function_name(argument_list)
{
	code;
}
```

Here *code* is one or more statements, each ending with a semicolon. Note that the function definition does not require a semicolon at the end.

One big difference between using C and C++ is your ability to declare variables wherever you need them with C++. Anywhere that you can include a statement in C++, you can also include a variable declaration.

**Even though you can include variable declarations almost anywhere, try to develop a standard way of using them. We declare them only at the beginning of code blocks. As a result, we can easily find the variable declarations.**

If a function returns a value, it must have one or more *return statements*. Return statements begin with the keyword `return` followed by an expression that evaluates to be the same data type as *return_type* and a semicolon. If you were to write a function that returned a float, this would be a valid return statement:

```
return 3.141592;
```

Upon reaching a return statement, the function terminates. You can have more than one return statement in a function. Here is a common procedure in a function:

```
if (condition)
	return expression1;
return expression2;
```

This code returns only *expression1* if the condition is `true`. Otherwise, it returns *expression2*.

You can use the variables created in arguments within a function. They are filled with the data that is passed when the function is called.

### Example—the add Function Continued

Now you are ready to define the add function. From the description of the function, you know that the sum of the two arguments must be returned. This definition then becomes a simple task:

```
int add(int a, int b)
{
     return a + b;
}
```

As you can see, this function is relatively short and simple. In the real programming world, functions can become very long, although it is good programming practice to keep your functions as short as possible.

## Calling a Function

In order to use a function in a certain section of code, you must call it from within that code. When you call a function, you are telling the computer to start executing another section of code (the code within the function) before continuing with this section.

To call a function, you write the function's name followed by the arguments you are passing. Here is the general syntax:

```
function_name(data1, data2, …);
```

Here *data1* and *data2* must be of the same data types as those in the function definition. For example, if the first argument in the function definition is an integer, *data1* also must be an integer, though exceptions occur wherever the value that you pass can be converted easily into the correct value. In the preceding example, you could pass a float or double value (for example, 3.56), and the value would be truncated to make an integer (for example, 3).

If the argument list in the function declaration and function definition is empty, you can use an empty set of parentheses (although it is better to use the void keyword, as we discuss later in this chapter):

```
function_name();
```

The values that you pass to the function are assigned to each of the variables in the argument list of the function declaration. For example, if your function declaration is

```
int my_Function(int first, int second)
{
     return first;
}
```

and you call the function somewhere else

```
my_Function(5,3)
```

the semantics of this function call are the same as the semantics of these two initializations:

```
int first = 5;
int second = 3;
```

The compiler first checks the type of data that you pass to the function against the type that the function requires. In this example, C++ checks to see whether you are passing `my_Function` two integers. If a conversion (cast) is required (for example, `float` to `int`), the conversion is done. If the two types of data are incompatible, the compiler returns an error. In this way, your function can access the data that you pass to it.

Return values are a little bit more confusing. When you call a function in your code, that call is replaced by the return value. Because `my_Function` returns an integer, you can call `my_Function` anywhere within code where you would normally use an integer. Here is an example:

```
my_Int = 5 + my_Function(5,3);
```

After `my_Function` finishes executing, the call is replaced by the value it returns (this replacement is not immediately obvious, so keep it in mind as you program):

```
my_Int = 5 + 5;
```

## Example—the add Function Continued

You now have enough information to write the function call to the `add` function. Here is a program that asks the user for two values and uses the `add` function to output the sum:

```
#include <iostream>
using namespace std;
```

```
int main (void)
{
      int number1, number2;
      cout << "Enter the first value to be summed: ";
      cin >> number1;
      cout << "\nEnter the second: ";
      cin >> number2;
      cout << "\nThe sum is: " << add(number1, number2) << endl;
}
```

This program first asks the user for two numbers and then gives the sum.

## Putting It All Together

A complete program that contains a function has three basic components:

- An optional function declaration
- The `main` function
- The function definition

A function must either be declared or defined before it can be called. If you put the function definition at the beginning of your program, a declaration is not needed. However, if the function definition is at the end of the program and you call the function prior to the function definition, you need to tell your computer that the function exists. You do so by placing the function's declaration at the beginning of the program.

Here is the complete "Add Program" with the `add` function. This program requires a function declaration because the function definition is at the end of the program:

```
//4.1 - The Add Program - Mark Lee - Premier Press
#include <iostream>
using namespace std;
//add declaration
int add(int a, int b);
//displays a sample use of the add function
int main (void)
{
      int number1, number2;
      cout << "Enter the first value to be summed: ";
      cin >> number1;
      cout << "\nEnter the second: ";
```

```
        cin >> number2;
        cout << "\nThe sum is: " << add(number1, number2)
            << endl;
}

// adds two numbers and returns the sum
int add(int a, int b)
{
        return a + b;
}
```

Until now, you have placed code inside `int main (void)` and its closing brace. (This section of code is called the `main` function.) Function declarations and definitions must go outside this section. (Don't worry if this seems confusing right now; it will become much clearer in time.)

Another way to write this program is to place the `add` definition at the beginning rather than at the end of the code. In this case, you don't need a function declaration because the function definition acts as its own declaration:

```
#include <iostream>
using namespace std;

int add(int a, int b)
{
        return a + b;
}

int main (void)
{
        int number1, number2;
        cout << "Enter the first value to be summed: ";
        cin >> number1;
        cout << "\nEnter the second: ";
        cin >> number2;
        cout << "\nThe sum is: " << add(number1, number2) << endl;
}
```

This way, having the definition at the beginning works just as well as adding a declaration and having the definition at the end of the program. Neither way offers a particular advantage, so which one you choose is just a matter of preference.

## Using the void keyword

Some functions do not necessarily return a value. Maybe the only purpose of one of your functions is to display some text. In this case, you do not need a return value.

Unlike arguments, if you don't have a return value, you cannot just leave the space before the function name blank in the function declaration or definition.

Here is where the `void` keyword comes into play. `void` is similar to zero in that it represents no value. For a non-returning function, put the term `void` where the return type would be:

```
void function_name(arg_list)
```

However, if you do this, you need to make sure that you do not try to return a value in your function. You can, however, have an empty `return` statement, as shown here:

```
return;
```

This statement terminates the function. An empty `return` statement for a `void` function is not required. If there are no `return` statements, the function ends when it runs out of code.

If your function has no arguments (regardless of whether it has a return value), you can use the `void` keyword as the argument list instead of leaving that field blank. You don't gain a particular advantage either way.

## Overloading Functions

What do you do when you are writing the `add` function for more than one possible data type? One approach is to write a separate function for each one, using a different name for each one. You might call one function `int_add()` to add two integers and another function `float_add()` to add two floats. This process can be quite tedious, and if you want to use the function, you must look up the proper name for the right data type.

Fortunately, C++ provides an alternative. Instead of giving each function a different name, you give them all the same name. This is called *overloading* the function. For example, every version of the `add` function is called `add`. But how does the computer tell them apart? When you call the `add` function, how does the computer know which version of the `add` function to use?

The answer is really quite simple. The computer just looks at the argument types and the number of arguments and attempts to match your function call to the correct function. Here is an example:

```
int add (int a, int b)
{
      return a + b;
}
float add (float a, float b)
{
      return a + b;
}
int main(void)
{
      cout << add(5,3);
      cout << add(5.5, 4.7);
      return 0;
}
```

The first call to `add` calls the integer version of the `add` function (the first one) because `5` and `3` are both integers and this matches the prototype for the integer version of `add`. The second call to `add` calls the floating-point version of the function.

## Defaulting Arguments

In C++, you can specify a default value for some parameters. If the calling procedure does not pass a complete argument list, the default arguments are used.

Here is the general syntax for implementing arguments in your code:

```
return_type function_name(arg_type arg_name = default_value)
```

Here *`default_value`* is the default value for the argument. Of course, you can still have more than one argument:

```
return_type function_name(arg1 = value1, arg2 = value2)
```

Here *`arg1`* and *`arg2`* are the argument types and names.

It is possible to have some arguments with default values and some without default values. The rule is that all the arguments without default values must come first in the argument list. In other words, for any particular argument with a default value, all the arguments following it in the argument list must also have default values.

To use such a function, you treat some of the arguments as nonexistent. If your function declaration is

```
int my_Function(int a, int b, int c = 0);
```

you can call this function two ways:

```
cout << my_Function(5, 3, 6);
cout << my_Function(5, 3);
```

In the first line, the value of `c` is `6`, but in the second the line, the value of `c` is `0`.

This device is useful for arguments that you don't use very often but need to include in order to maintain functionality. Maintaining functionality and convenience is an important step toward producing excellent code.

## Seeing Further with Variable Scope

All code that you write in a program can fit one of four categories, each with its own rules about which variables can access it:

- Code inside the `main` function
- Code in another function
- Code in a block of code, such as an `if` statement or a namespace
- Code outside functions

Within each of these categories are rules for how long a variable lasts *(variable lifetime)* and where it can be accessed *(variable scope).*

The general rules for variable scope and lifetime are as follows:

- If the variable is declared outside a block of code, it is called *global,* and its scope and lifetime are from the point of declaration until the end of the source file. (As we mentioned earlier in this chapter, a *block* of code is any code within curly braces.)
- If the variable is declared within a block of code, it is called *local,* and its scope and lifetime are until the end of the block.
- If the variable is declared within an argument list of a function, it is called a *parameter,* and its scope and lifetime are until the end of the function.

All this means that functions cannot access the variables declared within the `main` function unless they are passed as arguments to the function.

If a variable is declared within a block that is within another block, the scope of the variable is restricted to the inner block.

Perhaps this example will help clarify the preceding rules:

```
//4.2 - Variable Scope Example - Mark Lee - Premier Press
#include <iostream>
using namespace std;

int subtract (int a, int b);

int global = 5;

int main(void)
{
     int a, b;
     a = 5;
     b = 3;
     cout << "The value of main's a is: " << a << endl
          << "The value of main's b is: " << b << endl
          << "The value of global is: " << global << endl;
     global = 2 + subtract(a,b);
     cout << "The value of main's a now is: " << a << endl
          << "The value of global now is: " << global << endl;
     return 0;
}

int subtract(int a, int b)
{
     cout << "The value of subtract's a is: " << a << endl
          << "The value of subtract's b is: " << b << endl;
     a = a - b + global;
     return a;
}
```

**Output:**

```
The value of main's a is: 5
The value of main's b is: 3
The value of global is: 5
The value of subtract's a is: 5
The value of main's a now is: 5
the value of global now is: 9
```

In line 5, the global variable, `global`, is declared. In line 11, `main`'s two local variables, `a` and `b`, are declared. In line 17, the values in `main`'s `a` and `b` are copied into subtract's a and b. subtract then finds the difference and assigns it to a in line 27. When this value is returned from the subtract function, global = 2 + subtract(a,b), you have the following:

```
global = 2 + 7;
```

In other words, because subtract returns the value of subtract's a, line 17 is just adding 2 to the returned value, which is 7 in this case.

Remember that two separate, unrelated versions of a and b are in this code; main's a has nothing to do with subtract's a.

## Specifying with the Scope Resolution Operator

Sometimes you might come across situations where a global variable and a local variable have the same name. This is legal in C++, but it can cause some confusion. Here is an example:

```
int intVar;
int main(void)
{
	int intVar;	// Different from the global named intVar
	intVar = 5;
	return 0;
}
```

It is hard to tell at first glance which version of intVar is assigned the value 5, but a rule does exist. If a local variable has the same name as a global variable, the local variable is said to *shadow* the global variable. All operations performed on a variable by that name are performed on the local variable. How then do you access the global variable in these situations?

The answer is by using the *scope resolution operator.* If you want to make sure that the global version of the variable is used, just put two colons (::) in front of it. For example, to make the preceding code use the global version, you change the previous code to the following:

```
int intVar;
int main(void)
{
	int intVar;
	::intVar = 5;
	return 0;
}
```

This shadowing effect can also happen with subblocks. For example, if you have an `if` statement within the `main` function, a variable declared within the `if` block can shadow a global variable or a local variable of `main`. However, the scope resolution operator can be used only to specify a global variable. For example, if an `if` statement variable shadows a `main` variable, you can access the `main` version of that variable. Here's an illustration:

```
#include <iostream>
#include <string>
using namespace std;

string str = "Humans and elves can coexist. ";

//exemplifies the scope resolution operator(::)
int main(void)
{
      string str = "Elves often live in the woods. ";
      cout << str.c_str() << "---" << ::str.c_str() << endl;
}
```

**Output:**

```
Elves often live in the woods.---Humans and elves can coexist.
```

## Using Static Variables

You will sometimes find it convenient to use the same variable within a function every time the function is called. Local variables don't work because they are re-created every time the function is called. Global variables will work fine, except that sometimes they can be inconvenient. One solution is to use *static variables.*

Static variables have the same scope as normal variables, but their lifetime lasts until the end of the program. In this way, you can create a function that has a "memory."

You declare a static variable with the `static` keyword:

```
static var_type var_name;
```

The statement in which the static variable is created is executed only once for the whole program. This means that if you initialize the static variable on the same line

```
static var_type var_name = value;
```

this initialization will be executed only once.

Take a look at the following example:

```
//4.3 - Static Variables Example - Dirk Henkemans
//and Mark Lee - Premier Press
#include <iostream>
using namespace std;

int incrementFunction1(void);
int incrementFunction2(void);

//runs the increment functions
int main(void)
{
     for(int c = 0 ; c < 4 ; c++)
     {
          cout<<"incrementing both variables" <<endl;
          cout<< "value of function1 is: "
               << incrementFunction1() <<endl;
          cout<< "value of function2 is: " <<
               incrementFunction2() <<endl;

     }
     return 0;
}


//an increment function with a static variable
int incrementFunction1(void)
{
     static int x = 0;
     x++;
     return x;
}

//an increment function with a non-static variable
int incrementFunction2(void)
{
     int y = 0;
     y++;
     return y;
}
```

**Output:**

```
incrementing both variables
value of function1 is: 1
value of function2 is: 1
incrementing both variables
value of function1 is: 2
value of function2 is: 1
incrementing both variables
value of function1 is: 3
value of function2 is: 1
incrementing both variables
value of function1 is: 4
value of function2 is: 1
```

In this example, both `x` and `y` are local variables. While `x` is static and is initialized only once, `y` is initialized to `0` every time `incrementFunction2` is called. For this reason, `incrementFunction2` always returns `1`, whereas `incrementFunction1` will continue to increment `x`.

## Welcome to the Snail Races

Now, it's time to try out the skills you've gained from this chapter. In the "The Snail Racing Game," be sure to watch for instances that relate to the following points:

- There is only one global variable (`money`). It is global because it is declared outside of functions.
- `money` is used as a local variable in the `race()` function and as a global variable; the default is the local variable; however, whenever `money` is used as a global variable, the scope resolution operator (`::`) is used.
- This example has two versions of the `race()` function. They take different arguments. These two `race()` functions are an example of overloading functions.

Now, for some mood setting: Do you ever find yourself wishing that time would go just a little slower? Go to the snail races and that wish will come true. (Don't worry, eventually, one of the cute little critters will win, but you could be there a while.)

```
//4.4 - The Snail Racing Game -Dirk Henkemans
//and Mark Lee - Premier Press
#include <iostream>
```

```
#include <ctime>
using namespace std;

//function declarations
int main(void);
int race(int, int);
void race(void);
int menu(void);
int placeBet(int);
void ini(void);

//variables
int money = 200;

//the main function
int main(void)
{
     ini();

     int userResponse;
     cout<< "Welcome to the snail races!!!" <<endl;
     while(userResponse = menu())
     {
          switch(userResponse)
          {
          case 1:
          case 2:
          case 3:
               ::money +=
               race(placeBet(userResponse), userResponse);
               break;
          case 4: //the user did not bet
               race();
               break;
          }

     }

     return 0;
```

```
}

//displays the main menu and
//returns the user's selection
int menu(void)
{
      int userResponse;
      cout << "You have " << money << " dollars."<< endl;
      do
      {
            cout<< "Races Menu" <<endl
                  << "1) Bet on snail 1" << endl
                  << "2) Bet on snail 2" << endl
                  << "3) Bet on snail 3" << endl
                  << "4) Just Watch" << endl
                  << "0) leave the races" << endl;
            cin>> userResponse;
      }
      while(userResponse < 0 && userResponse > 4);
      return userResponse;
}

//decides how much a person will bet on the snail
int placeBet(int userResponse)
{
      int betAmount;
      cout<< "Snail " << userResponse << " is a good choice!"
            << endl;
      cout<< "How much would you like to bet on your snail "
            << userResponse <<"?";
      cin >> betAmount;
      return betAmount;
}

//if they are just watching the race
void race (void)
{
      race(0, 0);
}
```

```
//if they are betting money
int race (int money, int userResponse)
{
    //stores the random number
    int winner = rand() % 3 + 1;
    cout<< "And the snails are off" << endl
        << "Look at them GO!!!" << endl
        << "The winner is snail " << winner;
    if(winner == userResponse)
    {
        cout<< "You Win!" <<endl;
        return 2 * money;
    }
    cout<<"You loose " << money << " dollars." <<endl;
    return -1 * money;
}

//handles program initializations
void ini(void)
{
    srand(time(0));
}
```

This program is a basic racing program; feel free to add to it and make it more exciting.

## Revealing the main Function

You've probably noticed that we keep calling `main` a function. There is a reason for this: `main` is a function. "But, it can't be!" you say, "I just learned about functions, and I've been using `main` since Chapter 1 ("Starting the Journey")!" Fear not, young adventurer. This is a simpler concept than you might think.

You can broadly define a *function* as a section of code that breaks a program into smaller, more manageable tasks.

Think about your computer's operating system. If it is multitasking, it will have many programs running at once. Each of these programs has a `main` function (or a version of one).

Generally, every program begins when the `main` function begins and ends when the `main` function ends.

Now, think of your operating system as a program. From it, all the other `main` functions are called (as illustrated in Figure 4.2).

Are you beginning to see a parallel between your operating system and a program that you create? There are also parallels among the `main` function and the functions that you create. This is why `main` is a function.

In our experience, most programmers become confused at this point about exactly how a program runs. How does the computer decide where to start? We anticipated some confusion, so we now take you through the process, step by step.

## Examining the Sequence of Execution

Following is the order in which tasks are executed in any program:

1. All global variables are created. (Globals are initialized and stored inside the run-time code at compile time.)
2. The `main` function begins.
3. Each line of code in the `main` function executes sequentially.
4. The `main` function exits.
5. All local variables are destroyed.
6. When the program unloads, all global variables go away.

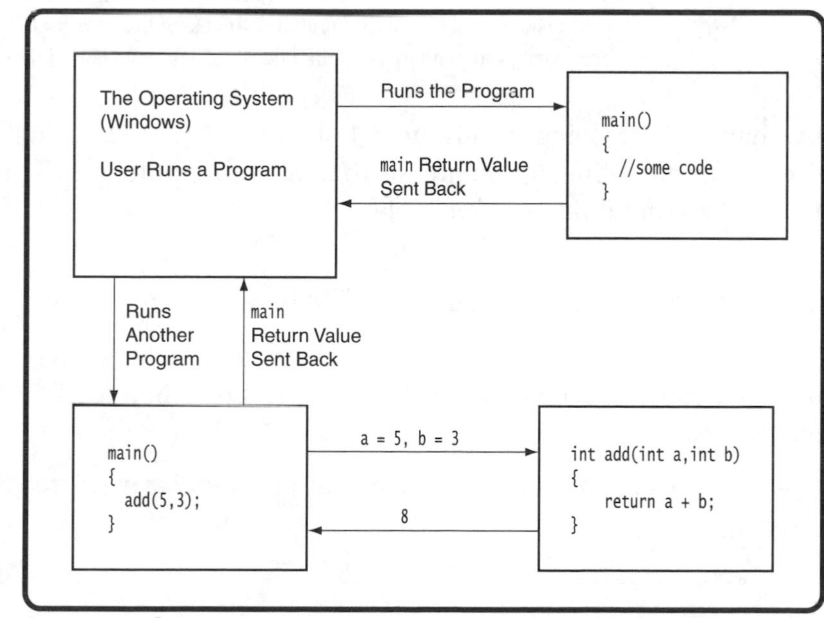


**FIGURE 4.2**

Here is how the operating system interacts with the `main` function.

Global variables are initialized before the `main` function is called because they are outside the `main` function. Their scope is larger than the `main` function's scope.

From the `main` function, all other functions are called. It is the container for the entire program (except for global variables). So, even though functions are written outside the `main` function, they are, in a sense, contained within it.

## Passing Arguments to main

When the operating system starts a program, the system sometimes passes information to that program. For the kind of programs that you are creating right now, only one kind of information can be passed; command-line arguments. But in other programs, such as a Windows-based program, many kinds of information can be passed.

In DOS or UNIX, you must type the program name at the command prompt in order to run a certain program. In some programs, you can provide additional information after the program name. For example, in an Internet browser, you might type a Web address after the program name, and then the browser will go immediately to that page.

**If you are using Windows as your operating system, you are probably not familiar with typing command lines at a command prompt (unlike those of you who use or have used DOS or UNIX). To access the MS-DOS prompt, from the Windows taskbar, click Start and from the menu that appears select Programs, MS-DOS Prompt (or your options might be Start, Programs, Accessories, Command Prompt). You can find command prompt tutorials on the Internet if you need more information.**

In Chapter 6, "Moving to Advanced Data Types," you learn how to respond to these command-line arguments so that your program can use them. For now, just realize that doing so is possible.

## Using the main Return Values

In all the programs presented so far, we have used `main` return `0`. This value is the one that you will see in nearly all programs, but other possible values have different meanings.

Often, the operating system's call to your program is structured like this:

```
if (call_program)
     error_message;
```

Here *call_program* is the call to your program, and *error_message* is a piece of code that displays some sort of error message.

Because all the programs so far have returned 0, this *error_message* line has not been executed. Returning 0 means that your program executed without errors. If you return a non-zero value, the *error_message* line will be executed, which means that your program has an error.

The return value of the main function tells the compiler whether your program executed with or without errors. This information becomes important in later chapters, but for now, just keep it in mind.

## Macros: Constants on Steroids

As shocking as this might be, you've already been introduced to one kind of *macro*: constants declared with the define keyword. Every macro is declared with this keyword. Macros provide a way to replace a short section of code with something much more convenient. The only purpose of macros is convenience. They do not add or subtract from your code's efficiency. In fact, the executable code is exactly the same. Here is an example:

```
#define PI 3.141592
```

This code tells the compiler to replace the word PI in your code with the number 3.141592. In Chapter 2, we define this statement as a constant. However, it can be more generally defined as a macro. A constant declared with the define keyword is a kind of macro.

You can use macros for much more than creating constants, however. Generally, macros are used to replace a common, short piece of code with something even shorter. A macro can replace any single code statement, as illustrated here with the macro PRNT, which replaces cout <<:

```
#define PRNT cout <<
...
PRNT("Hello World");
```

This code sample replaces every instance of the text PRNT with cout <<, essentially making your statements much more readable. Notice that parentheses are required around the argument, "Hello World", just as with a function. Without a macro, the preceding code would look like this:

```
cout << "Hello World";
```

Recall that the data sent to a function is called an *argument*. Macros are similar to functions in this respect. In the preceding example, the string, `"Hello World"` can be thought of as an argument sent to the macro. Actually, this is not entirely true because the compiler simply replaces the code; the string is not actually sent anywhere. This macro does not return a value, but it is possible to have macros that do.

One of the most common returning macros is `MAX`. Given two numbers, it will return the maximum. If the two numbers are equal, it will return either one of them. Here is `MAX` in all its glory:

```
#define MAX(a,b) (a>b) ? a : b
```

This macro takes two arguments, `a` and `b`. The section of code

```
MAX(a,b)
```

is like a function declaration except that the type is not required. The rest of the line

```
(a>b) ? a : b
```

can be thought of as the code that goes inside the function.

Here's an example of how you might use this macro in your code:

```
int x = 5;
float y = 5.5;
cout << MAX(x, y);
```

**Ouput:**

```
5.5
```

Here is how this code looks without a macro:

```
int x = 5;
float y = 5.5;
cout << (x > y) ? x : y;
```

Notice that `a` and `b` in the macro are replaced by `x` and `y` when the macro is used. `a` and `b` are used to represent whatever argument was sent to the macro.

How does this relate to functions? In a general sense, macros are a simplified version of functions. The concepts are similar. Macros can take arguments, and they can return a value just like functions do. To call a macro, as you do when calling functions, you use its name followed by its arguments.

## Creating the Cave Adventure Game

After emerging from the Dark Macro Forest, you see some smoke in the distance. You venture closer and realize that a village is burning. Some goblins are attacking a gnome village! Noble adventurer, will you journey forth to the goblin cave and rid this world of the evil attackers? The gnomes need your help, and you will need to use everything you now know about functions in order to help them!

```
//4.5 - The Cave Adventure Game - Dirk Henkemans - Premier Press
#include <iostream>
using namespace std;

bool intro(void);
void room(bool enemy, bool treasure, string description);
//player stats
string name = "";
//enemy stats
string enemyName = "";
//treasure stats
string treasureName = "";
//room descriptions;
const string room1 = "You enter the mouth of the caves.";
const string room2 = "You adventure deeper into the caves.";
const string room3 = "You have reached the depths of the caves.";

int main( void )
{
     if (intro())
          return 0; //if they choose not to do it exit the program
     treasureName = "gold sword";
     enemyName = "goblin";
     room(true, true, room1);
     enemyName = "wombat";
     room(true, false, room2);
                enemyName = "hobgoblin lord.";
     treasureName = "treasure horde.";
     room(true, true, room3);
     return 0;
}
```

```
bool intro(void)
{
     cout<<"Brave knight!!! What is your name? \n";
     cin>>name;
     cout<<"We are in need of your help "<< name
          <<", our village is being over run \nby "
          <<"the goblins of the northern caves.  Will "
          << " you accept the challenge? \n \n";
     cout<<"1) yes \n"
          <<"2) no \n \n";
               int response;
     cin>>response;
               return !(response == 1);
}


//Displays the description for the room and gives the options
void room(bool enemy, bool treasure, string description)
{
     while(true)
     {
          cout<<description.c_str()<<endl<<endl;
          int response = 0;
          do
          {
               cout<<"What would you like to do? \n"<<endl;
       if(enemy)
                    cout<<" 1)Attack the evil "<<
                         enemyName.c_str()<<endl;
               else if(!enemy)
                    cout<<" 1)Move to the next room.";
               if(treasure)
                   cout<<" 2)Pick up the "<<treasureName.c_str()
                         <<endl;
               cin>>response;
          }
         while(response < 1 || response > 2);
                    switch(response)
         {
              case 1:
```

```
                if(enemy)
                {
                    enemy = !enemy;
                    cout<<"You slay the deadly "
                        <<enemyName.c_str()<<endl;
                }
                else if(!enemy)
                    return;
                break;
            case 2:
                treasure = !treasure;
                cout<<"You pick up the "
                        <<treasureName.c_str()<<endl;
                break;
        }
    }
}
```

Take some time. Study this code. Figure out how it works. Try compiling it. Then try making some changes to it. Make it yours. Look at how it relates to the concepts presented in this chapter.

## Summary

You have learned some important concepts in this chapter, and with every word, you've come one step closer to being a professional programmer. You have learned how to create and use functions and variable scope, and you've found out exactly why `main` is a function.

You are at a point now where you have the basic set of tools needed to create your own programs. Try programming on your own and discover what you can do. Use this book as a reference, but try to remember as much as possible on your own.

If you're feeling overwhelmed, just scan this chapter again. You want to be comfortable with the information in this chapter before moving on.

## CHALLENGES

1. Write a function, called `multiply`, that multiplies two numbers and returns the result.
2. Change the function you wrote in Challenge 1 so that it remembers how many times you called it.
3. What is the difference between a global variable and a static variable? Which is better in which situation and why?
4. Try rewriting "The Cave Adventure Game" so that it does not use functions (an exercise to convince you how useful functions are).
5. If you actually made it through the last question, buy yourself a Slurpee.

CHAPTER 5

# Fighting with OOP

C++ enables you reuse code so that you don't have to write the same code again and again. Although most programming languages allow you to reuse code, in other languages, you often have to modify the reused code quite a bit to make it work. C++'s support of object-orientated programming (OOP) makes reusing an object, such as a game's hero, almost as easy as dropping the object into your next program. You could even clone the hero multiple times into an army of fire-wielding super heroes with little additional code.

In this chapter, you learn how to do the following:

- Declare classes
- Create objects
- Create a test chassis for your objects
- Add public and private methods and members to your classes
- Utilize the fundamental principles of OOP
- Construct a multiplayer strategy game

## Introduction to Object-Oriented Programming

Picture a programming object just like any normal object in the real world. Each real-world object has its own properties and specific things that you can do with it. For example, a bow has specific properties—such as color, number of arrows, and weight—and specific capabilities—such as the ability to fire. If you request a bow from an armory, you do not yet know what the properties of the specific bow will be. However, once you see the bow, you can determine its color, weight, and quiver size. As you will learn in the following section, this is very similar to the way objects work in the programming world.

Before continuing with OOP, you need to understand some key terms.

A *class* is like a general model from which you can create objects. For example, if you create a `dog` class, you describe the characteristics related to the general idea of a dog.

Creating a class is the same as creating a new data type. When you create a class, you tell the computer the kind and amount of data this new type can hold. You also tell the computer what actions the new type can perform. Then you can use the class you've created to create variables from this new type (as you will see, these variables are called *objects*). As complicated as this might seem now, creating your own classes is an easy process, as you will learn in the following sections.

You declare all the data members and methods inside a class. Figure 5.1 shows an example of what a `Bow` class might look like. The `Bow` class describes the general properties and capabilities of a bow. A `Bow` class tells the computer what a bow is in terms of programming so that the computer knows what to do the next time it encounters one.

*Objects* are a specific instance of a class. That is, the class *declares* what the properties of an object are, whereas the object stores specific values for each of these properties. For example, a `Bow` class describes that a bow has a certain color, but it doesn't identify the color. That way, each `Bow` object can have a different color. Figure 5.2 shows two `Bow` objects. Each is declared using the `Bow` class, but whereas the `Bow` class describes the properties of a bow, each of the two `Bow` objects has distinct values for these properties.

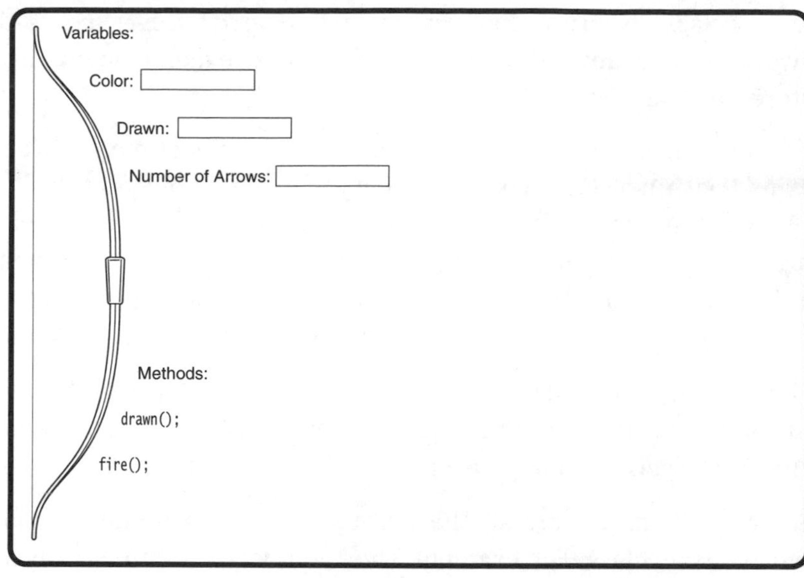


**FIGURE 5.1**

Here is the `Bow` class with its object methods and attributes.

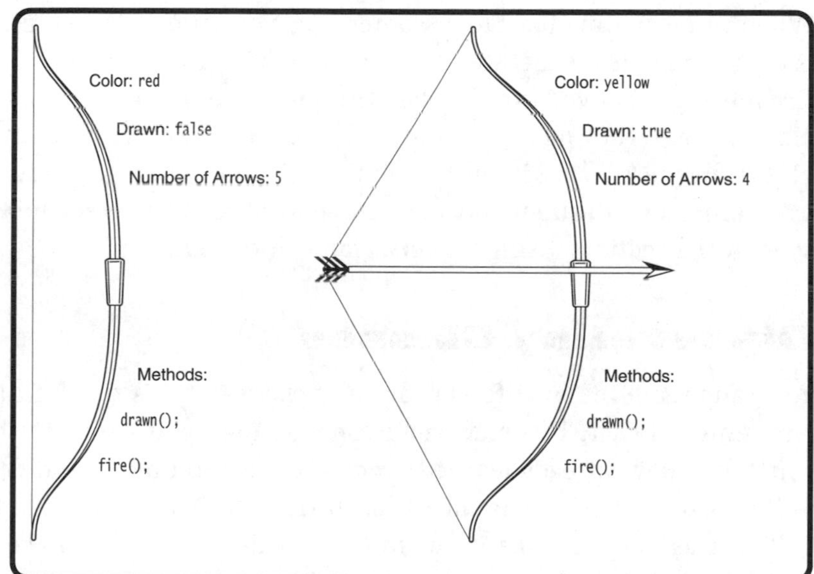


**FIGURE 5.2**

Here are two `Bow` objects derived from the `Bow` class.

Another analogy is a `Knight` class. You know that knights save princesses, slay dragons, are charming, and find magical items. Describing the attributes in this manner is very similar to creating the `Knight` class. If you create a specific knight, for example, Sir Lancelot, you have created an object. Sure, Sir Lancelot can save princesses, slay dragons, and find magical items with King Arthur at his side just as his class specifies. However, his actual *attributes*—such as the name of his sword, how many princesses he saved, and exactly how charming he is—are stored by the `SirLancelot` object.

*Methods* (also known as *member functions* or *object methods*) are functions contained within a class that define how you can use objects of the class. In the example `Bow` class, you might want to have methods such as `draw()` and `fire()`. Methods are like the functions that we previously used, except that methods are *part* of the object. The methods enable you to know what the object is capable of, and they are focused primarily on manipulating the object's data *(data members).*

*Data members* of a class are the variables that define what kind of data an object of the class can store. For example, an object created from the `Bow` class can store the color, weight, and quiver size.

A class's *members* are all the methods and data members that are contained within that class. For example, the members for the `Bow` objects are the data members—color, weight, and quiver size—and the methods— `fire()` and `draw()`.

When you want an object to do something, you send it a *message*. This is how you execute the object's methods. For example, if you want `bow1` to fire, you send it a fire message that will execute the `fire()` method. You can do this because the `Bow` class has a `fire()` method. In other words, `bow1` knows how to fire because all objects in the `Bow` class know how to fire. It's your job, as the programmer, to send `bow1` a message to fire if you want the bow to fire. You'll see how to send a message in the section "Using Objects," later in this chapter.

## Discovering Classes

You can create many different forms of classes, so it's time to dive directly into the center of OOP. This may be a little frightening at first, but think about how much you have already learned. Once you start to understand the concepts, you will realize that OOP is not nearly as difficult as it seems at first. It's really not as difficult as people make it out to be. In this section, we make learning about classes easy by teaching you how to declare a class, how to create methods, how to control access to objects, and how to organize your classes into different files.

### Declaring Classes

The following code is the general syntax for declaring a class. We go through it step by step following the code, but check it out carefully before moving on:

```
class ClassName
```

```
{
      memberList
};
```

Here *memberList* is the list of class members, and *ClassName* is the name of the class. Notice that *ClassName* begins with a capital letter. This is the most common convention, and we recommend it because your code will be very readable. Notice also that the class declaration ends with a semicolon. Forgetting the semicolon can cause strange errors, so be sure to include it.

*memberList* consists of a list of member declarations. These can be data member or method declarations. Data member declarations are normal variable declarations. For example, `int x;` is a data member declaration when inside a class. However, you cannot initialize data members where you declare them. They must be initialized either in a method or outside the class. For example, `int x = 5;` as a data member declaration causes an error. The scope of all data members is the same as the scope of the object created from the class. However, data members cannot always be accessed from outside a class. In the `Bow` class, these data members could store how many arrows are left, the color of the bow, and whether the bow is drawn. The data members of a class define and describe the class properties (also called *attributes*). Therefore, each bow object's color is a property of that object.

Method declarations are just as easy to understand as are data member declarations. *Method declarations* are function declarations placed inside a class (recall that a function declaration can also include the implementation, or you can implement it separately). All methods can be accessed only through an object of the class (with the exception of static methods, which we discuss later in the chapter in "Using Static Members").

Two special kinds of methods, the constructor and the destructor, can be in a class. Both are optional, but they provide special functionality that other methods cannot provide.

A *constructor* is executed every time a new instance of the class is created—that is, every time you declare a new object. The constructor is normally used to set initial values for the data members. For example, in the `Bow` class, a constructor might set the `drawn` boolean variable to be `false` and the number of arrows to `20`. A constructor always has the same name as the class and cannot have a return value (not even `void`).

**To understand classes and constructors, you might compare the classes you declare with the built-in data types that C++ already understands, such as `float` and `int`. All data have something like constructors, even C++'s built-in data types. For example, when you define an integer variable, you use the `int` keyword. C++ knows the properties of an integer. Therefore, C++ sets up a variable that can take only integer values. C++ does not, however, know what a `Bow` object is supposed to look like when you first define one. So your `Bow` class tells C++ what properties a `Bow` object will take on, and the constructor creates an initial `Bow` object with initial values.**

A *destructor* is the opposite of a constructor and is executed when the object is destroyed. The destructor is always named the same name as the class, but with a tilde (~) at the beginning (`~ClassName()`). The destructor cannot have arguments or a return value. In the example `Bow` class, the destructor would be `~Bow()`. A destructor is often used to perform any necessary cleanup tasks.

Here is what the `Bow` class looks like so far:

```
class Bow
{
	//data member declarations
	string color;
	bool drawn;
	int numOfArrows;

	Bow(string aColor);	//constructor
	~Bow();				//destructor

	//methods
	void draw();
	int fire();
};
```

The `Bow` class now has three data members that describe the attributes that each `Bow` object will take on. In addition, the `Bow` class contains four methods—`Bow()`, `~Bow()`, `draw()`, and `fire()`—but you have not, as yet, added the code to those methods. The preceding code fragment will compile (because the compiler assumes that the implementation of the methods is somewhere else), but if you try to use it, the program will crash and burn because there is no implementation of the declared methods.

## Creating Methods

You have, in general, walked through class declarations. Now, it is time to take a more detailed look at methods. This section provides some special rules and syntax, as well as hints on what to look out for when designing methods for classes.

First of all, you can declare a method two ways. The most common way is to declare a method inside the class declaration and then implement it outside. The second way is to declare and implement the method at the same time inside the class declaration.

You should declare most of your methods the first way. However, there is special syntax for the method implementation. Here is the general syntax for a method implementation that occurs outside a class:

```
return_type ClassName::methodName(argumentList)
{
      methodImplementation
}
```

Here *ClassName* is the name of the class, and *methodImplementation* is the code that goes inside the method. As you can see, this syntax is very similar to the function definition syntax. Notice that this is another use for the scope resolution operator (::). Here you are telling the computer to use the class's scope by putting the class's name in front.

Now, you are ready to implement the `draw()` and `fire()` methods of the `Bow` class. Here are the implementations:

```
//draws the bow
void Bow::draw()
{
      drawn = true;
      cout<< "The "<<color<<" bow has been drawn." <<endl;
}
//fires the bow if drawn
int Bow::fire()
{
      if(!drawn)
      {
            cout<< color << " has not been drawn "
                  << "and therefore could not fire." << endl;
            return 0;
      }
```

```
    int score;
    score = rand() % (10 - 0 + 1) + 0;
    if(score == 0)
        cout<<color<< " missed the target!!!" <<endl;
    else
        cout<< color << " scored " << score
            << " points!!!" <<endl;
    return score;
}
```

Remember that these implementations must be outside the class declaration. Also, they must be placed after the class declaration.

The second way to declare a method is to declare and implement the method at the same time. The syntax for this is nothing new to you. Here is an example:

```
class Hello
{
    void Display() { cout << "Hello World.\n"; }
};
```

Declaring a method this way is pretty simple. The catch is that a method declared this way is defined as an *inline* method. Because there is no keyword reminding you that it is inline, be on the lookout for methods declared this way.

If you implement a method outside a class, you can still make it an inline method by putting the `inline` keyword in front of the implementation. A method or function that is inline means that when the program is compiled, the compiler replaces all calls to the method or function with the code inside the method or function. Inline functions are similar to macros. They are used to increase speed, but they also increase the size of your program files.

## Designing Constructors and Destructors

Constructors and destructors are often an overwhelming concept for beginners, but in this section, we help you by cutting through the confusion.

Constructors are called automatically when an object is created, and destructors are called automatically when a function is destroyed. A constructor initializes the data members and performs all other required initialization tasks. A destructor performs all necessary cleanup tasks.

Both constructors and destructors are like methods; they can be declared and implemented at the same time or declared and implemented separately. Here is the syntax for declaring and implementing at the same time:

```
class ClassName
{
      //constructor
      ClassName(argumentList)
      {
            implementation
      }

      //destructor
      ~ClassName()
      {
            implementation
      }

      //other members
};
```

Here is the syntax for declaring and then implementing:

```
class ClassName
{
      ClassName(argumentList);
      ~ClassName();
      //other Members
};

ClassName::ClassName(argumentList)
{
      implementation
}

ClassName::~ClassName(argumentList)
{
      implementation
}
```

Notice that the constructor can have arguments. If you create a constructor with arguments, the user of your class must supply values for these arguments when creating an object. Having constructor arguments makes sense for many types of objects. For example, if you have a `Date` class, the arguments can specify which data a `Date` object will store.

The destructor, on the other hand, cannot have arguments. It is called automatically, so there isn't necessarily a chance for the user to provide arguments.

Because a constructor can have arguments, it might become necessary to overload the constructor. This is legal in C++ and is quite common in large classes. For example, in a `Date` class, you might want to enable a user to initialize a `Date` object with a string representation of the date or an integer version. Overloading the constructor in this way gives your class versatility and provides users of the class with many options.

The destructor cannot be overloaded. Having no return type or arguments, there is nothing with which the destructor can be overloaded.

A convenient and quick way to initialize data members in the constructor is to use an initializer list. An *initializer list* is a list of the data members you want to initialize, with the values to which you want to initialize them shown in parentheses. Here is the general syntax:

```
ClassName(argumentList) :
      dataMember1(value1), dataMember2(value2)
{
      implementation
}
```

You can have as many initializations as you want in an initializer list, though a great deal of them might make it hard to read. The syntax *`dataMember1(value1)`* is equivalent to *`dataMember1 = value1`* (that is, it does the same thing), but this syntax works only in an initializer list.

Here are the constructor and destructor for the `Bow` class:

```
Bow::Bow(string aColor)
{
      numOfArrows = 10;
      drawn = false;
      color = aColor;
       //seeds the time
      //(we need the rand() function in the fire() method)
      srand(time(0));
}

Bow::~Bow()
{
}
```

### Playing Safe with Constant Methods

Often, you will create methods that do not change the value of data members. You can make these methods constant. It is illegal (that is, impossible) to change the value of data members in a constant method. Trying to do so will cause a syntax error.

To declare a constant method, you place the keyword `const` after the argument list. Here is the syntax:

```
return_type methodName(argumentList) const;
```

Note that if you implement a constant method outside the class, the `const` keyword must be placed on both the declaration and the implementation.

The advantage of constant methods is that if a *constant object* is created (an object created with the `const` keyword), only constant methods can be accessed. This limited accessibility ensures that a constant object is indeed constant.

## Using Access Specifiers

C++ allows you to control where the data members of your class can be accessed. This control is a powerful tool because it allows you to protect data members from accidental change (you learn more about protecting data in the section "Learning the Principles of OOP," later in this chapter). An *access specifier* is a word that controls where the data members in a class can be accessed. The syntax for an access specifier is as follows:

```
class ClassName
{
      classMembers
      accessSpecifier:
      classMembers
};
```

An access specifier affects all members of the class (including methods) that come after it until another access specifier is encountered or until you reach the end of the class.

A class has two kinds of access specifiers: `public` and `private` (actually there are three; you learn about the third one, `protected`, in Chapter 8, "Introducing Inheritance"). The effects of these two access specifiers are outlined here:

- `public` members. Can be accessed anywhere that an object of the class can be accessed and from within the class (that is, in the class's methods).

- `private` members. Can be accessed only from within the class itself. An object of the class cannot access the `private` members, except through `public` methods. If no access specifier is provided in the class, all members default to `private`.

Here is an example of how you might use these specifiers:

```
class ClassName
{
     int x;
public:
     int y;
     int z;
private:
     int a;
};
```

In this example, `x` and `a` are `private` members, and `y` and `z` are `public`. You may have as many access specifiers as you want in your classes.

Here is how the `Bow` class looks with access specifiers:

```
class Bow
{
     //data member declarations
     string color;
     bool drawn;
     int numOfArrows;
public:
     Bow(string aColor);    //constructor
     ~Bow();                      //destructor

     //methods
     void draw();
     int fire();
};
```

## Separating Classes into Files

Classes often get pretty big, and having all your code in one file can quickly become unmanageable. Also, if you want to reuse your classes in other programs, you have to copy and paste them into the new program. This process can be quite a hassle.

Fortunately, there is a convention for separating classes into files. Normally, the class declaration is placed in one file, and the implementation of all the methods is put in another file. The class declaration file is normally called *ClassName*.h, where *ClassName* is the name of the class. You are familiar with using .cpp for C++ files, but .h is also a valid C++ file (however, it is used only in special situations, such as for class declarations, not for programs). The implementation is normally called *ClassName*.cpp.

If you use this convention, C++ allows you to do something really cool. Because you put your class into a file separate from where you are using your class, you must include it in your program with an #include directive. The syntax for the #include directive is as follows:

```
#include "filename"
```

However, instead of including two files (*ClassName*.h and *ClassName*.cpp), you have to include only ClassName.h. The compiler will include the .cpp file automatically (provided that the two files are in the same directory). Isn't that convenient?

Here is how the Bow class looks separated into different files:

```
//Bow.h
class Bow
{
      //data member declarations
      string color;
      bool drawn;
      int numOfArrows;
public:
      Bow(string aColor);   //constructor
      ~Bow();                      //destructor

      //methods
      void draw();
      int fire();
};


//Bow.cpp
Bow::Bow(string aColor)
{
```

```
    numOfArrows = 10;
    drawn = false;
    color = aColor;
    //seeds the time
    //(we need the rand() function in the fire() method)
    srand((unsigned)time(0));
}

Bow::~Bow()
{
}

//draws the bow
void Bow::draw()
{
    drawn = true;
    cout<< "The "<<color<<" bow has been drawn." <<endl;
}
//fires the bow if drawn
int Bow::fire()
{
    if(!drawn)
    {
        cout<< color << " has not been drawn "
            "and therefore could not fire." << endl;
        return 0;
    }
    int score;
    score = rand() % (10 - 0 + 1) + 0;
    if(score == 0)
        cout<<color<< " missed the target!!!" <<endl;
    else
        cout<< color << " scored " << score
            << " points!!!" <<endl;
    return score;
}
```

## Class Tactics 101

This section provides some guidelines to make OOP programming a bit easier. You can use these tactics to make your code easy to debug and understand.

- Start every class name with an uppercase letter. This convention is used not only in C++, but also in almost every other object-orientated programming language.
- Add a comment at the beginning of each method and class telling the user what the following member or class does.
- Make sure that each method does only one thing. The general rule is that if a method is more than 20 lines, you are trying to do too much in that method.
- Have each class model only one concept. For example, keep the `Weapon` class separate from the `Soldier` class.
- Test each class to be sure that it works before adding it to the project. Once you know that a class works, debugging a project is simply a matter of making sure that the interaction between the classes works as it should and not making sure that the classes themselves work as well (because you already know that they do).

Follow these rules, and you will be much more productive—and you will save yourself time when debugging.

# Using Objects

After all the preceding discussion on how to create classes, you must be eager to learn *about* classes. Soon you will be creating your own objects from your own classes, but for now, you learn just how to create objects. In this section, you learn about object variables, default constructors, how to access members of a class, how to create a test chassis for your classes, and how to use static members.

## Using Object Variables

Earlier, we wrote that creating a class is a lot like creating a data type. This relationship becomes evident when you start learning about objects. You can use the name of a class exactly like the name of a primitive data type (the data types that are built into C++). An *object variable* is a variable that stores the object of a certain class.

Follow these three steps to create objects:

1. Program the class that will become the template for the object. You completed this step when you created the Bow class.
2. Create an identifier for the object variable and determine what kind of object it will store (from what class it will be created). This process is similar to the way you declare a variable.
3. Add the arguments required by the constructor (if needed).

You can use two basic syntax forms to create objects:

**Method 1:**

```
className objectIdentifier(arguments);
```

**Method 2:**

```
className objectIdentifier = className(arguments);
```

Okay, you've waited long enough. It's time to start creating objects. Following are examples of how to create two different Bow objects:

```
Bow blue("Blue");
Bow red = Bow("Red");
```

You just created two bows, one named red and one named blue. Each of these object variables stores an object with several properties (such as a color and 20 arrows each), and each knows how to do two things: draw and fire (using the draw() and fire() methods). You can change the object stored in an object variable with the assignment operator (=), just as with normal variables. Here is an example:

```
Bow b1("blue");
Bow b2("red");
b1 = b2;
```

b1 and b2 will then each store a separate copy of a red bow.

## Taking the Easy Way Out with Default Constructors

If no arguments are provided when creating an object variable, the computer will execute the default constructor. A *default constructor* can be one of two things. If the class has no constructor, the default constructor is a blank constructor with no arguments; if you provide a constructor that has no arguments, the default constructor is this constructor.

An empty default constructor is present in all classes until you create a constructor. If every constructor requires arguments, the class does not have a default constructor. Unless you create your own default constructor, a default constructor does nothing but create a new object variable that conforms to that object's class declaration. Here is an example of a default constructor:

```
Cpoint3d::Cpoint3d()
{
}
```

## Accessing Members

When a member is public, you can access it from anywhere that an object can be accessed. You can access a public member by using the member access operator (.) between the object identifier and the member. To assign a value to a public data member, use this syntax:

```
objectIdentifier.dataMemberName = value;
```

To retrieve the value of a public data member of an object, you switch the operands like this:

```
variable = objectidentifier.variableName;
```

As you can see, objects are quite similar to normal variables. Here is an example of this syntax:

```
class S
{
public:
      int x;
};

int main(void)
{
      S s;
      s.x = 99;
}
```

Because the s object's data member x is public, all code in the program can use or change the x member (as long as the code can access the s object). As long as an s object exists, all code in the program with access to s can directly change s's data member x.

Public methods are accessed similarly. Here is the syntax to call a public method:

```
object.method(arguments)
```

Here is an example of calling a public method:

```
class S
{
      int x;
public:
      int getValue() { return x; }
      void setValue (int temp) { x = temp; }
      S(int temp) : x(temp) {}
      ~S() {}
};

int main (void)
{
      S s(5);
      cout << s.getValue();
}
```

**Output:**

```
5
```

You cannot access private members outside a class. However, through public methods, you can usually gain limited access to private data members. Because of this limited access, the designer of the class can make sure that the data members are not misused.

## Creating a Test Chassis

When you create a class, you must test it. One of the benefits of OOP is the ease with which you can test and debug classes. The idea is to test each class independently of all other classes. If the class does what it is supposed to, it should cause no more errors (in theory ☺) when combined with the rest of the more robust program. To test a class, you create what is called a test chassis.

A *test chassis* is a program that tests all the capabilities of a class. The test includes all the methods, constructors, and destructors.

An example test chassis for the `Bow` class appears in the following code (the full program is on the CD-ROM at the back of this book). This file is named bowTest.cpp.

```
//5.1 - The Bow Class Test Chassis - Dirk Henkemans
//Premier Press
#include <iostream>
using namespace std;

int main( void );
void bowTest(void);

//bow class is here….

//the main function
int main( void )
{
      bowTest();
      return 0;
}

//tests the bow class
void bowTest(void)
{
      cout<<"yellow bow created"<<endl;
      Bow yellow("yellow");
      cout<<"attempting to fire yellow bow"<<endl;
      yellow.fire();
      cout<<"drawing the bow"<<endl;
      yellow.draw();
      cout<<"attempting to fire yellow bow"<<endl;
      yellow.fire();
}
```

Notice that there are lots of `cout` statements, so you can be sure that the class works as expected. If the program crashes for some reason, you will know exactly which line it crashed on because of the most recent `cout` message. Follow a similar process for each class by creating a test chassis for every class you create. Doing so will prevent many errors.

## The Archery Competition

The King Nolan Bard all high and mighty has requested an archery competition to commemorate his daughter Anastasia's sixteenth birthday. The winner of the archery contest will receive the princess's hand in marriage.

To create "The Archery Competition" game, you will create the competition class. Each competition will have three contestants and an arbitrary number of rounds. The rounds will execute and then declare a winner. Study the following code and make sure that you understand what is going on.

```
//5.2 - The Archery Competition - Dirk Henkemans - Premier Press
#include <iostream>
#include <cstring>
#include "bow.h"
using namespace std;

class ArcheryCompetition
{
//member variables
private:
	//variables
	int rounds;
	float redScore;
	Bow red;
	float blueScore;
	Bow blue;

public:
	//constructor
	ArcheryCompetition(int lrounds);
	//destructor
	~ArcheryCompetition();

	//methods
	int compete(void);
};

//constructs an ArcheryCompetition object
ArcheryCompetition::ArcheryCompetition(int lrounds) :
	rounds(lrounds), red(Bow("red")),
	blue(Bow("blue")), redScore(0), blueScore(0)
{
}

//the destructor
ArcheryCompetition::~ArcheryCompetition()
```

```
{
}

//the heart of the game.
//Walks the player through an entire competition
//and figures out who won
int ArcheryCompetition::compete()
{
      //go through each round, keeping track of the score
      for(int i = 0; i < rounds; i++)
      {
            cout<<"now on round "<<i+1<<"."<<endl;
            red.draw();
            blue.draw();

            redScore = (red.fire() + redScore * i)/(i+1) ;
            blueScore = (blue.fire() + redScore * i)/(i+1);

      }

      //figure out who won
      if(redScore == blueScore)
            cout<<"We have a tie!!! \n";
      else if(redScore < blueScore)
            cout<<"blue wins her hand!! \n";
      else
            cout<<"red wins her hand!! \n";
      return 1;
}

void main(void)
{
      //the driver function
      //constructs the object and
      //calls the appropriate methods
      ArcheryCompetition plymouthSquare(2);
      plymouthSquare.compete();
      int get = 0;
      cin>>get;
}
```

## Using Static Members

So far, each object has had its own unique variables. But what would happen if you wanted the same value for all objects of a particular class? You could use one global variable, but doing so violates the goal of data abstraction. To declare a single variable that exists across all objects in a class and to make that variable take on OOP's safety properties discussed earlier, use static members. A *static member* is a variable that will be the same for all instances of that class. The syntax for a static declaration member is as follows:

```
class ClassName
{
static variableType variableIdentifier;  //declaration
     //other code.....
};
//global initialization

variableType ClassName::variableIdentifier = x;
```

See Figure 5.3 for a conceptual diagram of how static variables work.

Remember that to use a static member, you need to declare the variable in the class and also initialize the variable outside the class. That is, it *must* be initialized outside a class.

Imagine that you have a `Horse` class, and all the horses work together to pull one wagon. The speed of all the horses must be the same, but the speed might increase and decrease depending on the slope. The code for the `Horse` class looks something like this:

```
//5.3 - The Static Variable Demonstration program
// Dirk Henkemans - Premier Press
#include <iostream>
#include <string>
using namespace std;
//
class Horse
{
public:
     static int speed;
     //the remainder of the horse class
};
```

```
int Horse::speed = 3;//notice the global initialization

int main(void)
{
      Horse horse1;
      Horse horse2;
      Horse::speed = 5;
      cout<<horse2.speed<<endl<<horse1.speed<<endl;
      Horse::speed = 6;
      cout<<horse2.speed<<endl<<horse1.speed<<endl;
      return 0;
}
```

**Output:**

5
5
6
6

Notice that the speeds for both horse1 and horse2 are the same regardless of from which horse you access the speed member. This is because there is only one instance of the speed member regardless of how many horses you create to pull the carriage.

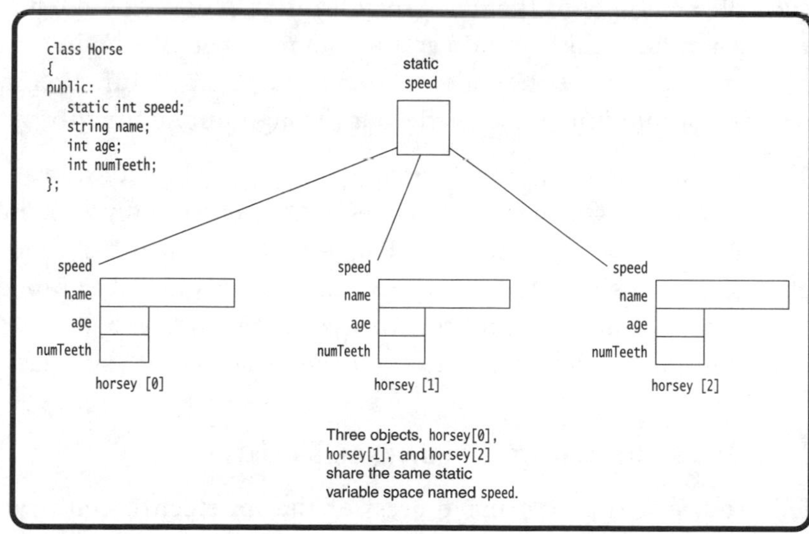


**FIGURE 5.3**

Static variables are the same in every object of a class.

## Learning the Principles of OOP

The following three aspects of OOP make your programs easy to maintain and also make it easy to reuse objects:

- Data abstraction
- Encapsulation
- Polymorphism

You've already seen the first two OOP terms used because data abstraction and encapsulation occur when you create classes that contain private data. The following sections help further explain what these tough-sounding, but relatively simple, concepts are all about.

### Understanding Data Abstraction

When you buy a certain cookie from Subway, you can identify it as a white-chocolate macadamia nut cookie. You probably can't tell what brand of flour or how much baking soda was used to make the cookie—and you probably don't care. The cookie tastes good, which is the purpose for which it was designed.

Likewise, it is often not important to know exactly how a class works, as long as it does what it is designed to do. This is the principle of data abstraction (also known as *data hiding*). *Data abstraction* is the process of hiding the data members and implementation of a class behind an interface so that the user of the class doesn't corrupt the data. The idea is that data is hidden inside the implementation for a class. You do access data members through the implementation by accessing the data members through the member function interface. That is, data is not manipulated directly, but through public functions.

The general rule is to use the smallest scope possible for all variables and members. Also, use as few global variables as possible. In doing so, only the code that should have access to data can change that data. If other code needs to use or change data inside a private object, that object's member functions can supply the routines that allow this kind of access. It is up to you, as a designer of a class, to decide exactly how much access to data the user of your class needs.

### Understanding Encapsulation

Picture the manufacturing process of the nineteenth century. Individuals did everything needed to create their products. No division of labor existed. For example, a sweater maker had to do everything, from creating the wool (well . . . the sheep did that part, but you know what we mean) to marketing the finished product, which meant, of course, that everything took a long time to make. With the advent of specialization, people became proficient at one thing and let other people worry about the rest.

This is similar to *encapsulation*. Each class that you create should represent one specific thing or concept. Multiple classes then come together to represent combinations of things or concepts. Remember when you created the archery contest? The contest used multiple bows from the `Bow` class and a class to represent the contest itself.

Here's another example of encapsulation. Say that you want to build a car. You must take and build the smaller subassemblies before you can build the finished product. Each small assembly does one small thing, but they all combine to produce a car. Figure 5.4 shows the different parts of a car. Each part serves a unique purpose.

## Understanding Polymorphism

*Polymorphism* is a nasty-sounding word that simply means "many forms." Polymorphism refers to a principle of OOP in which each object can be used in more than one program. The primary principle of polymorphism is that your code will analyze the conditions in which you use it and adjust to those conditions. The `Bow` class will always do what it is supposed to do, even if you use it on a 64-bit alpha computer or a Cray supercomputer. In Chapter 8, we cover polymorphism in greater detail. In this chapter, we continue to lay more of the C++ groundwork.

If you use these three OOP concepts (data abstraction, encapsulation, and polymorphism), your programming life will greatly improve—and so will your social life because of the time saved debugging.

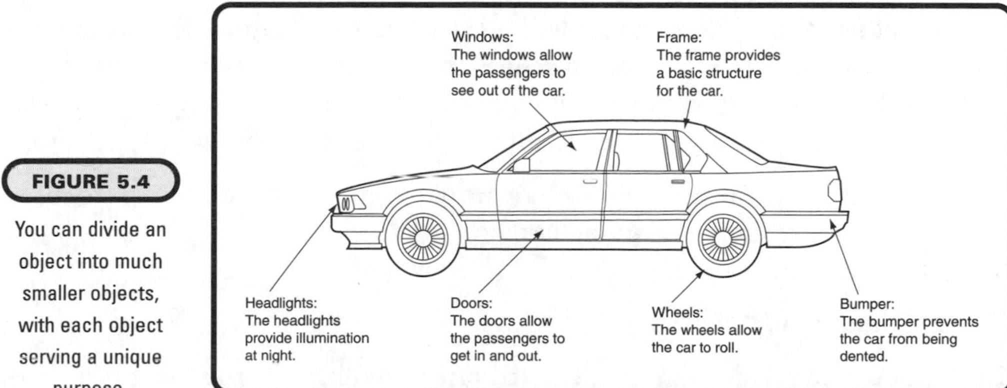


**FIGURE 5.4**

You can divide an object into much smaller objects, with each object serving a unique purpose.

## Debugging

Your code will not always be perfect. Things will go wrong. Sometimes, it's hard to know what is wrong with your code. Other times, you find the problem instantly. In this section, we discuss the kind of errors you can encounter while programming and how to prevent them.

There are four kinds of errors, each with different causes, and each with different ways of being fixed.

Here are the four kinds of errors and what they mean:

- **Insignificant errors.** Errors that don't affect the operation of your program. These errors generally don't cause problems. An insignificant error might occur if you do not follow a convention or forget to add comments to a section of code. These errors often go undetected until they cause obvious problems.
- **Compile-time errors.** Errors in the syntax of the programming language. For example, if you don't include the `t` in `int` while trying to declare an integer, you go against the syntax of the programming language and will receive the nasty error screen when you try to compile.
- **Run-time errors.** Errors that do not show up until you run the program, causing your program to crash. These errors are hard to debug—for example, errors such as declaring a constructor and forgetting to program it in. They are often hard to find and make your program crash with an unpleasant little Windows message. The compiler will not pick these up; however, the compiler might provide a *warning* (an error that doesn't stop the compile process). We recommend that you listen to the warnings your compiler gives and that you try to eliminate the errors from your code.
- **Semantic errors.** Errors that result in your program not doing what it is supposed to do. The compiler will not pick up these errors. The program functions and will not crash but does the wrong thing. For example, imagine that the orcs you programmed are all attacking themselves. Normally, these errors are easy to remove, although sometimes that is not the case.

Debugging is by far the most annoying part of programming, and in some cases, it can be the most time-consuming part.

## The Black Box

The black box method of object-orientated programming uses the three principles listed earlier in this section on OOP principles: data abstraction, encapsulation, and

**In the Real World**

**Semantic errors can cause a very large headache. They sometimes seem impossible to fix. Many moons ago, I (Dirk Henkemans) developed my first game using DirectX. (DirectX is a library by Microsoft that you will learn about in Chapters 13, "Using DirectX," and 14, "Creating the Pirate Adventure.") After producing five pages of code, my application displayed only a blank screen. I sat in front of the program trying to debug it for a whole week. I reviewed all my notes on DirectX; the syntax was right and so was the linking. After a whole week, I figured it out. I forgot, get this, two quotation marks. The error occurred while I was entering the filename of my sprites into my IDE. This problem was such an easy thing to miss, yet such a difficult thing to find.**

polymorphism. The idea behind the black box method is that you send an object a message and the object always does the right thing, even though you don't know how it does so. This happens because the object controls all its own data. This control allows the object to protect itself from invalid parameters and data. You don't need to know and might never know what's inside the class, but by the time you finish testing with the black box, the object is well tested and works as it should.

Black box testing makes debugging much easier. If you debug smaller sections of code and ensure that they work under all circumstances, the only errors that you might receive are those that occur when your smaller sections of code interact with the other, already debugged sections of code.

## Linking Errors

*Linking* occurs when the computer takes all the files you have used in your program, including those from the standard libraries, and compiles them into an executable file (.exe). Linking errors are normally hard to debug, and there is no specific formula for debugging them. However, as ominous as this sounds, only two things normally cause linking errors:

- You didn't include the library files correctly, both the standard libraries and all other libraries that you use in your program.
- You tried to declare a command that doesn't exist, and the compiler didn't pick it up. For example, if you declare a constructor for an object but do not add the code, you will produce a linking error when you try to compile.

**If you can't figure out how to fix one particular error, try fixing any other existing errors. Sometimes, doing so will make the first error "go away."**

## Creating the Conquest Game

You now use your skills in OOP to create the game of "Conquest," a strategic text adventure game that places you, the king, on the throne in order to conquer your enemies. You create a `Nation` class for each player, and each player goes through his or her turn building the nation and attacking his or her enemies.

```
//5.4 - Conquest - Dirk Henkemans - Premier Press

#include <iostream>
#include <string>

using namespace std;

//handles each nation for each player
class Nation
{
public:
     int land;
     int troops;
private:
     string name;

     int food;
     int gold;
     int people;
     int farmers;
     int merchants;
     int blacksmiths;

public:
     Nation(string lName);
     Nation();

     bool takeTurn(void);

private:
```

```
     void menu(void);
};

Nation nation1;
Nation nation2;

//sets the default nation values
Nation::Nation(string lName) :
     name(lName), land(20), food(50), troops(15),
     gold(100), people(100), farmers(0),
     merchants(0), blacksmiths(0)
{

}

//a default constructor
Nation::Nation()
{

}

//takes a turn for player
bool Nation::takeTurn()
{
     cout << "Its now " << name << "'s turn.\n";
     people += land * 0.2;
     food += farmers - people * 0.25;
     gold += merchants * 20;
     troops += blacksmiths;

     menu();

     if (nation1.land <= 0 || nation2.land <= 0) return false;
     return true;
}

//displays and handles the menu options
void Nation::menu()
{
while (true)
```

```
{
	int input = 0;
	cout << "food " << food << endl
		<< "gold " << gold << endl
		<< "land " << land << endl
		<< "merchants " << merchants << endl
		<< "troops " << troops << endl
		<< "unemployed " << people << endl;

	cout << "1) buy land \n"
		<< "2) hire farmers \n"
		<< "3) hire merchants \n"
		<< "4) hire weaponsmiths \n"
		<< "5) attack! \n"
		<< "6) take turn \n";
	cin >> input;

	switch (input)
	{
	case 1: //buys land
		cout << "You buy " << gold/20
			<< " sections of land. \n";
		land += gold/20;
		gold %= 20;
		cout << "You now have " << gold << " gold. \n";
		break;
	case 2: //hires farmers
		farmers += people;
		cout << "You hired " << people << " farmers. \n";
		people = 0;
		break;
	case 3: //hires merchants
		merchants += people;
		cout<< "You hired " << people << " merchants. \n";
		people = 0;
		break;
	case 4: //hires blacksmiths
		blacksmiths += people;
		cout << "You hired " << people << " blacksmiths. \n";
		people = 0;
```

```
            break;
        case 5: //handles the battle
            cout << "The war wages into"
                " the night and all die! \n";
            if (nation1.troops < nation2.troops)
            {
                nation2.land += 10;
                nation1.land -= 10;
            }
            else if (nation1.troops > nation2.troops)
            {
                nation2.land -= 10;
                nation1.land += 10;
            }

            nation1.troops = 0; //war is bloody thing!!!
            nation2.troops = 0;

            break;
        case 6:return; //ends the turn
        }
    }
}


//the main game function
int main(void)
{
    string tempString;

    cout << "Welcome to the Conquest \n";
    cout << "What is your name player 1? \n";
    cin >> tempString;
    nation1 = Nation(tempString);

    cout << "What is your name player 2? \n";
    cin >> tempString;
    nation2 = Nation(tempString);

    while(nation1.takeTurn() && nation2.takeTurn())
```

```
    {

    }

    return 0;
}
```

## Summary

In this chapter, you learned a lot about objects. Understanding OOP requires that you approach programming from a unique perspective. Hiding data in classes and protecting that data takes a little forethought, but it pays off later in maintainability and object reuse. Test your understanding of the OOP concepts by trying the following challenges and reviewing extra-demanding sections of this chapter before moving on to the next chapter.

### CHALLENGES

1. **Create a class that can be used to represent a character in a role-playing game. Store the character's name, class, and race.**
2. **Explain the three main principles of OOP.**
3. **What is the difference between a class and an object?**
4. **If you have a choice between declaring something public, private, global, or local without loss of functionality, which scope should you pick?**
5. **What attributes present in constructors and destructors are not present in other functions?**

# Moving to Advanced Data Types

Now good reader, we are moving from the basics of C++ and venturing into uncharted territory. You are ready to learn some of the more advanced aspects of the C++ language. Do not fear, however, for although these concepts might be challenging, with practice, you will find them as easy as the concepts in Chapter 1, "Starting the Journey."

In this chapter, you learn how to use the following:

- Arrays
- Pointers
- C-style strings
- References
- Dynamic memory basics

## Working with Arrays

All the variables covered in earlier chapters can store only one particular data type. If you want to store a second piece of information, you must create another variable. These types of variables are called *scalar* variables. But what happens when you have to store a long list of related data? It wouldn't be convenient to create a new variable for every single piece of data. What if you have to work with thousands and thousands of employee records? The task quickly would become overwhelming.

Fortunately, most problems have a solution. In this case, arrays are the solution. *Arrays* are a special group of variables that can hold many pieces of data and that all have the same data type and name, but different values.

Each individual variable within an array is called an *element*. Each element has a particular index associated with it. An *index* is a number that indicates which element of the array you are accessing.

Beginners often have difficulty with a seemingly odd thing about arrays: The numbering of the index starts at zero. So, if you have an array with five elements, the indexes will be 0, 1, 2, 3, and 4. After you work with arrays for a while, you will get used to this weird numbering, and it will start to feel natural. Figure 6.1 shows an array as boxes lined up in a row, with the array name `charArray[]` and individual array elements (such as `char_array[0]`) in each of the boxes.

## Creating Arrays

Creating arrays is an easy process, especially now that you've learned about variables. To create an array, type the data type and then the variable name followed by the subscripting operator. Here is how the resulting code might look:

```
data_type array_name[number_of_elements];
```

This creates an array called *`array_name`* of type *`data_type`* with *`number_of_elements`* elements. For example, to create an array of integers called `int_array` with ten elements, you type

```
int Int_array[10];
```

Remember that the indexing starts at 0, so the elements will be numbered 0 to 9. Element 10 does not actually exist in this array, even though it appears to when you are looking at the declaration.

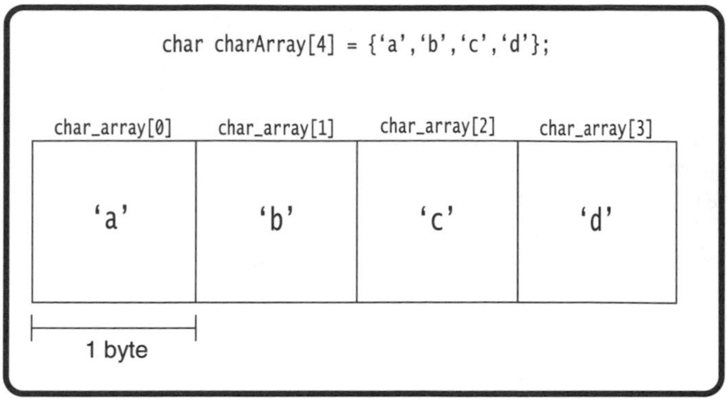

**FIGURE 6.1**

You can picture arrays as a row of boxes of memory lined up side by side.

You can create arrays of all data types, including user-defined types. If you have a class called `my_class`, you can create an array of ten `my_class` objects like this:

```
my_class my_class_array[10];
```

The number between the square brackets must be a *constant expression*, which means that you cannot use a variable to define the number of elements in your array. As you will discover in later chapters, their inability to resize is one of the major drawbacks to using arrays—as opposed to other advanced data types.

Here are some examples of array declarations:

```
int int_array[10];
float float_array[60];
char char_array[6];
```

## Initializing Arrays

You can fill an array with data a couple of ways. First, you can initialize the array at the same time that you declare it. You do this with an initializer list, which is a list of values used to fill the array. Here is the syntax you use:

```
array_type array_name[number_of_elements] = {value1, value2, value3, ...};
```

Here *`value1`*, *`value2`*, and so on are all values of type *`array_type`*. Note that if you initialize in this way, you can leave *`number_of_elements`* blank. The computer will decide how large to make the array based on the number of elements in the initializer list. Here are some examples:

```
float float_array[3] = {0.25, .876, 3.0};
char char_array[5] = {'H','e','l','l','o'};
```

If you don't include the number of elements that an array will have but include an initializer list, the array will default to the number of elements in the initializer list. In the following line of code, char_array2 will automatically assume that the array size is 6:

```
char char_array2[] = {'d','r','a','g','o','n'};
```

If you do not have as many values in the initializer list as *number_of_elements*, the rest of the values are assumed to be 0. For example, typing

```
int my_array[5] = {1,2,3};
```

is the same as typing

```
int my_array[5] = {1,2,3,0,0};
```

Another way to initialize arrays is with a for loop. To do so, first declare the array as you normally would and then create a for loop to fill it with a value. Here is an example:

```
int int_array[10];
for (int i = 0; i < sizeof(int_array)/sizeof(int); i++)
{
     int_array[i] = i;
}
```

Notice that the loop repeats until i is less than sizeof(int_array)/sizeof(int). This is another way of saying loop until you reach the end of the array. sizeof(int_array) evaluates to the number of bytes in the entire array, and sizeof(int) evaluates to the number of bytes in each element. So, if you divide the two, you get the number of elements in the array. In this example, the fact that you can increment using the sizeof() operator is trivial because you already know the size of the array; but in much of your code, you cannot tell how many elements are in the array.

## Using Arrays

Accessing elements of an array is similar to creating an array. Each element in an array acts as a separate scalar variable. To access a particular element, you use the array's name, followed by the index number within the subscripting operator:

```
array_name[Index_number];
```

This is equivalent to using just the name of a scalar variable. For example, if you declare the array

```
char char_array[10];
```

and you want to display the value of the fourth element (index number 3), you do the following:

```
cout << char_array[3];
```

You can also access the values of an array with a pointer, as you will learn later in this chapter in the section "Relating Arrays to Pointers."

## Multidimensional Arrays

Although multidimensional arrays can be a difficult concept at first, thinking of them as *arrays of arrays* is helpful. Looking at Figure 6.2, you see five primary elements (the big boxes) in the array, and each primary array element contains an array four elements long. This form is a 5 x 4 multidimensional array.

To create a two-dimensional array, you put a subscripting operator at the end of the declaration, as shown here:

```
array_type array_name[number_of_elements][number_of_elements2];
```

This code creates an array of *number_of_elements* arrays with *number_of_elements2* elements of type *array_type*. For example

```
int my_Array[5][4];
```

creates an array with five elements. Each of these five elements will be an array of four integers. Picture multidimensional array elements as boxes of memory, each containing an array; again, this concept is illustrated in Figure 6.2.

You can have as many dimensions on an array as you want. However, too many arrays of arrays can quickly use up a computer's memory.

**FIGURE 6.2**

Picture a two-dimensional array as boxes of boxes. Inside each array of larger boxes is an array of smaller boxes. Arrays inside arrays are the foundation to multidimensional arrays.

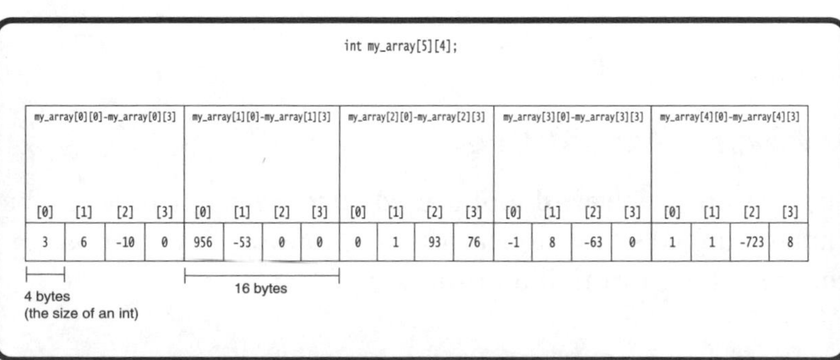

Any multidimensional array can also be represented as a single dimensional array simply by multiplying all the sizes. If you have a two-dimensional array such as

```
char my_Array[10][10];
```

you can create a single-dimensional array equivalent by multiplying 10 and 10 to get 100. Thus, the array

```
char my_Array[100];
```

will have the same number of integer elements (total) as the previous two-dimensional array.

The common way to scroll through all the elements in a multidimensional array is to use a for loop within a for loop. The following example will initialize all the elements in a multidimensional array:

```
//6.1 - Multidimensional Arrays - Dirk Henkemans and Mark Lee - Premier Press
#include <iostream>
using namespace std;
int main(void)
{
int numbers[10][10];
     for (int i = 0; i < sizeof(numbers)/(sizeof(int)*10); i++)
          for (int c = 0;c < sizeof(numbers)/(sizeof(int)*10); c++)
               cout << (numbers[i][c] = (i * 10) + c) << endl;
     return 0;
}
```

**Output:**

```
0
1
...
98
99
```

## Using Pointers

Pointers are a powerful tool if used effectively, but they can be one of the more challenging C++ tools to learn to use. However, we promise to guide you slowly through the information in this section.

The simplest definition of a pointer is this: A *pointer* is a variable that holds a memory address. Although this definition of a pointer is pretty straightforward, its implications are far more complex.

The memory address that the pointer stores is the address of another variable. So a pointer is said to "point to a variable."

The syntax for declaring a pointer is as follows:

```
type* pointer_name;
```

Here, `type` is the type of the variable being pointed to, and `pointer_name` is the name of the pointer. However, declaring pointers is only a start; *using* them is the complicated part.

First, you must learn about a new operator, the *address of operator* (`&`). You put it directly in front of a variable, and it evaluates to the memory address of the variable. This operator is useful for assigning values to a pointer. Here is an example of how to use the address of operator:

```
int my_int;
int* my_int_pointer = &my_int;
```

This code makes `my_int_pointer` point to `my_int`. Soon you will actually be able to do something with this pointer, but for now just learn the basics.

Note that if a pointer has the value `0` assigned to it, the pointer does not point to a variable. This case is called a *null pointer* or an *undeclared pointer*.

If you are having trouble picturing these concepts, try this example:

```
//6.2 - Pointers - Dirk Henkemans and Mark Lee - Premier Press
#include <iostream>
using namespace std;
int main(void)
{
	int an_int = 5;
	int* a_pointer = &an_int;
	cout << "The value of an_int is: " << an_int
		<< "\nThe address of an_int is: " << &an_int
		<< "\nThe value of a_pointer is " << a_pointer
		<< "\nThe address of a_pointer is: " << &a_pointer;
}
```

## Elevating to the Indirection Operator

You're halfway through learning about pointers. Next, you learn about the indirection operator. The *indirection operator* (*) is used to refer to the object pointed to by the pointer. You place the indirection operator right in front of a pointer (or an expression that evaluates to a pointer), and it evaluates to the value of the variable that the pointer points to. Although this operator is different from the * used to declare a pointer, you'll be able to tell which is which because of the context. If it's in the pointer declaration, it's not being dereferenced.

**In the last section, you saw a pointer named `a_pointer` initialized using the *, but don't confuse the indirection operator with the pointer declaration. Even though there is an * symbol before the pointer when you declare it, the pointer is not actually being dereferenced.**

For example, if you declare an integer and a pointer as

```
int a = 78;
int* pb = &a;
```

you can use the indirection operator to access the value of `a` through `pb` like this:

```
cout << "The value of a is: " << *pb;
```

This code displays the number `78` onscreen. You can think of the indirection operator (sometimes called the *dereferencing operator*) as the opposite of the address of operator.

To help clarify the relationship between the address of and indirection operators, look at this example:

```
int x;
int* px  = &x; // px points to x
*px = &x; // x now contains the value &x
```

In the second line, the value `&x` is assigned to `px`, not `*px`, as it is in the third line. Note that when you change the value of `*px`, you are changing the value of `x`.

It is also possible to have pointers to pointers. A declaration of a pointer to a pointer to an integer looks like this:

```
int** ppi;
```

It can be initialized like this:

```
int * pi;
ppi = &pi;
```

A pointer to a pointer holds the address of a pointer, which holds the address of a variable. Thus, it is possible to access the value of the variable through the pointer to a pointer. To access this value, you use the indirection operator twice:

```
cout << **ppi;
```

This code displays the value of the integer that `pi` points to. The concept of pointer to pointer is not always intuitive at first. It is like a road sign that points out another road sign so that you know where that road sign is located.

`*ppi` gives the value of the pointer `pi`; then using the indirection operator again, gives the value that `pi` points to. You could go even further, using it as many times as you want, but doing so isn't practical.

## Using Pointers and Objects

It is also possible to have pointers to objects and structures. For example, you can have a pointer to a string object like this:

```
string* ps;
```

As you can see, pointers of this type are much like other types of pointers in that pointers to strings can be used in exactly the same way. However, you need to notice some qualities. First, no object is actually being created, just a pointer to one. Because of this, you are not calling the string's constructor. (C++ calls a constructor when you declare a string because `string` is a class, not a built-in data type.)

Second, if you have a `Point` class defined as

```
class Point
{
public:
      int X,Y;
      Point (int lX, int lY) : X(lX), Y(lY){}
      void print();
};
void Point::print()
{
      cout << "The value of X is: " << X
            << "/nThe value of Y is: " << Y << endl;
}
```

and you create an object from the class

```
Point p(5,3);
```

you can create a pointer to this object as

```
Point* pp = &p;
```

It is possible to access the members of this object using the pointer like this:

```
pp->X = 6;
pp->Y = 5;
```

This code introduces a new operator, the *Member Selection operator* (`->`). It is just like the other member selection operator (.), except that it is for pointers to objects rather than member objects. You can also call member functions using this operator:

```
pp->print();
```

This code causes the `print` method to be executed, as you might suspect.

### Using the this Pointer

Every object of a class has a constant pointer to itself called the `this` pointer. With a `this` pointer, you can access any of the public data members or functions of the class. The syntax for using the `this` pointer is the same as the syntax for any other pointer to an object.

For example, in the `Point` class (declared in the last section), you can rewrite the `print()` method to use the `this` pointer:

```
void Point::print()
{
     cout << "The value of X is: " << this->X
          << "/nThe value of Y is: " << this->Y << endl;
}
```

This change, however, does not change the meaning of the method. It is simply a way of explicitly stating which instance of the class you are referring to.

Interestingly enough, you can also use `this` to get the object:

```
Point p = *this;
```

This information does not have any use to you at the moment, but it might in the future.

## Relating Arrays to Pointers

Arrays and pointers are closely linked. In fact, in a strict definition, arrays are pointers. Consider this array:

```
float f[10];
```

The name of the array, `f`, acts as a pointer to the first element. The following displays the value of the first element:

```
cout << *f;
```

If you declare a pointer to the same type as the array's type, you can assign the pointer to the first element of the array like this:

```
float* pf = f;
```

This code snippet is synonymous to the following one:

```
float* pf = &f[0];
```

Then you can go through every element in the array by incrementing the pointer. Wait a second! You increment a pointer just like you do any other variable. Because a pointer stores a memory address, incrementing a pointer changes the memory address. Instead of going up by one, however, the value of the memory address is increased by the size of the pointer type. This effectively moves on to the next element in the array, as shown in this example:

```
float f[] = {5.5, 0.5 , 6.7};
float* pf = f;
cout << *pf;
cout << " " << *(++pf);
cout << " " <<*(++pf);
```

This code displays `5.5 0.5 6.7` onscreen. Every time you increment a pointer, it moves on to the next element of the array. If the increment operator is used on a pointer, C++ assumes that the pointer points to the array, but it doesn't actually check, so be careful that you increment pointers only to array elements.

The decrement operator (--) works the same way (see Chapter 2, "Descending Deeper . . . into Variables"). Every time it is used on a pointer, it will move the pointer one element back in the array. Take care not to go past the beginning of the array; doing so can cause quite a few errors that might be difficult to find and debug.

You can also add to or subtract from pointers. If `p` is a pointer to an array, `p+`*n* moves *n* elements forward in the array, and `p-`*n* moves *n* elements back in the array.

Here is an example of how to increment through an array using a pointer:

```
int n[] = {0,1,2,3,4,5};
int* pn = n;
cout << *(pn+3) << endl;
cout << *++pn << endl;
*pn--;
cout <<*pn << endl << *(pn+4);
```

**Output:**

```
3
1
0
4
```

**C++ will not prevent you from trying to access values that are no longer in the array. For example, if you increment the pointer beyond `5` in the preceding `n[]` array, C++ will be happy to return all the data that your computer has stored there. Worse, if you try to manipulate the data and the data is required by Windows or another program, you might wind up causing the computer to crash. Accessing data that is no longer in the array is called *walking off the array.***

## Constructing Constant Pointers and Pointers to Constants

You can have a *constant pointer,* a pointer that cannot change the memory address it stores. However, with a constant pointer, you can still change the value that the pointer points to. To create a constant pointer, place the `const` keyword after the `*` operator, as shown here:

```
char* const p; // constant pointer to char
```

This code creates a constant pointer. However, because a constant pointer is a type of constant, you must initialize the pointer at the same time that you declare it:

```
char p;
char* const pc = &p;
```

The memory address that `pc` stores (`&p`) cannot be changed after this point. But you can change the value of `p` with `pc`:

```
*pc = 'd'; //this is legal, actually changes p
pc = 0; //this is illegal
```

You can also have pointers to constants. With a pointer to a constant, you can change the memory address the pointer stores, but not the constant pointed to. To declare a pointer to a constant, you add the `const` keyword before the * operator, as shown here:

```
char const* pcc; // pointer to a constant char
const int* pci; // pointer to a constant int
```

In the preceding code snippet, `pcc` can change which constant character it points to, but not the value of this constant character. Pointers to constants do not need to be initialized when declared because the pointer is still variable, but the variable pointed to isn't, as shown here:

```
char c;
pcc = &c;
*pcc = 'd'; // this is illegal
pcc = 0; // this is legal
```

You can also have constant pointers to constants, where neither the memory address nor the thing pointed to can be changed. To create such a pointer, you put the keyword `const` before and after the * operator, as shown here:

```
int x;
const int* const cpci = x;
```

The only thing you can do with `cpci` is read its value and the value of the variable it points to (`x`).

## Introducing Pointers and Functions

Pointers can be very useful as function parameters and return values. Having a pointer as a function parameter can make your programs much more efficient.

Normally, when you pass an argument to a function, a new copy of this argument is made and assigned to the appropriate parameter. However, if you have a pointer as a parameter, only the memory address must be copied, which can save a lot of extra copying for large data types.

Another advantage to having pointers as function parameters is that you are altering the original and not a copy that has been passed. Take a look at this example of what *not* to do:

```
#include <iostream>
using namespace std;
class Point
```

```
{
     public:
          int X = 0,Y=0;
     Point() : X(0), Y(0) {}
}
Point MoveUp(Point p)
{
     p.Y+=5;
     return point;
}
int main(void)
{
      Point point;
     point = MoveUp(point);
     cout << point.X << point.Y;
     return 0;
}
```

**Output:**

```
05
```

This code is not very good for two reasons. First, the entire `point` object must be copied twice in order to call the function `MoveUp()`. Second, the line `point = MoveUp(point);` is fairly awkward. From a design standpoint, the user of the function has to do a lot.

However, with a pointer as the parameter of `MoveUp()`, you can improve the function as shown here:

```
//6.3 - Passing a Pointer - Dirk Henkemans and Mark Lee - Premier Press
#include <iostream>
using namespace std;
class Point
{
     public:
          int X,Y;
     Point() : X(0), Y(0) {}
};
void MoveUp(Point* p)
{
```

```
    p->Y+=5;
}
int main(void)
{
    Point point;
    MoveUp(&point);
    cout << point.X << point.Y;
    return 0;
}
```

**Output:**

```
05
```

The efficiency of the `MoveUp()` function is greatly increased. Now, instead of making two copies of the `Point` object for each call, one copy is made of the memory address for each call. Also, the call to `MoveUp()` is simplified greatly. Instead of having an awkward assignment statement to call the method, you simply call the method. This is much easier for the user of the function to understand.

## Strings Revisited

We cover strings earlier in this book (refer to Chapter 1, for example). However, you have only scratched the surface of strings. Here you revisit strings for a more detailed view on how strings work and what you can do with them.

You are now ready to for some advanced concepts regarding strings. In C, strings are represented as character arrays, instead of objects as they are in C++. Because of this, you will commonly see strings represented as character arrays. As a result, we will go into some detail about how C-style strings work so that you will be able to read all C++ code.

### String Literals

The official type of string literals (such as `"Hello"`) is `const char []`. The string `"Hello"` is of type `const char [6]`. But, wait! The word *Hello* has five letters, not six! Don't worry, we didn't make a mistake. The extra character is there because you must have a terminating null character, `'/0'` (the value `0`), that tells the computer the length of the string.

Every string literal has a hidden null character (`'/0'`) at the end so that certain algorithms will know the length of the string and when they reach the end of the string. Not all algorithms need to know the length of the string, but most do.

You can assign a string literal to a variable of type `char*`, as shown here:

```
char* x = "Hello";
```

However, the value pointed to by `x` cannot be manipulated. If it is not a constant, the code will produce an error, as shown in the following example.

```
*x = 'S';
```

This code causes an error because you *cannot* change the value of a constant. If you need to point to a string that you can modify, you must assign a string literal to a string object or to a character array. Here is an example of a way that you can change the value in a character array:

```
char s[] = "Hello";
s[0] = 'S';
```

This code is okay, and the new value of the string is `"Sello"`.

Many of the C standard library functions for strings take `char*` as an argument. However, if a string is stored in a character pointer, its length is lost, which is why a string literal has a null character at the end. Without it, you will not be able to tell where the string ends.

### Character Arrays

As you have seen, arrays of characters are another way of representing strings. You can initialize a character array with a string literal, as shown in the following example:

```
char s[] = "Hello World!";
```

Because you don't have to provide the length of the array within the subscripting operator, declaring a string this way is almost as convenient as using the string class from the standard library. C++ will allocate enough characters in the `s` array to hold the null zero that appears at the end of the string.

### Determining String Length

To obtain the length of the string `s[]` (from the previous section "Character Arrays"), you could use the usual method for determining the length of an array—use the `sizeof` operator. For example, to obtain the length of s in the example in the preceding section, you do the following:

```
cout << sizeof(s);
```

This code displays the number 13 onscreen. We didn't divide by the size of char as you normally would to obtain array length because the size of char is always 1.

There is a slight problem with this method. The length of the string is 12, not 13. If you obtain the size through the sizeof operator, the null character is included in your length. To obtain the length of the string without the null character, you can subtract 1 from the length you obtain, or you can use the standard library.

A function called strlen() returns the length of any string. For example, to find the length of s in the preceding examples (char s[] = "Hello World!";), write this code:

```
cout << strlen(s);
```

This code displays the proper string length, 12, onscreen, rather than 13 because strlen() determines the length by counting the elements up to the first null character. For example, for a string such as

```
char weird_string = "Hello/0 World";
```

strlen() returns 5, going up to only the first null character. If you determine the length of the string with the sizeof operator, however, you get 14 (two null characters).

The prototype for the strlen() function is as follows:

```
int strlen(const char*)
```

To use this function, you must include <string> in your program.

### Using Other C-Style String Functions

You can find many other C-style string functions in the standard library. This section goes through a couple of them, just as a form of introduction to these many functions. The functions you will go through in this section are strcopy(), which is used for copying strings, and strcat(), which is used for concatenating strings.

To use these functions, you need to include <cstring> or <string.h>. To copy one string into another string, use the function strcpy() (string copy). The prototype for this function is as follows:

```
char* strcpy(char* p, const char* q);
```

This function puts every element in `q` into `p`. For example, calling the function as follows

```
char s[6];
strcpy(s, "Hello");
```

causes `s` to hold the value `"Hello"` (including the terminating null character). The `char*` that this function returns is the value of `q` (the value that is copied).

This function does not check to make sure that the array you pass in `p` is large enough to hold all the values in `q`. It just copies away. Because of this, you must make sure that the array you pass in for `p` is at least as large as `q`.

Here is an example of how to copy strings using the `strcpy()` function:

```
char s[6];
char t[] = "Hello";
cout << strcpy(s, t);
```

This code displays `Hello` onscreen and copies `s` with the string `"Hello"`.

To *concatenate* two strings (to append one string to the end of another), you use the function `strcat()`. The prototype for the `strcat()` function is as follows:

```
char* strcat(char* p, const char* q);
```

This function appends the string in `q` to the end of `p`. For example, if you use the function

```
char s[12] = "Hello";
cout << strcat(s, " World");
```

`s` holds the value `"Hello World"` (with a null character at the end). The `char*` that this function returns is the entire concatenated string. In the example, `Hello World` is displayed onscreen.

The function `strncpy()` will do a `strcpy()`, but will copy only a certain amount of `q` into `p`. The prototype for `strncpy()` is as follows:

```
char* strncpy(char* p. const char* q, int n);
```

This prototype copies *n* characters from `q` to the end of `p`. For example, writing

```
char s [7]= "Say ";
char t[]= "Hi";
cout << strncpy(s, t, 2);
```

causes the new value of `s` to become the character array `"Say Hi"`. This string also displays onscreen because it is the value that `strncpy()` returns.

### Converting Strings to Numbers

You can also use a couple of functions to convert strings that contain numeric values to the numeric value (for example, "5" to 5). You declare these functions in <cstdlib> or <stdlib .h>.

To convert a string representation of an integer to an integer, use the atoi() function. The prototype for this function is as follows:

```
int atoi(const char* p);
```

To use this function, you pass in a string, and the function returns an integer. Here is an example:

```
char s[] = "567";
int x = atoi(s) + 3;
cout << x;
```

This code displays the number 570 onscreen.

You can also use functions to convert a string to a double and a string to a long; they are, atof() and atol(), respectively. Their prototypes are about the same as the prototype for atoi():

```
double atof(const char* p);
long atol(const char* p);
```

These functions also work the exact same way as atoi() does.

If the string does not contain a number (for example, "HI"), 0 is returned.

These functions can be useful for receiving user input. Instead of assuming that users will enter valid numbers, you can let them enter a string. Then you can check to see whether this string can be converted to a number. This is a much safer way to receive user input.

## Beginning with References

You've come a long way. Congratulations! Now, you are ready to learn how to use references. A *reference* is an alias, or an alternative name, for a variable. You can think of a reference as a constant pointer that is always dereferenced. References are much like constants in that they must be initialized when declared and their value cannot be changed after that.

To create a reference, you use the reference (&) operator. Don't confuse this operator with the address of operator. You will be able to tell which is which according to the current context. Here is the syntax for declaring a reference:

```
data_type& reference_name;
```

Here *data_type* is the type of variable that the reference is a reference to and *reference_name* is the name of the reference. To initialize a reference (as you must do when you declare it), you assign a variable of type *data_type* to the reference creation:

```
data_type& reference_name = variable;
```

Here is an example of how to create and initialize a reference:

```
int x ;
int& rx = x;
```

The preceding code causes `rx` to be a reference to the variable `x`.

Strangely enough, operators do not act on a reference. They act only on the variable referenced by the reference. For example, if you increment `rx` as

```
rx++;
```

`x` is incremented by one. `rx` is just another name for `x`.

You use references mainly as function parameters and return types.

## Using References in Function Parameters

You can legally make any function parameter a reference. This can be useful if you want to write a function that can change the argument passed to it. For example, you can write a function called `decrement` that has a reference parameter like this:

```
void decrement(int& x)
{
      x--;
}
```

You can then use this function as follows:

```
int a = 5;
decrement(a);
cout << a;
```

**Output:**

```
4
```

Because `x` becomes a reference to `a` when `decrement` is called, decrementing `x` changes the value of `a`. As you can see, this looks much cleaner than using references to do the same thing.

## Using References as Function Return Values

As you might suspect, you can return a reference to a variable in a function. However, the implications of doing so are not so obvious. Consider the following example.

```
//6.4 - Reference Example - Dirk Henkemans and Mark Lee - Premier Press
#include <iostream>
using namespace std;
class Point
{
	int X,Y;
	public:
		Point(int lX, int lY):X(lX),Y(lY) {}
		int& GetX() {return  X;}
		int& GetY() {return Y;}
};
int main(void)
{
	Point p(5,3);
	p.GetX() = 3;
	p.GetY() = 5;
	cout << p.GetX() << p.GetY();
}
```

**Output:**

```
35
```

Because `GetX()` and `GetY()` return references to the member variables `X` and `Y`, you can use these function calls as `lvalues` (*`lvalues`* are values, or variables, that can be changed). Changing the value of these references changes only the values of the member variables, `X` and `Y`.

# Explaining Dynamic Memory

So far in your programming experience, you have put data only into static memory and automatic memory. *Static memory* is where all global and static variables are stored. Everything stored in static memory is declared once and then exists until the end of the program. *Automatic memory* is where all function parameters and local variables are stored. Items stored in automatic memory are automatically created and destroyed as needed.

However, you can use a third kind of memory: *free store memory* (or the *heap* or *dynamic memory*). The program must explicitly request memory for items stored in the free store, and the program can free the memory when finished with it. Learning to use dynamic memory effectively is a difficult, but useful task.

You must understand a couple of concepts in order to use the free store memory successfully. First, you must explicitly request memory to be *allocated* (memory is allocated for a variable when space is found and marked as used for that variable in memory) for whatever you want to store by using the `new` operator. Second, you must *free* all memory (when it is no longer marked as being used) that you request when you are done with it by using the `delete` operator.

All items stored in dynamic memory exist until freed or until the end the program (whichever comes first). Because of this, the variables stored in dynamic memory are not destroyed when they lose their scope. This is useful because you can create a variable in a function and use it outside the function. Most advanced programmers use dynamic memory almost exclusively, out of habit.

## Allocating Dynamic Memory with the new and delete Operators

As we just said, you allocate memory in the free store using the `new` operator. This operator returns a pointer to the newly allocated memory. The syntax for the `new` operator is as follows:

```
new data_type;
```

Here *`data_type`* is any valid data type or class. To use this memory, you must assign it to a pointer variable. Dynamic memory is where pointers come in really handy. For example, to create an integer in the free store, you can do the following:

```
int* a = new int;
```

That's really all there is to it. The `new` operator is actually very easy to use. The C equivalent of this operator is the `malloc()` function, which is in `<cstdlib>` (or `<stdlib.h>`):

```
int* a = (int*)malloc(sizeof(int));
```

As you can see, this is much more intimidating. You no longer have a reason to use the `malloc()` function, but it's there in case you need it or come across it in someone else's program.

All memory that you allocate with the `new` operator must be deallocated with the `delete` operator. If you do not free the memory you use, this memory will not be available to use later in the program. Forgetting to free dynamic memory is called a *memory leak*, and you should always avoid it.

The `delete` operator acts on a pointer to a section of memory allocated with the `new` operator, or `0`. If the `delete` operator is used on anything else, it will cause an error. The syntax for the `delete` operator is as follows:

```
delete pointer;
```

For example, to free the memory allocated in the preceding example, do the following:

```
delete a;
```

Once you free the memory allocated with `new`, set the value of the pointer to `0`. This ensures that you will not accidentally try to delete something that you have already deleted. Using the `delete` operator on `0` does nothing, so it is harmless.

If you are creating objects on the free store memory within a class, the best place to free their memory is in the destructor for the class. Deallocating memory on the free store memory is one of the main reasons why the destructor was created in C++.

## Creating Dynamic Arrays

Normally, when creating an array, you must supply a constant expression that is the number of elements in the array. If you try to use a variable expression, the compiler will issue an error. For example, if you try to create the array

```
int x = 5;
char s[x];
```

CodeWarrior will respond with an error saying that a constant expression was expected.

If you create an array on the free store, you can use a variable expression for the number of elements, as shown here:

```
int x = 5;
char* s = new char[x];
```

To deallocate the memory for the preceding array, you use the `delete[]` operator. The `delete[]` operator works just like the `delete` operator:

```
delete[] s;
```

This frees the entire array, so you don't have to worry about each element.

## Re-Creating the Tic Tac Toe Game

Now, you get to use your newfound array and pointer skills as you follow along with us to create the classics of classics: "Tic Tac Toe." To make it a little easier to understand, we did not fully optimize this version of "Tic Tac Toe." Later, you might want to see how you can improve on the design.

```
//6.5 - Tic Tac Toe  - Dirk Henkemans and Mark Lee - Premier Press
#include <iostream>
#include <string>

using namespace std;      //introduces namespace std
enum SquareState { blank = ' ', X = 'X', 0='0'};
class gameBoard
{
     private:
          const int WIDTH;
          const int HEIGHT;
          int* GameBoard;
     public:
           gameBoard() : WIDTH(3), HEIGHT(3)
           {
                GameBoard = new int[9];
                for (int i = 0; i < 9; i++)
                     *(GameBoard + i) = blank;
           }
          ~gameBoard() {delete[] GameBoard;}
          void setX(int h, int w);
          void set0(int h, int w);
          bool isTaken(int h, int w);
          SquareState isLine();
          void draw();
};

void gameBoard::setX(int h, int w)
{
     *(GameBoard + h*HEIGHT + w) = X;
}

void gameBoard::set0(int h, int w)
{
     *(GameBoard + h*HEIGHT + w) = 0;
```

```
}

bool gameBoard::isTaken (int h, int w)
{
     return *(GameBoard + h*HEIGHT + w) != ' ';
}

SquareState gameBoard::isLine()
{
     if(*GameBoard==X && *(GameBoard +1)==X && *(GameBoard +2)==X)
          return X;
     if(*GameBoard==0 && *(GameBoard +1)==0 && *(GameBoard +2)==0)
          return 0;
     if(*(GameBoard +3)==X && *(GameBoard +4)==X && *(GameBoard +5)==X)
          return X;
     if(*(GameBoard +3)==0 && *(GameBoard +4)==0 && *(GameBoard +5)==0)
          return 0;
     if(*(GameBoard +6)==X && *(GameBoard +7)==X && *(GameBoard +8)==X)
          return X;
     if(*(GameBoard +6)==0 && *(GameBoard +7)==0 && *(GameBoard +8)==0)
          return 0;

     if(*GameBoard==X && *(GameBoard +3)==X && *(GameBoard +6)==X)
          return X;
     if(*GameBoard==0 && *(GameBoard +3)==0 && *(GameBoard +6)==0)
          return 0;
     if(*(GameBoard +1)==X && *(GameBoard +4)==X && *(GameBoard +7)==X)
          return X;
     if(*(GameBoard +1)==0 && *(GameBoard +4)==0 && *(GameBoard +7)==0)
          return 0;
     if(*(GameBoard +2)==X && *(GameBoard +5)==X && *(GameBoard +8)==X)
          return X;
     if(*(GameBoard +2)==0 && *(GameBoard +5)==0 && *(GameBoard +8)==0)
          return 0;

     if(*GameBoard==X && *(GameBoard +4)==X && *(GameBoard +8)==X)
          return X;
     if(*GameBoard==0 && *(GameBoard +4)==0 && *(GameBoard +8)==0)
          return 0;
     if(*(GameBoard +2)==X && *(GameBoard +4)==X && *(GameBoard +6)==X)
          return X;
```

```
    if(*(GameBoard +2)==0 && *(GameBoard +4)==0 && *(GameBoard +6)==0)
        return 0;
    return blank;

}

void gameBoard::draw()
{
    cout << endl;
    for(int i=0; i < HEIGHT; i++)
    {
        cout << (char)*(GameBoard + i*HEIGHT);
        for(int c=1; c < WIDTH; c++)
            cout << " | " << (char)*(GameBoard + i*WIDTH + c);
        cout << endl << "------" << endl;
    }
}

class Game
{
public:
    gameBoard* doInput(string player, gameBoard* gb);
    bool inRange(int test);
};

gameBoard* Game::doInput(string player, gameBoard* gb)
{
    gb->draw();

    string letter;
    if (player.compare("one") == 0)
        letter = "X";
    else if (player.compare("two") == 0)
        letter = "O";
    else return gb;

    int input1, input2;

    do {

        do {
```

```
                cout << "\nPlayer " << player.c_str()
                    << ", please enter a row number to put an "
                    << letter.c_str() << ": ";
                cin >> input1;
            }while(!inRange(input1));

            do {
                cout << "\nPlease enter a column number to put an "
                    << letter.c_str() << ": ";
                cin >> input2;
            }while(!inRange(input2));

    }while (gb->isTaken(input1,input2));

    if (player.compare("one") == 0)
        gb->setX(input1, input2);
    else gb->setO(input1, input2);

    return gb;

}

bool Game::inRange(int test)
{
    return test > -1 && test < 3;
}

int main( void )
{
    gameBoard* gb = new gameBoard;
    Game g;
    string player1, player2;
    cout << "Welcome to Tic Tac Toe!"
        << "\nPlayer one, please enter your name: ";
    cin >> player1;
    cout << "\nPlayer two, please enter your name: ";
    cin >> player2;

    while (gb->isLine() == ' ')
    {
        gb = g.doInput("one",gb);
        gb = g.doInput("two",gb);
```

```
        }
        gb->draw();
        if(gb->isLine() == X)
              cout << "\nPlayer one, you win!"
                    << "\nGame Over.";
        else cout << "\nPlayer two, you win!"
                    << "\nGame Over.";
        return 0;
}
```

## Summary

In this chapter, you learned many concepts. You started with pointers and learned how they are the basis for arrays. Then you covered how to use references and dynamic memory. Finally, you revisited strings to learn the difference between C-style strings and the C++ strings you have used so far. Your adventure is not over though. Now, it's time to continue to Chapter 7, "Building Namespaces."

### CHALLENGES

1. **What is the size of the string `"Hello World"`? What is the length of this array named `s`?**

   ```
   char s[] = "Hello World";
   ```

2. **List five reasons to use pointers.**
3. **What are the problems with the "Tic Tac Toe" game at the end of the chapter? How can you improve the game?**
4. **List three reasons to use dynamic memory.**

# Building Namespaces

Imagine that you have ventured into an unknown land, attracting many followers along the way. Your followers grow tired and decide to set up a new town on the banks of a mighty river. However, you are not sure what to name the settlement; you aren't familiar with the other towns in this country and don't want to choose a name identical to one of those towns. The solution is to declare a new country so that the name of your town is the only name in the country. In programming, this tactic is similar to naming one variable the same as another variable by using namespaces.

In this chapter, you learn the following:

- The purpose of namespaces
- How to declare a namespace
- The effects of duplicate namespaces
- How to use unnamed and named namespaces
- Why namespaces will benefit you
- The standard and global namespaces

## Understanding Namespaces

The easiest way to grasp the concept of namespaces is to think of them as classes. When you use a class (refer to Chapter 5, "Fighting with OOP," for more on classes), you create a small private area of scope in which you declare your public and private variables. You then use the scope resolution operator (::) to specify that an object is in a class or is global (refer to Chapter 4, "Writing Functions," for more on the scope resolution operator). Namespaces are like this because when you use a namespace, you can divide a scope into smaller subscopes.

## Declaring Namespaces

The syntax for declaring a namespace is similar to the syntax for declaring a class. When you declare a namespace, you are declaring a name for the scope in which each of the namespace's members will be contained. An analogy is the area code for a phone number, which differentiates identical phone numbers.

The general syntax for declaring a namespace is as follows:

```
namespace name
{
     MemberList
}
```

Here, *MemberList* can consist of functions, classes, and variables. In fact, anything that can be part of the global namespace can be part of *MemberList*.

You can't have two identifiers with the same name in the same scope. For example, you could not place two `fire()` functions, one to light a torch and the other to fire the user's crossbow, in the same program, except by using namespaces. Namespaces enable you to place these two functions in different scopes without confusing the compiler. Furthermore, you can put all of the functions with a similar idea into the same namespace. For example, the `fire()` that lights the torch will go in the `exploration` namespace with all other exploration functions, and the `fire()` that fires the user's crossbow will go in the `combat` namespace.

Here is an example of the code for the two different `fire()` functions:

```
//stores all the combat functions, classes and variables
namespace combat
{
      void fire()
      {
            cout << "You fire your cross bow." << endl;
      }
}

//stores all the combat functions, classes and variables
namespace exploration
{
      void fire()
      {
            cout << "You light your torch." << endl;
      }
}
```

Figure 7.1 provides another example of namespaces. This figure shows an integer variable, `subGlobalInt`, being declared in the `subGlobal` namespace. This declaration makes `subGlobalInt` part of the `subGlobal` namespace. For this reason, you must refer to `subGlobalInt` with the namespace identifier in front (`subGlobal::subGlobalInt`) when referring to it outside the `subGlobal` namespace.

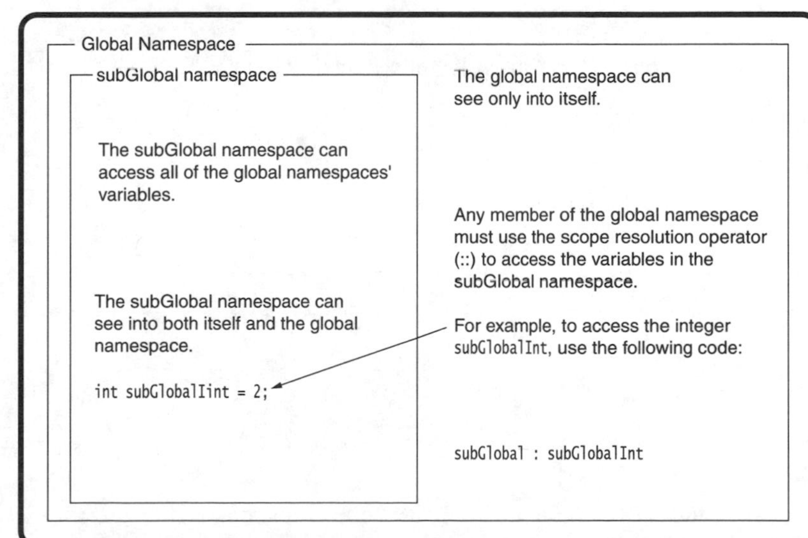


**FIGURE 7.1**

The global scope has a namespace called `subGlobal`. The global namespace needs the scope resolution operator to see data inside the `subGlobal` namespace, but the `subGlobal` namespace can see everything.

## Using Namespaces

You use the namespaces' members (functions, classes, and variables) with the scope resolution operator. This syntax is exactly like the syntax for a class:

*namespace*::*member*;

For example, to call each of the `fire()` functions from the previous example, you can write something similar to the following code:

```
//7.1 - The Fire Functions - Dirk Henkemans - Premier Press
#include <iostream>
using namespace std;

//stores all the combat functions, classes and variables
namespace combat
{
      void fire()
      {
            cout << "Whoosh, you unleash a bolt"
                  " from your crossbow." << endl;
      }
}

//stores all the combat functions, classes and variables
namespace exploration
{
      void fire()
      {
            cout << "You set your torch ablaze." << endl;
        }
}

int main(void)
{
      combat::fire();
      exploration::fire();
      return 0;
}
```

**Output:**

```
Whoosh, you unleash a bolt from your crossbow.
You set your torch ablaze
```

## Introducing the Global Namespace

The global namespace is the official name for the largest level of scope (the one that you have been declaring as global variables). In order to refer to a member as the global namespace, you sometimes have to use the scope resolution operator (::). Doing so is necessary if duplicates are among the local namespace and the global namespace because the default is always the variable with the smallest scope. The syntax to specify the member of the global namespace is as follows:

```
::globalMember;
```

**IN THE REAL WORLD**

**Besides the obvious usefulness of namespaces for dividing games into more manageable segments, you can use namespaces to create versatile databases. For example, imagine that you work in a library and you want to create a database to keep track of library books. You are working with the library's computerized inventory application, which uses a different sorting function for fiction and nonfiction books, and you perceive a problem because you want to name both versions of the method `sort()`. However, you can solve this problem by placing the two functions inside two different namespaces.**

# Declaring Duplicate Namespaces

If two namespaces are declared with identical identifiers, the second namespace is counted as an extension of the first. The computer treats

```
namespace x
{
	func1() {}
}
namespace x
{
	func2() {}
}
```

the same as

```
namespace x
{
	func1() {}
	func2() {}
}
```

C++ puts both namespaces into the same scope when the program is compiled, which means that you cannot have duplicate members inside duplicate namespaces.

## Gaining Explicit Access to a Namespace

If you are sure that a namespace contains no repeated identifiers, you can merge a namespace into the global namespace. Doing so saves time because you don't have to continuously type the namespace identifier and the scope resolution operator.

You can use two methods to obtain explicit access to a namespace:

- The `using` declaration
- The `using` directive

### The using Declaration

The `using` declaration declares that you are going to use a particular member of its subscope. The result is that the need for explicit scope qualification is eliminated. The syntax for the `using` declaration is as follows:

```
using namespaceName::member;
```

Here is an example of the `using` declaration:

```
namespace dragon{int gold = 50;}
int main(void)
{
      using dragon::gold;
      cout << gold;
}
```

With this `using` declaration, you no longer need to preface `gold` with the `dragon` qualifier.

### The using Directive

The `using` directive declares that you are going to use all the members of a particular namespace. The `using` directive works like the `using` declaration, except that it applies to all the members of that namespace. Once you've used the `using` directive, you no longer have to qualify any of the members of that namespace in the rest of the program. To utilize the using directive, you must make sure that no duplicate identifiers are in the namespace that you incorporate into the global namespace. The syntax for the `using` directive is as follows:

```
using namespace namespaceName;
```

You have already seen an example of this syntax, and you've used it in all your programs thus far:

```
using namespace std;
```

We explain this line in more detail in the section, "Rediscovering std Namespaces," later in this chapter.

## Creating the Menu Utility

You have created a new menu for each program. Now, you are ready to create a general menu program that can be used again and again. The ability to reuse code is the principle of *polymorphism* (a principle of OOP in which each object can be used in more than one program; see Chapter 5 for more on polymorphism). The `menu()` function is encapsulated in the `menuNamespace` namespace because the `menu` function is a common function and you don't want the menu utility's `menu()` function to conflict with the program's `menu()` functions.

The following code consists of three files. The files are marked with comments that tell you the files' names and where they start. The code must be in three different files, or it will not work. Include the first file, hello.cpp, in your project, and when the project compiles, it will automatically link to the other files because of the `#include` statements.

```
//7.2 - MenuUtility Test Chassis (hello.cpp)
//Dirk Henkemans - Premier Press
#include <iostream>
#include "MenuUtility.h"
using namespace std;      //introduces namespace std

int main( void )
{
      using namespace menuNamespace;

      string example[] = {"attack","retreat"};
      menu(example, 2);

      return 0;
}
```

The following code is for the header file for the Menu Utility. Save this code as MenuUtility.h.

```
//7.3 - MenuUtility.h - Dirk Henkemans - Premier Press
#include <iostream>
#include <string>
using namespace std;

namespace menuNamespace
{
     int menu(string* strArray, int size);
}
```

Last comes the source code for the Menu Utility. Save this as MenuUtility.cpp.

```
//7.4 - MenuUtility.cpp - Dirk Henkemans - Premier Press
#include <iostream>
#include <string>
using namespace std;

namespace menuNamespace
{
     int menu(string* strArray, int size)
     {
          int userResponse;

          cout << "Your choices are:"
          while(userResponse < 1 || userResponse > size)
          {
               for(int i = 0; i < size; i++)
               {
                    cout<< i + 1 << ")" << strArray[i] << endl;
               }
               cin>> userResponse;
          }
          return userResponse;
     }
}
```

Try working with this code because you'll use it a lot in the future.

## Creating Unnamed Namespaces

How can you be sure that the identifier you are using for a namespace is accurate? By not naming the namespace. Sounds counterintuitive, doesn't it? Trust us; it's not. If you don't give an identifier for a namespace, C++ automatically gives it a unique one. The syntax for declaring an unnamed namespace is as follows (just use the keyword `namespace`):

```
namespace
{
     members
}
```

Without an identifier, C++ allows you to access the members of an unnamed namespace by placing an implied `using namespace` declaration after the unnamed namespace. So the code is more similar to this:

```
namespace a
{
     members
}
using namespace a;
```

Here *a* is a unique identifier (which you don't know and can't find).

Here is an example of using an unnamed namespace:

```
#include <iostream>
using namespace std;

namespace
{
     void func(void) {cout << "::func" << endl; }
}


int main(void)
{
     ::func();
}
```

**Output:**

```
::func
```

## Rediscovering std Namespaces

The standard namespace is a namespace that encapsulates the entire C++ standard library, including the iostream library and the string library that you have been using so far. The `using namespace std` brings the standard namespace into the global namespace.

This is a very useful line because it enables you to use the code without concern about it being of a different scope than the global namespace. Here, as an example, is a relatively simple program:

```
#include <iostream>
#include <string>
using namespace std;

int main(void)
{
      string name;
      cout<< "What is your name my lord?" <<endl;
      cin>> name;
      cout<< "\nHello Sir " << name.c_str() << endl;
      return 0;
}
```

If you try to create the equivalent program without using the standard namespace in the global namespace, you have to use the scope resolution operator. In this example, you must use the scope resolution operator eight times to keep the same functionality.

```
#include <iostream>
#include <string>

int main(void)
{
      std::string name;
      std::cout<< "What is your name my lord?" <<std::endl;
      std::cin>> name;
      std::cout<< "\nHello Sir " << name.c_str() << std::endl;
      return 0;
}
```

The moral of this story is to use standard namespaces; they make your life much easier.

## Creating the Pirate Town Game

After hard months of plundering the Caribbean, your ship, the BloodWind, docks in St. Marie. Getting off the ship for the first time, what do you do? Some of your options get pretty weird. Well, here is the game for you.

As you study this game, notice the use of namespaces to encapsulate each major section. To create a really great game, you will want each section to be much, much longer. After checking this one out, see how you can improve upon it. Don't forget to include the menu files in you project. Happy plundering!

First, save the following code as a header file named pirateTown.h.

```
//7.5 - Pirate Town (pirateTown.h) - Dirk Henkemans - Premier Press
#include <iostream>
#include <string>
#include "MenuUtility.h"
using namespace std;

//function declarations
namespace street
{
     void menu(void);
}

namespace weaponShop
{
     void menu(void);
}

namespace wharf
{
     void menu(void);
}

namespace tavern
{
     void menu(void);
}
```

Now, enter and run the following source code file called pirateTown.cpp.

```
//7.6 - Pirate Town (pirateTown.cpp) - Dirk Henkemans
//Premier Press
#include <iostream>
#include <string>
#include "MenuUtility.h"
#include "pirateTown.h"
using namespace std;

//includes our menu utility into the global namespace
using menuNamespace::menu;

//the code
//handles everything at the wharf
namespace wharf
{
      void menu()
      {
            string options[] =
            {"Jump In the Water",
            "Grab a rowboat and row into the sunset.",
            "Board the BloodWind.",
            "Head into town"};
            int userResponse = ::menu(options, 4);

            switch(userResponse)
            {
                  case 1:
                        cout << "You jump in to the water."
                              << " Suddenly you hear"
                              << " laughing and \n"
                              << "realize that you forgot"
                              << " to take off your clothes."
                              << " You emerge \n"
                              << "from the water sopping wet. \n" ;
                              menu();
                        break;
                  case 2:
                        cout << "You grab a little red dingy"
                              << " and row off into the sunset."
                              << "Oh the glory." << endl;
                        break;
```

```
                case 3:
                    cout << "You re-board the BloodWind"
                         << " and wait for your mates to"
                         << " return after having fun. \n";
                    break;
                case 4:
                    street::menu();
                    break;
            }
        }
}

//handles the tavern scene
namespace tavern
{
    void menu(void)
    {
        string options[] =
        {"Order a Drink",
        "Start a rowdy brawl.",
        "Walk back into the street."};
        int userResponse = ::menu(options, 3);

        switch(userResponse)
        {
            case 1:
                cout << "You order a drink called"
                     << " \"Mikes\"\n";
                menu();
                break;
            case 2:
                cout << "You start a nice rowdy fight.\n";
                menu();
                break;
            case 3:
                street::menu();
                break;
        }
    }

}
//handles everything that happens in the street
```

```
namespace street
{
      void menu(void)
      {
            string options[] =
            {"Head to the wharf",
            "Enter the tavern.",
            "Enter the weapons shop.",
            "Start a fight."};
            int userResponse = ::menu(options, 4);

            switch(userResponse)
            {
                  case 1:
                        wharf::menu();
                        break;
                  case 2:
                        tavern::menu();
                        break;
                  case 3:
                        weaponShop::menu();
                        break;
                  case 4:
                        cout<< "You start a nice healthy"
                              << " brawl in the street. \n";
                        street::menu();
                        break;
            }
      }

}

//allows you to buy weapons
namespace weaponShop
{
      void menu(void)
      {
            string options[] =
            {"Buy a jewel encrusted dagger for 300.",
            "Buy the beautiful flint-lock musket for 300",
            "Buy a standard English fighting saber for 100",
            "Leave the shop."};
```

```
        int userResponse = ::menu(options, 4);

        switch(userResponse)
        {
            case 1:
                cout << "You purchase a dagger"
                    << " and slip it into you pocket after \n"
                    << "paying the scrawny man"
                    << " across the counter \n";
                menu();
                break;
            case 2:
                cout << "After paying for the musket"
                    << " you try it out and "
                    << "it works perfectly!!! \n";
                menu();
                break;
            case 3:
                cout << "After taking it for "
                    << "a couple test swings"
                    << " you realize that it wasn't \n"
                    << "even worth the gold"
                    << " you paid for it \n";
                menu();
                break;
            case 4:
                street::menu();
                break;
        }
    }

}

//starts the game
int main( void )
{
    cout<< "Your ship, the BloodWind docks in St. Marie."
        << " You get off the \n"
        << "ship and are standing on the wharf. \n \n";
    wharf::menu();

    return 0;
}
```

## Summary

In this chapter, you learned how to subdivide scope into smaller, more contained sections. You continued by learning about the standard namespace and why it is a good habit to use it. You also learned how to gain access to a namespace and how to create an unnamed namespace. Although you'll have few uses for namespaces in smaller programs, in larger programs, they can help you avoid having to debug to remove duplicate naming errors.

### CHALLENGES

1. **Explain why someone would want to use a namespace.**
2. **What is the advantage of an unnamed namespace over a named namespace?**
3. **What are the two ways that you can gain explicit access to a namespace and how do they differ?**
4. **Looking at the code that follows, how do you call the `breathFire()` function from each of the following places?**
   a. **From the global namespace**
   b. **From inside the dragon namespace**
   c. **From inside another namespace**

```
namespace dragon
{
        void breathFire() {cout<< "The dragon breaths fire \n"; }
}
using dragon::breathFire();
```

CHAPTER 8

# Introducing Inheritance

Earlier chapters cover the basics of object-oriented programming (OOP) and intermediate C++. In this chapter, you continue your OOP training with a very important concept: inheritance. *Inheritance* is the derivation of one class from another. Once you understand this concept, you will be well on your way to reading any C++ code that you come across and to designing efficient, worthwhile code. In this chapter, you learn about the following:

- The concept of inheritance
- How to access a base class's members
- Multiple inheritance
- More on polymorphism
- Virtual functions
- Abstract classes

## Understanding Inheritance

As we mention in Chapter 5, "Fighting with OOP," classes tend to model concepts or things. However, we haven't mentioned that these concepts or things tend to have certain relationships. As do other relationships, these relationships help clarify and provide a logical order for the world.

When you are designing classes for your programs, be sure to focus on these relationships, both for convenience and logic. In this chapter, you will learn how to express these relationships in your code.

When two things are related, they have some point in common. For example, a cat and a dog are both animals, they have tails, they have fur, and they have whiskers. A manager and a salesperson are both paid employees, they clock into work, and they have Social Security numbers.

To express this commonality in C++, you must define three classes—two for the related things and one for what they have in common. Using animals as an example, you create an `Animal` class, a `Dog` class, and a `Cat` class to express the relationship between dogs and cats. Then you must link these classes together with inheritance.

First, however, you need to study a new type of relationship, called the *derives-from* relationship. Again, use the relationship between the concept of a dog and the concept of an animal as an example. From the concept of an animal, you can derive the concept of a dog simply by adding a few ideas. You can also call this relationship the *type-of* relationship. A dog is a type of animal.

In C++, you create a *base class* (also called a *superclass* or *parent class*), which usually models some general idea or type of thing (in the current example, the base class is the `Animal` class). Other classes are derived from base classes. *Derived classes* (also called *subclasses* or *child classes*) inherit all the members of their base class and more. Figure 8.1 illustrates these concepts.

If you are confused at this point, don't worry. After you learn how to write code for inheritance, all of this information will be much clearer.

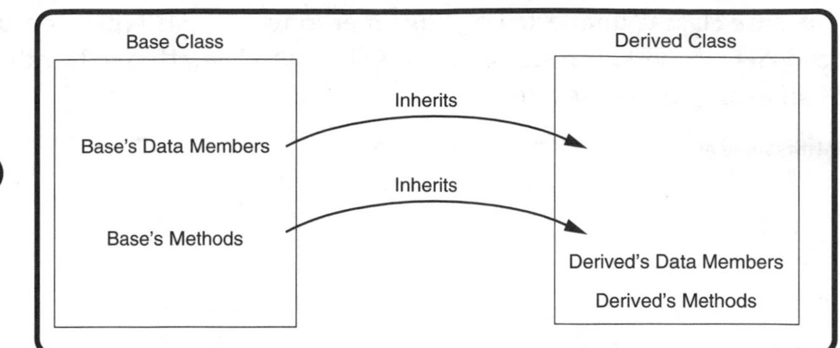


**FIGURE 8.1**

A derived class inherits member information from its parent, or base, class.

## Writing Code for Inheritance

If you have a class with one data member, such as

```
class aClass
{
      public:
            int anInt;
};
```

you can use this class to derive another one, as follows:

```
class aDerivedClass : public aClass
{
      protected:
            float aFloat;
};
```

`aDerivedClass` then has two members: `aFloat`, which is specified, and `anInt`, which this child class inherits from `aClass`.

Here is the general syntax for creating a derived class:

```
class derived_class_name : scope_modifier base_class_name
```

Here *`derived_class_name`* is the name of the derived class, and *`base_class_name`* is the name of the base class. *`scope_modifier`* can be `public`, `private`, or `protected`; but for now, you will just use `public`. We discuss the results of using different scope modifiers later in this chapter in the section, "Modifying Access to Base Classes."

A derived class inherits all the members from its base class. It is almost as though these members were declared in the derived class (but not quite, as you'll see in the next section).

The base class is unaffected by this inheritance. It is still just a normal class with its own members. The derived class is the only class affected by inheritance. Here is an example to illustrate:

```
class Base
{
     public:
          int base_int;
};

class Derived : public Base
{
     public:
          int derived_int;
};

int main ( void )
{
     Derived d;
     d.base_int = 5; // legal
     d.derived_int = 10; //legal
     Base b;
     b.base_int = 6; //legal
     b.derived_int = 12; //illegal - Base only has one member
     return 0;
}
```

As you can see, the base class, `Base`, inherits nothing. `Base` contains only one member, `base_int`, so the statement that attempts to assign `6` to `b.derived_int` is illegal because `b` does not have a member named `derived_int`. On the other hand, the derived class, `derived_int`, contains *two* members, the base class's member named `base_int` and the member declared in the derived class named `derived_int`.

## Accessing Class Members through Inheritance

Although the rules for what a derived class can access are straightforward, they are often difficult for a beginner (and even advanced programmers at times). In this section, we attempt to minimize the confusion and maximize your enjoyment (or at least one of the two).

First of all, recall that both public and private members are in a class. There is actually a third kind of member called *protected.* In this section, we also discuss the use and limitations of this scope.

A derived class can access the following:

- Its own members
- All global variables
- All public and protected members of its base class

See, that's not so bad. If you are ever in doubt, just consult this list. A derived class has almost as much access to members as does a base class because the derived class inherits most of the base class's functionality. The only items that a derived class cannot access are the base class's private members.

As the preceding list implies, a derived class can access all the public and protected members of its base class. However, it cannot access the private members. Here is an example:

```
class Base
{
      private:
            int private_int;
      protected:
            int getInt() { return private_int;}
};

class Derived : public Base
{
      protected:
            //Error - cannot access private_int
            int getInt() { return private_int; }
            int getInt() { return Base::getInt(); } // The right way
}
```

In this example, the `Derived` class cannot access `private_int` because `private_int` is private. It can, however, access the protected member function `getInt()`. Using the base class's public and protected member functions to access the private data is the proper way to access this data. Keep in mind that a `Derived` object still has a `private_int` member. It just can't access it.

In almost all other aspects, the protected scope is treated as private. For example, if you create a `Derived` object, you cannot access the `getInt()` function through this object (from outside the class). See Table 8.1 to find out what can and can't be accessed from a class.

**TABLE 8.1 ACCESSING CLASS MEMBERS**

| Access Specifier | Inside Class | Outside Class | In Derived Class |
|---|---|---|---|
| private | Can access | Can't access | Can't access |
| protected | Can access | Can't access | Can access |
| public | Can access | Can access | Can access |

Most of the time, you will still want to use the private access specifier for data members.

## Overriding Functions

Sometimes a derived class might need a slightly different implementation of a method that it inherits from its base class. There can be many reasons for this. A derived class might need a more specific implementation, or you might want to extend the functionality of the base class's function. Fortunately, C++ provides an easy way, called *overriding,* to do this.

To override a function you simply create a function with the same signature in the derived class. Then, if you call the function, the derived class's version will be called. Thus, it effectively takes over for the base class's function. Here is an example:

```
//8.1 - Overriding Functions - Mark Lee - Premier Press
#include <iostream>
using namespace std;
class Base
{
      public:
            void display() { cout << "Base Class\n"; }
};

class Derived : public Base
{
      public:
            void display() { cout << "Derived Class\n"; }
```

```
};

int main( void )
{
      Derived d;
      d.display();
      Base b;
      b.display();
      return 0;
}
```

**Output:**

```
Derived Class
Base Class
```

In this example, when `d`'s display method is called, `Derived` class's version of display is used. First, the derived class is searched for the method, and if the method is not found, the base class is searched. Notice that the base class member function does not change when you override it in the derived class. The base class is not affected.

## Extending the Scope Resolution Operator

Sometimes when you override a function, you may still need to access the base class's version of the function. If this is the case, you must use the scope resolution operator (`::`) to explicitly denote which class's member you are trying to access. The syntax for the scope resolution operator in this case is

*`class_name::member`*

where *`member`* is the name of the member and *`class_name`* is the name of the class that contains the member. Here is an example:

```
//8.2 - Using the Scope Resolution Operator - Mark Lee
//Premier Press
#include <iostream>
using namespace std;
class Base
{
      public:
            void display() { cout << "Hello World.\n"; }
};
```

```
class Derived : public Base
{
      public:
            void display()
            {
                  // Executes base display() function
                  Base::display();
                  cout << "Goodbye World.";
            }
};

int main(void)
{
      Derived d;
      d.display();    // Executes derived display() function
      return 0;
}
```

**Output:**

```
Hello World.
Goodbye World.
```

In this example, the line `Base::display()` explicitly calls the base class's `display()` method. Keep in mind that, in order to use this operator to access a member, you must have access to the member to begin with. This operator will not give you permission to access something that you normally couldn't.

## Creating Constructors and Destructors in Derived Classes

The constructors and destructors of classes involved in inheritance are a little bit more complicated than normal functions, so we're treating them as a special case.

The first rule is this: If a base class does not have a constructor or one of the base class's constructors does not require arguments, no constructor is needed in the derived class. An empty constructor is implied for the base class. Here is an example:

```
class Base
{
      protected:
            int an_int;
```

```
};

class Base2
{
     Base2() { cout << "Hello"; }
     protected:
          int an_int;
};

class Derived : public Base
{
     //no constructor needed
};

class Derived2 : public Base2
{
     //must have a constructor
     public:
     Derived2() {}
};

int main( void )
{
     Derived2 d2;
     return 0;
}
```

Second, if all the base class's constructors require arguments, the derived class must have a constructor, and the constructor must explicitly invoke the base class's constructor in the initializer list. Here is an example:

```
class Base
{
     public:
          Base(int a) {}
};

class Derived : public Base
{
     public:
```

```
        Derived(int a, int b) : Base(a) {} //correct
        Derived(int a, int b) {Base(a)} //incorrect
        Derived(int a, int b) {} //incorrect
};
```

Third, the derived class's constructor cannot initialize the variables that it inherits from the base class in an initializer list. It must either use the base class's constructor or initialize the relevant variables in the braces ({ and }). Here is an example:

```
class Base
{
    public:
        Base (int a);
    protected:
        int an_int;
        int an_int2;
};
//the base class's constructor:
Base::Base(int a) : an_int(a) {}

class Derived : public Base
{
    public:
        Derived(int a, int b);
    protected:
        int an_int3;
};
//the Derived class's constructor
//the right way
Derived::Derived(int a, int b) : Base(a), an_int3(b) {}
//also right
Derived::Derived(int a, int b) : Base(a) {an_int2 = b;}
//error
Derived::Derived(int a, int b) : Base(a), an_int2(b) {}
```

In the first version of `Derived` class's constructor, the base class's constructor is called, and then `Derived` initializes its own variables. This is what you normally will see, and it is the proper way to initialize a class.

However, the second version is also correct. You can initialize the base class's members if the initialization is within the braces rather than in the initializer list.

The order of construction is as follows: first the base class and then the derived class. Destruction happens in the reverse order. The derived class is destroyed and then the base is destroyed. Here is an example to clarify:

```
class Base
{
      public:
            Base() { cout << "Base's constructor\n"; }
            ~Base() { cout << "Base's destructor\n"; }
};

class Derived : public Base
{
      public:
            Derived() { cout << "Derived's constructor\n"; }
            ~Derived() { cout << "Derived's destructor\n"; }
};

int main ( void )
{
      Derived d;
      return 0;
}
```

**Output:**

```
Base's constructor
Derived's constructor
Derived's destructor
Base's destructor
```

See, that wasn't so bad! If you're comfortable with all of these basics, the rest is easy.

## Extending Inheritance

The simple inheritance that we have taught so far is not particularly useful, but it is the base from which your knowledge will grow. The following concepts are actually incredibly simple, so if you understand the past few sections, you should be on easy street.

First, a derived class can also be a base class for another derived class. Through multilevel derivation, you can get an inheritance chain. An *inheritance chain* is a sequence of derived classes, each of which is also a base to the class below it. The idea here is to begin with a general concept for the base class and then become more specific as you move down the chain.

The following code illustrates how this inheritance structure looks in C++:

```
class Vehicle
{};

class LandVehicle : public Vehicle
{};

class Car : public LandVehicle
{};

class HondaInsight : public Car
{};
```

As with normal inheritance, the constructors are executed from the base down, and the destructors are in reverse. For example, in the preceding inheritance chain, the order is as follows: `Vehicle` constructor, `LandVehicle` constructor, `Car` constructor, `HondaInsight` constructor; then `HondaInsight` destructor, `Car` destructor, `LandVehicle` destructor, and `Vehicle` destructor.

Figure 8.2 shows a conceptual diagram of the `Vehicle` inheritance chain. Notice how the arrows point up rather than down. This is because the arrows show the direction that classes can access other classes. A base class does not have access to a derived class, but a derived class has access to a base class.

When you call a method of a class, the computer first checks that class, then its base class, then the base's base, and so on up the chain until it finds the method.

A base class can have more than one derived class under it. In this way, you can create tree-like structures of inheritance. These structures are called *class hierarchies*. The MFC (Microsoft Foundation Class) is an example of a large, advanced class hierarchy. If you create advanced Windows applications, you will learn how to use it.

**FIGURE 8.2**

The arrows in this diagram represent the direction from which classes can access other classes.

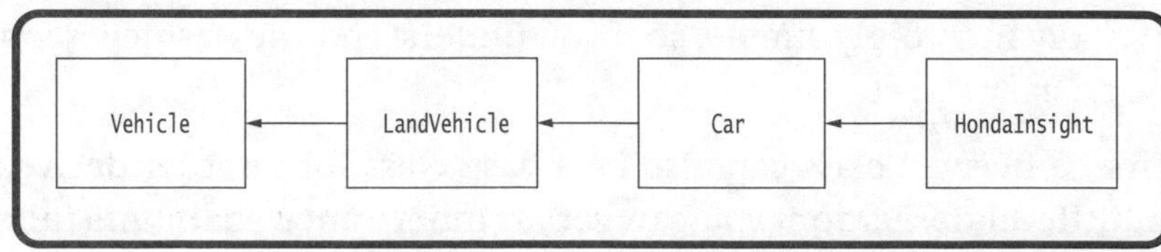

A class hierarchy is not incredibly complex. The main thing is that *siblings* (classes with the same base class) are not affected by each other. No class has any of its siblings' members. Figure 8.3 shows a class hierarchy for vehicles.

The following code shows how this hierarchical structure looks in C++:

```
class Vehicle
{};

class LandVehicle : public Vehicle
{};

class WaterVehicle : public Vehicle
{};

class Car : public LandVehicle
{};

class Bike : public LandVehicle
{};

class Boat : public WaterVehicle
{};

class Submarine : public WaterVehicle
{};
```

You can divide this fancy class hierarchy into a bunch of inheritance chains, as illustrated in Figure 8.4.

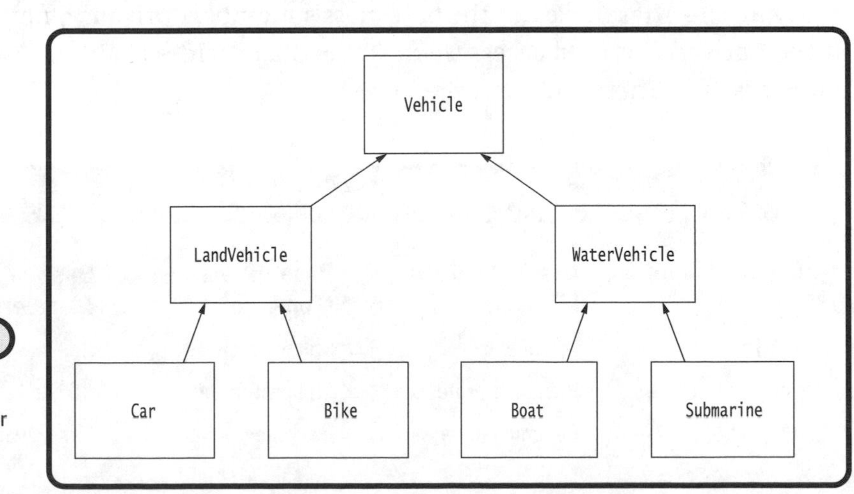


**FIGURE 8.3**

You can design a class hierarchy for vehicles to look like this one.

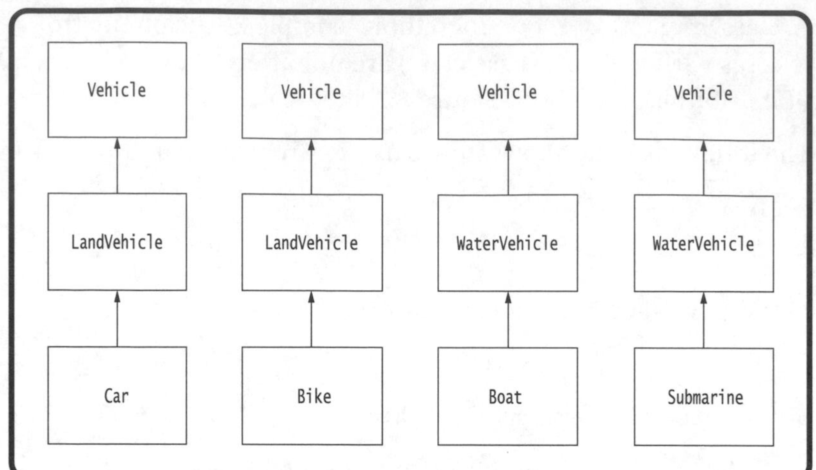


**FIGURE 8.4**

A hierarchy consists of many inheritance chains.

## Modifying Access to Base Classes

Remember when we wrote that the access specifier right before the name of the base class can be public, private, or protected? Well, now you learn how to do that. When using a public specifier, all the base class's public and protected members can be accessed freely by the derived class or by a derived class object.

However, when you use a private or protected specifier, this all changes. If you use a protected specifier, all the base class's public members become protected when the derived class inherits them. Keep in mind that the base class remains unchanged. It's the derived class's version of the base class's members that changes.

A private specifier makes all the base class's members private. Only the members of the derived class can access them. Table 8.2 provides a summary of the different access specifiers and their meanings.

**TABLE 8.2 ACCESS SPECIFIERS IN INHERITANCE**

| Access Specifier | Base's Public Members | Base's Protected Members | Base's Private Members |
|---|---|---|---|
| `public` | Still public | Still protected | Still private |
| `protected` | Becomes protected | Still protected | Still private |
| `private` | Becomes private | Becomes private | Still private |

Here is an example of using these access specifiers in code:

```
class Base
{
private:
      int x;
protected:
      int y;
public:
      int z;
};

class Derived1 : public Base
{
      void f()
      {
            x = 5; //error because x is private in base
            y = 10; //ok
            z = 15; //ok
};

class Derived2 : protected Base
{
      void f()
      {
            x = 5; //error
            y = 10; //ok
            z = 15; //ok
};

class Derived3 : private Base
{
      void f()
      {
            x = 5; //error
            y = 10; //error
            z = 15; //error
};

int main(void)
{
```

```
    Derived1 d1;
    Derived2 d2;
    Derived3 d3;
    //error - cannot access private member outside of class
    d1.x = 4;
    //error - cannot access protected member outside of class
    d1.y = 8;     d1.z = 12; //ok
    d2.x = 3; //error - private member
    d2.y = 6; //error - protected member
    d2.z = 9; //error - protected member
    d3.x = 2; //error - private member
    d3.y = 4; //error - private member
    d3.z = 6; //error - private member
    return 0;
}
```

Try to picture the access specifier as functioning like a dimmer switch. If you use public inheritance, the light is on its brightest setting, so you are unable to see only the darkest things. If you use protected inheritance, the light is on its middle setting, so you must move closer to some things in order to see them. If you use private inheritance, the light is off, so you can see only the most reflective things—most things are too dark to be seen at all.

## Using Multiple Inheritance

Everything that you have studied so far in this chapter has been part of single inheritance. *Single inheritance* occurs when a derived class has only one base class. However, there is another kind of inheritance, called *multiple inheritance.* It occurs when a derived class has more than one base class. This is a new concept, even to some advanced programmers, so we'll move slowly through these dark waters.

The idea behind multiple inheritance is to merge base classes into one subclass, and as unbelievable as it might be at this point, multiple inheritance does have some practical uses.

The code for multiple inheritance is relatively straightforward. Instead of listing only one base class in the derived class declaration, you list more than one. Here is an example:

```
class A
{
    int a;
```

```
};

class B
{
      int b;
};

class AB : public A, public B
{
      int ab;
};
```

This code produces the derived class AB with three private members: a, b, and ab. Notice that each base class is separated by a comma. Instead of having all the members of a single base class plus its own, a derived class has all the members of all its base classes plus its own.

Imagine that you are creating an application to store employee records for a computer game company. You might have a Programmer class for one kind of employee and an Artist class for another. But what do you do if one employee does both? A programmer-artist employee might belong to both the Programmer and the Artist classes. If you were to choose one class in which to store this type, you would lose information. The solution is to use multiple inheritance. You can create a Programmer_Artist class that is derived from the Programmer and the Artist classes. In this way, you can create an accurate representation of employees.

## Resolving Ambiguity

When using multiple inheritance, the base classes of a derived class might have members of the same name, creating an ambiguity that must be resolved. Take a look at the following example:

```
class A
{
      public:
            int x;
};

class B
{
      public:
            int x;
```

```
};

class AB : public A, public B
{};

int main( void )
{
     AB ab;
     ab.x; // which x does this refer to?
     return 0;
}
```

As you can see, the line `ab.x` can refer to the `x` of either `A` or `B`.

The easiest way to resolve this ambiguity is to use the scope resolution operator (::). Using this operator, you can tell the computer explicitly which member you are referring to. Here is an example to illustrate this use:

```
class A
{
     public:
          int x;
};

class B
{
     public:
          int x;
};

class AB : public A, public B
{};

int main( void )
{
     AB ab;
     ab.A::x = 5; // use A's x
     ab.B::x = 6; // use B's x
     return 0;
}
```

The scope resolution operator is a practical way to differentiate between the two instances of x. However, using this operator every time you need to access the members can be a pain.

A better solution is to resolve the ambiguity within the derived class so that the users of your class do not even know ambiguity exists. You resolve ambiguity within the class a little differently for every class, but the following is an example of how it might work.

```
//8.3 - Resolving Ambiguity - Mark Lee - Premier Press
#include <iostream>
using namespace std;
class Hello
{
      public:
            void g() { cout << "Hello World\n";}
};

class Goodbye
{
      public:
            void g() { cout << "Goodbye World\n";}
};

class HelloGoodbye : public Hello, public Goodbye
{
      public:
            void g() //override both Hello::g() and Goodbye::g()
            {
                  Hello::g();
                  Goodbye::g();
            }
};

int main( void )
{
      HelloGoodbye hg;
      hg.g();
      return 0;
}
```

**Output:**

```
Hello World
Goodbye World
```

The derived class in this example overrides both the `Hello` version of `g()` and the `Goodbye` version of `g()`. This technique is effective for getting rid of the ambiguity. Now users of the `HelloGoodbye` class have to worry about only one version of the function.

## Replicated Base Classes

When using multiple inheritance, you might have more than one copy of a base class. For example, suppose that both the `Hello` and `Goodbye` classes are derived from a `Display` class that contains a function to display a string. The `Display` class might look like this:

```
class Display
{
      protected:
            void output(string s) { cout << s.c_str();}
};
```

The `Hello` and `Goodbye` classes will look like this:

```
class Hello : public Display
{
      protected:
            void g() { output("Hello World.\n"); }
};

class Goodbye : public Display
{
      protected:
            void g() { output("Goodbye World.\n");}
};
```

Finally, the `HelloGoodbye` class will look like this:

```
class HelloGoodbye : public Hello, public Goodbye
{
      public:
            void g()
            {
                  Hello::g();
```

```
            Goodbye::g();
        }
};
```

So far, so good. The only hard part is remembering that two separate copies of the `Display` class are within the `HelloGoodbye` class. If you want to use any members of the `Display` class, you must specify which copy of the `Display` class you want. Figure 8.5 shows a diagram of this class structure.

In order to specify which copy of the `Display` class you are referring to, you must use the scope resolution operator twice: once to denote which copy of the `Display` class you want (`Hello`'s or `Goodbye`'s) and once to specify which member within that class. Here is an example:

```
class HelloGoodbye : public Hello, public Goodbye
{
    public:
        void g() { Hello::Display::ouput("Hello.\n");}
};
```

As you can see, this double usage of the scope resolution operator can be annoying. Multiple inheritance can be dangerous ground for programmers, but if used correctly, it can be an important tool.

**Some experts believe that you should never use multiple Inheritance, so you might want to avoid using it whenever you can.**

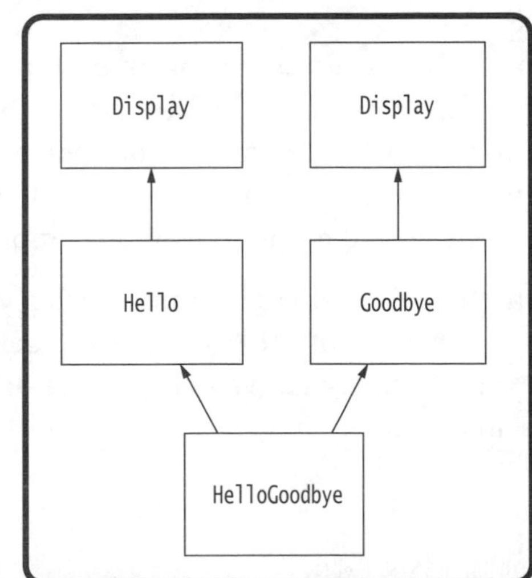


**FIGURE 8.5**

Here is how `HelloGoodbye` looks with a replicated base class.

# Accessing Objects in a Hierarchy

Now that you know how to create derived classes and have gone through the rules and tricks of creating inheritance from the inside out, it is time to study inheritance from the outside in. You need to know how to work with objects created from classes involved in inheritance and what to watch for when accessing objects that are involved in inheritance. The following sections provide some important concepts and new ideas, so keep your eyes on the target. You will learn how to access objects involved in inheritance and how to create true polymorphism.

## Revisiting Polymorphism

One of the most important aspects of inheritance is a derived class's capability of acting as any of its base classes do in certain situations. This capability, called *polymorphism,* is one of the main components of OOP in that it allows each object to be used in more than one situation.

You will often use polymorphism when working with pointers to objects of base classes. In the next section, you learn how and when this polymorphism occurs.

### Pointers to Base Classes

One of the best examples of polymorphism occurs when working with pointers to objects involved in a hierarchy. A pointer to a base class can store the address of a derived object. Here is an example:

```
Base* b;
Derived d;
b = &d; //this is ok
```

This capability of storing two kinds of addresses is an important part of inheritance, and it makes C++ a very powerful language. One place where this ability might be useful is in an array. You can make an array of pointers to `Vehicle` objects, and this array can store all types of vehicles. Otherwise, you would have to create a separate array for each type of vehicle, and doing so would be annoying.

Using polymorphism has some drawbacks. For example, after you store a `Car` object in a `Vehicle` pointer array, the type of the `Car` is hard to get back. In other words, it is difficult to figure out which type of vehicle you are dealing with in a `Vehicle` pointer array. Here is an example:

```
void f(Vehicle* v)
{
     //v could be a Car, Boat, Bike, etc.
}
```

Another problem is that the computer assumes the object stored in a pointer to a base class is a base object. If you've overridden a function in the derived class, the pointer will ignore it. Here is an example to clarify our point:

```
class Base
{
      public:
            void Display() { cout << "Base's Display";}
};

class Derived : public Base
{
      public:
            void Display() { cout << "Derived's Display";}
};

int main( void )
{
      Derived d;
      Base* b = &d;
      b->Display();
      return 0;
}
```

**Output:**

```
Base's Display
```

As you can see, the computer has no way of knowing whether the object stored in b is a derived object or a base object. Because of this, the computer must assume that the stored object is a `Base` object.

These rules can be confusing. Basically, you can store a derived object as a base object, but then the object loses its identity (it is assumed to be a base object).

## Virtual Functions

Fortunately for C++ programmers, there is a solution to the problem of the computer ignoring overridden functions. If you use *virtual functions*, an overridden function will not be ignored. Virtual functions enable the computer to figure out which function is the appropriate one to call, even if the computer does not know the kind of object with which it is dealing.

To create a virtual function, use the `virtual` keyword. Here is the general syntax:

```
virtual return_type function_name(argument_list);
```

You put the `virtual` keyword in front of the function only when it is first declared. If you declare the function and then define it later, the `virtual` keyword goes only in front of the declaration. If the function is defined at the same time that it is declared, you put the `virtual` keyword in front of the function definition.

You need to put the `virtual` keyword only in front of the base class's version of the function. Making functions virtual tells the computer to search for the correct version of the function to call. Take a look at the following example:

```
//8.4 - Virtual Functions - Mark Lee - Premier Press
#include <iostream>
using namespace std;
class Base
{
	public:
		void Display() { cout << "Base's Display\n";}
};

class Derived : public Base
{
	public:
		void Display() { cout << "Derived's Display\n";}
};

class Base2
{
	public:
		virtual void Display() { cout << "Base2's Display\n";}
		virtual void f(); // this is also correct
};

void Base2::f() // virtual not needed here
{}

class Derived2 : public Base2
{
	public:
		void Display() { cout << "Derived2's Display\n";}
```

```
};

int main ( void )
{
     Derived d;
     Base* b = &d;
     b->Display();

     Derived2 d2;
     Base2* b2 = &d2;
     b2->Display();
     return 0;
}
```

**Output:**

```
Base's Display
Derived2's Display
```

As you can see from the output, using a virtual function corrected the problem. The `Base` class used a non-virtual `Display()` function, so the incorrect function was called. Because `Base2`'s `Display()` is virtual, the call to `b2->Display()` produces the correct output.

Virtual functions are an important part of C++'s OOP. Without virtual functions, polymorphism would be much more difficult (if not impossible) in C++.

## Using Abstract Classes

Some classes that you design in a hierarchy might not make sense as objects. For example, although the `Vehicle` class works well as a parent class to define common elements of objects derived from `Vehicle`, creating a `Vehicle` object does not have any meaning.

Another example is when you have hierarchy of shape classes with a general `Shape` class at the top. Creating a `Shape` object does not make sense. It is a shape without shape. These classes represent abstract concepts. In contrast, a `Car` class can represent an actual object. Another possibility is to create a `Comparable` class that has the basic interface needed to make an object comparable with another object. If you derive classes from this base class, you are guaranteed to be able to compare them. However, making an object from the `Comparable` class wouldn't have much meaning.

C++ provides a way, called *abstract classes*, to represent these abstract concepts without accidentally mistaking them for normal objects. You create an abstract class by putting a pure virtual function inside the class. (You cannot create an object from an abstract class.)

A *pure virtual function* is a virtual function that is not implemented but is used only to create abstract classes (the base class does not provide a definition for it). To create the syntax for a pure virtual function, you simply put `= 0` at the end of the virtual function declaration:

```
virtual return_type function_name(argument_list) = 0;
```

**Remember not to implement pure virtual functions. Doing so will cause errors.**

If a class has one of these pure virtual functions as one of its members (or it does not override one from its base class), the class is an abstract class. It is illegal in C++ to create an object from an abstract class. The pure virtual function just helps to ensure that you don't accidentally attempt to create an object from that base class. The base class exists, therefore, only to provide a structure for derived classes. Here is an example:

```
class Abstract
{
      public:
            virtual void draw() = 0;
};

int main(void)
{
      Abstract a; //illegal - causes an error
      return 0;
}
```

If a class has an abstract base class, the class can override all the pure virtual functions so that it is not also an abstract class. Here is an example:

```
class Abstract
{
      public:
            virtual void draw() = 0;
};
```

```
class Derived : public Abstract
{
      public:
            //overrides Abstract::draw()
            void draw() { cout << "Hello World.";}
};

int main( void )
{
      Derived d; // legal
      Abstract a; // illegal
      return 0;
}
```

However, if a derived class does not override all the pure virtual functions from its base class, it inherits them and becomes an abstract class. Here is an example:

```
class Abstract
{
      virtual int f() = 0;
      virtual float g(float) = 0;
};

class Derived : class Abstract
{
      int f(); //override pure virtual from base
      //g() is not overridden
};

int main (void)
{
      Abstract a; //illegal - abstract class
      Derived d; // illegal - also an abstract class
}
```

## Creating the Dragon Lord Game

While wandering through a great kingdom, some noble messengers approach. "Noble Knight," they say, "You must help us!" Before you have a chance to explain that you aren't a knight, they explain their situation: "An evil dragon has kidnapped our princess! You must rescue her. We're desperate."

You can't refuse to help, so before you know it, you are riding to the dragon's lair. Can you defeat the dragon? Compile the following program and find out. Note that this program is made up of more than one file.

First, you create and save Dragon.cpp, RedDragon.cpp, BlueDragon.cpp, and BlackDragon.cpp in the same directory as the rest of the project. Then replace the .cpp file generated by CodeWarrior with DragonLord.cpp (remove the old one from the project and then add DragonLord.cpp). Next, include each file in your project. Finally, compile and run the project like any other program.

```
//8.5 - Dragon Lord - Mark Lee - Premier Press
// Dragon.cpp
#include <string>
#include <ctime>
#include <cstdlib>

#define MAX(a,b) a>b? a:b

using namespace std;
class Dragon
{
private:
      int speed;
      string name;
      int hitPoints;
      int armour;
      int treasure;
      int clawDamage;
      int size;
protected:
      Dragon(int theSize);
      int getArmour() {return armour;}
      int& getHitPoints() {return hitPoints;}
      int getClawDamage() { return clawDamage;}
      int getSize() { return size;}
      virtual int attack(int targetArmour, int specialDamage);
public:
      virtual int attack(int targetArmour) = 0;
      virtual void defend(int damage) = 0;
      int getTreasure() {return treasure;}
      virtual string getName() {return name;}
```

```
    int getSpeed() {return speed;}
    bool isAlive() { return hitPoints >0;}
};

Dragon::Dragon(int theSize) :
    size(theSize)
{
    if (size < 1 || size > 4)
        size = 3;
    clawDamage = 2 * size;
    speed = 3 * size;
    hitPoints = 4 * size;
    armour = size;
    treasure = 1000 * size;
    srand(time(0));
}

int Dragon::attack(int targetArmour, int specialDamage)
{
    int useSpecial = rand() % 2; // 0 or 1
    int damage;
    if (useSpecial)
        damage = specialDamage;
    else damage = getClawDamage();
    return MAX(damage - targetArmour,0);
}

//RedDragon.cpp
class RedDragon : public Dragon
{
private:
    int fireDamage;

public:
    RedDragon(int theSize);
    int attack(int targetArmour);
    void defend(int damage);
    string getName() {return "Red Dragon";}
};
```

```
RedDragon::RedDragon(int theSize) :
     Dragon(theSize)
{
     fireDamage = 4 * getSize();
}

int RedDragon::attack(int targetArmour)
{
     return Dragon::attack(targetArmour, fireDamage);
}

void RedDragon::defend(int damage)
{
     getHitPoints() -= (damage - getArmour())/3;
}

//BlueDragon.cpp
class BlueDragon : public Dragon
{
private:
     int iceDamage;

public:
     BlueDragon(int theSize);
     int attack(int targetArmour);
     void defend(int damage);
     string getName() {return "Blue Dragon";}
};

BlueDragon::BlueDragon(int theSize) :
     Dragon(theSize)
{
     iceDamage = 3 * getSize();
}

int BlueDragon::attack(int targetArmour)
{
     return Dragon::attack(targetArmour, iceDamage);
}
```

```
void BlueDragon::defend(int damage)
{
     getHitPoints() -= (damage - getArmour())/2;
}

//BlackDragon.cpp
class BlackDragon : public Dragon
{
private:
     int poisonDamage;

public:
     BlackDragon(int theSize);
     int attack(int targetArmour);
     void defend(int damage);
     string getName() {return "Black Dragon";}
};

BlackDragon::BlackDragon(int theSize) :
     Dragon(theSize)
{
     poisonDamage = getSize();
}

int BlackDragon::attack(int targetArmour)
{
     return Dragon::attack(targetArmour, poisonDamage);
}

void BlackDragon::defend(int damage)
{
     getHitPoints() -= damage - getArmour();
}

//DragonLord.cpp
#include <iostream>
#include <ctime>
#include <cstdlib>
#include "Dragon.cpp"
#include "RedDragon.cpp"
#include "BlueDragon.cpp"
```

```
#include "BlackDragon.cpp"

using namespace std;

int menuChoice();

int main (void)
{
     srand(time(0));
     Dragon* dragons[3];
     int hp = 15;
     int armour = 2;
     int tempArmour;
     int tempAttack;
     dragons[0] = new RedDragon(rand()%4+1);
     dragons[1] = new BlackDragon(rand()%4+1);
     dragons[2] = new BlueDragon(rand()%4+1);
     Dragon* d = dragons[rand()%3];
     cout << "Welcome noble knight.\n"
          << "You must save a princess."
          << " She has been captured by a "
          << d->getName() << ".\n"
          << "You must defeat the dragon.\n";
     cout << "Your hit points are: " << hp << endl;
     while (d->isAlive() && hp>0)
     {
          int choice = menuChoice();
          if (choice == 3) goto RUN;
          else if (choice == 1)
          {
               tempAttack = rand()%16+5;
               tempArmour = armour;
          }
          else {
               tempAttack = rand()%11;
               tempArmour = armour + 4;
          }
          hp -= d->attack(armour);
          d->defend(rand()%16-5);
```

```
            cout << "\nYou deliver a mighty blow and deal "
                 << tempAttack << " damage.\n";
            cout << "Your hit points are: " << hp;
        }
        if (d->isAlive())
            cout << "\nYou have perished before"
                 << " the might of the dragon.\n";
        else
            cout << "\n\nYou have slain the dragon!"
                 << " Congratulations.\n"
                 << "The princess is saved.\n";
        return 0;
        RUN:
        cout <<"\nYou have fled in cowardice.\n";
        return 0;
}

int menuChoice()
{
        int choice;
        do {
            cout << endl
                 << "[1]Attack\n"
                 << "[2]Defensive Mode\n"
                 << "[3]Run Away\n";
            cin >> choice;
        } while (choice < 1 && choice > 3);
        return choice;
}
```

## Summary

This chapter has been a whirlwind of new concepts. You have learned about basic inheritance, the protected access modifier, multiple inheritance, virtual functions, and abstract classes. Knowing and being able to use the information in this chapter are crucial to becoming an advanced C++ programmer. If you ever move on to other programming languages, you will find that the concepts in this chapter also apply to most of those languages.

## CHALLENGES

1. Create a weapon hierarchy, with at least four weapons derived from a single parent class. What kind of data members should each contain? What about methods?
2. Give an example of a situation in which multiple inheritance might be useful. Is it easier to program with single inheritance than with multiple inheritance?
3. When would you use protected and private inheritance?
4. Design and fully implement an abstract `Shape` class. What should be included? What should be left to the derived classes?

# Using Templates

If you started at the beginning of this book, you are well on your way to becoming a professional programmer. You have learned the basics of C++ programming, and now you're ready for more advanced concepts. In this chapter, you learn about templates, which will serve as a springboard to the C++ standard library. You study some of the main components of the standard library. If you've ever considered designing libraries for other programmers to use, this chapter is crucial. In this chapter, you learn the following:

- How to create class templates
- How to create function templates
- How to make template use invisible
- How to use the standard library
- How to use strings
- How to use vectors

## Creating Templates

Imagine that you are a renowned weapon maker, famous for your excellent weapons across the land. A king has come to you and asked for a bow that can shoot any kind of arrow. Foolishly, you agree to make such a bow, not realizing that the task is impossible. How can any one bow shoot every kind of arrow? Unfortunately, the bow is due tomorrow. But while studying some ancient texts on weapon making, you come across a magic spell . . . called the *Template*. "Cast this spell on a weapon," the book notes, "and the weapon will become completely versatile, able to handle any kind of ammo." You're saved! You will be able to finish the bow easily by tomorrow.

In C++, templates enable you to generalize a class or function so that it doesn't use a particular data type, and just as you might use the magic "Template" in our (newly coined) fable to create a bow that will handle all kinds of arrows, you can use templates in C++ to create a function or class that can handle all kinds of data types.

For example, each version of the `add` function we discuss in Chapter 4, "Writing Functions," is specific to a certain kind of data (two integers, two floating-points, and so on). With templates, however, you can create a single version that covers every C++ data type (and even user-defined data types, such as classes). Sound powerful? It is.

The theory is that when you use templates, you are performing essentially the same operation on the data no matter what data type you are working with. As a result, there's no particular reason why you can't program this operation only once. In this way, templates enable you to generalize an operation to avoid redundant programming.

Now, let us share with you the basics of programming with templates.

## Creating Class Templates

A *class template* is a class that utilizes a template in order to make the class more general. Well, that doesn't provide very much enlightenment, does it?

First, take a look at this `Storage` class, which stores an array of integers (without using a template):

```
class Storage
{
     int* data;
     int numElements;
     Storage();
     Storage(int* array, int num) :
          data(array), numElements(num) {}
     Storage(int num) {data = new int[num];}
     void AddElement(int newElement);
     int ElementAt(int location);
     int RemoveElementAt(int location);
     ~Storage();
};
```

This class stores an array of integers and provides methods to add, view, and remove the elements. But what would you do if you wanted to store floats or characters? You'd have to copy the preceding code and change the integers to floats or characters, which would be inefficient. Or you might somehow pass the data type that you want to store as a parameter. Then you might have a switch statement to handle each case. This would quickly become complicated and unmanageable.

The best solution to this problem is to use templates. A template version of the `Storage` class can store any kind of data. Templates are a simple way to pass the data type as a parameter without the methods becoming complicated and unmanageable. Here is how the `Storage` class looks when you use a template:

```
template<class T> class Storage
{
     T* data;
     int numElements;
     Storage();
     Storage(T* array, int num) :
          data(array), numElements(num) {}
     Storage(int num);
     void AddElement(T newElement);
     T ElementAt(int location);
     T RemoveElementAt(int location);
     ~Storage();
};
```

As you can see, this code is fairly different. It might look a little unfamiliar to you at the moment, but soon it will become more familiar. The only thing that has changed is the replacement of `int` with `T` (but not all instances of `int`) and the addition of `template<class T>` immediately before the class.

The uses of `T` are easy to explain. They act as a placeholder for whichever kind of data the user of the class decides to store. So, if the user decides to store integers, all instances of `T` will be `int`s. Some uses of `int` remain because they aren't all part of the data. Some of them are just for the number of elements (which should always be an integer value).

The code, `template<class T>`, tells the computer that this class is using a template and that `T` is being used as a placeholder for the data type being stored. Even though you write `class T`, `T` doesn't have to be a class. It can be any data type.

Another way to think about a template is as an argument list. The preceding example has one argument, `class T`. When the class is used, the user passes the type of data to store "almost" as an argument. Then `T` is filled with this data type. As you can see, `class T` is much like an argument declaration. Here, the keyword `class` is used in a different way to mean "data type." In this case, you can use the keyword `typename` rather than `class` if you want (it has the exact same meaning here).

After you declare `T` in the first line, you can use it anywhere within the class just like any other type name (such as `int` or `float`). This means that you can declare new variables and make pointers, arrays, or anything else for which you might use a type name.

When you create an object from this class template, you must specify which type of data you are going to store. Here is an example for storing integers:

```
Storage<int> intStore;
```

As you can see, specifying the type of data for a template is much like passing an argument. When `intStore` is created, `int` takes the place of all the `T`s in the class. You can use `Storage<int>` just like you use the name of any other class. In the same way, you can store any other kind of data:

```
Storage<float> floatStore; //stores float's
Storage<string> stringStore; //stores strings
Storage<Shape*> shapeStore; //stores pointers to Shape's
```

Take a look at the syntax for creating a class template:

```
template<class TypeName> class ClassName
```

```
{
    ClassDeclaration
};
```

Here *TypeName* is an arbitrary placeholder for a data type, *ClassName* is the name of the class, and *ClassDeclaration* is the declaration of the class (just like normal classes from Chapter 5, "Fighting with OOP"). Keep in mind that *TypeName* can be any valid identifier, but it is usually a single capital letter, such as `T` or `C`.

If a method is implemented outside the class template, you must use the template syntax again for it. Here is the syntax for methods that are implemented outside of the class template:

```
template<class parameter> returnType
    ClassName<parameter>::methodName(args)
{
    methodImplementation
}
```

Here *parameter* is the name of the parameter (such as `T`), and *methodImplementation* is the implementation of the method.

Because the constructor implementation uses the name of the class twice (once for the class name and once for the method name), you would normally have to put `<parameter>` after each use of the class name. However, this is a bit redundant, so for the name of the method, you don't have to (but you can if you like). Here is the syntax for a constructor implemented outside of a class template:

```
template<parameter>
    ClassName<parameter>::ClassName<parameter>(args)
{
    constructorImplementation
}
```

Or you could use this, more common, syntax:

```
template<parameter> ClassName<parameter>::ClassName(args)
{
    constructorImplementation
}
```

Both ways are exactly the same. It is a matter of personal preference. The first way is more formal, but the second way is more common.

**If you are making a class template, we suggest first designing the class for a specific data type. Then you can work out all the bugs and design flaws before you generalize with a template. This approach makes programming much easier.**

## Using Template Parameters

The declaration inside the angle brackets (for example `<class T>`) is a *template parameter*. As you have seen, the template parameter behaves almost the same way that a function argument does. As with function arguments, you can have more than one template parameter. In fact, you can have as many as you want.

One example of where multiple template parameters are useful is when you are creating an associative array. An *associative array* is like a normal array, except that two different objects are at each element. One of the two might be a string, and the other might be an integer representing the number of occurrences of the string in a section of text. Think of associative arrays as side-by-side arrays with the same number of elements. Here is how an associative array class might look:

```
template<class T, class C> class AssociativeArray;
AssociativeArray<string, int> wordFrequency;
```

In addition, a template parameter does not have to be a general type. It can be something specific, such as an integer or a floating-point. Here is an example of using a specific data type in a template parameter:

```
template<class T, int i> class Array
{
      T data[i];
      //...
};
```

You can then use this class template as follows:

```
Array<int, 10> intArray;
```

This code snippet creates an array of ten integers. Notice how the array is created with the size given from the template parameter? Doing this might be confusing. You can't create dynamic sized arrays from function arguments because an array must be declared with a constant size (except an array on the free store). A function argument does not have to be constant; however, a template parameter does. A template parameter can be a constant or a pointer. Also, a template parameter used within a class must be treated as a constant (you can't change its value).

Here is an example to illustrate these concepts:

```
int i = 10;
//error - non-constant value used for template parameter
Array<int, i> intArray;
Array<int, 10> intArray; //ok - constant value used
```

The compiler has to know the size of all arrays created before the program actually runs. If you provide a constant expression, such as `20 - 10`, the compiler will be able to evaluate the expression, so it is acceptable to use constant expressions.

However, the compiler can check only syntax errors when a template is compiled. That is, the compiler can check whether a particular type works in the template code only when you use that template with a particular data type. The point in time in which you use a template with a specific type is called the *point of instantiation.*

Say that you design a class template and, accidentally assuming that the type will always be a string, you use the function `c_str()`. In doing so, you might wind up with a problem. If an object is created with string as the type, no errors will occur. However, if the data type is not a string, problems will occur. Though assumptions of this nature do not always present a problem, they often do, so be on the lookout for them. If you design a class template that works for only certain types, make this condition very clear to the user.

## Creating Function Templates

Functions can also use templates similarly to the way classes use them. A good example is a function such as the `add` function covered in Chapter 4. Admittedly, `add` is a trivial function (because it adds only two numbers), but we can easily expand the concept of functions like this to something more complex.

As you do with class templates, you create a function template by putting the keyword `template` and the parameter list at the beginning of the function. Function templates are similar to overloaded functions, except that you can create one function template to handle every case rather than a different function for each case. Here is how the `add` function might look with a template:

```
template<class T> T add (T a, T b)
{
    return a + b;
}
```

Unfortunately, this add function is not universal. You cannot provide arguments of two different types. In the section, "Overloading Function Templates," later in this chapter, you learn ways to provide almost any argument and get the desired results.

You can use the template parameters as you do with all other data types anywhere within the function. Here is an example:

```
template<class T> void swap(T* a, T* b)
{
      T temp = *a;
      *a = *b;
      *b = temp;
}
```

This function exchanges the values of two pointers. Here is an example of how you might use this function:

```
int x = 5;
int y = 6;
swap<int>(&x, &y);
```

x now contains the value 6, and y contains the value 5. <iostream> includes a standard library version of this function called swap, which takes two of the same type argument (regardless of which type, because the standard library swap is a function template).

### Understanding Argument Resolution

Function templates are not quite the same as class templates. With function templates, you do not always have to provide a template parameter when you call the function. Sometimes, the computer can figure out what the parameters are supposed to be simply from the arguments you pass. Here is an example:

```
add(5,3);
```

Don't be fooled, brave reader; this is not the add function from Chapter 4. The version with the template is being called here. Because the arguments are both integers, the computer can deduce that the parameter (T) is supposed to be int. Now, you're venturing into the land of truly programming; however, for now, you don't even have to know that the add function has a template. You simply call it like any other function.

If the arguments for the preceding function were not so clear (for example, if one were an integer and the other a floating-point), the compiler would return an error. Computers have a limited intelligence, and they can't quite decide whether the integer should be converted to a floating-point or the floating-point should be converted to an integer. If you choose not to provide parameters for function template calls, be sure that the arguments clearly designate what the parameters are supposed to be.

Also, if all the parameters are not contained in the argument list (for example, one parameter is used only for a return type), you must provide a full parameter list for the function call.

Now, as a case study, you are ready to create a function to type-cast for you. (In Chapter 2, "Descending Deeper . . . into Variables," we define *type casting* as the act of converting data from one type to another, retaining almost the same value.)

This function is an example of where one of the parameters is not used in the argument list, as shown here:

```
template<class C, class T> C cast(T a)
{
     return (C)a;
}
```

This function works only if a normal cast will work for the argument. Here are some examples of how you might use this function:

```
cout << cast<int, float>(3.5); //converts 3.5 to 3
cout << cast<float, int>(9); //converts 9 to 9.0
//error - cannot cast an int to a char*
cout << cast<char*, int>(35769);
```

In cases like these, you can assume from the function argument what the second template parameter is. However, as with default function arguments, you can leave out a template parameter only at the end of the parameter list. For example, if there are three parameters, you leave out the last one, the last two, or all three, provided that they can be assumed. Here is an example of how you can leave out parameters:

```
//converts 3 to 3.0 - second parameter deduced to be int
cout << cast<float>(3);
//converts 3.5 to 3 - second parameter assumed to be float
cout << cast<int>(3.5);
cout << cast(35); //error - what to cast it to?
```

## Specializing Templates

Sometimes, you might want a function template to work in a specialized way for a particular kind of data. One data type might be an exception to the rule that all other types follow. In this case, you must provide a different version of the template for that particular type. This different version is called a *specialization*. You use it whenever the data type in question is used.

In the section "Using Vectors," later in this chapter, you study vectors. A *vector* is a class template. Here is the basic declaration for the `vector` class template:

```
template<class T> class Vector;
```

This declaration seems pretty simple. It's just a normal class template. However, the `vector` class template has a specialization as well as this more general declaration. A vector must treat an array of void pointers differently in some way. Here is the declaration for the `Vector` class's specialization:

```
template<> class Vector<void*>;
```

The preceding code essentially denotes a specialization of `Vector` to be used whenever `void*` is used as the parameter type. That is, when you use `void*` as a parameter, the specialization is used. The specialization basically takes over. If you use any other type, the first version will be used. Here is an example of using specializations:

```
#include <iostream>
#include <string>
using namespace std;
template<class T>class SayHi
{
     T data;
public:
     SayHi(T a) : data(a) {}
     void display() { cout << data << endl; }
};

template<> class SayHi<string>
{
     string data;
public:
     SayHi(string a) : data(a) {}
     void display() {cout << data.c_str() << endl; }
};
```

```
int main (void)
{
      SayHi<int> hi(5);
      hi.display();
      SayHi<string> hs("Hello World");
      hs.display();
      return 0;
}
```

**Output:**

```
5
Hello World
```

You can specialize a function template in the same way. Here is the syntax for this:

```
template<> returnType functionName<specialType>(args) {}
```

Here `specialType` is the type for which you are specializing.

## Simplifying Template Use

Templates can become annoying to users of your classes and functions. Fortunately, you can hide the fact that templates are used.

The first and easiest way is to use `typedef`. Because you can use `ClassName <parameters>` just as you use the name of a normal class, you can `typedef` the name of a class template to something shorter. For example, rather than use `Vector<int>`, use `IntVec`. Then, when users want a vector of integers, they can use `IntVec`. Users do not have to be aware that `IntVec` is part of a template. Here is how you might accomplish this renaming:

```
typedef Vector<int> IntVec;
```

An example of where `typedef` is used like this is in the standard library string class. The actual name of the class template for a string is `basic_string`. This class template takes one template parameter: the type of character being stored. Here is the `typedef` for this class:

```
typedef basic_string<char> string;
```

Isn't that interesting? This means that you can use `basic_string<char>` rather than `string` if you want to (if you want useless inconvenience).

A second common method of simplifying template usage is with default template parameters. As with function arguments, template parameters can have default values. The format is exactly the same:

```
template<class A, class B = int, class C = float> class ABC;
```

In this example, `B` and `C` default to `int` and `float`, respectively, if no type is passed when an object is created. Here are some ways to use this class template:

```
ABC<int> a1; //A is int, B is int, C is float
ABC<int, string, char> a2; //A is int, B is string, C is char
//A is double, B is double, C is float

ABC<double, double> a3;
```

You must place all default template parameters at the end of the list (as you have to with function arguments).

In the section "Understanding Argument Resolution," earlier in this chapter, we talked about the third way to make function templates less complicated.

If no parameters are provided with the function call, the computer can sometimes deduce what they should be. In this way, you can make a function template seem like a normal function.

The fourth way applies just to function templates and is discussed in the following section.

### Overloading Function Templates

Function templates can be overloaded, just like normal functions can. In fact, you can create many versions of a function with the same name, some being function templates and some being just normal functions.

Wait a minute! If everything we've said about templates is true (that they make a function general for every kind of data type), why would you ever need to overload a function template? Surprisingly, there are some reasons for doing so. One of the main reasons is to make a function template behave exactly like a normal function. You can write overloaded versions of a function template that handle cases where template parameters would otherwise have to be called. This ensures that the correct version is always called.

Say that you add two integers together and you want to return a floating-point (just because). Here is the new complete `add` function:

```
template<class T> T add (T a, T b)
```

```
{
     return a + b;
}

float add (int a, int b)
{
     return (float) a+b;
}
```

Now, if you call the add function with two integers, the overloaded version (the second one) will be called. For every other data type, the second version is ignored. But how does the computer decide which version to call? The computer follows specific rules to decide. For every function call to an overloaded function template, the computer must follow these steps:

1. Find all the versions of the function that could possibly apply to the arguments. For a call of add(5,3), this rule leaves both versions as possibilities. For a call of add(75, 'a'), this rule leaves no possibilities (because both versions take two of the same data type).
2. If one function template is a specialization of another, choose the specialization.
3. Apply the normal overload rules for functions to everything that is left.
4. If a function and a function template are left, choose the function. For a call of add(5,3), both the function and the function template were candidates until this step. The function is chosen.
5. If no possibilities remain, the call was an error. If two or more possibilities remain, the call was ambiguous and is an error.

Earlier, we said that if the parameters are not clear from the argument list, you must provide parameters when you call the function—for example, if you call the add function with an integer and a floating-point. Fortunately, there are some ways around having to provide parameters. One way is to provide overloaded versions of the add function that call the function template with the parameters. This way, the user does not have to worry about the function template parameters. Here is an example of how you can overload the add function:

```
inline float add(int a, float b) { return add<float>(a,b);}
inline float add(float a, int b) { return add<float>(a.b); }
```

Now, if you call the add function with an integer and a floating-point and you don't provide a parameter, the computer will be able to figure out what to do. Notice how the preceding functions are declared inline. This is so that no extra memory is taken up for the convenience of not having to provide a parameter. You are telling the computer that when you add an integer and a floating-point, you want a floating-point to be returned. Here are some examples of using this new version of the add function:

```
cout << add(3.5, 7); //returns 10.5
cout << add(7, 3.5); //returns 10.5
```

Do not be overwhelmed by function template overloading. It really is just like normal overloading, except that you must apply a few more rules. If you are ever in doubt, just consult the list of rules.

## Using the Standard Library

The C++ standard library was designed to be useful for almost every C++ user. Because of this, it must be as general as possible. For example, if the standard library vector were designed for a specific data type, then its usefulness would be severely limited.

When the designers of the C++ language were creating the standard library, they set these requirements:

- It must be convenient, efficient, useful, and safe for all users.
- Users should not have to reprogram the library in order to find it useful.
- The library must provide a simple interface.
- The library must be complete in what it tries to do.
- The library must blend well with built-in data types and keywords.

Knowing these requirements, the designers then constructed the library. In our opinion, they succeeded in meeting every one of the requirements.

The standard library is organized into a set of header files, each serving a different purpose. They can be divided into ten categories: containers, general utilities, iterators, algorithms, diagnostics, strings, streams, locales, language support, and numerics.

In this section, we discuss a few of the containers and the string that has been used since Chapter 1, "Starting the Journey." *Containers* are types that store a set of values. *Strings* (as you know) store text.

Because templates are used specifically to make code more general, the standard library is a rich source for examples of how you can use templates.

## Using Strings

All the C++ standard string facilities are included in <string>. As we mentioned previously in this chapter, string is a synonym for basic_string<char>. basic_string is a class template that can accept any kind of character. For example, you might create a class to store Egyptian characters called E_char. Then you can create a string object using Egyptian characters like this:

```
basic_string<E_char> egyptian;
```

All characters that are used as a parameter for basic_string must have their properties defined by another class template called char_traits. The basic declaration of char_traits is as follows:

```
template<class Ch> struct char_traits{};
```

A struct is exactly like a class, except that all its members are public by default rather than private. Strangely enough, this template class is never used. Every kind of character has a specialization for this template, including this example:

```
template<> struct char_traits<char>;
```

This code is the specialization for the char character type. This char_traits class template stores the properties of a particular character type. Take a look at a simplified version of the implementation of char_traits<char>:

```
template<> struct char_traits<char> {
    typedef char char_type; //call it by a standard name
    //standard name for the integer representation
    typedef int int_type;
    //copy the second argument into the first
    static void assign(char_type& a, const char_type& b);
    //convert int to char
    static char_type to_char_type(const int_type& a);
    //convert char to int
    static int_type to_int_type(const char_type& a);
    //are the two ints the same character?
    static bool eq_int_type(const int_type& i,
        const int_type& j);
    //are the two chars equal?
    static bool eq(const char_type& a, const char_type& b);
    //is the first char less than the second?
    static bool lt(const char_type& a, const char_type& b);
    //move n copies of s2 into s
```

```
    static char_type* move(char_type* s,
         const char_type* s2, size_t n);
    //move n copies of s2 into s
    static char_type* copy(char_type* s,
         const char_type* s2, size_t n);
    //copy n copies of a into s
    static char_type* assign(char_type* s,
         size_t n, char_type a);

    //compares 2 characters
    static int compare(const char_type* s,
         const char_type* s2, size_t n);
    //returns the length of the character array
    static size_t length(const char_type* c);
    //find c in s
    static const char_type* find(const char_type* s,
         int n, const char_type& c);
};
```

You've had your first glimpse at libraries. At first they can seem unreadable, but with practice, you will become used to them. The main annoyance is that most libraries use variable names such as `_E`, making it hard to remember what they do. The libraries use names like this is to make sure that their names don't conflict with any other names.

As you can see, `char_traits<char>` defines the basic operations when using a `char` or `char` array.

The first few lines of code you see in this definition are two `typedefs`. They give standard names to the character type and integer type so that the string class can refer to `char_traits::char_type` or `char_traits::int_type` regardless of which kind of character is used.

Because you haven't seen `size_t` before, you might be wondering what it is. You can think of it as an unsigned integer.

Implementing the methods in this class template is fairly straightforward. For example, here is the implementation for the first version of `assign`:

```
template<> void char_traits<char>::assign(char_type& a,
     char_type& b)
{
     a = b;
}
```

Every character that is used as a basic_string must define a specialization of char_traits and must implement all these functions. This guarantees that the basic_string class will be able to perform these operations on any character.

The second most common character type is the wide character (wchar_t). It is similar to a normal character, except that it takes up 2 bytes (to allow more characters in the character set).

Here is the basic declaration for the basic_string class template:

```
template<class C, class T = char_traits<C>,
     class A = allocator<C>> class std::basic_string;
```

As you can see, the class is part of the std namespace (as everything in the standard library is), and the template takes three parameters. Two of these parameters are default parameters, so you have to provide a minimum of only one. C is the type of character, T is the char_traits associated with that character, and A is a type called an *allocator* that deals with allocating memory for the character. By default, T and A are the specializations of their respective classes for the character type. You should leave them alone in almost all cases.

Just as the char_traits class defines standard names for things with typedef, so does the basic_string class. Here is the list of these typedefs:

```
//type of char_traits used (char_traits<char> usually)
typedef T traits_type;
//type of memory manager (allocator<char> usually)
typedef typename A allocator_type;

//kind of character being stored (char usually)
typedef typename T::char_type value_type;
//some kind of unsigned type (unsigned int maybe)
typedef typename A::size_type size_type;

//reference to individual character (char& usually)
typedef typename A::reference reference;
//pointer to individual character (char* usually)
typedef typename A::pointer pointer;

//the type used for a standard iterator
typedef compiler_dependant iterator;
//the type used for a reverse iterator
typedef std::reverse_iterator<iterator> reverse_iterator;
```

```
//used to represent every character of a string
static const size_type npos;
```

You must use typename at the beginning of a template parameter when you use the parameter to access things inside it. For example, to define value_type, you need to access char_type from inside the char_traits class. *compiler_dependant* indicates that the code placed there is based on which compiler you are using. The code is different for every compiler, but regardless of what it is, it will indicate some type of standard iterator. npos represents "all characters." That is, whenever you need to supply the number of characters to use for an operation, you can use npos to mean all of them (from whatever point to the end). Keep in mind that this doesn't necessarily mean the whole string. The most accurate meaning is "all the string."

### Constructing a String

The standard library provides many ways to construct a string object. You can use another string object, a character array, a string literal, an empty constructor, and more. We cover these constructors one by one. The first is when you want to construct one string from another:

```
//construct a string from another whole or partial string
basic_string(const basic_string& s, size_type pos = 0,
    size_type n = npos, const A& a = A() );
```

The first argument is simply another string. You can use any kind of basic_string here. The second argument is the position (treating the string as a character array) from which to start taking values. The third argument is the number of characters to take. This argument defaults to npos, which loosely correlates to the largest possible value of a string. This means "go to the end of s." pos = 0 means "start at the beginning" and n = npos means "take every character." The fourth argument relates to the way memory is allocated for this string. Although we don't cover the fourth argument here because it is too complicated for a beginner, here are some examples of how you might use this constructor:

```
string s = "Hello World:"; //declare a string to work with
string s1(s); //s1 and s both contain the value "Hello World"
//start at position 6, take two chars - s2 contains "Wo"
string s2(s, 6, 2);
string s3(s, 6); //error - need third argument too
```

The last call to the constructor fails because the computer mixes it up with the second constructor (explained next). The second and third constructors create a string from a character array, as shown here:

```
basic_string(const C* p, size_type n, const A& a = A());
basic_string(const C* p, const A& a = A());
```

The first argument, p, is the character array. n is the number of characters to use, and a has to do with the way the string is allocated (just let it have its default value, unless you feel like learning about allocators). If you don't supply n, the whole C-style string is used to construct the string. Here are some examples of how you might use these constructors:

```
char* p = "Hello World";
string s1(p); //s1 contains "Hello World"
string s2(p, 5); //s2 contains "Hello"
string s3(p+6, 5); //s3 contains "World"
```

The last constructor creates a string from a sequence of characters. You pass the sequence of characters with an iterator. You learn about iterators in detail in the next section, but here are the basics. For a container or a string, you can call the methods begin() and end() to get pointers to the first and last elements stored in the container or string. You can use these two values to copy the entire set of characters into the new string. Here is the constructor:

```
//uses all of the characters from first to last
template<class I> basic_string(I first, I last,
      const A& a = A());
```

Here are some ways that you can use this constructor:

```
string s = "Hello World";
char* c = "Hello World";
string s1(s.begin(), s.end()); //s1 contains "Hello World"
string s2(c, c+5); //s2 contains "Hello"
string s3(c+6, c+11); //s3 contains "World"
```

You can use any two pointers to characters in a sequence for this constructor. Every element between them will be used. Take care to make sure that the first argument comes before (in memory) the second and that every value between them is actually a character.

As well as constructors, the basic_string class has a destructor to do the cleanup that is required:

```
~basic_string();
```

## Iterating through a String

Iterators are common to all containers and strings. Iterators enable you to navigate through the values stored in a container or string. All iterators provide a similar interface, which is one of the main strengths of the standard library. If you learn about the interface for one container, you can easily use any container. For a `basic_string`, the individual characters in the string are the values navigated through by the iterator. All the code for these iterators is included with `<iterator>`.

Some containers (for this discussion, a string is being treated as a container of characters) can provide certain operations efficiently and some cannot. For example, a list cannot access any particular value that it stores at any given time. In other words, a list does not have *random access*. A vector, on the other hand, does. There are five categories of iterators, dependant on the kind of access operations that are available. They are input, output, forward, bi-directional, and random access.

Input can only read values from the elements and navigate forward through the container (input from the container to you). Output can only write values to the elements and navigate forward through the container (output from you to the container). Forward can read, write, and navigate forward through the container. Bi-directional can read, write, and navigate forward and backward. Random access can read, write, and navigate to any element at random.

The operations available to each type of iterator are summarized in Table 9.1.

**TABLE 9.1 ITERATOR OPERATIONS**

| Operation Type | Out | In | Forward | Bi | Rand |
|---|---|---|---|---|---|
| Forward iteration (++) | Yes | Yes | Yes | Yes | Yes |
| Backward iteration (--) | No | No | No | Yes | Yes |
| Random access ( [ ], +=, -=, +, - ) | No | No | No | No | Yes |
| Read ( *`Iterator`) | No | Yes | Yes | Yes | Yes |
| Write (*`Iterator` =) | Yes | No | Yes | Yes | Yes |
| Member access (->) | No | Yes | Yes | Yes | Yes |
| Comparison (==, !=) | No | Yes | Yes | Yes | Yes |
| More comparison (<, >, <=, >=) | No | No | No | No | Yes |

As you can see from the operations in Table 9.1, iterators are similar to pointers to arrays. In fact, a pointer to an array is an iterator for the array. All iterators provide operators that match those of pointers. To the untrained eye, an iterator can appear to be a pointer because it is used exactly like one.

The categories of iterators form a hierarchy:

```
struct input_iterator_tag {};
struct output_iterator_tag {};
struct forward_iterator_tag : public input_iterator_tag {};
struct bidirectional_iterator_tag :
     public forward_iterator_tag {};
struct random_access_iterator_tag :
     public bidirectional_iterator_tag {};
```

This hierarchy matches the capabilities of each type. For example, a random access iterator can function as an input iterator, but not vice versa. Output iterators are left out of the hierarchy because they don't quite fit with the rest. If one were included, it would become a second base class to `forward_iterator_tag`, but that does not create any significant advantages, so it's not.

Now, you are ready for the basic iterator class. After a few minutes of study, it will seem fairly simple, so here it is:

```
template <class C, class T, class Dist = ptrdiff_t,
     class Ptr = T*, class Ref = T&>
struct iterator {
     //a class from the hierarchy above
     typedef C iterator_category;
     //the type of element being iterated upon
     typedef T value_type;
     //type of distance between two elements
     typedef Dist difference_type;
     typedef Ptr pointer; //pointer to element type
     tyepdef Ref reference; //reference to element type
};
```

Here `C` is the kind of iterator (indicated by a type from the preceding hierarchy), `T` is the type of element, `Dist` is the type used to measure the distance between elements, `Ptr` is the type used as a pointer to an element, and `Ref` is the type used as a reference to an element. `ptrdiff_t` is defined to be the standard distance between two pointers. As you can see, all that this class does is define names, because it is just a base class from which each container can derive its own version. You use this class to define all these types to meet your requirements, whatever they are.

Just as each character class has a `char_traits` associated with it, each iterator has an `iterator_traits` associated with it. Here is the `iterator_traits` template class:

```
template<class Iter> struct iterator_traits {
     typedef typename
          Iter::iterator_category iterator_category;
     typedef typename Iter::value_type value_type;
     typedef typename Iter::difference_type difference_type;
     typedef typename Iter::pointer pointer;
     typedef typename Iter::reference reference;
};
```

When a programmer designs an algorithm that uses iterators, she can use `iterator _traits<Iter>::iterator_category` to design different behavior for each different iterator type. That way, the user of the code does not have to be aware of iterators. The most appropriate version of the code is automatically used. It is one more powerful way to make the implementation invisible to the user.

All strings and containers provide standard methods to generate an iterator of their elements. Here are the iterator methods for the `basic_string` class:

```
//generates an iterator which points at the first element
iterator begin();
//iterator that points at one past the last element
iterator end();
```

Often, both these methods are required if you are using the iterator as a sequence of characters. For example, the string constructor that takes an input sequence can use the results of these two methods to produce a string:

```
string s = "Hello World";
string s1(s.begin(), s.end()); //s1 now contains "Hello World"
```

Sometimes, you might want to iterate through a container in reverse order. A class template, called `reverse_iterator`, accomplishes this feat. This class template is derived from the iterator class. Here is the `reverse_iterator` class template:

```
template<class Iter> class reverse_iterator :
public iterator<iterator_traits<Iter>::iterator_category,
iterator_traits<Iter>::value_type,
iterator_traits<Iter>::difference_type,
```

```
iterator_traits<Iter>::pointer,
iterator_traits<Iter>::reference> {

protected:
     //used to internally iterate backwards with
     //a normal iterator
     Iter current;
public:
     //give the iterator type a standard name
     typedef Iter iterator_type;

     reverse_iterator() : current() {} //default constructor
     //constructor from a normal iterator
     reverse_iterator(Iter x) : current(x) {}
     //construct from another reverse_iterator
     template<class U> reverse_iterator(
          const reverse_iterator<U>& x) : current(x.base()) {}

     //return the normal iterator that this class uses
     Iter base() const {return current;}

     //dereferencing
     reference operator* () const { Iter tmp = current;
          return *--tmp;}
     pointer operator-> () const; //access member operator
     reference operator[] (difference_type n) const;

     //go backwards(reverse)
     reverse_iterator& operator++ () {--current;
          return *this; }
     reverse_iterator operator++ (int) {
          reverse_iterator t = current; --current; return t;}
     //go forwards (reverse)
     reverse_iterator& operator-- () {++current;
          return *this;}
     reverse_iterator operator-- (int) {
          reverse_iterator t = current; ++current; return t;}

     reverse_iterator operator+ (difference_type n) const;
     reverse_iterator operator+= (difference_type n);
```

```
    reverse_iterator operator- (difference_type n) const;
    reverse_iterator operator -= (difference_type n);
};
```

The reverse_iterator contains an iterator, called current, that reverse_iterator uses to iterate. reverse_iterator increments and decrements this iterator internally and uses its value whenever the user requests a value. The meaning of the ++ operator for an iterator is "go to the next element." However, a reverse_iterator goes through the elements backward, so a ++ on a reverse_iterator is equivalent to a -- on a normal iterator (both move the same direction in the container). This is why current is decremented in the implementation of the ++ operator function.

Normally, when an iterator reaches the end of a container, the iterator is pointing to one past the last element of the container. However, because a reverse_iterator moves backward, the end will be when the iterator points to 1 before the first value. This is an illegal value to access and might cause problems. To avoid this complication, current points to one element after whatever the iterator points to. In other words, when the iterator is at the end, current will point to the first element of the container. This design is much safer than pointing to 1 before the first element.

A reverse_iterator, like all iterators, supports operators that make it behave exactly like a pointer.

To create a reverse iterator from a container or string, you use the rbegin() and rend() methods. Here they are for the basic_string class:

```
//reverse iterator starting at end of string
//and moving backwards
reverse_iterator rbegin();
//reverse iterator starting at the beginning of the string
reverse_iterator rend();
```

Here are some examples of how you might use a reverse_iterator:

```
string s = "Hello World";
cout << *s.rbegin(); //"d" is displayed
cout << *++s.rbegin(); //"l" is displayed
cout << s.rbegin()[4]; //"W" is displayed
```

## Accessing Strings

The standard library provides numerous ways to access the data contained in a string. In this section, we go through each of them to give you a thorough understanding of the basic_string class.

Because a basic_string is really just an advanced character array, it stands to reason that you should be able to access a basic_string like an array, and, fortunately, you can. You can access individual elements of an array two ways: with the subscripting operator ([]) or with the at() method. Here are the declarations for both:

```
reference operator[] (size_type n);
reference at(size_type n);
```

n is the index indicating the position in the string for both these methods (starting at 0, just like an array). The difference between the two is that the at() method checks to make sure that the index is within the string (an error occurs if it's not). The subscripting operator does not. It assumes that a character is stored there and accesses the position in memory. Here are some examples of how you might use these methods:

```
string s = "Asus Motherboards Rule!!";
cout << s[3]; //the fourth character - 's'
cout << s.at(2); //the 3rd character - 'u'
```

As you can see, these methods are straightforward and easy to use.

Another common way to access a string is to convert it to a C-style string. In Chapter 1, you learned about one of the methods, c_str(), for doing this. There are also two others, data() and copy(). Here are the declarations for all three:

```
const C* c_str() const;
const C* data() const;
size_type copy(C* p, size_type n, size_type pos = 0) const;
```

The data() method returns a pointer to a constant array of characters. The string maintains ownership of the array, so you cannot change it in any way. It is just for viewing purposes. The c_str() method does the same thing, except that it adds a null character at the end of the array (making the array a proper C-style string). You use the copy() method to copy the elements into an array so that you can then manipulate them. This method copies n elements into array p, starting with element pos. The number of elements copied is returned. Here are some examples of how you might use these methods:

```
string s = "SyncMaster 3";
char array[15];
s.copy(array, 4, 7); //array now contains "ster"
array[4] = 0; //now it is a proper c-style string
cout << s.c_str(); //an old favorite
```

```
const char* p = s.data();
p[4] = 'a'; //error, can't manipulate the array
```

These functions have limited use, unless you are using the functions for C-style strings.

One way to obtain information about a string is to compare it to another string. A `basic_string` can be compared to another `basic_string` and to character arrays (of the same character type). You use the method `compare()` to compare two strings. It is overloaded to provide many possibilities:

```
int compare(const basic_string& s) const;
int compare(const C* p) const;
int compare(size_type pos, size_type n,
     const basic_string& s) const;
int compare(size_type pos, size_type n,
     const basic_string& s, size_type pos2,
     size_type n2 = npos) const;
```

Every version of the `compare()` method returns an integer. This integer is `0` if the things being compared are equal (as defined by `char_trait<C>::compare()`), negative if the first is less than the second, and positive if the first is greater than the second. The idea of one string being greater than another might seem strange, but it is the integer values of the characters that are actually compared (so `a` is less than `b`).

The first two versions are pretty clear-cut. Simply provide a string or a character array, and the `compare()` method will compare them. However, sometimes you want to compare only parts of a string. This is where the last two versions come in. `pos` is the position from which you start comparing, and `n` is the number of characters to compare. In the third version, part of a string is being compared to all of `s`. In the fourth, only parts of both strings are being compared. Here are some examples:

```
string s1 = "Get the Fish";
string s2 = "Getting Started";
char array[] = "5-Port Starter Kit";
cout << s1.compare(s2); //-1 is displayed
cout << s2.compare(array); //1 is displayed
cout << s1.compare(0,3,s2); //-1 is displayed
cout << s1.compare(0.3.s2.0,3); //0 is displayed
```

These methods are very important if you ever want to sort a set of strings (for example, to put a list of names in alphabetical order).

The standard library also provides functions for the standard comparison operators (==, !=, <, >, <=, and >=). These are declared outside the basic_string class. Here are a few of the declarations:

```
template<class C, class T, class A> bool operator==(
     const basic_string<C,T,A>&, const basic_string<C,T,A>&);
template<class C, class T, class A> bool operator==(
     const C*, const basic_string<C,T,A>&);
template<class C, class T, class A> bool operator==(
     const basic_string<C,T,A>&, const C*);
```

From these functions, you can test the equality of two strings or of a string and a character array. Here is an example of testing a string and a character array:

```
string continent = "Europe";
if (continent == "Europe") //true
     cout << "The continent is Europe!";
```

Don't worry too much about how the computer decides whether two strings are equal. Basically, if they hold an equal set of characters, they are equal.

At times, you will need to search for a particular sequence of characters (a *substring*) within a string. The basic_string class provides 24 different ways to do this. The first is the find() method. It searches from a particular point in a string and returns the position (the index) if it finds the sequence. If it does not, it returns npos (which represents an illegal index). The sequence that you are looking for can be a string, a character array, or a single character. Here are the declarations for all the versions of the find() method:

```
size_type find(const basic_string& s, size_type i = 0) const;
size_type find(const C* p, size_type i, size_type n) const;
size_type find(const C* p, size_type i = 0) const;
size_type find(C c, size_type i = 0) const;
```

Here i is the position to start searching from, and n is the number of characters from the character array to search for. Here are some examples:

```
string s = "The basic_string class is extremely versatile.";
string s1 = "basic_string";
cout << s.find(s1); //displays 4
//displays 4294967295 - indicating that
//the string wasn't found
cout << s.find(s1, 5);
//displays 17 - match found for "class"
```

```
cout << s.find("classes", 17, 5);
//displays 4294967295 - couldn't find "classes"
cout << s.find("classes", 17);
//displays 19 - started searching past the first 'a'
cout << s.find('a', 6);
```

It is sometimes more convenient (or efficient) to search backward from the end of the string. You can use the `rfind()` method in this case. It searches for a particular character sequence, from a specified point, just like `find()`, except that it searches backward. Here are the declarations for the `rfind()` functions:

```
size_type rfind(const basic_string& s,
     size_type i = npos) const;
size_type rfind(const C* p, size_type i, size_type n) const;
size_type rfind(const C* p, size_type i = npos) const;
size_type rfind(C c, size_type i = npos) const;
```

As you can see, not much has changed, other than the method name. The default values for the arguments are a notable exception. For `find()`, the default value for the start position was `0` (start at the beginning), but for `rfind()`, it is `npos` (start at the end). Here are some examples:

```
string s = "The string class sure has a lot of methods.";
string s1 = "of";
cout << s.rfind(s1); //displays 32
//displays 4294967295 - couldn't find it
cout << s.rfind(s1, 31);
//displays 35 - the position of "meth"
cout << s.rfind("methane", string::npos, 4);
```

You can also search for a particular character from a sequence of characters. The method `find_first_of()` does this job. It searches forward from a given point, and if it runs across a character also in the character sequence, the function returns the position of that character. The method `find_last_of()` does the same thing, except that it searches backward (just as `rfind()` does). Here are the declarations for the `find_first_of()` functions:

```
size_type find_first_of(const basic_string& s,
     size_type i = 0) const;
size_type find_first_of(const C* p, size_type i,
     size_type n) const;
size_type find_first_of(const C* p, size_type i = 0) const;
size_type find_first_of(C c, size_type i = 0) const;
```

```
size_type find_last_of(const basic_string& s,
     size_type i = npos) const;
size_type find_last_of(const C* p, size_type i,
     size_type n) const;
size_type find_last_of(const C* p, size_type i = npos) const;
size_type find_last_of(C c, size_type i = npos) const;
```

Here are some examples of this group of functions:

```
string s = "We need a bigger gun.";
string s1= "Mercenaries.";
//displays 1 - the position of 'e'
cout << s.find_first_of(s1);
//displays 15 - the position of 'r' in "bigger"
cout << s.find_last_of("tree.", 16);
```

You might want to do the opposite at times. You can search for the first (or last) character in a string that isn't also in a particular sequence of characters. You do so using the `find_first_not_of()` and `find_last_not_of()` methods. Here are the declarations:

```
size_type find_first_not_of(const basic_string& s,
     size_type i = 0) const;
size_type find_first_not_of(const C* p, size_type i,
     size_type n) const;
size_type find_first_not_of(const C* p,
     size_type i = 0) const;
size_type find_first_not_of(C c, size_type i = 0) const;

size_type find_last_not_of(const basic_string& s,
     size_type i = npos) const;
size_type find_last_not_of(const C* p, size_type i,
     size_type n) const;
size_type find_last_not_of(const C* p,
     size_type i = npos) const;
size_type find_last_not_of(C c, size_type i = npos) const;
```

Here are examples of using this group of functions:

```
string s = "The sock is on the floor.";
string s1 = "These rocks";
//displays 9 - the position of 'i' in "is"
cout << s.find_first_not_of(s1);
```

```
//displays 20 - the position of 'l' in "floor."
cout << s.find_last_not_of("roof.");
```

You can create new strings from parts (substrings) of a string. For example, if you have a string that stores "Hello World", you could create another string from it that stores "World". You use the substr() method to accomplish this task. By indicating a position and a length, you can specify exactly which part of the string you want. Here is the declaration for substr():

```
basic_string substr(size_type i = 0,
      size_type n = npos) const;
```

Here i is the position to start from, and n is the number of characters to use. Here is an example:

```
string s = "annihilation";
string s1 = s.substr(4,2);
cout << s1.c_str(); //displays "hi"
```

Notice that the default values for the arguments create a copy of the string.

As a counterpart to substr(), the standard library provides a way to put two strings together to form a new one. You use the + operator for this task. Putting two strings together is called *concatenation*. All the concatenation functions are declared outside basic_string. Here are the concatenation functions for strings:

```
template<class C, class T, class A> basic_string<C,T,A>
      operator+ (const basic_string<C,T,A>&,
      const basic_string<C,T,A>&);
template<class C, class T, class A> basic_string<C,T,A>
      operator+ (const C*, const basic_string<C,T,A>&);
template<class C, class T, class A> basic_string<C,T,A>
      operator+ (C, const basic_string<C,T,A>&);
template<class C, class T, class A> basic_string<C,T,A>
      operator+ (const basic_string<C,T,A>&, const C*);
template<class C, class T, class A> basic_string<C,T,A>
      operator+ (const basic_string<C,T,A>&, C);
```

With these functions, you can create a string from two strings, a string and a character array, or a string and a character. Here are some examples:

```
string s = "Hello";
string t = "World";
cout << s + ' ' + t; //displays "Hello World"
cout << s + ' ' + "Everyone!"; Displays "Hello Everyone!"
```

The basic_string class also provides some memory functions to handle the memory used for the data and statistics about the string. One such statistic is the size() method. It returns the number of characters stored in the string. The length() method does the same thing. The empty() method returns true if the string is empty (otherwise, it returns false). The max_size() method returns the largest possible size that a string can be. Here are the declarations for these methods:

```
size_type size() const;
size_type length() const {return size();}
bool empty() const { return size == 0;}
size_type max_size() const;
```

## Manipulating Strings

The capability of manipulating strings in a number of different ways is essential for a string class. Fortunately, basic_string more than fulfills this requirement. You have many options when you need to manipulate a string.

One of the simplest and most useful ways to change a string is to use the assignment operator (=). The basic_string class overloads these operators to make the string seem more like a built-in data type. Here are the declarations for these assignment methods:

```
basic_string& operator= (const basic_string& s);
basic_string& operator= (const C* p);
basic_string& operator= (C c);
```

These functions enable you to assign a string, a character array, or a single character to a string object. Keep in mind that whatever was stored in the string before the function call is destroyed.

For these operations, a normal method called assign() allows more flexibility in arguments. Here are the declarations for the assign() method:

```
basic_string& assign(const basic_string&); //a whole string
//a partial string, starting at position pos
//and taking n characters
basic_string& assign(const basic_string& s, size_type pos,
     size_type n);
//the first n elements from p
basic_string& assign(const C* p, size_type n);
basic_string& assign(const C* p); //all of p
basic_string& assign(size_type n, C c); //n copies of c
```

```
//everything from first to last
typedef<class I> basic_string& assign(I first, I last);
```

This mimics the versatility of the constructor. It wouldn't make sense to create an object a certain way and not be able to assign that way as well. The `basic_string&` that is returned is the same as the value that is assigned, but you can ignore it if you don't need it.

*Appending* (adding characters to the end) is an operation commonly performed on a string. The `basic_string` class provides either the += operator or the `append` method to append things to strings. Here are the declarations for the appending functions:

```
basic_string& operator+= (const basic_string& s);
basic_string& operator+= (const C* p);
basic_string& operator+= (C c);

basic_string& append(const basic_string& s);
//append partial string
basic_string& append(const basic_string& s, size_type pos,
     size_type n);
//append partial character array
basic_string& append(const C* p, size_type n);
//append whole character array
basic_string& append(const C* p);
basic_string& append(size_type n, C c); //append n copies of c
//append values from iterator
template<class I> basic_string& append(I first, I last);
```

Using the += operator, you can append a string, character array, or character to a string. Using the `append` method, you can append a string, a partial string, a partial character array, a whole character array, `n` copies of a character, or the values from an iterator.

If the values that you want to add don't necessarily go at the end of the string, you can use the `insert` method to put them somewhere in the middle. Here are the declarations for the `insert` method:

```
//insert string right before character at pos
basic_string& insert(size_type pos, const basic_string& s);
//insert partial string right before character at pos
basic_string& insert(size_type pos, const basic_string& s,
     size_type pos2, size_type n);
```

```
//insert partial array at pos
basic_string& insert(size_type pos, const C* p, size_type n);
//insert array at pos
basic_string& insert(size_type pos, const C* p);
//insert n copies of c at pos
basic_string& insert(size_type pos, size_type n, C c);

//insert c right before character at pos - return iterator at c
iterator insert(iterator pos, C c);
//insert n copies of c at pos
void insert(iterator pos, size_type n, C c);
//insert sequence at pos
template<class I> void insert(iterator pos, I first, I last);
```

Every version of the `insert` method inserts the specified characters before the character at `pos`. Every character after this is moved up to make room.

You can use the `replace()` method to change part of a string to something else. Here are the declarations:

```
//replace characters from pos to pos+n
basic_string& replace(size_type pos, size_type n,
     const basic_string& s);
basic_string& replace(size_type pos, size_type n,
     const basic_string& s, size_type i2, size_type n2);
basic_string& replace(size_type pos, size_type n,
     const C* p, size_type n2);
basic_string& replace(size_type pos, size_type n, const C* p);
basic_string& replace(size_type pos, size_type n,
     size_type n2, C c);
//replace characters from pos to pos2
basic_string& replace(iterator pos, iterator pos2,
     const basic_string& s);
basic_string& replace(iterator pos, iterator pos2,
     const C* p, size_type n);
basic_string& replace(iterator pos, iterator pos2,
     const C* p);
basic_string& replace(iterator pos, iterator pos2,
     size_type n, C c);
template<class I>basic_string& replace(iterator pos,
     iterator pos2, I first, I last);
```

You can also just get rid of a substring from your string if you desire. To do so, you use the `erase()` method. Here are the declarations:

```
//erase all characters from position i to i+n
basic_string& erase(size_type i = 0, size_type n = npos);
//erase single character at position i
iterator erase(iterator i);
//erase all characters from first to last
iterator erase(iterator first, iterator last);
```

The first version of this method clears the string by default.

## Using Vectors

As your programs get more complex, the need for more advanced data storage arises. Arrays are not bad for storing data, but they are pretty low-level. In other words, you have to deal with many of the inconveniences yourself.

The standard library containers provide an optimal solution to this problem. There are many different containers to suit many different needs. In your programming experience, you will encounter most of them. To get you started, this section presents the most common one: the *vector*. The vector has properties that make it ideal in some situations and quite inefficient in others. It is up to you to decide which container suits your needs.

Vectors are similar to arrays. They hold a series of values, each of which can be accessed as though it were its own variable (and not part of a data structure). In fact, the data in a vector is stored in a single dimensional array. Because of this, you can easily access any element in the vector simply by providing the index number. This kind of access to the elements is called *random access*, because you can access any random element easily.

A vector automatically resizes itself if you add elements to it. It does so by creating a new, larger array and copying each element from the old array to the new one. This procedure is inefficient and is one of the main disadvantages of the vector.

If you insert or remove an element from the middle of the vector, every element must be shifted up or down, respectively, to make sure that no empty spots are in the array. This shifting up or down of all the elements can be costly.

A vector is a class template and is in the header `<vector>`. The declaration looks fairly similar to `basic_string`:

```
template <class T, class A = allocator<T>> class std::vector;
```

### IN THE REAL WORLD

**Many programmers ignore or don't know about all the utilities provided by the standard library. When I (Mark) started programming my first computer game, I needed to figure out a way to store units. The number of units in a game is not something a programmer can predict (at least not without great difficulty), so I needed to store the units dynamically, which was a complicated concept for me at the time. As a result, I did a great deal of research to find a way. When I stumbled onto vectors in the standard library, I was pleasantly surprised. Not only had programmers already encountered this problem, but also they had provided a solution. Without a doubt, the standard library can save you immeasurable time and is well worth careful study.**

The allocator for `vector` behaves much the same way that it does for `basic_string` (that is, in most cases, you won't need to access it). `T` is the type of data stored in the vector.

Like `basic_string`, `vector` uses `typedef` to define some standard names:

```
typedef T value_type; //the type of data stored
typedef A allocator_type; //the type of memory allocator
typedef typename A::size_type size_type;

//a way to iterate through the elements
typedef compiler_dependent iterator;
//iterates backwards
typedef std::reverse_iterator<iterator> reverse_iterator;

typedef typename A::pointer pointer; //pointer to an element
//reference to an element
typedef typename A::reference reference;
```

Though these names can come in handy, they are used mostly for internal implementations, so you don't have to worry about them too much (as long as you know what each one refers to).

The constructors for `vector` provide a variety of ways to create a `vector` object:

```
vector(const A& = A());
//vector with n copies of val
vector(size_type n, const T& val = T(), const A& a = A());
//vector copied from input sequence
```

```
template<class I> vector(I first, I last, const A& a = A());
vector(const vector& a); //vector created from another vector
```

The first constructor creates a designated number of elements. Each element is initialized with a default constructor (or a constructor of your choosing). The second acts exactly like the basic_string constructor that takes a sequence of characters. It takes a sequence of elements of the same type that the vector stores (obviously). You use the third constructor to create a vector from another vector. Here are some examples of how you might construct a vector:

```
vector<float> fv; //default constructor - empty vector
vector<string> sv(10); //vector of 10 strings
//vector of 10 ints, each initialized to 3
vector<int> iv(10,3);
string s = "Hello World";
vector<string> sv2(s.begin(), s.end());
vector<int> iv2(iv);
```

The vector class also has a destructor:

```
~vector();
```

### Accessing and Manipulating Vectors

Using vectors is similar to using strings. Most of the interface is the same. For example, here are the methods to obtain a vector iterator:

```
iterator begin(); //points to first element
iterator end(); //points to one past the last element
reverse_iterator rbegin(); //points to last element
reverse_iterator rend(); //points to one before first element
```

As you can see, iterators work here exactly the same as they do for strings. Note that these iterators are random access iterators, because strings and vectors have random access to their elements.

To access individual elements in a vector, you can use the subscripting operator or the at() method, as with strings. You can also access the first element in the vector with the front() method and the last element with the back() method. Here are the declarations for these two methods:

```
reference front();
reference back();
```

The vector has two methods of assigning values to it: with the assignment operator or with the assign() method. Here are the declarations:

```
vector& operator=(const vector& x); //copy a vector
//assign all values from first to last
template<class I> void assign (I first, I last);
//assign n copies of val
void assign(size_type n, const T& val);
```

The `vector`'s `assign()` methods are similar to the string versions and, so, are fairly self-explanatory.

Two of the operations that a vector can perform are referred to as *stack operations*. They are `push_back()` and `pop_back()`. `push_back()` adds a value to the end of a vector, and `pop_back()` removes the last element from a vector. Here are their declarations:

```
void push_back(const T& x);
void pop_back();
```

Three of a vector's operations are called *list operations*. They are `insert()`, `erase()`, and `clear()`. `insert()` includes a set of values at a certain position in the vector, `erase()` deletes a sequence of elements from a vector, and `clear()` deletes all the elements from the vector. Here are the declarations:

```
iterator insert(iterator pos, const T&); //insert x at pos
//insert n x's at pos
void insert(iterator pos, size_type n, const T& x);
//insert a sequence at pos
template <class I> void insert(iterator pos, I first, I last);
iterator erase(iterator pos); //erase element at pos
//erase a sequence of elements
iterator erase(iterator first, iterator last);
void clear(); //erase all elements
```

The `vector` class provides the `size()`, `empty()`, and `max_size()` methods. These methods behave the same way they do in the `basic_string` class.

Finally, the `vector` class provides the comparison operators (==, !=, <, >, <=, >=) just like the `string` class does.

## Creating the Mysterious Store Game

While stumbling through the vast wilderness known as Vector Valley, you come across a small town. This town is not like other towns you have seen. Everyone in this town appears to have everything they need. No one is short of supplies. While pondering this oddity, you come across a strange little store. The store appears to be the source of everyone's supplies. Looking at your own supplies, you decide that you could use more, so without another thought you enter the store. Compile the following code to see what happens.

```
//9.1 - The Mysterious Store - Mark Lee - Premier Press
#include <iostream>
#include <vector>
#include <string>

using namespace std;

#define MAX(a,b) a<b ? b: a //the common macro

struct Item //used to store a single item from the store.
{
     string name;
     int price;
};

class Store //used to handle everything to do with the store
{
     vector<Item> inventory;
     vector<Item> forSale;
     int money;
public:
     Store(Item* itemList, int n);

     ~Store() {}

     string BuyItem(int item);

     string viewInventory();

     string ListItems();

     int getMoney()
     {
          return MAX(money,0);
     }

};
```

```
Store::Store(Item* itemList, int n)
{

     for(int i = 0; i < n; i++)
          forSale.push_back(itemList[i]);
     money = 20;
}

string Store::BuyItem(int item)
{
     money -= forSale[item-1].price;
     if (money < 0)
          return "\nSorry, you don't have enough money.\n\n";
     inventory.push_back(forSale[item-1]);
     return "You bought a " + forSale[item-1].name + '\n';

}

string Store::ListItems()
{
     string s;
     for(int i = 0; i < forSale.size(); i++)
     {
          s += "[";
          s += i + 49;
          s+="]Buy a ";
          s+= forSale[i].name;
          s+= " ($";
          s+= forSale[i].price + 48;
          s+= ")\n";
     }
     return s;
}

string Store::viewInventory()
{
     string s;
     for(int i = 0; i < inventory.size(); i++)
          s += inventory[i].name + '\n';
     return s + '\n';
```

```
}

int main(void)
{
     int input;
     Item f[3];
     f[0].name = "Clown";
     f[0].price = 2;
     f[1].name = "Cracker Jack";
     f[1].price = 6;
     f[2].name = "Camel";
     f[2].price = 9;
     Store s = Store(f,3);
     while(true)
     {
          do {
               cout << "Welcome to the store.\n"
                    << "You have " << s.getMoney()
                    << " dollars.\n"
                    << "\nWhat would you like to do?\n"
                    << s.ListItems()
                    << "[4]View your inventory\n"
                    << "[5]Leave\n";
               cin >> input;
          }while(input<1||input>5);
          switch(input)
          {
               case 4:
                    cout << s.viewInventory();
                    break;
               case 5:
                    goto END;
               default:
                    cout << s.BuyItem(input);
          }
     }
END:
     cout << "See ya!";
     return 0;
}
```

## Summary

In this chapter, we covered many important topics, including templates, strings, and vectors. Consider this chapter your first major introduction to the C++ standard library, a powerful tool that you will probably want to delve into more deeply over time. You don't have to memorize every method of the `basic_string` class or know everything about a vector; just knowing where to find the information is the important first step.

### CHALLENGES

1. **Create a vector that stores a set of vectors that each store a set of integers.**
2. **Create a template class called `store` that stores an array of `T` (where `T` is the template parameter).**
3. **Create an iterator called `random_iterator` that uses another iterator to iterate through a container in random order.**
4. **Name three places where you can get quick information about the components of the standard library (not including this book).**

# Using Streams and Files

Streams and files are two of the most complex subjects in the C++ language. However, in this chapter, we intend to make learning about these topics painless. Although much more can be written about these topics, when you finish this chapter, you definitely will be able to complete tasks using streams.

In this chapter, you learn about the following:

- The vocabulary associated with streams and I/O
- The various kinds of manipulators
- Binary files and text files
- Dividing a data type into smaller bit fields
- The wonders of bit shifting
- Creating an encryption program

## Understanding the Vocabulary of I/O

The core of this chapter is I/O (input/output). *I/O* refers to sending (outputting) and receiving (inputting) data from various hardware devices, such as hard drives, modems, and keyboards.

**Although C++ does not directly support I/O operations as part of the base language, it does include I/O as part of the standard library. Even with I/O as part of the standard library, C++ leaves much of the application of streams up to programmers. By this, we mean that C++ has a very basic support for I/O, so programmers must adjust this low-level support to meet their needs.**

Although C++ does not directly support I/O operations as part of the base language, it does include I/O as part of the standard library. Even with I/O as part of the standard library, C++ leaves much of the application of streams up to programmers. By this, we mean that C++ has a very basic support for I/O, so programmers must adjust this low-level support to meet their needs.

In order to learn I/O, you need to know the terminology. Here are several of the definitions we use throughout this chapter:

- **Stream object.** Acts as both a source and a destination for bytes. The stream object manipulates an ordered linear sequence of bytes. This series of bytes can represent a screen, a file, or anywhere else the programmer wants bytes to go. You find the classes that handle streams in several of the library files: `<fstream>`, `<iomanip>`, `<ios>`, `<iosfwd>`, `<iostream>`, `<istream>`, `<ostream>`, `<sstream>`, `<streambuf>`, and `<strstream>`.
- **Manipulator.** Manipulates the data of the stream in some way. For example, a manipulator can make all characters uppercase or can convert numbers using decimal notation to hexadecimal notation.
- **Insertion.** Places bytes into the stream. The methods that perform the insertions are called *inserters.*
- **Extraction.** Takes bytes from the stream. The methods that perform the extractions are called *extractors.*

## Understanding the Header Files

In the preceding section's bullet on stream objects, we listed several header files. Each of these header files encapsulates a section of the overall C++ stream architecture. All these files come together with each other to give the complete I/O support provided by C++. Each of these files completes its specific task to give C++ the most diverse I/O functionality of any programming language. The purpose of each of the headers is as follows:

- `<fstream>`. Contains the definition for several template classes that support the iostream header file's operations on sequences stored in external files.
- `<iomanip>`. Contains several single-argument manipulators.
- `<ios>`. Contains a majority of the format manipulators basic to the operation of iostream header file's classes.
- `<iosfwd>`. Contains the forward declarations for the iostream header file's classes.
- `<iostream>`. Contains the declarations for the standard global stream objects such as `cin` and `cout`.
- `<istream>`. Contains the extractors for inputting data from streams and includes the template class `basic_istream`. In other words, `<istream>` puts the I in I/O.
- `<ostream>`. Contains the inserters for outputting a series of bytes and includes the template class `basic_ostream`. Basically, `<ostream>` puts the O in I/O.
- `<sstream>`. Supports the iostream header file's classes' operations on several sequences stored in character arrays with several template classes.
- `<streambuf>`. Defines the `basic_streambuf` template class.
- `<strstream>`. Defines classes that support the iostream header file's classes' operations on sequences stored in C-style character arrays.

With the exception of the `ios_base` class, each template class has a specialization class for characters. Figure 10.1 shows the most commonly used template classes and their character specialization classes. However, this is not a complete list because several of the stream classes are beyond the scope of this book.

### The ios_base Class

The `ios_base` class contains the byte storage common to all streams and the methods that are not dependent on template parameters. This byte storage stores the bytes that are being input and output until they reach their final destination.

**FIGURE 10.1**

The class contained within each header file and the classes from which they are derived. Terms in bold represent header files, and terms without bold represent classes. The lines that link the classes indicate from which classes each class is inherited.

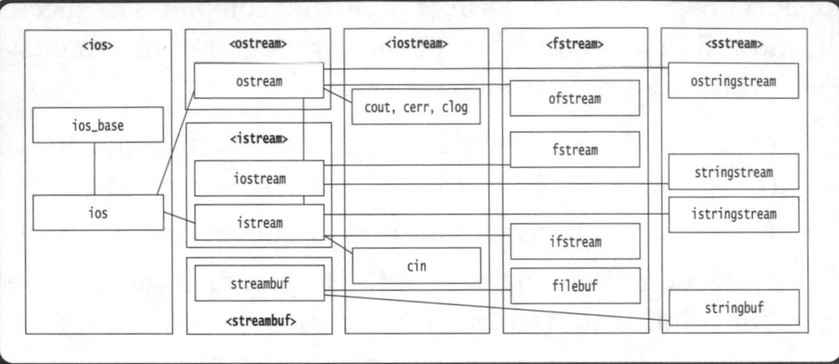


The several data types contained within the `ios_base` class provide the basis for controlling streams.

The following list outlines the purpose of several data types that can be used to control streams:

- `event`. Use the event information in the data type `event` to store callbacks. *Callbacks* are pointers to methods that are registered with and called by the operating system when a specified significant event happens.
- `fmtflags`. Use format flags in the data type `fmtflags` to specify information about the format of the stream.
- `iostate`. Use I/O state information in the data type `iostate` to keep track of the current state of I/O operations. Use the `iostate` data type to check for stream corruption.
- `openmode`. Use open mode to specify a stream's type of read/write access.
- `seekdir`. Use seek direction to specify where the stream data should be sought and store it in the type alias `seekdir`.

In addition, you can use several methods provided by the `ios_base` and in its derived classes (all other stream classes). Here they are in alphabetical order:

- `flags()`. Sets or returns format flag information.
- `getloc()`. Returns an internal local object that encapsulates the stream's information.

- imbue(). Stores a local object that encapsulates the stream's information and returns its previously stored object.
- ios_bas(). This is the constructor.
- iword(). Returns a reference to a specified element of the extensible array having elements of type long.
- operator =() (overloaded assignment operator). Copies everything in the object to a new stream object including formatting information and extensible arrays.
- precision(). Determines the number of decimal places in the display's precision.
- pword(). Returns a reference to a specific element of the void* array.
- register_callback(). Stores callback information for stream callback events.
- setf(). Sets new flags for the stream and returns the previously set flags.
- unsetf(). Clears all flags.
- width(). Sets or retrieves the field width of a stream.
- xalloc(). Returns a unique static variable to be used in iword() or pword() as an array index.

Much more could be written about the ios_base class. However, to keep this book interesting and within its intended page count, we decided to focus on applying streams to their most common uses. However, if, like us, you are one of those strange individuals who can't learn enough about streams, you can extend your knowledge in the Library section on the MSDN Web site at http://www.MSDN.Microsoft.com.

## Introduction to File Streams

To increase the functionality of games, you often need to store millions of pieces of data—for example, map information or data for a player's last saved game. You store this data by using several specialized file I/O classes: ofstream, ifstream, and fstream, contained in the ofstream, ifstream, and fstream header files, respectively.

### Opening Files

Generally, your first action with a file stream object, such as one derived from the ofstream, ifstream, and fstream classes, is to associate it with the file with which you want to work. You make the association using the open() method or the constructor of each of the classes.

The `open()` method's prototype looks like this:

```
void open (const char * filename, openmode mode);
```

*filename* is a string of characters representing the filename, and *mode* is a combination of the flags shown in Table 10.1.

Flags are connected with the bitwise or (|) operator. Say that you want to open `"level1.map"` to output in binary mode. The `open` function might look like this:

```
ofstream file;
file.open ("level1.map", ios::out | ios::binary);
```

Each of the file classes includes the `open()` method; however, each stream has several default flags specifying its use. The default values, however, are applied only if the method is called without flags. The default flags are shown in Table 10.2.

You can also open a file by including the filename in the constructor. The class constructors use the same argument as the `open()` method:

**TABLE 10.1 FLAGS FOR OPENING A FILE**

| Flag | Function |
|---|---|
| `ios::in` | Opens file for reading. |
| `ios::out` | Opens file for writing. |
| `ios::ate` | Initial position is at the end of the file. |
| `ios::app` | Appends every output at the end of the file. |
| `ios::trunc` | Erases file, if one already existed. |
| `ios::binary` | Access to the file is in binary mode. |

**TABLE 10.2 DEFAULT FLAGS FOR THE FILE CLASSES**

| Class | Flags |
|---|---|
| `ofstream` | `ios::out \| ios::trunc` |
| `ifstream` | `ios::in` |
| `fstream` | `ios::in \| ios::out` |

For example, if you use the ifstream class, the prototype for the constructor will look like this:

```
ifstream::ifstream(const char * filename, openmode mode);
```

Here *filename* and *mode* mean the same thing as in the open() method.

You can check whether a file opened correctly by calling to the method is_open():

```
bool is_open()
```

is_open() returns true if the file is properly open and false if not.

Here are the usual reasons why a file does not open correctly:

- A bad filename—for example, a name for a file that doesn't exist.
- A corrupt file—for example, one on a bad sector of a hard drive.
- Another program has exclusive access; this means that only the program with exclusive access can access the file. The file is therefore unusable by other programs until the program with exclusive access relinquishes its exclusive access privileges.
- Windows protects the file. Windows sometimes automatically protects files in particular folders or of certain types. Contact your system administrator if this happens.

### Closing Files

In order to make a file accessible to other programs, you must close the file. Also, an object can open only one file at a time. To close a file, you use the close method. For each of the three classes, use the close member to close a file, as follows:

```
void close();
```

If a file stream object is destroyed, its destructor will automatically close the file associated with that object.

## Working with Text Files

Inputting and outputting to files is exactly like inputting and outputting onscreen because the cin and ifstream classes are both derived from the istream class, as shown earlier in Figure 10.1. Likewise, cout and ofstream are both derived from the ostream class. Both use the overloaded insertion operator <<.

The following code exemplifies this point:

```
//10.1 - Outputting Text  - Dirk Henkemans - Premier Press
#include <fstream>
using namespace std;

int main( void )
{
     //contains the default flags ios::out | ios::trunc
     ofstream dragons("dragons.txt");

     if(dragons.is_open())
     {
          dragons << "Copper Dragon" << endl
               << "Bronze Dragon" << endl
               << "Silver Dragon" << endl
               << "Gold Dragon" <<endl;
     }

     dragons.close();

     return 0;
}
```

**Output:**

```
Copper Dragon
Bronze Dragon
Silver Dragon
Gold Dragon
```

`"dragons.txt"` will normally be in the same folder as your project. However, if you don't find it there, go to the Windows taskbar, click Start, Find (or Search), Files or Folders. A window entitled something like Find: All Files will appear. Type the name of the file and select the drive on which it is stored. Then click Find Now, and Windows will find the file for you. (Note that your program might have slightly different names.)

If you run the program twice, you will notice that the text file always contains the same information. This is because the implied `ios::trunc` uses the `ofstream` class if you do not specify mode parameters. Remember that `ios::trunc` restarts a file if it already exists.

Although you can input from the file with the overloaded shift operator (>>), it becomes impossible to know when you reach the end of your file. The easiest way to input from a text file is to input the data line by line using the `istream::getline()` method. This is also the most useful method because most data are stored line by line, so you input the line and then dissect the line of data into its respective fields.

You have three options for using the `istream::getline()` method:

```
istream& getline(char* pch, int nCount, char delim = '\n');
istream& getline(unsigned char* puch, int nCount, char delim = '\n');
istream& getline(signed char* psch, int nCount, char delim = '\n');
```

The parameter placeholders mean the following:

- *pch, puch, psch.* A pointer to a `char` array. Remember that the `getline` method overwrites data stored in the array.
- *nCount.* The maximum numbers that the `getline` method should store, including the terminating null.
- *delim.* The delineating character to which `getline()` goes.

Last, you probably want to read to the end of a file, except how do you know where the end is? You use the `ios::eof()` method:

```
int eof();
```

The `eof()` method returns a non-zero integer when the end of the file is reached.

You can put it all together now and read from the `"dragon.txt"` file. A sample implementation of this is shown here:

```
//10.2 - InputtingDragons - Dirk Henkemans
//Premier Press
#include <fstream>
#include <iostream>
using namespace std;

int main( void )
{
      //contains the default flags ios::in
      ifstream dragons("dragons.txt");

      char buffer[50];
```

```
    if(!dragons.is_open())
    {
        cout<<"Error opening file";
        //none 0 exit means there was an error (normally)
        exit(1);
    }

    while(!dragons.eof())
    {
        dragons.getline(buffer, 49);
        cout<< buffer <<endl;
    }

    dragons.close();

    return 0;
}
```

**Output:**

```
Copper Dragon
Bronze Dragon
Silver Dragon
Gold Dragon
```

The `getline()` method deletes the delineators (in this case, the default line breaks), so the program compensates by adding a line break after reading each line.

You now have read your first file!

## Verifying Stream

When you send a message asking a stream to perform a task, how do you know that the stream accomplished the task? The interface with stream objects provides several methods that enable you to know whether a stream successfully completes its tasks. Table 10.3 provides several of the stream verification methods.

In order to reset all the preceding stream verification methods, use the `ios::clear()` method (no parameters).

**Table 10.3 Verification Methods**

| Method | Description |
|---|---|
| `bad()` | Returns `true` if a severe error occurs when you are trying to read or write from a file. For example, this might occur when you are trying to write to a device with no space left. |
| `eof()` | Returns `true` if the stream reaches the end of the file. This works only when you are inputting from a file. |
| `fail()` | Returns `true` if there is a formatting error. For example, the stream tries to read an integer but finds an alpha character. |
| `good()` | This is a general method that returns `false` if any one of the preceding methods, `bad`, `eof`, or `fail`, returns `true`. |

## Working with Binary Streams

Although working with text is convenient, it is inefficient in many cases. When using a 28.8 modem, you often will send as little data as possible. In a game such as "StarCraft," by Blizzard, you can specify ahead of time what data types will be sent. This enables you to use more than one data type (such as characters).

The solution is *binary streams*, which can send multiple data types. The program *must* know the order and kind of data types being sent in order to read the data. Figure 10.2 shows a text stream and a binary stream.

In order to make correct interpretations, the program must know to which structure the bytes in a binary stream are related. This means that the binary stream must apply a programmed algorithm (such as `int`, `char`, or `long`) to decipher the data, but a text stream can assume that every byte is a character. In Figure 10.2, note that the top data stream is a text file, and each byte means the same thing—one character. The bottom stream is a data stream in which bytes are part of larger structures; your program must know what the structure is to use the byte properly.

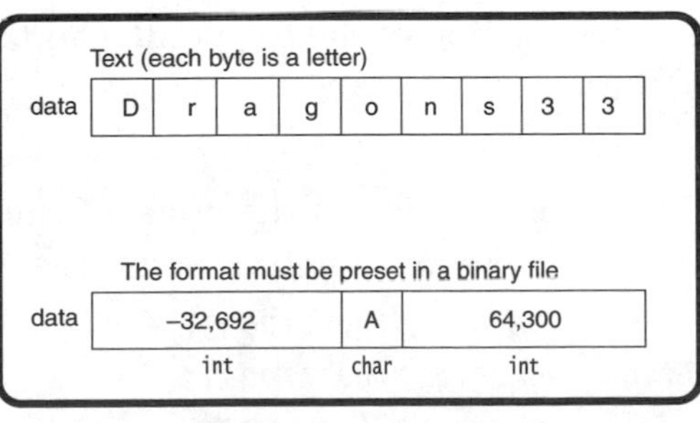


**FIGURE 10.2**

This figure shows the relationships between the different stream header files and the classes they contain.

## The get and put Stream Pointers

Memory is indexed for our enjoyment, but more importantly, it is indexed to ensure random access. Random access enables you to access portions of files of streams in any order. For example, you can read a file backward almost as easily as you can read it forward. Two pointers, generally referred to as *stream pointers,* indicate the location where you are reading or writing. These stream pointers are the `get` pointer and the `put` pointer. The `get` pointer indicates where you are reading, and the `put` pointer indicates where you are writing.

All I/O streams have at least one stream pointer, depending on the stream's method. Here are the ones for the common classes:

- `ifstream`. Like `istream`, this class has the `get` pointer.
- `ofstream`. Like `ostream`, this class has the `put` pointer.
- `fstream`. Because it is derived from `istream` and `ostream`, this class has both pointers.

## Interfacing with the Stream Pointers

The two stream pointers gain their functionality when an interface is created to adjust them. The interface consists of the following methods:

- `istream::tellg()`. Returns the number of bytes the `get` pointer is from the beginning of the file (not the address to which the `get` pointer is pointing). The `streampos` data type is effectively type alias for an integer. The prototype for this method is
  ```
  streampos tellg();
  ```
- `ostream::tellp()`. Returns the number of bytes the `put` pointer is from the beginning of the file. The prototype for this method is
  ```
  streampos tellp();
  ```
- `istream::seekg()`. Sets the position of the `get` pointer in the stream. The prototype for this method is
  ```
  seekg (pos_type position);
  ```
- `ostream::seekp()`. Sets the position of the `put` pointer in the stream. The prototype for this method is
  ```
  seekp (pos_type position);
  ```
- `seekg()` and `seekp()`. Sets the direction of the offset of the pointer and the amount of offset. The prototypes for these methods are
  ```
  seekg ( off_type offset, seekdir direction );
  seekp ( off_type offset, seekdir direction );
  ```

The offset directions specified in the second parameter, *direction*, are shown in Table 10.4.

**Table 10.4 Offset Directions**

| Direction | Description |
|---|---|
| ios::beg | The offset is specified from the beginning of the stream. |
| ios::cur | The offset is specified forward from the current position of the pointer. |
| ios::end | The offset is specified from the end of the stream. |

The following example uses a number of methods just seen to determine the size of a file:

```
//10.3 - BinaryFileSize - Dirk Henkemans - Premier Press
#include <iostream>
#include <fstream>
using namespace std;

int main( void )
{
     int n1, n2;
     ifstream dragons("dragons.txt", ios::in|ios::binary);
     n1 = dragons.tellg();
     dragons.seekg (0, ios::end);
     n2 = dragons.tellg();
     cout<<"The size of dragons.txt is " << n2 - n1 << endl;

     return 0;
}
```

**Output:**

```
The size of dragons.txt is 58
```

## Writing and Reading Binary Streams

File streams introduce two new methods that are designed especially for sequential input and output of data: `ostream::write()` and `istream::read()`. The prototypes of both these files are as follows:

```
write (char * buffer, streamsize size );
read( char * buffer, streamsize size );
```

`write()` places the number of bytes specified by size after the `put` pointer, thereby writing them to the file.

`read()` places the number of bytes specified by size taken from the `get` pointer and places the bytes after the buffer pointer parameter.

To exemplify these two methods, examine the following program, which takes the `"dragons.txt"` file and copies it to another file named `"dragons2.txt"`.

```
//10.4 - File Copier  - Dirk Henkemans - Premier Press
#include <iostream>
#include <fstream>
using namespace std;

int main( void )
{
      char buffer;
      int index = 0;

      //the file names
      const char filename1[] = "dragons.txt";
      const char filename2[] = "dragons2.txt";

      //opening the files
      fstream file1(filename1, ios::in);
      fstream file2(filename2, ios::out);

      //points to the beginning of the files
      file1.seekg(0, ios::beg);
      file2.seekp(0, ios::beg);

      //reads the first char
      file1.read(&buffer, 1);

      //writes the remainder of the chars
      while(file1.good() && file2.good())
      {
            file2.write(&buffer, 1);

            index++;
```

```
        file1.seekp(index);
        file2.seekg(index);

        file1.read(&buffer, 1);
    }

    //closes the files
    file1.close();
    file2.close();

    return 0;
}
```

When you open "dragons2.txt", it should be the same as "dragons.txt".

## Working with Common Manipulators

Manipulators are used to manipulate the data in a stream. For example, you can use some manipulators to turn all lowercase alpha characters to uppercase or to adjust the way a number displays. Most manipulators are included in the ios header file. In the following section, you use only the common manipulators found in the ios header file.

Although we can't list all the manipulators in this book, Table 10.5 lists several of the most common ones and their functions.

**Table 10.5 Common Manipulators in the <ios> Header**

| Flag | Function |
|---|---|
| dec() | Displays in the base10 numeric system. |
| hex() | Displays in the base16 numeric system. |
| oct() | Displays in the base8 numeric system. |
| fixed() | Inserts floating-point values. |
| scientific() | Inserts floating-point values in scientific format using exponents. |
| internal() | Pads to a field width as needed by inserting internal whitespace. |
| left() | Left-justifies characters by padding with white space on the right. |
| right() | Right-justifies characters by padding with white space on the left. |

## Table 10.5 Common Manipulators in the <ios> Header (continued)

| Flag | Function |
|---|---|
| boolalpha() | Symbolic representation of true and false. |
| noboolalph() | Cancels boolalpha(). |
| showbase() | Shows the base of the number prefixing octal and hex numbers with 0 and 0x, respectively. |
| noshowbase() | Cancels showbase(). |
| showpoint() | Displays a decimal point even if there is no fractional portion. |
| noshowpoint() | Cancels showpoint(). |
| showpos() | Inserts a positive (+) sign before non-negative numbers. |
| noshowpos() | Cancels showpos(). |
| skipws() | Skips white space. |
| noskipws() | Cancels skipws(). |
| unitbuf() | Flushes out after each insertion. |
| nounitbuf() | Cancels unitbuf(). |
| uppercase() | Inserts uppercase equivalents of lowercase alpha characters. |
| nouppercase() | Cancels uppercase(). |

You can use the manipulators in Table 10.5 on any stream by using the ios::setf() method and by placing a flag as the parameter. The next program clearly demonstrates this procedure and the results when used on the cout object.

```
//10.5 - Manipulators - Dirk Henkemans - Premier Press
#include <iostream>
#include <ios>
using namespace std;

int main( void )
{
     cout << "Default True, False \n"
          << true << " " << false << endl;

     cout.setf(ios::boolalpha);
     cout<<"\nwith ios::boolalpha:\n"
          <<true << " " << false << endl;
```

```
    cout <<"\n140 in hex\n";
    cout.setf(ios::hex, ios::basefield);
    cout.setf(ios::showbase);
    cout << 140 << endl;

    float f[2] = {1.0f, 775.374f};

    cout<< "\nDefault numeric formula\n"
        << f[0] << endl
        << f[1] << endl;


    cout.setf(ios::showpos);
    cout<< "\nand with showpos\n"
        << f[0] << endl
        << f[1] << endl;

    //indicates that cout should always use 6 digit precision
    cout.setf(ios::fixed);
    cout<< "\nand with a precision of 6\n"
        << f[0] << endl
        << f[1] << endl;

    return 0;
}
```

## Using Bit Fields

Standard data types are built into C++; however, often it is more efficient to divide a standard data type into several fields of bits in order to store multiple smaller values. These subsections of bits are called *bit fields.* For example, imagine that you want to subdivide an unsigned character into bit fields. An unsigned character is composed of 8 bits. This means that the sum of all the bit fields must contain 8 bits.

You declare a bit field by placing a colon after the declaration and specifying the number of bits that will be in the bit field. You must declare bit fields inside a structure, as shown here:

```
struct shortBits
{
```

```
    short member1 : 2;
    short member2 : 7;
    short member3 : 7;
};
```

`member1` can store only three values: `1 + 2`.

`member2` and `member3` can store 127 values: `1 + 2 + 4 + 8 + 16 + 32 + 64`.

Figure 10.3 visually represents what the `shortBits` structure might look like in memory.

## Fun with Bit Shifting

The << (left shift) and >> (right shift) are the bit shift operators. When you *bit shift*, you take the bits of a data type and shift them over 1 bit. For example, if you want to bit shift a `char` to the left by 2 bits, all the bits of the `char` are shifted to the left 2 bits. The leftmost 2 bits are truncated, and 2 false bits are added to the rightmost position, as illustrated in Figure 10.4.

Bit shifting one place right is the equivalent of multiplying by 2, and bit shifting one place left is the equivalent of dividing by 2 and truncating the reminder.

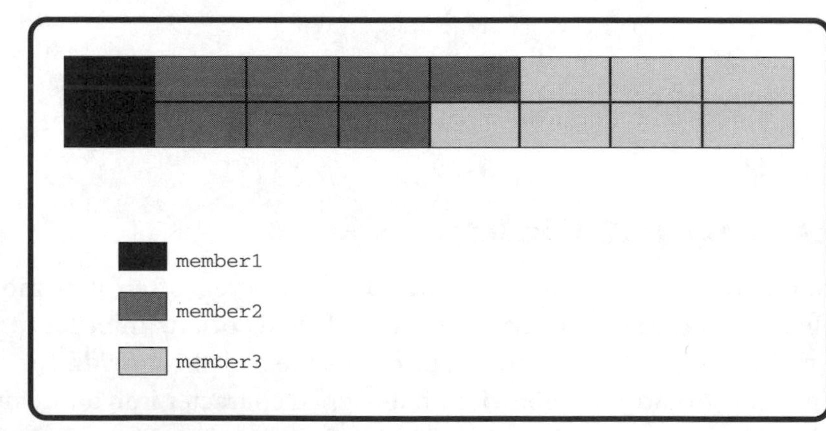


**FIGURE 10.3**

In this figure, the total memory for the short data type is divided into three individual members.

**FIGURE 10.4**

10110111 — Bit Shifted Left 2 Bits (<<2) — 11011100

Original char — Resulting char

10110111 — Bit Shifted Right 2 Bits (>>2) — 00101101

The original character on the left is shifted over two places to form the resulting character on the right.

## Creating an Encryption Program

You goal, agent, should you accept it, is to develop a high-security encryption program for the British S.A.S. covert operations force. The program must be quick and efficient, allowing S.A.S. agents the ability to work quickly in enemy territory. If you are caught, we, the authors, will deny all knowledge of your existence.

Good luck, agent!

The encryption algorithm used on this assignment is not difficult. Your program will take the first 4 bits and last 4 bits of every byte and switch them. You can do this using the bit shift operator and dividing by 128 while truncating the fractional section.

Try to solve the problem by yourself, but if you get stuck, you can check out the solution in the following "Encryption Program."

```
//10.6 - Encryption Program - Dirk Henkemans
//Premier Press
//A text data encryption program
#include <iostream>
#include <fstream>
using namespace std;

class Encryption
{
      fstream file1;//source file
      fstream file2;//destination file

      public:
      Encryption::Encryption(char* filename1, char* filename2)
      {
            file1.open(filename1, ios::in | ios::out | ios::binary);
            file2.open(filename2, ios::out|ios::binary);
      }

      //encrypts the file
      void Encrypt(void)
      {
            char currentByte;
            bool currentBit;

            int index = 0;
```

```
        //sets the pointers to the beginning of the file
        file1.seekg (0, ios::beg);
        file2.seekp (0, ios::beg);

        //reads the first value
        file1.read(&currentByte, 1);
        while(file1.good())
        {
            //loop for four bits
            for(int c = 0; c < 4; c++)
            {
                //finds out if the first bit is a one
                currentBit = (int)((unsigned char)currentByte / 128);
                //shifts the byte over
                currentByte <<= 1;

                //if the first bit was a one then we add it to the end
                if(currentBit)
                {
                    currentByte += 1;
                }
            }

            //writes the character
            file2.write(&currentByte, 1);

            //increments the pointer
            file1.seekg (++index);
            file2.seekp (index);

            //reads the next value
            file1.read(&currentByte, 1);
        }
    }

    //closes both of the files
    void close(void)
    {
        file1.close();
        file2.close();
```

```
        }
};

int main( void )
{
        cout<< "Welcome to the S.A.S encryption program.";
        Encryption delta("dragons.txt", "output1.txt");
        delta.Encrypt();
        delta.close();

        Encryption gamma("output1.txt", "output2.txt");
        gamma.Encrypt();
        delta.close();
        return 0;
}
```

**Don't try to use the "Encryption Program" on large or important files. Neither the authors nor Premier Press hold any responsibility for loss or alteration of data or for the program's security.**

**When you first use this program to encrypt a file, if you open the encrypted file in a text editor such as Notepad or DOS Edit, the file will look strange and often be all on one line. For example, it might look like this (no kidding):**

```
@##%$%^&*7gfh@#$#4
```

**When you run the program the second time, the program should decrypt the file, causing it to look the same as the original file.**

## Summary

You started this chapter by looking at the hierarchy and learning the definitions for streams. Then you used the file streams on some text files in text mode. Later, as you expanded your knowledge, you continued to use file streams to copy files and learned about the `get` and `put` pointers. With some common manipulators from the `<ios>` header library, you manipulated the `cout` stream and produced several cool outputs. Last, you developed an encryption program.

## CHALLENGES

1. Create a program to write the following two lines of text to a file called "Question1.txt":

```
Programming is fun.
I love programming.
```

2. What method can you use to test whether a file has reached its end? What method can you use to test whether a file has an error? What method can you use to test whether a file has reached its end *and* has an error?
3. What is the result when the letter A is bit-shifted to the left three places (<<3)? What is the result when the letter A is bit-shifted to the right two places (>>2)?
4. Explain why the encryption program needs to be run a second time in order to decrypt the file placed into the program.

CHAPTER 11

# Errors and Exception Handling

You've learned much about C++ so far, good reader. Now, you are ready to find out how to make your programs secure and safe from crashing. In this chapter, you learn how to ensure that certain conditions remain true. You learn how to safeguard against going out of array bounds. In short, you learn how to make your programs very stable, capable of handling the unexpected. In this chapter, you learn the following:

- How to use assertions
- How to handle exceptions
- How to catch every exception

## Asserting Conditions

Sometimes, certain operations can be dangerous. They can corrupt memory, freeze your computer, or worse. Normally, you know what must be true in order for the operation to succeed. You know that certain conditions must be true. If these conditions are not true, the results could be disastrous. It is your duty, as a programmer, to test for these conditions before proceeding with the operation. If the condition fails, you must immediately end the program or risk catastrophe.

Okay, that was a little melodramatic. It's true that some operations can cause problems, but it is rare for them to be permanent or disastrous. However, to make your program execute successfully, it is a good idea to test to be sure that conditions are true before performing a major operation (or a potentially risky one). If a condition fails while you are testing your program, you might simply exit the program and have the program display a message saying what happened and on which line.

C++ provides a special macro, called an *assertion,* for exiting the program and displaying a specified message for a specified condition. Assertions are macros that test a condition and exit the program if the condition fails. A standard version of this macro is defined in `<cassert>` and `<assert.h>` header files. The prototype for an assertion is as follows:

```
void assert(int expression);
```

Even though `expression` is an integer, it is treated as a boolean expression (for example, `5 <3`). Thus, testing a condition might look like this:

```
assert (y > 0);
```

This assertion does nothing if `y` is greater than `0`, but if `y` is not greater, the program stops, and an error message is displayed. To see this error message for yourself, try compiling the following program:

```
//11.1 - An Assertion Failure - Mark Lee - Premier Press
#include <cassert>

int main(void)
{
      assert(5>6); //always fails
      return 0;
}
```

This assertion will always fail, no matter what, because 5 is never greater than 6. So, what happens when this assertion fails? First, this message is displayed:

```
Assertion failed: 5>6, file C:\Projects\Temp\Test13\Test13.cpp, line 5
```

On my computer (I'm using Windows 2000 Professional and Visual Studio 6.0) a window pops up displaying a message saying that the program terminated abnormally, as shown in Figure 11.1.

The assert macro ends the program when it fails by calling a function called abort(). The abort() function is included in <cstdlib> and <stdlib.h>. This function takes no arguments and returns no value. It simply ends the program. This is the function that caused the message box in Figure 11.1 to appear. This function also outputs the message, abnormal program termination.

If this assertion does not meet your needs or you want your program to keep running after a failed assert, you need to define your own assertion. However, if you are using the assert macro just to debug your programs, you should be fine.

Here is an example of how a user-defined ASSERT macro might look:

```
#define ASSERT(a) if (!a) {
   cerr << "\nAssertion failed. The condition: " << #a << " was not true."
        << "\nThe assertion failed on line " << __LINE__ << " of the file:"
        << "\n\t\"" << __FILE__ << "\"\n";
```

cerr behaves exactly like cout, except that it is used for reporting errors. It is included with <iostream>. The code #a converts the failed condition into a string. The code __LINE__ and __FILE__ return the line number and filename, respectively.

Here is an example of how you might use this macro:

```
int array[] = {5,4,2,7,5};
for (int i = 0; i <5; i++)
{
     ASSERT(i <sizeof(array)/sizeof(int));
     array[i] = i;
}
```

The preceding code uses a for statement to initialize all the elements of an array. However, before i is used as an index, you use an assertion to make sure that i is within the bounds of the array.

You can use assertions, as in the previous example, to ensure that you don't walk off the end of an array. You also use them at the beginning of functions to ensure that the user applied the function correctly, and you use them to validate the result of code that you are not sure is correct.

FIGURE 11.1

If you have an assertion failure in your programs, you will see a message box like this one. The filename and directory of the executable file are displayed.

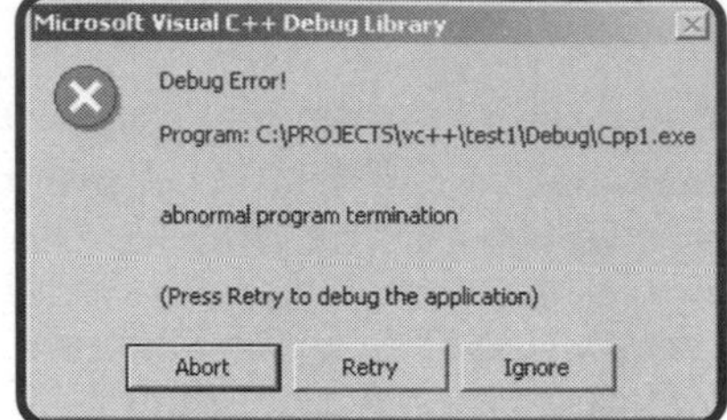


Keep in mind that you use assertions to debug code, so before you release something or give it to other people to use, be sure to remove all the assertions. (The users of your program do not need to know that an assertion failed on line 675 of a code file.) If you want to handle unexpected errors happening in your program when you release it, use exception handling.

## Handling Exceptions

When you write code that is not a complete program (such as a class or a set of functions), unexpected errors can happen in your code. You can't always count on the values that you expect, and you can't always assume that users of your code will know what they are doing. A graceful piece of code will prevent a program from crashing when these kinds of things happen. One way to make your code "graceful" is by using *exception handling,* which enables you to manage non-routine circumstances in a program.

With exception handling, you can actually prevent unpredictable occurrences and exceptional events. Exceptions mean that a part of your code cannot perform a task that it was asked to do. Exception handling enables you to try another method of completing the task or to attempt to fix the problem.

An exception occurs because a section of code *throws* an exception. One example of an unexpected event, or exception, is a computer running out of hard drive space. However, running out hard drive space does not mean that a program will necessarily crash or completely fail at its task. You can write code that handles such exceptions by specifying that the program *catch* a certain kind of exception.

In order to catch an exception, you must use a try-block. A *try-block* is a section of code with the keyword `try` at the beginning. This keyword keeps track of whether an exception is thrown. The syntax for a try-block is as follows:

```
try
{
      someCode
}
```

Using a try-block tells the computer that the code inside a try-block might throw an exception, so watch out.

After you establish a try-block, you can use it to catch an exception. You do this by using a `catch` statement. Here is the syntax for the `catch` statement:

```
catch(exceptionName)
{
      whatToDo
}
```

Here *exceptionName* is the name of an exception. When the code inside a try-block throws an exception, the computer starts executing the code inside the `catch` statement. In order for a `catch` statement to be connected with a `try` statement, the `catch` statement must occur immediately after the `try` statement. You cannot have any code between them:

```
try
{
      someCode
}
catch (exceptionName)
{
      whatToDo
}
```

You can have as many `catch` statements after `try` statements as you want:

```
try
{
      someCode
}
catch (exceptionName1)
{
      whatToDo1
}
catch (exceptionName2)
{
      whatToDo2
}
```

When an exception is thrown, the appropriate `catch` statement is called.

An exception is thrown using the `throw` statement. Here is the syntax:

```
throw exception;
```

Here *exception* is the exception.

*exceptionName* (from the `catch` statement) is the name of a type, any type at all. It can be `int`, `char*`, or `string`. In fact, it is very similar to a function argument, except that it doesn't need a variable name.

*exception* must be an expression. Using a `throw` statement is like calling a function. Think of all the `catch` statements as an overloaded function. Based on the type of *exception*, the computer can decide which `catch` statement is the most appropriate one to use (if any).

Here is an example:

```
#include<iostream>

using namespace std;

int main (void)
{
	try
	{
		int x = 10;
		if (x == 10)
			throw x;
	}
	catch(int x)
	{
		cerr << "Oh No! x equals " << x << "!!!!";
	}
	catch(float f)
	{
		cerr << "How did I get here?";
	}
	return 0;
}
```

In the preceding example, the variable `x` is initialized to `10`. Then the program checks to see whether `x` is `10` and throws an exception if so. This is obviously a useless example, but it illustrates our point.

The *exceptionName*s for the `catch` statements are not just type names. There is also a variable declaration, because `catch` statements work exactly like functions. The value of `x` (10) is passed to the `catch` statement so that the `catch` statement can deal with the error properly (it helps if the `catch` statement knows what the error is).

Also, even though there are two `catch` statements, the computer, using the rules for function overloading, figured out which statement is the correct one to call.

Using a built-in data type for an exception is usually not a good idea. When an integer is thrown, you can't tell exactly what the error is. You might assume that the error is related to the value of an integer, but you can't tell for certain.

Fortunately, there is a standard way to pass this information. Normally, you define a new type for every kind of exception. Here is an example:

```
class FileError
{};
```

Notice how this class is completely empty? This is because the class doesn't need anything in it. The class is just being used for its name. Here is an example of how you might use this:

```
#include <iostream>
#include <istream>
#include <fstream>

using namespace std;

class FileError
{};

int main (void)
{

      try
      {
            char* filename = "hello.txt";
            fstream file;
            file.open(filename, ios::in) ;
            if (!file.is_open())
            throw FileError();
      }
      catch (FileError)
```

```
    {
        cerr << "Error with file.";
    }
    return 0;
}
```

If your code throws an exception that is not caught (there is no appropriate `catch` statement), the computer decides what to do. Unfortunately, a computer is not very forgiving. It thinks the best way to handle an exception is to immediately close the program. To do so, the computer calls the `terminate()` or `unexpected()` functions; both are included with `<exception>`. Also, neither of the two have arguments or a `void` return type. To see what happens when these functions are called, compile and run the following program:

```
int main (void)
{
    throw 5; //an arbitrary value
    return 0;
}
```

You might have noticed that the error message displayed is exactly the same as for the `abort()` function. This is because `terminate()` calls `abort()`. You can make `terminate()` call a custom function as well by calling the `set_terminate()` function. Here is the declaration:

```
typedef void (*terminate_function)();
terminate_function set_terminate(terminate function term_func);
```

This declaration looks really complicated, but you just pass the name of the function as the parameter. Here is an example:

```
#include <exception>
#include <iostream>

using namespace std;
void error_handler();
void error_handler()
{
    cerr << "There was an uncaught error.";
}

int main (void)
{
    set_terminate(error_handler);
```

```
    throw 5;
    return 0;
}
```

**Output:**

```
There was an uncaught error.
```

## Building an Exception Hierarchy

If you use really specific exceptions for a large program, you can quickly have an unmanageable number of exceptions. Having a ton of `catch` statements after every try-block is annoying at best. You can easily forget to include one and wind up with quite a problem. Fortunately, as you program, you will discover personal techniques to alleviate this problem.

However, one common way is to use inheritance (refer to Chapter 8, "Introducing Inheritance," for more on that topic). If you make a hierarchy of exceptions, you can deal with only the most general one, rather than be specific. Or you can be very specific for some and very general for others. This technique gives you the flexibility to design your programs so that they adapt to meet any situation.

Here is an example of such a hierarchy:

```
class MathError {};
class DivideByZero : public MathError {};
class Overflow : public MathError {};
```

With this hierarchy, you can choose to handle a specific exception, such as `DivideByZero`, or deal only with all math errors in one `catch` statement. Here is an example:

```
#include <iostream>

using namespace std;
int divide(int a, int b);

class MathError {};
class DivideByZero : public MathError {};
class Overflow : public MathError {};

int divide(int a, int b)
{
    if (b == 0)
    {
```

```
        throw DivideByZero();
        return false;
    }
    return a/b;
}

int main (void)
{
    try
    {
        if (!divide(5,0))
            throw MathError();
    }
    catch(DivideByZero)
    {
        cerr << "Whoops! You tried to divide by zero";
    }
    catch (MathError)
    {
        cerr << "There was an unexplained math error.";
    }
    return 0;
}
```

**Output:**

```
Whoops! You tried to divide by zero
```

Here you see that if you try to divide by zero, a `DivideByZero` exception is thrown, but if there is some other problem, a general `MathError` is thrown.

This example also illustrates another important point. If you call a function within a try-block and that function throws an error, the try-block can catch it.

## Catching Every Exception

You can catch every possible exception in your programs, making them virtually crash-proof. To do so, you use a form of the `catch` statement that can handle any exception that hasn't already been handled. Rather than an exception type as the argument for the `catch` statement, you use an ellipsis (. . .). When the computer searches the `catch` statements for one that will handle an exception, the computer will use this one as a last resort (if you include it). Here is the syntax:

```
catch(...)
{
	handleTheException
}
```

Here is an example of how you might use the default catch statement:

```
#include <iostream>

using namespace std;

int main (void)
{
	try
	{
		throw 6;
	}
	catch(...)
	{
		cerr << "There was an exception, but it was caught!";
	}
	return 0;
}
```

**Output:**

```
There was an exception, but it was caught!
```

If you use this version of the catch statement with other catch statements, it must be at the end of the list. If not, no subsequent catch statements beyond the default catch statement will ever have the possibility of being called. However, if the default catch statement is used at the end of the list of catch statements, the default catch statement will be used only as a last resort.

## Creating the MineField Game

You are part of the elite Soviet team XJ77. You have been sent out to disarm a deadly minefield. The work is extremely dangerous. Only the best and brightest will survive a day in the minefield. Compile this program, and see whether you have what it takes.

```
//11.2 - MineField - Mark Lee - Premier Press
#include <iostream>
```

```
#include <exception>
#include <string>
#include <vector>
#include <cstdlib>
#include <ctime>
#include "MenuUtility.h"

using namespace std;
using namespace menuNamespace;

class StepOnMine{};
class FailedDisarm{};

class MineField
{
      vector<bool> minefield;
      //stores where the player has been
      vector<bool> beenThere;
      int location; //current location of player
public:
      MineField()  //4X4 minefield
      {
            srand(time(0));
            location = 0;
            for (int c = 0; c <16; c++)
            {
                  minefield.push_back(false);
                  beenThere.push_back(false);
            }
            for (int i = 0; i <10; i++) //place 10 random mines
                  minefield[rand()%15+1] = true;
            beenThere[0] = true;
      }

      bool IsAMine(int location)
      {
            return minefield[location];
      }

      string draw()
      {
```

```
        string s;
        for (int i = 0; i <4; i++)
        {
            for (int c=0; c<4; c++)
            {
                if (location == i*4+c)
                    s+='P';
                else {
                    if (beenThere[i*4+c])
                        s+= "X";
                    else s+= " ";
                }
                s+="|";
            }
            s+= '\n';
        }
        return s;
    }

    bool moreMines()
    {
        for (int i-0; i<16; 1++)
            if (beenThere[i]) return true;
        return false;
    }

    int Directions()
    {
        string options[4];
        options[0] = "North";
        options[1] = "East";
        options[2] = "South";
        options[3] = "West";
        return menu(options, 4);
    }

    int& place() {return location;}

    void goThere(int place) {beenThere[place] = true;}
};
```

```
void Detonate()
{
     cout << "You detonated the mine. Ka-boom!!!\n";
}

void disarm()
{
     int temp = rand()%2+1;
     if (temp-1)
          throw FailedDisarm();
}

int main (void)
{
     set_terminate(Detonate);
     MineField m; //create the minefield

     string input;
     cout << "Welcome to the MineField!!\n"
          << "You are part of the elite Soviet mine team "
          <<"XJ77,\n sent to clear a deadly minefield full"
          <<" of remote heat-sensing claymore mines.\n"
          << "Most of your team will not survive.\n"
          << "Only the best of you will see then end of "
          << " the day.\n Do you have what it takes?\n";
     cin >> input;
     if(input == "no" || input == "No")
          goto TOO_BAD;
     cout << "You are in the NorthWest corner.\n";
PLAY:
     try
     {
          int goTo;
          while(m.moreMines()){
               cout << endl << m.draw();

               cout << "Your position is marked with a P.\n"
                    << "Which direction would you like to go?"
                    <<endl;
               bool proper = false;
               do {
```

```
                    goTo = m.Directions();
                    if (goTo == 1 && m.place() >3)
                          proper = true;
                    if (goTo == 2 && (m.place()-3)%4 != 0)
                          proper = true;
                    if (goTo == 3 && m.place() <12)
                          proper = true;
                    if (goTo == 4 && m.place()%4 != 0)
                          proper = true;
                    if (!proper)
                          cout<<"\nYou cannot go that way.\n";
              }while (!proper);

              if (goTo == 1)
                    m.place() -= 4;
              if (goTo == 2)
                    m.place()++;
              if (goTo == 3)
                    m.place() += 4;
              if (goTo == 4)
                    m.place()--;

              m.goThere(m.place());

              if (m.IsAMine(m.place()))
                    throw StepOnMine();
        }
  }
  catch(StepOnMine)
  {
        int input;
        do {
        cout << "\nYou have encountered a mine.\n"
              << "What would you like to do?\n"\
              << "[1]Attempt to Disarm it.\n"
              << "[2]Run Away.\n";
        cin >> input;
        }while(input <1 && input >2);
        if (input == 1)
        {
              try { disarm(); }
```

```
                catch(FailedDisarm) {terminate();}
                cout << "You have disarmed the mine!!!\n";
                goto PLAY;
            }
            cout << "You have failed the XJ77 team.\n";
            goto TOO_BAD;

    }

    return 0;
TOO_BAD: cout << "\nMaybe next year kid.\n";
    return 0;
}
```

## Summary

This chapter, although short, is an important one. Even the most advanced programmers too often ignore the concept of this chapter, and it is true that exception handling does not add to the functionality of your program. However, exception handling makes your programs stable, and if you want to advance from being a good programmer to being an excellent one, we strongly suggest that you make a habit of using it.

### CHALLENGES

1. What does the keyword `try` do?
2. What is the purpose of an exception hierarchy?
3. How can you design your programs so that they will not crash?
4. What is the definition of an exception?
5. At what point in your program's development should you use assertions?

CHAPTER 12

# Programming with Windows

The preceding chapters thoroughly introduce you to the C++ language. In the next two chapters, we cover much more recent programming concepts. In this chapter, you learn how to create Windows programs using the Windows Application Programming Interface (API), which will prepare you for Chapter 13, "Using DirectX." In Chapter 13, you learn how to use a Microsoft library with DirectX to program games. In this chapter, you learn the following:

- How to create a Windows program
- How to use `WinMain`
- How to use `WndProc`
- How to create a window
- How to process messages

## Introducing the Windows API

When Microsoft designed Windows, the company decided to provide a library of functions so that people could design Windows programs. This library is called the *Windows API* (Application Programming Interface). To use the Windows API, you must be using Windows 95, 98, NT 4, or 2000. You can find complete documentation for the Windows API at http://www.msdn.microsoft.com/library/default.asp. Look under the section named Platform SDK.

A subset of this library is called the *Windows GUI* (Graphic User Interface). Using the Windows GUI, you can make your programs more interesting by adding command buttons, scrolling lists, icons, and other Windows elements that users can employ to interact with your programs.

## Creating a Windows Program in CodeWarrior

Congratulations, reader; you're in for a treat. You're about to enter a whole new world of programming in the land of Microsoft. Programming for Windows is much more exciting than boring, old console applications because you get to see most of what you do right away. Also, because about 98 percent of computer users work on Windows, your programs will be highly portable.

The steps to generating a Windows program are inherently different from those of a console application. In Chapter 1, "Starting the Journey," we tell you to open the New Project dialog box (the one right after you choose the project name) and choose C++ Console App. This step tells CodeWarrior that you do not want your program to be a Windows application. Now, however, you explore one of the other options in this dialog box, Win32 C++ App.

To help you become familiar with this process, we now walk you through it step by step. In this set of steps, you create a program that displays the message `Hello from Win32` onscreen.

1. Open CodeWarrior and choose New from the File menu. The New dialog box opens with the Project tab selected.
2. In the Project name text box, enter **WinHelloWorld** as the name of the project (see Figure 12.1).

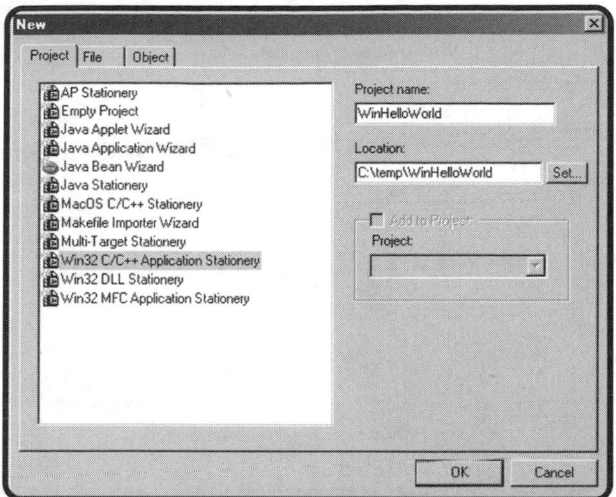


**FIGURE 12.1**

You can designate your project's name, location, and type in the New dialog box.

3. In the Location text box, type an appropriate directory or click the Set button to browse to the directory.
4. In the directory at the right side of the New dialog box, select Win32 C/C++ Application Stationery as the type of project.
5. Click OK to open the New Project dialog box (see Figure 12.2).
6. Select Win32 C++ App from the list of options.
7. Click OK. The project window opens, which means that you have finished creating the skeleton application.
8. The project window displays the source code for a Windows program (see Figure 12.3).
9. Compile and run the program the same way you compile and run a console application. The CodeWarrior Win32 Stationery window appears with the message `Hello from Win32` shown onscreen (see Figure 12.4). You have now completed your first Windows application.

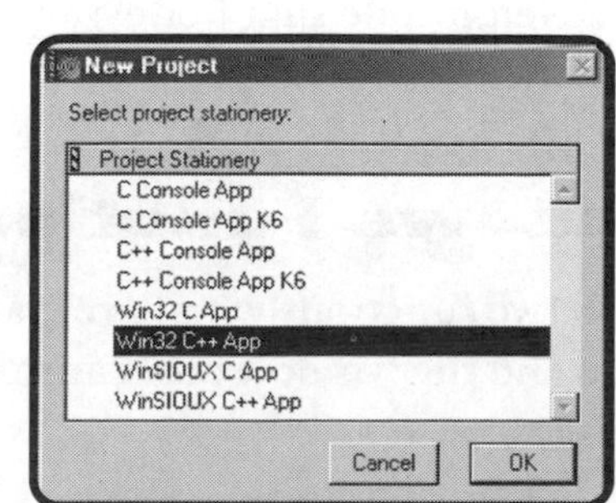


**FIGURE 12.2**

The New Project dialog box.

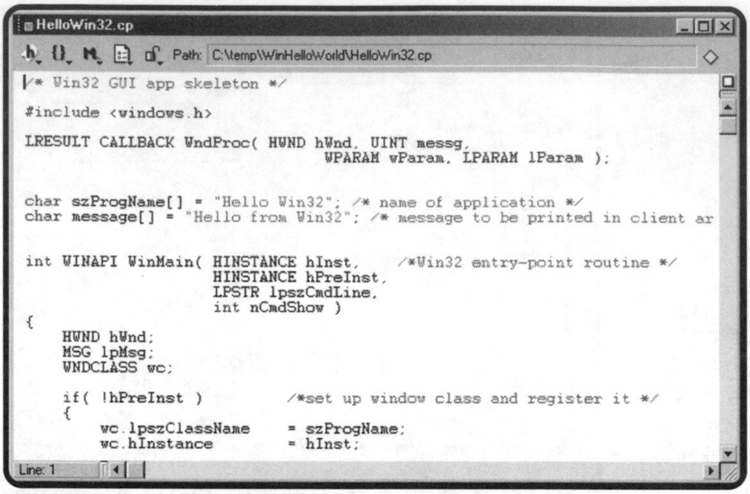

FIGURE 12.3

This window displays the skeleton code that CodeWarrior generates for a Windows program.

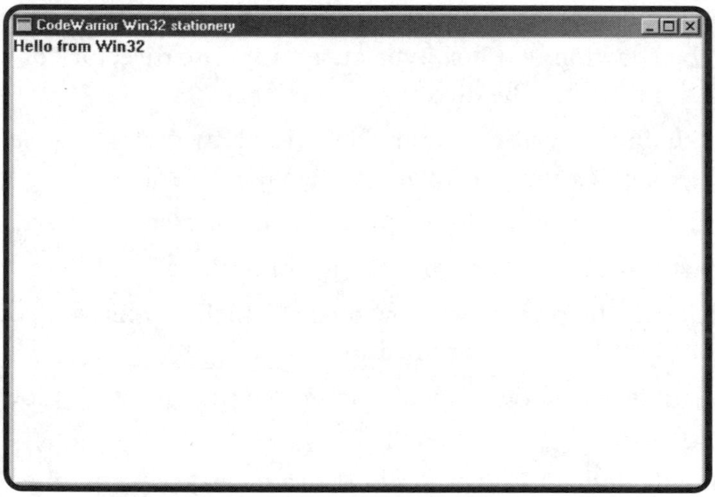

FIGURE 12.4

The skeleton code generated by CodeWarrior produces a window that can be moved, maximized, minimized, and resized.

Though more is involved, Windows programs aren't too difficult to create. In the next few sections, you examine the skeleton code that CodeWarrior generated in the preceding steps.

## Examining the Windows Functions

You will become quickly familiar with two functions when programming in Windows. These two functions are `WinMain` and the window procedure. In this section, you learn about both these functions.

In the steps in the preceding section, you probably noticed that CodeWarrior generates a great deal of code for you. Here, in its entirety, is the code that CodeWarrior generates:

```
/* Win32 GUI app skeleton */

#include <windows.h>

LRESULT CALLBACK WndProc( HWND hWnd, UINT messg,
                                WPARAM wParam, LPARAM lParam );


char szProgName[] = "Hello Win32"; /* name of application */
/* message to be printed in client area */
char message[] = "Hello from Win32";


int WINAPI WinMain(/*Win32 entry-point routine */
                    HINSTANCE hInst,
                    HINSTANCE hPreInst,
                    LPSTR lpszCmdLine,
                    int nCmdShow )
{
    HWND hWnd;
    MSG lpMsg;
    WNDCLASS wc;

    if( !hPreInst ) /*set up window class and register it */
    {
        wc.lpszClassName = szProgName;
        wc.hInstance = hInst;
        wc.lpfnWndProc = WndProc;
        wc.hCursor = LoadCursor( NULL, IDC_ARROW );
        wc.hIcon = LoadIcon( NULL, IDI_APPLICATION );
        wc.lpszMenuName = NULL;
        wc.hbrBackground = (HBRUSH)
            GetStockObject( WHITE_BRUSH );
        wc.style = 0;
        wc.cbClsExtra = 0;
        wc.cbWndExtra = 0;
```

```
		if( !RegisterClass( &wc ) )
			return FALSE;
	}

hWnd = CreateWindow(/* now create the window */
		szProgName,
		"CodeWarrior Win32 stationery",
		WS_OVERLAPPEDWINDOW,
		CW_USEDEFAULT,
		CW_USEDEFAULT,
		CW_USEDEFAULT,
		CW_USEDEFAULT,
		(HWND)NULL,
		(HMENU)NULL,
		(HINSTANCE)hInst,
		(LPSTR)NULL
	);

	ShowWindow(hWnd, nCmdShow );
	UpdateWindow( hWnd );


	/* begin the message loop */
	while( GetMessage( &lpMsg, NULL, 0, 0 ) )
	{
		TranslateMessage( &lpMsg );
		DispatchMessage( &lpMsg );
	}
	return( lpMsg.wParam);
}

/*callback procedure */
LRESULT CALLBACK WndProc( HWND hWnd, UINT messg,
					WPARAM wParam, LPARAM lParam )
{
	HDC hdc; /* handle to the device context */
	PAINTSTRUCT pstruct; /*struct for the call to BeginPaint */

	switch(messg)
	{
```

```
        case WM_PAINT:
        /* prepare window for painting*/
        hdc = BeginPaint(hWnd, &pstruct );
        /*print hello at upper left corner */
        TextOut( hdc, 0, 0, message,
             ( sizeof(message) - 1 ) );
        /* stop painting */
        EndPaint(hWnd, &pstruct );
        break;

        case WM_DESTROY:
        PostQuitMessage( 0 );
        break;

        default:
        return( DefWindowProc( hWnd, messg,
             wParam, lParam ) );
    }

    return( 0L );
}
```

With the knowledge of C++ that you have gained so far, you probably recognize parts of this code. First of all, it contains one `include` statement:

```
#include <windows.h>
```

This statement includes the standard Windows library needed to create a Windows program. The Windows API contains many other libraries, but this file is the main one. Just remember that `windows.h` must be included in every Windows program.

You probably also noticed the two global character array variables, `szProgName` and `message`:

```
char szProgName[] = "Hello Win32"; /* name of application */
char message[] = "Hello from Win32";
/* message to be printed in client area */
```

Windows does not require these two variables. They exist only for convenience. As the comments explain, `szProgName` stores the name of the program, and `message` holds the text that is displayed. Notice that if you change the value of `message`, you can change what is displayed! Perhaps that's not as exciting to you as it is to us, but at least now you know that you have a choice.

Another thing you can immediately gather from this code is that it has two functions, `WinMain` and `WndProc`:

```
int WINAPI WinMain(
     HINSTANCE hInst,       /*Win32 entry-point routine */
     HINSTANCE hPreInst,
     LPSTR lpszCmdLine,
     int nCmdShow );
LRESULT CALLBACK WndProc( HWND hWnd, UINT messg,
     WPARAM wParam, LPARAM lParam );
```

You probably will not recognize some terms in these function declarations—for example, `WINAPI`, `HISTANCE`, `LPSTR`, `LRESULT`, `CALLBACK`, `HWND`, `UINT`, `WPARAM`, and `LPARAM`. `WINAPI` and `CALLBACK` are special terms that you can ignore for now (just pretend they aren't there).

The rest of the terms are Windows data types, each with a different purpose. For example, `WinMain` is the Windows equivalent of the `main` function. It does exactly the same thing in Windows that `main` does in console applications—provides the starting function for the program. All the arguments passed to `WinMain` (by Windows to your application) are Windows equivalents to command-line arguments. They provide all the information your program needs to perform normal Windows functions.

The `WndProc` function handles special events, such as when you click a button. The arguments that `WndProc` receives contain information about the type of event and the circumstances.

### In the Real World

**In Windows programming, *events* take on a special meaning. Normally, when you open a Windows program, it will load and sit, waiting for your input. This is different from, say, a real-time strategy game, where the computer opponents will build up an army to destroy you whether you do anything or not. This programming style is called *event-driven programming*.**

**Events in Windows happen frequently and in specified circumstances—for example, when the clock changes to a certain time or the user presses Enter or clicks the mouse. Events are happening all the time when Windows is running.**

**When Windows programmers design programs, they design functions called *event-handlers* (see "Handling Events," later in this chapter, for more on event-handlers). Windows calls these functions whenever a certain event takes place. For example, when the user clicks a program's Exit button, the program immediately exits.**

## Investigating WinMain

As we stated previously, `WinMain` is the Windows equivalent of the `main` function. Windows calls `WinMain` when a program starts. When the program exits `WinMain`, the program is done. In this section, you examine `WinMain` in detail.

Windows passes these four arguments to your application when the application begins: `HINSTANCE hInst`, `HINSTANCE hPreInst`, `LPSTR lpszCmdLine`, and `int nCmdShow`.

`hInst` is a handle to your application. A *handle* is a lot like a pointer or a reference and keeps track of various Windows elements, such as your application, your application's program windows, and other things. `Inst` stands for *instance*. If two copies of your application are running at the same time, each one will be a different instance of the same application. `hInst` is a handle to this particular instance of the application. It can be useful for calling some of the Windows API functions.

`hPreInst` is a handle to the previous instance of your application. This is outdated and no longer has use, so just ignore it. The only reason that it is still here is for backward compatibility. *Backward compatibility* occurs when a new version of some software is still compatible with older versions. This way, people using older versions won't have to buy the newer version.

`lpszCmdLine` is just a null-terminated string that stores the command-line arguments. If you go to the Start menu and select Run, you can type anything you want after the program name. For example, if your program is named Hello.exe, you can type **Hello.exe Goodbye**. Then you can design the program to use this command-line argument to display whatever message is supplied, in this case `Goodbye`. Notice that the name of the program, Hello.exe, is not part of `lpszCmdLine`.

`nCmdShow` is an integer specifying how the window will display. You can treat this as a suggestion from Windows as to how your window should look. Like most suggestions, this one can be ignored. This argument has too many possible values to list here, but Table 12.1 lists the ones generally needed.

Knowing all the possible values is nearly impossible (Table 12.1 shows approximately 5 percent of them). However, you'll probably use only the first three values in Table 12.1 in roughly 99 percent of your programming.

However, if you need to know the other possible values, you can find them in many places. One good place to find them is the Microsoft Developer Network (MSDN). You can find it on the Web at http://www.msdn.microsoft.com. For more detailed information about Windows programming, you might go to your library and look up *Platform SDK*.

**TABLE 12.1 POSSIBLE VALUES FOR NCMDSHOW**

| Value | Description |
|---|---|
| SW_SHOWNORMAL | Activates and displays a window normally (takes up only part of a screen). |
| SW_SHOW | Activates and displays a window in its current size and position. |
| SW_HIDE | Hides the window. |
| SW_MAXIMIZE | Maximizes the window. |
| SW_MINIMIZE | Minimizes the window. |
| SW_RESTORE | Activates and displays a minimized window. Brings it back to its original size and position. |

## Investigating WndProc

`WndProc` is the function called by Windows whenever an event occurs that affects your program. Windows passes arguments to `WndProc` that explain what the event is. You, as the programmer, have an option of letting Windows handle the event in its own way or handling it yourself. It is not possible to handle all the events yourself—there are just too many of them.

`WndProc` supports these four arguments: `HWND hWnd`, `UINT messg`, `WPARAM wParam`, and `LPARAM lParam`.

`hWnd` is a handle to the window the event is relevant to. You will not need to use this argument often, but if you have multiple windows that use the same version of `WndProc`, `hWnd` enables you to tell which window should receive which message. You use the data type `HWND` to refer to a window in Windows programming. Handles are used in a similar way as classes are used. For example, to refer to a bitmap (a kind of image), you use the `HBITMAP` data type.

`messg` is the ID number of the message. There are hundreds of different messages. Table 12.2 shows some of the possible messages.

In the section "Handling Events," later in this chapter, you learn how to use some of these message IDs; right now, you just need to know they exist and that there are hundreds of them.

`wParam` and `lParam` are extra information about an event. These arguments are different for every event and may or may not be filled with values, depending on the type of message.

**Table 12.2 Common Message IDs**

| ID | Action |
| --- | --- |
| WM_ACTIVATE | Sent when a window is activated or becomes the focus. |
| WM_CLOSE | Sent when a window is closed. |
| WM_CREATE | Sent when a window is created. |
| WM_DESTROY | Sent when a window is about to be destroyed. |
| WM_MOVE | Sent when a window is moved. |
| WM_MOUSEMOVE | Sent when the mouse is moved. |
| WM_KEYUP | Sent when a key (on the keyboard) is released. |
| WM_KEYDOWN | Sent when a key is pressed. |
| WM_TIMER | Sent when a timer event occurs. |
| WM_USER | Special message sent when you create your own events. |
| WM_PAINT | Sent when a window needs to be redrawn onscreen. |
| WM_QUIT | Sent when a Windows application is terminating (not just a window). |
| WM_SIZE | Sent when a window has changed size. |

The return type, LRESULT, is a standard return type for many Windows functions. It is a type used to store the result of a function.

# Creating a Window

One of the most important things to learn in Windows programming is how to actually create a window and display it onscreen. In this section, you investigate this process and discover some of the possible options.

## Creating a Message Box

Before you can investigate the rest of the code generated by CodeWarrior, you need to learn a little bit more about creating windows.

You have two main options for creating a window. You can create a fully functional one that can do almost anything, or you can create simpler ones that only display a message. In this section, you examine the simpler windows, called *message boxes,* as an introduction to creating windows in general.

You create a message box with the `MessageBox` function. `MessageBox` has four arguments that specify the necessary information about how it is to be created. Here is the function declaration for the `MessageBox` function:

```
int MessageBox (HWND hWnd, LPCTSTR lpText, LPCTSTR lpCaption, UINT uType);
```

`hWnd` specifies the handle to the window that you want to control the message box. For example, if you have an application that has an error, you can use a message box to display the error. In this case, the main window of the application will control the message box. A window that controls another window is called a *parent window,* and a window that is controlled is called a *child window.* If you pass the value `NULL` (`0`) for this argument, the Windows desktop is assumed to be the parent window.

`lpText` is the string that you want to display. For example, if you want to display the message `Hello Win32`, you pass this string as the argument.

`lpCaption` is the string that is displayed in the title bar of the window. For example, if you open CodeWarrior and look at the top of the screen, you will see the text `Metrowerks CodeWarrior`. This string is the caption for the CodeWarrior window. For the caption of the main application window, you generally use the title of the application (or something equally appropriate).

`uType` is an integer, like `nCmdShow` for the `WinMain` function, that specifies the style of the message box you want to display. You can specify which buttons the message box has and which icon displays beside the message. Table 12.3 lists a few of the possible button combinations for `uType`, and Table 12.4 lists the possible icons for `uType`.

You can combine buttons and icons by using the or operator. For example, if you want a message box with an OK button, a Cancel button, and a stop icon, you pass `MB_OKCANCEL | MB_ICONSTOP`.

**TABLE 12.3 POSSIBLE BUTTONS FOR UTYPE**

| Value | Description |
|---|---|
| `MB_OK` | Default value. The message box has an OK button. |
| `MB_OKCANCEL` | The message box has an OK button and a Cancel button. |
| `MB_RETRYCANCEL` | The message box has a Retry button and a Cancel button. |
| `MB_YESNO` | The message box has a Yes button and a No button. |
| `MB_YESNOCANCEL` | The message box has a Yes button, a No button, and a Cancel button. |

**Table 12.4 Possible Icons for uType**

| Value | Description |
|---|---|
| MB_ICONEXCLAMATION | The message box has an icon with an exclamation mark. |
| MB_ICONINFORMATION | The message box has an icon with an i in a circle. |
| MB_ICONQUESTION | The message box has an icon with a question mark. |
| MB_ICONSTOP | The message box has an icon with a stop sign. |

Here is an example of how you can create a message box:

```
//12.1 - The Message Box Program - Mark Lee
//Premier Press
#include <windows.h>
int WINAPI WinMain( /*Win32 entry-point routine */
                            HINSTANCE hInst,
                            HINSTANCE hPreInst,
                            LPSTR lpszCmdLine,
                            int nCmdShow )
{
     MessageBox(NULL, "Windows Programming is Easy!!",
          "My First Message Box",
          MB_OKCANCEL | MB_ICONINFORMATION);
}
```

Figure 12.5 shows the output of this program. Notice how the title of the message box is displayed in the taskbar. This is because the parent of the message box is the Windows desktop.

## Setting the Properties of a Window

Before you can actually create a window, you must define the window's properties. You can use two structures, WNDCLASS and WNDCLASSEX, to define the window's properties. These structures contain a number of data members that store the relevant information. You first fill these members and then pass the information to Windows so that it can create the window.

When you create a Win32 Application in CodeWarrior, you use the default structure WNDCLASS. However, this structure is rather old and will likely soon be replaced by the newer WNDCLASSEX. We use WNDCLASSEX in this book's examples.

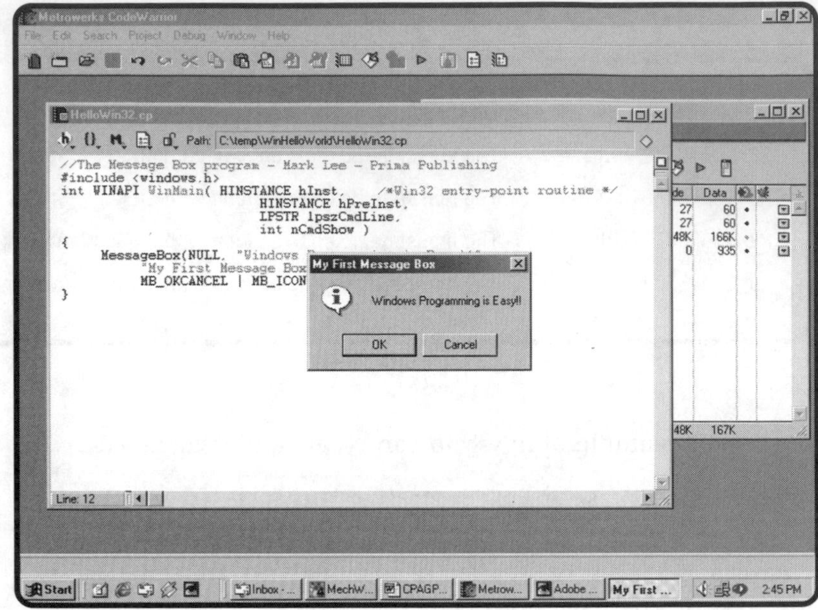


**FIGURE 12.5**

Your code determines what the icon and buttons look like in this message box.

Here is the definition of `WNDCLASSEX`:

```
typedef struct _WNDCLASSEX
{
    UINT cbSize; //the size of this structure
    UINT style; //the style of the window
    WNDPROC lpfnWndProc; //the function that handles events
    int cbClsExtra; //extra info
    int cbWndExtra; //extra window info
    //handle to the instance of the application
    HANDLE hInstance;
    HICON hIcon; //the window's icon
    HCURSOR hCursor; //the cursor used for the window
    //specifies how to fill the background of the window
    HBRUSH hbrBackground;
    //the name of the menu (if there is one)
    LPCTSTR lpszMenuName;
    //the name you want to give to the class
    LPCTSTR lpszClassName;
    //the icon used (when a smaller icon is needed)
    HICON hIconSm;
} WNDCLASSEX;
```

If you look at the code generated by CodeWarrior, you'll see a line that looks like this:

```
WNDCLASS wc;
```

This line creates an object from this structure called `wc`. You modify this line to use `WNDCLASSEX` instead:

```
WNDCLASSEX wc;
```

Once you have an object created from the structure, you fill all the members with the appropriate values. After filling `wc`, here is how it looks in the code generated by CodeWarrior:

```
wc.lpszClassName = szProgName;
wc.hInstance = hInst;
wc.lpfnWndProc = WndProc;
wc.hCursor = LoadCursor( NULL, IDC_ARROW );
wc.hIcon          = LoadIcon( NULL, IDI_APPLICATION );
wc.lpszMenuName = NULL;
wc.hbrBackground = (HBRUSH)GetStockObject( WHITE_BRUSH );
wc.style          = 0;
wc.cbClsExtra = 0;
wc.cbWndExtra = 0;
```

When you do fill this structure yourself, it might look slightly different. The first member of the `WNDCLASSEX` structure is the `cbSize` member. This member stores the size of the object. Why would you need to store the size of an object? If you pass the object as a pointer, you can use this member to determine exactly how much memory the object uses. Doing so is mostly a precautionary measure, but you should always fill it. Here is how you set the appropriate value for `cbSize`:

```
wc.cbSize = sizeof(WNDCLASSEX);
```

The next member is `style`. This member sets how your window behaves. You fill this member with constants that can be combined with the or operator. Table 12.5 lists a few of the possible values you can use.

This overview gives you a taste of some Windows program possibilities. The values you choose to use depend on the kind of application you are designing. For your purposes, you can ignore all of these and just set this member to `0` (just as the code generated by CodeWarrior does):

```
wc.style = 0;
```

The next member specifies which function will handle events sent by Windows.

**Table 12.5 Possible Window Styles**

| Value | Action |
|---|---|
| CS_HREDRAW | Redraws the entire window if a movement or size adjustment changes the width of the window. |
| CS_VREDRAW | Redraws the entire window if a movement or size adjustment changes the height of the window. |
| CS_OWNDC | Makes drawing in the window more convenient. |
| CS_DBLCLKS | Sends a double-click message when the user double-clicks somewhere within the window. |
| CS_NOCLOSE | Disables the Close command on the system menu. |

In the code generated by CodeWarrior, this function is `WndProc`. However, you are free to name the function anything you want. Here is how you set this member:

```
wc.lpfnWndProc = WinProc;
```

When you set this value, you are telling Windows which function to call. After you do so, Windows takes care of the rest and calls the function automatically.

The next two members, `cbClsExtra` and `cbWndExtra`, are designed to give your window some extra functionality; however, they are beyond the scope of this book. For your purposes, you can set these members to `0`:

```
wc.cbClsExtra = 0;
wc.cbWndExtra = 0;
```

The next member, `hInstance`, is a handle to the instance of your application. Fortunately, Windows provides it. You simply use `hInst`, which is passed to `WinMain`:

```
wc.hInstance = hInst;
```

Calling the Windows function `LoadIcon` sets the next member, `hIcon`. You can use any icon you want, but for your purposes, you can use a *system icon* (an icon that is built into Windows). Table 12.6 lists some of the possible system icons that you can use.

The code that CodeWarrior generates uses the `IDI_APPLICATION` icon. This is fine if you are content to just sit in the back seat and let life go where it may. But some of us have a need for speed. If this is the case, you should use the `IDI_EXCLAMATION`

**Table 12.6 System Icons**

| Value | Description |
|---|---|
| IDI_APPLICATION | Default application icon (pretty boring) |
| IDI_ASTERISK | Asterisk icon |
| IDI_EXCLAMATION | Exclamation point (very exciting) |
| IDI_HAND | Hand-shaped icon |
| IDI_QUESTION | Question mark |
| IDI_WINLOGO | Windows logo |

icon. Careful, though; it's not recommended if you have a heart condition. Here's how you set it:

```
wc.hIcon = LoadIcon(NULL, IDI_EXCLAMATION);
```

You set `hCursor` almost exactly the same way. You use the `LoadCursor` function. `hCursor` determines how the mouse looks when it is within the window. Again, you can define a custom cursor, but for your current purposes, you don't need to. Table 12.7 shows some of the possible system cursors.

**Table 12.7 System Cursors**

| Value | Description |
|---|---|
| IDC_ARROW | Standard arrow |
| IDC_APPSTARTING | Standard arrow and small hourglass |
| IDC_CROSS | Crosshair |
| IDC_IBEAM | Text I beam |
| IDC_NO | Slashed circle |
| IDC_SIZEALL | Four-pointed arrow |
| IDC_SIZENESW | Double-pointed arrow pointing northeast and southwest |
| IDC_SIZENWSE | Double-pointed arrow pointing northwest and southeast |
| IDC_SIZENS | Double-pointed arrow pointing north and south |
| IDCSIZEWE | Double-pointed arrow pointing west and east |
| IDC_UPARROW | Arrow pointing up |
| IDC_WAIT | Hourglass |

The next member, hbrBackground, defines how the background of your window will look. You can use special effects to make it striped (ugly), but most people just use a solid color. You define the way the window background is painted with a brush. A brush is the Windows way of storing a certain way to fill an area with color. You can define a custom brush if you need to, but most people do not. Table 12.8 lists some of the different brushes you can use.

You request a handle to one of these brushes by using the GetStockObject function. It takes one argument: the name of the brush. Here is how you do this:

```
wc.hbrBackground = GetStockObject(WHITE_BRUSH);
```

To have a menu in your window (such as the File menu in CodeWarrior), you use the lpszMenuName member to define what the menu contains. However, if you do not, you must set this value to NULL:

```
wc.lpszMenuName = NULL;
```

The next member gives a name to the class from which your window is created. Each window is an object. When you fill a WNDCLASSEX structure with values, you are creating a new class. Your window will then be created from this class. You can use any name you like for your window class (it really doesn't matter that much). Many people use simple names, such as WINCLASS1. Here is how you set this member:

```
wc.lpszClassName = "WINCLASS1";
```

Use the last member to store the small version of the icon. This is the icon you see on the title bar and the taskbar. You set this member exactly the same way that you set the hIcon member:

```
wc.hIconSm = LoadIcon(NULL, IDI_EXCLAMATION);
```

**Table 12.8 System Brushes**

| Value | Description |
|---|---|
| BLACK_BRUSH | Solid black |
| WHITE_BRUSH | Solid white |
| GRAY_BRUSH | Solid gray |
| LTGRAY_BRUSH | Solid light gray |
| DKGRAY_BRUSH | Solid dark gray |
| NULL_BRUSH | Nothing |

Okay, that's all. Take a look at the complete code for filling the WNDCLASSEX structure:

```
WNDCLASSEX wc;

wc.cbSize = sizeof(WNDCLASSEX);
wc.style = 0;
wc.lpfnWndProc = WinProc;
wc.cbClsExtra = 0;
wc.cbWndExtra = 0;
wc.hInstance = hInst;
wc.hIcon = LoadIcon(NULL, IDI_EXCLAMATION);
wc.hbrBackground = GetStockObject(WHITE_BRUSH);
wc.lpszMenuName = NULL;
wc.lpszClassName = "WINCLASS1";
wc.hIconSm = LoadIcon(NULL, IDI_EXCLAMATION);
```

## Registering and Creating Windows

After you design a window class by filling in a WNDCLASSEX structure, you must register the class with Windows. You do so by calling the function RegisterClassEx. This function takes one argument, which is a reference to the WNDCLASSEX object (wc).

If you are creating a window using the WNDCLASS structure, you must register the class by calling the RegisterClass function.

Here is how you register a window class:

```
RegisterClassEx(&wc);
```

This function returns a boolean value, indicating whether the function succeeded (True if it did, False if not).

When your window class is registered, you are free to create a window from it. You do so by calling CreateWindow or CreateWindowEx. CreateWindowEx has more options and is a little newer (like WNDCLASSEX is to WNDCLASS).

Here is the function declaration for the CreateWindowEx function:

```
HWND CreateWindowEx
(
     DWORD dwExStyle, // extended styles
     LPCTSTR lpClassName, // name of class
     LPCTSTR lpWindowName, // name of window
     DWORD dwStyle, //style
     int x, // distance of window from left side of screen
```

```
    int y, // distance of window from top of screen
    int nWidth, // width of window
    int nHeight, // height of window
    HWND hWndParent, // handle to parent of this window
    HMENU hMenu, // handle to menu
    HINSTANCE hInstance, // handle to instance of application
    LPVOID lpParam // window creation data
);
```

Here is how the code generated by CodeWarrior creates the window:

```
HWND hWnd;
hWnd = CreateWindow(/* now create the window */
                                    szProgName,
                                    "CodeWarrior Win32 stationery",
                                    WS_OVERLAPPEDWINDOW,
                                    CW_USEDEFAULT,
                                    CW_USEDEFAULT,
                                    CW_USEDEFAULT,
                                    CW_USEDEFAULT,
                                    (HWND)NULL,
                                    (HMENU)NULL,
                                    (HINSTANCE)hInst,
                                    (LPSTR)NULL           );
```

Both `CreateWindow` and `CreateWindowEx` return `NULL` if the function fails or a handle to the newly created window if the function succeeds. This is why you must create a variable to store a handle to a window. You must be able to access the newly created window later so that you can do things with it. You create the variable like this:

```
HWND hWnd;
```

The first parameter, `dwExStyle`, stores all advanced options that you want your window to have. For example, you can always make the window be on top. If you want to see some of the other options, you can find them in the Windows API documentation. You can set this parameter to `NULL` if you don't want extra options.

The second parameter is the name of the class that you are using to create this window. For this window, you are using `"WNDCLASS1"`.

The third parameter is the title of the window. For example, the title of the CodeWarrior window is `Metrowerks CodeWarrior`. The code generated by CodeWarrior uses `CodeWarrior Win32 stationery` as a title.

The fourth parameter, dwStyle, defines how the window looks and behaves. Keep in mind that the style options in the WNDCLASSEX structure define the appearance and behavior of every window created from the class, but dwStyle defines only the appearance and behavior of one window. You might be confused, because you've already completed this step. The difference is that now you are defining more specific properties. Table 12.9 lists some of the options you can use with this parameter.

The parameters x and y specify the distance from the upper-left corner of the screen to the upper-left corner of the window. If you want Windows to decide this for you, you can use CW_USEDEFAULT rather than a number.

The parameters nWidth and nHeight specify the width and height of the window. You can use CW_USEDEFAULT if you want to let Windows decide.

hWndParent specifies the handle to the parent window, if there is one. Use NULL if you want the Windows desktop to be the parent.

hMenu specifies a handle to any menu that you would like to attach. Use NULL for now.

hInstance is the instance of the application. Use hInst from WinMain.

lpParam is for advanced options. Set to NULL for now.

**Table 12.9 Window Styles**

| Value | Description |
|---|---|
| WS_POPUP | A pop-up window. |
| WS_OVERLAPPED | An overlapped window that has a title bar and a border. |
| WS_OVERLAPPEDWINDOW | An overlapped window with the WS_OVERLAPPED, WS_CAPTION, WS_SYSMENU, WS_THICKFRAME, WS_MINIMIZEBOX, and WS_MAXIMIZEBOX styles. |
| WS_VISIBLE | A window that is initially visible. |
| WS_SYSMENU | A window that has a window menu on its title bar (when you click the little icon). The WS_CAPTION option must also be specified. |
| WS_BORDER | A window that has a thin-line border. |
| WS_CAPTION | A window that has a title bar (the WS_BORDER style is included). |
| WS_MINIMIZE | A window that is initially minimized. |
| WS_MAXIMIZE | A window that is initially maximized. |

That covers all the parameters. Here is the final function call:

```
HWND hWnd;
hWnd = CreateWindowEx (
      NULL, //extended styles
      "WINCLASS1", //name of class
      "A Basic Window", //title of window
      WS_OVERLAPPEDWINDOW | WS_VISIBLE, //styles
      CW_USEDEFAULT, CW_USEDEFAULT, //initial position
      CW_USEDEFAULT, CW_USEDEFAULT, //initial size
      NULL, //parent is Windows desktop
      NULL, //no menu for this window
      hInst, //handle to application instance
      NULL) //extra parameters
```

You've now created a window. Notice how the `WS_VISIBLE` style is used. This option makes the window initially visible. If you did not use this option, you would have to call the function `ShowWindow` in order to display the window. The `ShowWindow` function takes two parameters, the handle to the window and the `nCmdShow` parameter that you received from `WinMain`. Here is how you manually display a window:

```
ShowWindow(hWnd, nCmdShow);
```

You might remember that Windows recommends what your window should look like in `nCmdShow` (see "Investigating WinMain," earlier in this chapter). You can use `ShowWindow` if you want to use the recommendations contained in `nCmdShow`. Officially, you are supposed to use these recommendations to create a window.

Finally, you need to call the function `UpdateWindow` to ensure that the window is redrawn on the screen right away (this is a standard procedure). This function sends a `WM_PAINT` event (you learn more about events in the next section). Here is how you call `UpdateWindow`:

```
UpdateWindow();
```

Congratulations! You've now created your first real window (without the aid of CodeWarrior).

## Processing Messages

After creating a window, the next step is to handle all the incoming events. As you have learned, you use `WndProc` to do this. However, there is a little more to it than that.

CodeWarrior provides the following code when you generate a Windows application:

```
/* begin the message loop */
while( GetMessage( &lpMsg, NULL, 0, 0 ) )
     {
          TranslateMessage( &lpMsg );
          DispatchMessage( &lpMsg );
     }
```

Although it might not look like it, this code segment is the heart of your program. After the window is created, the program enters this `while` loop and does not exit until the program finishes.

The main function that keeps this loop going is `GetMessage`. This message gets the next message that needs to be processed from Windows. If there are no more messages (the program has ended), `GetMessage` returns `0`, and the `while` loop ends.

Here is the function declaration for `GetMessage`:

```
BOOL GetMessage (LPMSG lpMsg, HWND hWnd,
     UINT wMsgFilterMin, UINT wMsgFilterMax);
```

This function fills `lpMsg` with the next message. You can ignore the other three parameters. They are not very important (except for advanced programming).

For the first parameter, you must pass a reference to an `MSG` structure (no, not the stuff that's bad for you). Here is the `MSG` structure:

```
typedef struct tagMSG
{
     HWND hwnd; // window where message occurred
     UINT message; // message id
     WPARAM wParam; // extra message info
     LPARAM lParam; // extra message info
     DWORD time; // time of message event
     POINT pt; // position of mouse
} MSG;
```

First, you create a `MSG` object; then you pass it to `GetMessage`. Here is the code so far:

```
MSG msg;
while (GetMessage(&msg, NULL, 0, 0))
{
}
```

You now have a working event loop. This is a very important step. Now that you have the messages, you probably want to do something with them. You do so with the TranslateMessage and DispatchMessage functions.

These functions take a reference to the MSG object as an argument. TranslateMessage prepares all input that was received. Don't worry too much about how TranslateMessage works; just remember that you have to call it.

DispatchMessage sends the message away to WndProc to be handled. Take a look at the code now:

```
MSG msg;
while (GetMessage(&msg, NULL, 0, 0))
{
      TranslateMessage(&msg);
      DispatchMessage(&msg);
}
```

That's message processing in a nutshell. Windows programming isn't so bad, is it? You just have to get used to it.

## Handling Events

Once the messages (indicating an event) are sent to WndProc, you must handle them in some fashion. The usual way to do so is to create a switch statement. Then you can handle a different event for each case.

Earlier in this chapter (refer to the section "Investigating WndProc"), you learned that the messg argument of WndProc holds the ID of the message (with things such as WM_PAINT). Having the message identifier means that you can use this argument in the switch statement. Here is the basic structure:

```
switch (messg)
{
}
```

Now you can test messg against each kind of message to figure out which is being sent. This procedure works fine, except for one flaw: There are too many different kinds of messages. You could spend years programming what to do for every case, and your code would be huge.

Fortunately, you can ask Windows to handle messages that you don't want to handle. You do so by calling the function DefWindowProc. You are saying, "I don't want to deal with this; can you? Here's all the information you need." The arguments that DefWindowProc takes are the same as those that WndProc takes, so you can just pass those arguments along. Here's how the call to DefWindowProc looks:

```
DefWindowProc( hWnd, messg, wParam, lParam );
```

Although you want Windows to handle most of the messages, you want to handle some of them yourself. To do so, you put the call to DefWindowProc in the default case of the switch statement, like this:

```
switch (messg)
{
      default:
            DefWindowProc( hWnd, messg, wParam, lParam );
}
```

The return value of DefWindowProc works the same way as the return value for WndProc, so you can just return what DefWindowProc returns. Here is the finished version:

```
switch (messg)
{
      case WM_SOMETHING:
            //do something
      default:
            return (DefWindowProc(hWnd, messg, wParam, lParam));
}
return 0;
```

Now you are ready to learn how to handle some of the different messages.

WM_CREATE occurs when a window is first created. You can use this message to perform all initialization tasks that need to be done (this is the official, proper place to initialize things).

WM_DESTROY occurs when a window is about to be destroyed. Usually, this means that the application must end (you must end it yourself). To end the application, you call the function PostQuitMessage. This sends a WM_QUIT message (where you can put more code) and ends the program. Here is an example:

```
case WM_DESTROY:
      PostQuitMessage(0);
      break;
```

## Being on Time

Often you want to do something at a particular interval in time. For example, you might want to refresh the screen every 1/26 second. Fortunately, Windows provides a convenient way for you to do this.

You must create what is called a *timer*. A timer sends a WM_TIMER message to your program after a certain interval. In fact, you can have more than one timer. One might have a 2-second delay, and one might have a 3-second delay.

To create a timer, you call the function SetTimer. This function takes four arguments. Here is the function declaration:

```
UINT SetTimer (HWND hWnd, UINT nIDevent, UINT nElapse,
          TIMERPROC lpTimerFunc);
```

hWnd is the handle to the window of which this timer is a part. nIDevent is the ID of the timer. The timer ID can be any integer. You use it to identify the timer. nElapse is the delay that you want your timer to have. This argument is measured in milliseconds (1000 milliseconds = 1 second). The last parameter, lpTimerFunc, is the name of a function that is called every time the timer goes off. If you don't want to use a function, you can use the WM_TIMER message instead, and you can set this parameter to NULL.

The best place to put the call to SetTimer is in the WM_CREATE message.

After you create the timer, you can respond whenever it goes off by using the WM_TIMER event. The WM_TIMER event occurs whenever a timer goes off. The WndProc argument, wParam, stores the ID of the timer so that you respond differently to different timers.

Finally, when you are done with a timer (most likely when the program ends), you can destroy it by calling KillTimer. Here is the declaration to do so:

```
BOOL KillTimer (HWND hWnd, UINT uIDEvent);
```

The first argument is the handle to the window, and the second one is the ID of the timer. You will most likely call this function in the WM_DESTROY message (before the call to PostQuitMessage).

Here is an example of how you might use a timer:

```
case WM_CREATE:
     SetTimer (hWnd, 1, 1000, NULL);
     break;
case WM_TIMER:
     switch (wParam)
```

```
    {
        case 1:
            //do something
            break;
    }
    break;
case WM_DESTROY:
    KillTimer (hWnd, 1);
    PostQuitMessage(0);
    break;
default:
    return (DefWindowProc(hWnd, messg, wParam, lParam));
```

### Painting in the Window

You can use the `WM_PAINT` message to draw things inside your window. You can draw all kinds of things. Of course, you don't have to draw things inside the `WM_PAINT` event. You can do it anywhere.

The `WM_PAINT` event occurs whenever your window needs to be redrawn. This can be because it was resized, because it used to be behind another window, or for any number of reasons.

You can call two main functions in order to draw. You can use either `BeginPaint` or `GetDC`. You use `BeginPaint` when you are drawing in the `WM_PAINT` event, and you use `GetDC` when you are painting anywhere else.

Both these functions create what is called a *device context*. Device contexts are complicated. For now, all you need to know is that they give permission to draw. You can't draw anything without one.

When you are done with a device context, you must release it, with `EndPaint` (if you used `BeginPaint`) or with `ReleaseDC` (if you used `GetDC`).

`BeginPaint` takes two parameters, a handle to the window and a reference to a `PAINTSTRUCT` object. This function fills the `PAINTSTRUCT` object with information about what needs to be repainted. You really don't need to worry about this. You can just repaint the whole window if you want (although this is a bit inefficient). Here is how you call `BeginPaint`:

```
HDC hDC;
PAINTSTRUCT ps;
hDC = BeginPaint(hWnd, &ps);
```

`EndPaint` takes the exact same arguments. Here is how you call it:

```
EndPaint(hWnd, &ps);
```

`GetDC` takes a handle to the window as a parameter. Here is how you call it:

```
HDC hDC;
hDC = GetDC(hWnd);
```

Finally, `ReleaseDC` takes two arguments. One is the handle to the window, and the other is the device context. Here is how you call it:

```
ReleaseDC(hWnd, hDC);
```

This is how the code for the `WM_PAINT` message might look:

```
case WM_PAINT:
      HDC hDC;
      PAINTSTRUCT ps;
      hDC = BeginPaint(hWnd, &ps);
            //draw on the window with hDC
      EndPaint (hWnd, &ps);
      break;
```

This is how painting in other events might look:

```
case WM_OTHER:
      HDC hDC;
      hDC = GetDC(hWnd);
            //draw on the window with hDC
      ReleaseDC(hWnd, hDC);
      break;
```

Now that you have the preparation out of the way, it's time for the fun part. You get to draw things.

The easiest thing to draw is a line. First, you set the starting position. Then you tell Windows where to draw the line. Here is an example:

```
MoveToEx(hDC,20,20,NULL);
LineTo(hDC, 20, 30);
```

The first parameter for these functions is the device context with which to draw. The next two are the `x` (`x` position starts at `0` and increases as you move right on the screen or device context) and `y` (`y` starts at `0` and increases as you move down the screen or device context) positions. The last `NULL` on `MoveToEx` is for storing where you started (don't worry about it for now). The upper-left corner of the window is at position (0,0).

When you call the function `LineTo`, it moves your current position. So, if you call `LineTo` again, it will draw a new line starting where the last one ended.

The next thing you can draw onscreen is a rectangle. You do this by calling the `Rectangle` function. Here is the declaration:

```
BOOL Rectangle (HDC hdc, int x1, int y1, int x2, int y2);
```

`x1` and `y1` denote the position of the upper-left corner, and `x2` and `y2` denote the position of the lower-right corner. Here is an example:

```
Rectangle(hDC, 20, 20, 50, 50);
```

This function call draws a square. You can also draw a filled rectangle that doesn't have an outline with the `FillRect` function. Instead of taking the coordinates of the rectangle as parameters, `FillRect` takes a pointer to a `RECT` structure. A `RECT` structure stores four integer values: `top`, `left`, `right`, and `bottom`. The last parameter is a handle to a `BRUSH` object (which specifies how the rectangle should be filled). Here is an example:

```
FillRect(hDC, &rect, brush);
```

The last thing you can draw is an ellipse with the `Ellipse` function. To draw an ellipse, you provide the coordinates of the rectangle that bound it. Windows automatically figures out how the ellipse should look. The parameters for the `Ellipse` function are actually exactly the same as for the `Rectangle` function. Here is an example:

```
Ellipse (20, 20, 30, 30);
```

This function call creates a circle with a center at (25,25) and a radius of 5.

Well, that's about it for our crash course in drawing. Drawing in Windows is pretty easy once you get used to it.

### Reading Keyboard Input

You can use the `WM_KEYDOWN` message to read keyboard input. The `wParam` parameter of `WndProc` stores the virtual key code, which identifies the key being pressed. Table 12.10 lists the virtual key codes for a standard keyboard.

First, you convert `wParam` to an integer like this:

```
int virtualCode = (int)wParam;
```

**Table 12.10 Virtual Key Codes**

| Constant | Value (hex) | Description |
|---|---|---|
| VK_BACK | 08 | Backspace key |
| VK_TAB | 09 | Tab key |
| VK_RETURN | 0D | Enter key |
| VK_SHIFT | 10 | Shift Key |
| VK_CONTROL | 11 | Ctrl key |
| VK_PAUSE | 13 | Pause key |
| VK_ESCAPE | 1B | Esc key |
| VK_SPACE | 20 | Spacebar |
| VK_PRIOR | 21 | Page Up key |
| VK_NEXT | 22 | Page Down key |
| VK_END | 23 | End key |
| VK_HOME | 24 | Home key |
| VK_LEFT | 25 | Left arrow key |
| VK_UP | 26 | Up arrow key |
| VK_RIGHT | 27 | Right arrow key |
| VK_INSERT | 2D | Insert key |
| VK_DELETE | 2E | Delete key |
| VK_HELP | 2F | Help key |
| No virtual key codes | 30 through 39 | 0 through 9 keys |
| No virtual key codes | 41 through 5A | A through Z keys |
| VK_F1 through VK_F12 | 70 through 7B | F1 through F12 keys |

Then you can use a `switch` statement on `virtualCode` to decide how to respond. That's really about all there is to it.

## Creating the Bouncing Ball Program

In this section, your skills in Windows programming are tested to the extreme! Are you ready? You create a window, process messages, use a timer, and draw to the screen. Your specific task is to create a ball that bounces inside your window. Check out Figure 12.6 to see what it should look like in its finished form.

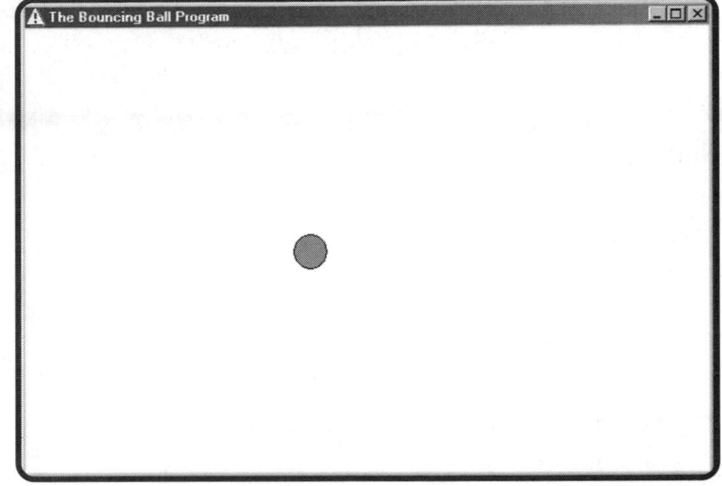


FIGURE 12.6

Here is the completed "Bouncing Ball Program."

Can you program it? Take a look at the following code for one solution.

```
//12.2 - Bouncing Ball Program -Mark Lee -Premier Press
#include <windows.h>

LRESULT CALLBACK WndProc(HWND hWnd, UINT nMsg, WPARAM wParam,
                                          LPARAM lParam);

int WINAPI WinMain(HINSTANCE hInst, HINSTANCE hPreInst,
                         LPSTR lpszCmdLine, int nCmdShow)
{
     HWND          hWnd;
     MSG               msg;
     WNDCLASSEX     wc;

     //fill the WNDCLASSEX object with the appropriate values
     wc.cbSize = sizeof(WNDCLASSEX);
     wc.style = CS_HREDRAW | CS_VREDRAW;
     wc.lpfnWndProc = WndProc;
     wc.cbClsExtra = 0;
     wc.cbWndExtra = 0;
     wc.hInstance = hInst;
     wc.hIcon = LoadIcon(NULL, IDI_EXCLAMATION);
     wc.hCursor = LoadCursor(NULL, IDC_ARROW);
     wc.hbrBackground = (HBRUSH)GetStockObject(WHITE_BRUSH);
     wc.lpszMenuName = NULL;
```

```
    wc.lpszClassName = "BouncingBall";
    wc.hIconSm = LoadIcon(NULL, IDI_EXCLAMATION);

    //register the new class
    RegisterClassEx(&wc);

    //create a window
    hWnd = CreateWindowEx(
        NULL,
        "BouncingBall",
        "The Bouncing Ball Program",
        WS_OVERLAPPEDWINDOW | WS_VISIBLE,
        CW_USEDEFAULT,
        CW_USEDEFAULT,
        CW_USEDEFAULT,
        CW_USEDEFAULT,
        NULL,
        NULL,
        hInst,
        NULL
    );

    //event loop - handle all messages
    while(GetMessage(&msg, NULL, 0, 0))
    {
        TranslateMessage(&msg);
        DispatchMessage(&msg);
    }

    //standard return value
    return (msg.wParam);
}

LRESULT CALLBACK WndProc(HWND hWnd, UINT nMsg, WPARAM wParam,
                                            LPARAM lParam)
{
    //static variables used to keep track of
    //the ball's position
    static int dX = 5, dY = 5; //stores direction
    //stores position
```

```
static int x = 0, y = 0, oldX = 0, oldY = 0;
//device context and brush used for drawing
HDC hDC;
HBRUSH brush;

//find out which message is being sent
switch(nMsg)
{
     case WM_CREATE:
          //create the timer (0.02 seconds)
          SetTimer(hWnd, 1, 20, NULL);
          break;

     case WM_TIMER: //when the timer goes off (only one)
          //get the dc for drawing
          hDC = GetDC(hWnd);
          //use pure white
          brush = (HBRUSH)SelectObject(hDC,
               GetStockObject(WHITE_BRUSH));

          //fill a RECT object with the
          //appropriate values
          RECT temp;
          temp.left = oldX;
          temp.top = oldY;
          temp.right = oldX + 30;
          temp.bottom = oldY + 30;

          //cover the old ellipse
          FillRect(hDC, &temp, brush);
          //get ready to draw the new ellipse
          brush = (HBRUSH)SelectObject(hDC,
               GetStockObject(GRAY_BRUSH));
          //draw it
          Ellipse(hDC, x, y, 30 + x, 30 + y);
          //update the values
          oldX = x;
          oldY = y;
          //prep the new coordinates for next time
          x += dX;
```

```
            y += dY;
            //get the window size and store it in rect
            RECT rect;
            GetClientRect(hWnd, &rect);
            //if the circle is going off the edge then
            //reverse its direction
            if(x + 30 > rect.right || x < 0)
            {
                  dX = -dX;
            }
            if(y + 30 > rect.bottom || y < 0)
            {
                  dY = -dY;
            }
            //put the old brush back
            SelectObject(hDC, brush);
            //release the dc
            ReleaseDC(hWnd, hDC);
            break;

      case WM_DESTROY:
            //destroy the timer
            KillTimer(hWnd, 1);
            //end the program
            PostQuitMessage(0);
            break;

      default:
            //let Windows handle every other message
            return(DefWindowProc(hWnd,
                  nMsg, wParam, lParam));
      }

      return 0;
}
```

## Summary

This chapter is definitely important if you want your programs to be up-to-date. The Windows API has existed for more than a decade and will continue for a long time. You have learned how to write a Windows program, create a program window, respond to messages, create a timer, display graphics, and respond to keyboard input.

If this chapter intrigued you and you want to know more about the Windows API, you might want to check out these books: *Beginning Direct3D Game Programming* by Wolfgang Engel and Amir Geva, *Isometric Game Programming with DirectX 7.0* by Ernie Pazera, and *The Zen of Direct3D Game Programming* by Peter Walsh. Also, you eventually might want to investigate MFC (Microsoft Foundation Classes) to learn about a much more advanced library made by Microsoft. To investigate MSDN and learn more about MFC, go to http://msdn.Microsoft.com/. Then go to the Libraries section, and select Visual Tools and Languages, C/C++ and Visual C++, Visual C and C++ (General), Product Documentation, Visual C++ Programmer's Guide, Adding Program Functionality, Details, MFC Topics (General).

### CHALLENGES

1. **Write a Windows program that displays a circle that changes to different random locations every second.**
2. **Name four messages that can be sent to `WndProc`.**
3. **What are the steps for creating a window?**
4. **Name five virtual key codes from memory.**

# Using DirectX

In this chapter, you work with C++ by using *DirectX,* a library of programming routines by Microsoft. Along the way, you will discover how much fun using DirectX can be. In addition, you can relax knowing that you can create games without worrying about specific hardware. In this chapter, you learn the following:

- Industry-standard game programming techniques
- How to store images in memory
- How to display images onscreen
- How to create composite images

## Understanding the Components of DirectX

The *DirectX SDK* (Software Development Kit) for C++ is on this book's CD-ROM. You must install the program on your computer's hard drive before you start programming. (See Appendix E, "What's on the CD," for installation instructions.) The SDK is slightly different from the version of DirectX that you probably have on your computer. Some of the differences relate to the way errors are presented and how you set adjustments. For example, error messages will look different and be much more detailed, most likely asking you whether you want to debug. You can adjust the DirectX SDK settings in the control panel.

The DirectX SDK includes seven components: *DirectDraw, DirectSound, Direct3D, DirectInput, DirectPlay, DirectSetup,* and *DirectMusic.* As you have probably already guessed, each DirectX component specializes in a particular part of multimedia development.

### Drawing Pictures with DirectDraw

DirectDraw provides direct access to video hardware. You use DirectDraw to store and display sprites, to display the visual component of videos, and generally to do anything that involves displaying onscreen. (*Sprites* are portions of images used to display units onscreen; see a "In the Real World" sidebar, later in this chapter, for more on

**IN THE REAL WORLD**

**Estimates have shown that before the advent of DirectX, games and certain other multimedia applications were not compatible with about 50 percent of the computers being used. DirectX solved this problem by developing a standard interface for developers, which enables you to program without worrying about the hardware an end user might be using. The first version of DirectX was known as the *Game Developers' Kit* or (*GDK*). However, Microsoft soon realized the potential for other multimedia applications and named the second version DirectX 2.0. DirectX still retains its value and is used in almost every game placed on the market, including, for example, "Starcraft" by Blizzard, "Diablo II" by Blizzard, "X-Wing vs. Tie Fighter" by LucasArts, "Age of Empires" by Microsoft, "Baldur's Gate" by Bioware, "WarCraft II" by Blizzard, and "MechWarrior 4" by Microsoft.**

sprites.) You can store the image data in video memory where it can be accessed quickly. Because DirectX follows the principles of object-orientated programming, the entire set of DirectDraw components are encapsulated around the `DirectDraw` object. You then use derived objects to interact with the `DirectDraw` object.



## Making Noise with DirectSound

DirectSound provides direct access to sound hardware. DirectSound enables game or other multimedia developers to utilize standard sound buffers. Developers can then mix these buffers to create multiple channel audio effects. DirectSound also provides support for 3D audio. With 3D audio, you can make sound effects seem like they are coming from many different directions.

## Expanding the World with Direct3D

3D applications are really cool. Direct3D is one of only two industry-standard techniques to create 3D graphics. The other one is *OpenGL* (more commonly referred to as the "Quake Engine"). Figure 13.1 shows the use of Direct3D to create a cool, realistic world in "MechWarrior 4 Vengeance," by Microsoft. Three-dimensional imaging creates triangles and then uses mathematics to predict how the light will bounce off the triangles.

## Responding to Input with DirectInput

DirectInput provides direct access to some of the input devices connected to computers. At this time, there is support for almost any input device including the mouse, keyboard, joystick, and force feedback devices.

### In the Real World

**In a game, each picture that is displayed onscreen is a composite of multiple images. The images that make up the picture are called *sprites*. For example, in "Solitaire" (the card game that comes with Windows), you display each of the cards using an individual sprite. Then you pile the sprites (cards) one on top of the other until you display the final picture. This is the picture you see when you play the game.**

**However, sprites are not limited to games. In corporate Web sites, for example, each image is used and loaded separately to create the entire picture on the Web site. This effect is really evident if you work with a 28.8 modem (that's right—those things of the past that required you to actually dial up in order to get on the Internet).**

FIGURE 13.1

The final level in "MechWarrior 4 Vengeance" produces stunning 3D graphics. *(MechWarrior 4 copyright 2000 Microsoft Corporation)*

## Entertaining the User with DirectMusic

DirectMusic gives programs the capability of directly accessing sound hardware, as does DirectSound. However, DirectMusic differs from DirectSound because it's developed especially for musical files and handles the nuances of music more accurately.

## Installing with DirectSetup

DirectSetup provides an easy way to add the setup for DirectX components to installation files. When combined with AutoRun, a Windows function that directly loads a program from a CD, your professional game programs install smoothly.

## Interacting with DirectPlay

DirectPlay offers support for networking capabilities. Some of the networking protocols supported are TCP/IP, IPX, serial, and modem. TCP/IP is currently the most commonly used networking protocol. DirectPlay makes creating network games easy to do. It handles all the underlying information, such as IP addresses and subnet masks. The ease of networking that DirectPlay enables "nongeeks" to connect in a user-friendly way.

**In the Real World**

In 1999, Microsoft introduced force feedback in its SideWinder joysticks. This was the beginning of mainstream force feedback devices.

Force feedback enables users of games to "feel" the game through the joystick, thereby experiencing games through a third medium. Using a WWII flight simulator, for example, you can see the other plane and hear your machine gun. With force feedback, you can also feel the recoil of the machine gun through your joystick. This is similar to the N64 rumble pack.

Unfortunately, we have seen force feedback only in computer games and simulators, so it's not yet useful in mainstream applications. However, in games and simulations, force feedback is out of this world!

## Setting Up DirectX

You will find the code for DirectX in several header files and a library file. To set up DirectX, you must do two things: Include the header files and include the library files in the project.

First, the only header file required for DirectDraw is `ddraw.h`. Include it as you do all other header files:

```
#include <ddraw.h>
```

Second, include the library files. They are in the library subdirectory of the directory that you installed with the DirectX SDK. Often I include all the library files because the compiler will use only what it needs; you will use only `ddraw.lib`.

You include the library file by clicking the Add Files option under the Project drop-down menu.

Now you are all set up and ready to rock with some cool graphics!

## Examining the DirectDraw Architecture

The DirectDraw architecture consists of multiple components. Each component is an object. Microsoft does not create all these objects; hardware drivers supply some of the information. Luckily, you don't need to know anything about this information (hardware drivers provide information that is specific to the device, telling DirectX how to communicate with the device), other than the fact that it exists and DirectX will handle it for you.

The software provided with your video card abides by the driver of the card's manufacturer (for example, the highly popular Quadra II Pro driver supplied by Nividia). These drivers convey the capabilities of the video card to DirectX.

Figure 13.2 shows the architectural overview of DirectDraw.

To begin with, you have the Windows application, which is the part of the program that you create. Your program interacts with the DirectDraw API (application interface). Remember that each of these components is encapsulated. You must, therefore, use the interface provided in order to make them work.

When you ask DirectDraw to do something, it has two options. First, it will query the video card drivers to see whether the video card contains hardware support. For example, some video cards come with memory and functions to store 32-bit palettes in memory. When the palette is stored in video memory, you can access it much faster than you can if it is stored in RAM.

This direct access to the hardware is called *HAL* (hardware abstraction layer). The video card determines HAL's capabilities, which means that you can't count on the advantages offered by some hardware (such as 32-bit textures). Depending on HAL can limit the number of computers that can use your program. Programs that count on HAL should have their limitations clearly marked on the box.

The second option available to DirectDraw is the use of *HEL* (hardware emulation layer). HEL mimics the hardware abstraction layer by artificially processing with the processor and RAM. HEL acts slower than the hardware abstraction layer because it uses the CPU to emulate video capabilities that are not supported by the underlying hardware.

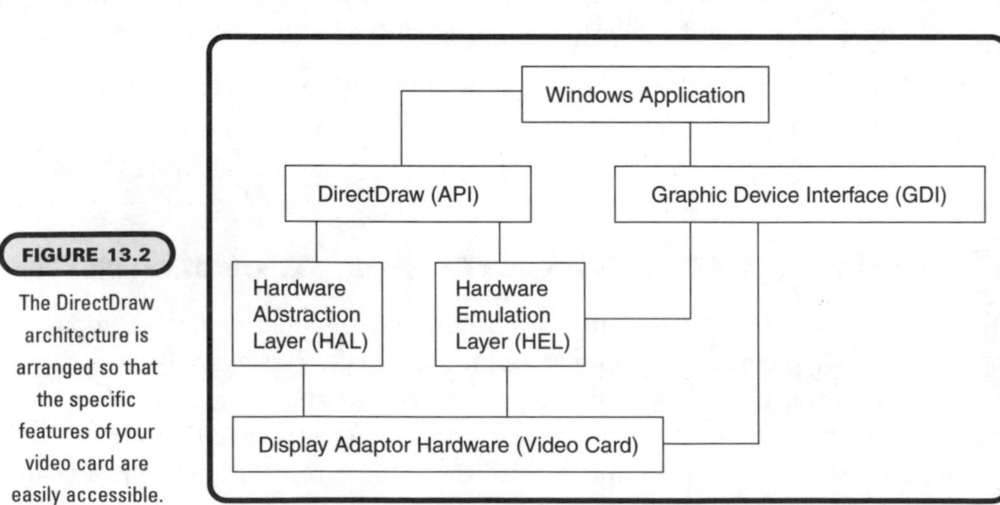


**FIGURE 13.2**

The DirectDraw architecture is arranged so that the specific features of your video card are easily accessible.

## Investigating DirectDraw Interfaces and Objects

After creating a Win32 application, you next create the DirectDraw object. You do so using the DirectDrawCreate method. Here is the prototype for this method:

```
HRESULT DirectDrawCreate(GUID FAR* lpGUID,
     LPDIRECTDRAW FAR* lplpDD, Iunknown FAR* pUnkOuter);
```

The DirectDrawCreate method takes three parameters:

- The first parameter is a pointer to a GUID (globally unique identifier) that tells DirectDraw which display driver the DirectDraw object will use. When this value is set to NULL, DirectDraw uses the default video card.
- The second parameter takes an address to the pointer of a DirectDraw object.
- The third parameter must be set to NULL. It is there to add more functionality in the future.

The function returns an HRESULT object. You can use the HRESULT object to tell whether an operation is successful. If the function is successful, the DirectDraw object returns DD_OK.

Here is a code snippet that can be used to set up a DirectDraw interface:

```
LPDIRECTDRAW lpDD = NULL;
HRESULT hs;
hs= DirectDrawDrawCreate(NULL, &lpDD, NULL);
if(hs != DD_OK)
     return;
```

### Examining the DirectDrawSurface Object

A DirectDrawSurface object represents an area in memory that is used for storing picture information. DirectDrawSurface includes the primary display surface, which represents the picture that is being displayed to the screen. To add functionality to a DirectX program, you must create a surface object. You create a DirectDrawSurface object using the createSurface method.

### Examining the DirectDrawPalette Object

A DirectDrawPallette object stores palette color information for the DirectDraw surfaces. It stores each color using three numbers, one red, one green, and one blue. Some image types store palettes because doing so makes the overall file size smaller. This object enables DirectDraw to use image types that use palettes.

## Examining the DirectDrawClipper Object

A `DirectDrawClipper` object represents rectangular portions of a `DirectDrawSurface` object that can be *blitted* (drawn) onto. You can draw only inside the rectangle. You create the `DirectDrawClipper` using the `CreateClipper` method.

## Examining the DirectDrawVideoPort Object

A `DirectDrawVideoPort` object enables DirectX to access a hardware video port from the CPU or PCI bus. You create a `DirectDrawVideoPort` object using the `QueryInterface` method and using the reference identifier, `IID_IIDVideoPort Container`. (We don't discuss this object here because of its complexity—and it would blow our page count!)

How one program interacts with other programs is called the *cooperative level*. For example, some programs are full-screen and require exclusive use of the video hardware in order to work. Others display in Windows and function well with other Windows programs. Some will not even allow the user to press Ctrl+Alt+Delete to reboot a computer.

To set the cooperative level, you use the `SetCooperativeLevel` function. You should call this function directly after the `DirectDraw` object is set up. The prototype for this function is as follows:

```
HRESULT SetCooperativeLevel (HWND hWnd, DWORD dwFlags);
```

The first parameter takes the window object that the program will be using. (You create this window object in Chapter 12, "Programming with Windows.")

The second parameter is made of flags that specify the mode settings. See Table 13.1 for a list of these flags.

The value returned is of type `HRESULT` and will equal `DD_OK` if the operation was successful.

You will want to create your games so that they have a full-screen window. To do so, you use the `DDSCL_FULLSCREEN` and `DDSCL_EXCLUSIVE` flags.

# Understanding Display Modes

When you set the display mode, you are giving the computer the screen's attributes. These four attributes make up a display mode:

- Width
- Height

- Color depth
- Refresh rate

The width and height specify the number of pixels wide and the number of pixels high for the screen. There should be a 4:3 width/height ratio, reflecting the ratio of standard monitors. This ratio is called the *aspect ratio*.

**Table 13.1 Flags Used to Set the Cooperative Level**

| Flag | Purpose |
|---|---|
| DDSCL_ALLOWMODEX | DDSCL_FULLSCREEN and DDSCL_EXCLUSIVE flags. ModeX is an antiquated game development mode, still available for backward compatibility. |
| DDSCL_ALLOWREBOOT | This flag specifies that users can reboot the computer by pressing the key combination Ctrl+Alt+Delete. |
| DDSCL_CREATEDEVICEWINDOW | This flag gives multi-monitor DirectDraw application support (Windows 98, WinNT 5.0, Windows NT 2000, and Windows ME/XP only). |
| DDSCL_EXCLUSIVE | This flag specifies that the DirectDraw object has exclusive access to the hardware. This must be used with the DDSCL_FULLSCREEN flag because no other applications can use the hardware. |
| DDSCL_FPUSETUP | This flag specifies that the DirectDraw object should be optimized in order to be used with Direct3D. |
| DDSCL_FULLSCREEN | This flag specifies that it's safe to multi-thread the DirectDraw object. We do not cover multi-threading in this book. |
| DDSCL_NORMAL | This flag specifies that the DirectDraw object is not given special privileges and must interact with all other Windows programs. This flag must not be used with the DSCL_ALLOWMODEX, DDSCL_EXCLUSIVE, and DDSCL_FULLSCREEN flags. |
| DDSCL_NOWINDOWCHANGES | This flag specifies that the DirectDraw object not minimize or restore the application's window. |
| DDSCL_SETDEVICEWINDOW | This flag specifies that the window handle given in the first parameter is the handle to the device window. This flag is useful when writing multi-monitor DirectDraw applications. |
| DDSCL_SETFOCUSWINDOW | This flag specifies that the window object given in the first parameter is the handle of the focus window. This flag is useful when writing multi-monitor DirectDraw applications. |

The color depth specifies the number of bits used to store a color. The more bits used to store color, the slower the program operation, but the more colors that can be displayed.

The refresh rate specifies in Hertz (cycles per second) how many times the monitor refreshes the screen. Refresh rates are very hardware-specific, so in most cases, they should be set to zero. Setting a refresh rate to zero means that the hardware can pick the refresh rate.

Setting the display mode was much harder before the advent of DirectX. However, now you can set the display mode in a single function:

```
HRESULT SetDisplayMode (DWORD dwWidth, DWORD dwHeight,
     DWORD dwBPP, DWORD      dwRefreshRate, DWORD dwFlags);
```

The first two parameters specify the width and height. The third parameter specifies the color depth, the fourth parameter specifies the refresh rate, and the fifth parameter specifies the flags.

For example, to set the display mode to a 800 x 600 resolution and a 16-bit color depth (a common game setting), you can use the function as follows:

```
hs = SetDisplayMode (800, 600, 16, 0, 0);
```

The function will return `DD_OK` if successful.

## Exploring Primary Surfaces

You have now set up the `DirectDraw` object for your application. You're not finished, however (which probably doesn't come as a surprise). Now you must give the `DirectDraw` object the resources needed to store what is on the screen. Primary surfaces provide those resources.

Primary surfaces are `DirectDraw` surface objects that use video memory and that can be displayed directly onscreen. Each primary surface must take on the characteristics of the display mode. For example, if your screen resolution is 640 x 480, the primary surfaces must be 640 x 480.

### Using a Front and Back Buffer

You should display graphics onscreen so that you find and eliminate unwanted flickering or image tearing. You can do so by using front and back buffers. Front and back buffers are made up of a primary surface. The front buffer is displayed while the program creates the next frame on the back buffer. Using front and back buffers is called *double buffering*. Essentially, double buffering works by using two primary surfaces and then flipping them. See Figure 13.3 for a diagram of double buffering.

Double buffering works because the `DirectDraw` object has a pointer to the front buffer. When the back buffer is ready to be displayed, DirectDraw can point the pointer to the back buffer. This is known as *flipping the buffers.*

## Creating Surfaces

The first step in creating a surface is to describe the surface you want to create. You do so using the `DDSURFACEDESC2` object, which was designed specifically for this purpose. The `DDSURFACEDESC2` object stores the following information:

- The capabilities of the surface
- The purpose of the surface
- How the surface acts

The `DDSURFACEDESC2` structure acts on a surface just as a `WNDCLASSEX` structure acts on a window class (see Chapter 12 for more on `WNDCLASSEX`). You fill the object with the necessary information and then pass it to a function. Instead of calling `RegisterClassEx` and then `CreateWindowEx` as you do when creating a window, you call `CreateSurface`.

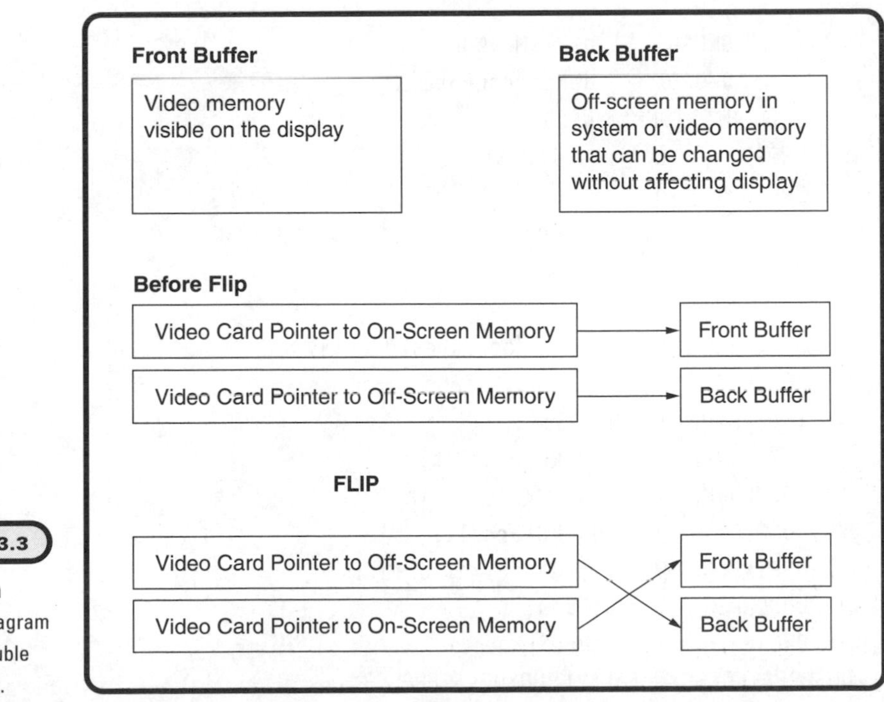


**FIGURE 13.3**

Here is a conceptual diagram of using double buffering.

Finally, after creating the primary surface, you must retrieve the attached back buffer from the primary surface by calling the `GetAttachedSurface` method. After you complete all these steps, you are ready to start drawing with DirectX.

## Filling the Structure

The first step in creating a surface is to fill an object of the `DDSURFACEDESC2` structure with the relevant information about the surface. Take a look at the declaration of this structure:

```
typedef struct _DDSURFACEDESC2 {
     DWORD       dwSize;
     DWORD       dwFlags;
     DWORD       dwHeight;
     DWORD       dwWidth;
     union
     {
          LONG      lPitch;
          DWORD      dwLinearSize;
     } DUMMYUNIONNAMEN(1);
     DWORD       dwBackBufferCount;
     union
     {
          DWORD      dwMipMapCount;
          DWORD      dwRefreshRate;
     } DUMMYUNIONNAMEN(2);
     DWORD       dwAlphaBitDepth;
     DWORD       dwReserved;
     LPVOID       lpSurface;
     union
     {
          DDCOLORKEY      ddckCKDestOverlay;
          DWORD      dwEmptyFaceColor;
     } DUMMYUNIONNAMEN(3);
     DDCOLORKEY      ddckCKDestBlt;
     DDCOLORKEY      ddckCKSrcOverlay;
     DDCOLORKEY      ddckCKSrcBlt;
     DDPIXELFORMAT      ddpfPixelFormat;
     DDSCAPS2      ddsCaps;
     DWORD       dwTextureStage;
} DDSURFACEDESC2, FAR* LPDDSURFACEDESC2;
```

Although this structure might look complicated, you need to know only a select few members within it, which we cover now. First, though, you must create an object from the preceding structure. Here is an example of how to create a DDSURFACEDESC2 object:

```
DDSURFACEDESC2 ddsd;
```

The first member you need to know about is dwSize. This member stores the size of the structure. The size of an object might seem like a strange thing to store, but errors can occur if you forget to fill this member. Filling in the dwSize member is not difficult. You fill it with sizeof(ddsd). Here is how this process might look:

```
ddsd.dwSize = sizeof(ddsd);
```

The next member that you need to focus on is dwFlags. This member specifies the rest of the members that you will use. In this way, DirectX looks only for information that you specify in this member. Table 13.2 lists some of the possible values for this member. You can use the or (|) operator on these values to combine them.

**Table 13.2 Possible Values for dwFlags**

| Value | Description |
|---|---|
| DDSD_ALL | All input members are valid. |
| DDSD_ALPHABITDEPTH | The dwAlphaBitDepth member is valid. |
| DDSD_BACKBUFFERCOUNT | The dwBackBufferCount member is valid. |
| DDSD_CAPS | The ddsCaps member is valid. |
| DDSD_CKDESTBLT | The ddckCKDestBlt member is valid. |
| DDSD_CKDESTOVERLAY | The ddckCKDestOverlay member is valid. |
| DDSD_CKSRCBLT | The ddckCKSrcBlt member is valid. |
| DDSD_CKSRCOVERLAY | The ddckCKSrcOverlay member is valid. |
| DDSD_HEIGHT | The dwHeight member is valid. |
| DDSD_LINEARSIZE | The dwLinearSize member is valid. |
| DDSD_LPSURFACE | The lpSurface member is valid. |
| DDSD_MIPMAPCOUNT | The dwMipMapCount member is valid. |
| DDSD_PITCH | The lPitch member is valid. |
| DDSD_PIXELFORMAT | The ddpfPixelFormat member is valid. |
| DDSD_REFRESHRATE | The dwRefreshRate member is valid. |
| DDSD_TEXTURESTAGE | The dwTextureStage member is valid. |
| DDSD_WIDTH | The dwWidth member is valid. |

At this stage, you need to be concerned about only two of these values: DDSD_CAPS and DDSD_BACKBUFFERCOUNT. Here is how you fill the dwFlags member:

```
ddsd.dwFlags = DDSD_CAPS | DDSD_BACKBUFFERCOUNT;
```

The ddsCaps member is an object of the DDSCAPS2 structure that stores the capabilities of the surface. The only member of ddsCaps that you have to be concerned with is dwCaps. dwCaps is a member of the DDSCAPS2 structure that stores flags representing different capabilities of the structure. Table 13.3 shows some of the values for this member.

**Table 13.3 Possible Surface Capabilities**

| Value | Description |
|---|---|
| DDSCAPS_PRIMARYSURFACE | The surface is a primary surface. |
| DDSCAPS_BACKBUFFER | The surface is a back buffer for a primary surface. |
| DDSCAPS_FLIP | The surface is capable of flipping (more on flipping later in this chapter in the section "Drawing to the Screen"). |
| DDSCAPS_COMPLEX | The surface is part of a complex flipping chain, having more than one surface attached to it. |

To create a primary surface that has an attached back buffer, you must use the DDSCAPS_PRIMARYSURFACE, DDSCAPS_COMPLEX, and DDSCAPS_FLIP values. Here is how this process will look:

```
ddsd.ddsCaps.dwCaps = DDSCAPS_PRIMARYSURFACE |
     DDDCAPS_COMPLEX | DDSCAPS_FLIP;
```

The last member to be filled is dwBackBufferCount. This member stores the number of back buffers attached to this surface. For a normal flipping chain, you will have only one back buffer. Here is how you set this value:

```
ddsd.dwBackBufferCount = 1;
```

That's it. You've filled the DDSURFACEDESC2 structure enough to create a working surface. Take a look at the completed code:

```
DDSURFACEDESC2 ddsd;
ZeroMemory(&ddsd,sizeof(ddsd));
ddsd.dwSize = sizeof(ddsd);
ddsd.dwFlags = DDSD_CAPS | DDSD_BACKBUFFERCOUNT;
ddsd.ddsCaps.dwCaps = DDSCAPS_PRIMARYSURFACE |
```

```
    DDSCAPS_COMPLEX | DDSCAPS_FLIP;
ddsd.dwBackBufferCount = 1;
```

The ZeroMemory function sets all the memory allocated for the ddsd object to 0, which is a good way to initialize objects.

## Creating the Surface

The next step in creating a surface is to actually create it. You do so by calling the CreateSurface method. This method is a member of the DIRECTDRAW7 object. Take a look at the method definition:

```
HRESULT CreateSurface (LPDDSURFACEDESC2 ddsd,
    LPDIRECTDRAWSURFACE7 FAR *lplpDDSurface,
    IUnknown FAR* pUnkOuter);
```

The first parameter is a pointer to the DDSURFACEDESC2 object, the second is a pointer to an LPDIRECTDRAWSURFACE7 object (this pointer will then point to the object), and the third is currently not used and must be set to NULL. So, you first must create an LPDIRECTDRAWSURFACE7 object and then call this function. Here is how this process might look:

```
LPDIRECTDRAWSURFACE7 lpPrimary;
g_pDD->CreateSurface(&ddsd, &lpPrimary, NULL);
```

Here you have an instant surface. CreateSurface returns DD_OK if successful.

## Retrieving the Back Buffer

At this point, you have created the primary surface and the back buffer. The final step is to retrieve a pointer to the back buffer so that you can actually use it. You do so by calling the GetAttachedSurface method, which is a member of the DIRECTDRAWSURFACE7 class. Here is the implementation for this method:

```
HRESULT GetAttachedSurface (LPDDSCAPS2 lpDDSCaps,
    LPDIRECTDRAWSURFACE7 FAR* lplpDDAttachedSurface);
```

The first parameter is a pointer to a DDSCAPS2 object, describing the capabilities of the attached surface. The second parameter is a pointer to a surface (this pointer will then point to the attached surface). To call this method, you must first fill a DDSCAPS2 object with the relevant values. Here is an example:

```
DDSCAPS2 ddsd;
LPDIRECTDRAWSURFACE7 lpBack;
```

```
ZeroMemory(&ddsc,sizeof(ddsc));
ddsc.dwCaps = DDSCAPS_BACKBUFFER;
g_pddsprimary->GetAttachedSurface(&ddsc,&lpBack);
```

You are now ready to draw on the surfaces.

## Drawing to the Screen

In order to draw things to the screen, you must follow a certain procedure. The first step is to prepare the back buffer. You make it an exact representation of how you want the screen to look. Next, you flip the primary surface and the back buffer. Your image displays instantly.

To prepare the back buffer, you usually must call the `Blt` (pronounced "blit") method. You can use the `Blt` method for many different tasks, including copying one surface to another, filling a surface with one color, or drawing an image to part of a surface. Take a look at the prototype for the `Blt` method:

```
HRESULT Blt (LPRECT lpDestRect,
     LPDIRECTDRAWSURFACE7 lpDDSrcSurface, LPRECT lpSrcRect,
     DWORD dwFlags, LPDDBLTFX lpDDBltFX);
```

The first parameter is a pointer to a `RECT` structure that describes what part of the surface on which to blit. If you want to use the entire surface, this parameter can be `NULL`.

`lpDDSrcSurface` is an `LPDIRECTDRAWSURFACE7` object from which you want to blit. If you do not want to blit from another surface, you can set this parameter to `NULL`.

The third parameter describes which part of the source surface from which to blit. You can pass `NULL` if you want to use the entire surface (or if you aren't using a surface).

The fourth parameter describes which members of `lpDDBltFX` you are using and other information about the blit. Table 13.4 lists some of the values that this member can contain.

You can also set this member to `NULL` if you do not need any of these styles.

The fifth parameter is a pointer to a `DDBLTFX` object that contains information about the blit. The `DDBLTFX` structure contains many members. Fortunately, you have to be concerned with only two of them: `dwSize`, `dwFillColor`.

`dwSize` is the size of the object. `dwFillColor` specifies the color with which to fill the surface (if you are filling the surface with a color). Every number corresponds

**Table 13.4 Possible Blit Styles**

| Value | Description |
|---|---|
| DDBLT_COLORFILL | Uses the dwFillColor member of the DDBLTFX structure as the RGB color that fills the destination rectangle on the destination surface. |
| DDBLT_DDFX | Uses the dwDDFX member of the DDBLTFX structure to specify the effects to use for this blit. |
| DDBLT_WAIT | Postpones the DDERR_WASSTILLDRAWING return value if the blitter is busy, and returns as soon as the blit can be set up or another error occurs. |

to a different color. Experiment with different numbers to see the kinds of colors you can get. 0 is black.

Here is an example of how you might blit to the back buffer:

```
DDBLTFX ddbltfx;
ZeroMemory(&ddbltfx,sizeof(ddbltfx));
ddbltfx.dwSize = sizeof(ddbltfx);
ddbltfx.dwFillColor = 2;
lpBackBuffer->Blt(NULL,NULL,NULL, DDBLT_COLORFILL, &ddbltfx);
```

After you prepare the back buffer, you must flip the primary surface and the back buffer. This makes the back buffer the primary surface and the primary surface the back buffer. You do so using the Flip method. Here is the prototype for the Flip method:

```
HRESULT Flip (LPDIRECTDRAWSURFACE7 lpSurfaceOverride,
     DWORD dwFlags);
```

The first parameter specifies a surface in the flipping chain. Set this parameter to NULL if you want to use the normal flipping mechanism (recommended).

The second parameter specifies special options for the flip. Set this to 0 if you do not want any of these special options.

Here is an example of how you might flip the surfaces:

```
lpPrimary->Flip(NULL,0);
```

Displaying your image to the screen is as simple as making one function call.

## Using Bitmaps

You will often find it useful to load the data from an image file onto the screen. This way, you can conveniently draw images ahead of time, store them on a disk, and display them as needed. One very common image file is the bitmap file. A bitmap file is a relatively simple image file and is supported by almost every computer. The extension for a bitmap file is .bmp.

You can load a bitmap onto a surface two ways. One way is to create a temporary surface, copy the bitmap to the surface, and then copy the surface to the other surface. The second way is to load the image into an HBITMAP structure and then copy this image onto the surface.

To use either one of these ways, you must include ddutil.h (which is on the CD-ROM at the back of this book). ddutil.h is a file produced by Microsoft that makes using bitmapping much easier. For the first option, you create the surface, call DDLoadBitmap to load the image, and then blit from one surface to the other. DDLoadBitmap takes four parameters: the DirectDraw object, the name of the image file (including the complete directory), the width of the bitmap, and the height of the bitmap. This function returns the newly created surface. Here is an example of calling this function:

```
lpTempSurface = DDLoadBitmap(g_pDD, "myImage.bmp", 800,600);
```

The second way to load a bitmap onto the screen is to use the Windows LoadImage function and then call DDCopyBitmap to copy the image to the surface. LoadImage takes six parameters. The first must be NULL, the second is the name and directory of the bitmap, the third must be IMAGE_BITMAP, the forth and fifth are the height and width, and the sixth must be LR_LOADFROMFILE | LR_CREATEDIBSECTION. LoadImage returns an HBITMAP object, which represents the image. Here is an example:

```
HBITMAP temp = (HBITMAP)LoadImage(NULL, "myImage.bmp",
      IMAGE_BITMAP, 800,600,
      LR_LOADFROMFILE | LR_CREATEDIBSECTION);
```

Notice that you have to cast the return value to HBITMAP. This is because LoadImage is a function for every type of image, not just bitmaps. Once you have this HBITMAP object, you can call DDCopyBitmap to copy it onto the surface. DDCopyBitmap takes six parameters. The first is the surface to copy to, the second is the HBITMAP object, the third and fourth specify the starting position on the bitmap to copy (you'll usually use 0,0), and the fifth and sixth specify the width and height of the bitmap (from the starting position). Here is an example:

```
DDCopyBitmap(lpBack,temp,0,0,800,600);
```

That's really all it takes to load a bitmap onto the screen. With a little practice, you will get the hang of it.

## Creating the Random Color Program

In this section, you create a program that displays a random color onscreen every three seconds. Can you guess which color will be next? This program tests your new skills using DirectX and provides an example of how to successfully integrate Windows programs with DirectX.

```
//13.1 - Random Color Program - Mark Lee - Premier Press
#include <windows.h>
#include <cstdlib>
#include <ctime>
#include <ddraw.h>

LRESULT CALLBACK WndProc(HWND hWnd, UINT nMsg, WPARAM wParam,
      LPARAM lParam);

LPDIRECTDRAW7 g_pdd; //the DirectDraw object
LPDIRECTDRAWSURFACE7 g_pddsprimary; //the primary surface
LPDIRECTDRAWSURFACE7 g_pddsback; //the back buffer
LPDIRECTDRAWSURFACE7 g_pddsone; //a temporary surface
DDSURFACEDESC2 ddsd; //used to store surface descriptions
DDSCAPS2 ddsc; //stores the capabilities of a surface
//used to temporarily store the result of a function
HRESULT hRet;


int WINAPI WinMain(HINSTANCE hInst, HINSTANCE hPreInst,
      LPSTR lpszCmdLine, int nCmdShow)
{
      HWND hWnd;
      MSG msg;
      WNDCLASSEX wc;

      //fill the WNDCLASSEX structure
      //with the appropriate values
      wc.cbSize = sizeof(WNDCLASSEX);
      wc.style = CS_HREDRAW | CS_VREDRAW;
```

```
    wc.lpfnWndProc = WndProc;
    wc.cbClsExtra = 0;
    wc.cbWndExtra = 0;
    wc.hInstance = hInst;
    wc.hIcon = LoadIcon(NULL, IDI_EXCLAMATION);
    wc.hCursor = LoadCursor(NULL, IDC_ARROW);
    wc.hbrBackground = (HBRUSH)GetStockObject(WHITE_BRUSH);
    wc.lpszMenuName = NULL;
    wc.lpszClassName = "RandomColor";
    wc.hIconSm = LoadIcon(NULL, IDI_EXCLAMATION);

    //register the new class
    RegisterClassEx(&wc);

    //create a window
    hWnd = CreateWindowEx(
          NULL,
          "RandomColor",
          "The Random Color Program",
          WS_VISIBLE,
          CW_USEDEFAULT,
          CW_USEDEFAULT,
          CW_USEDEFAULT,
          CW_USEDEFAULT,
          NULL,
          NULL,
          hInst,
          NULL
    );

    //event loop - handle all messages
    while(GetMessage(&msg, NULL, 0, 0))
    {
          TranslateMessage(&msg);
          DispatchMessage(&msg);
    }

    //standard return value
    return (msg.wParam);
}
```

```
LRESULT CALLBACK WndProc(HWND hWnd, UINT nMsg, WPARAM wParam,
     LPARAM lParam)
{

     //find out which message is being sent
     switch(nMsg)
     {
          case WM_CREATE:
               //create the timer (3 seconds)
               SetTimer(hWnd, 1, 3000, NULL);
               //create the DirectDraw object
               hRet = DirectDrawCreateEx(NULL,
                    (void**)&g_pdd,IID_IDirectDraw7, NULL);
               if(hRet != DD_OK)
                    MessageBox(hWnd,
                         "DirectDrawCreateEx Failed",
                         "Error", NULL);
               //Set the Cooperative Level
               hRet = g_pdd->SetCooperativeLevel(hWnd,
                    DDSCL_FULLSCREEN | DDSCL_EXCLUSIVE);
               if(hRet != DD_OK)
                    MessageBox(hWnd,
                         "SetCooperativeLevel Failed",
                         "Error", NULL);
               //Set the display mode: 800x600
               //with 16 bits per pixel
               hRet = g_pdd->SetDisplayMode(800, 600, 16,0,0);
               if(hRet != DD_OK)
                    MessageBox(hWnd, "SetDisplayMode Failed",
                    "Error", NULL);

               //prepare primary surface info
               ZeroMemory(&ddsd,sizeof(ddsd));
               ddsd.dwSize = sizeof(ddsd);
               ddsd.dwFlags =
                    DDSD_CAPS | DDSD_BACKBUFFERCOUNT;
               ddsd.dwBackBufferCount = 1;
               ddsd.ddsCaps.dwCaps = DDSCAPS_PRIMARYSURFACE |
                    DDSCAPS_FLIP | DDSCAPS_COMPLEX;
```

```
            //create the surface
            hRet = g_pdd->CreateSurface(&ddsd,
                &g_pddsprimary, NULL);
            if (hRet != DD_OK)
                MessageBox(hWnd, "CreateSurface Failed",
                    "Error", NULL);

            //prepare the back buffer info
            ZeroMemory(&ddsc,sizeof(ddsc));
            ddsc.dwCaps = DDSCAPS_BACKBUFFER;

            //get a pointer to the back buffer
            hRet = g_pddsprimary->GetAttachedSurface(&ddsc,
                &g_pddsback);
            srand(time(0));
            break;

        case WM_TIMER: //when the timer goes off (only one)
            DDBLTFX ddbltfx;
            ZeroMemory(&ddbltfx,sizeof(ddbltfx));
            ddbltfx.dwSize = sizeof(ddbltfx);
            ddbltfx.dwFillColor = rand()%16;
            g_pddsback->Blt(NULL,NULL,NULL,
                DDBLT_COLORFILL, &ddbltfx);
            g_pddsprimary->Flip(NULL,0);
            break;

        case WM_DESTROY:
            //destroy the timer
            KillTimer(hWnd, 1);
            //end the program
            PostQuitMessage(0);
            break;

        default:
            //let Windows handle every other message
            return(DefWindowProc(hWnd, nMsg, wParam,
                lParam));
    }

    return 0;
}
```

## Summary

In this chapter, you learned the basics for working with DirectX. With these new skills, you are on your way to creating professional-quality games that meet the highest standards of game producers. But that's not all. You're now also more experienced with using a development library, which is highly important because in your programming career, you will encounter many libraries. So, take heed, noble reader; in Chapter 14, "Creating the Pirate Adventure," you put these skills to the ultimate test.

### CHALLENGES

1. **What are the two ways to load a bitmap onto the screen?**
2. **Name the seven components of DirectX.**
3. **What are the steps for creating a DirectDraw surface?**
4. **What does the primary surface represent?**

# Creating the Pirate Adventure

Last chapter! If you started at the beginning of this book, you've traveled far, good reader. This chapter shows you how to apply all the information in the earlier chapters to design a computer game. In this chapter, you find the code for a basic game engine. You will use DirectX, covered in Chapter 13, "Using DirectX"; Microsoft Windows, covered in Chapter 12, "Programming with Windows"; and much of the C++ programming covered in the rest of this book. It is up to you, as a new programmer, to develop this code, make it your own, and produce a fully functional game. Good luck!

In this chapter, you learn about the following:

- Declaring the global variables of the game engine
- Creating the `Ship` class, which is used to represent a ship
- Creating the game chassis
- Moving the ship across the screen
- Drawing the game to the screen
- Visiting towns within the game

## Getting an Overview of the Game

When you are designing a game, we suggest creating the graphics first because the graphics help give the game shape. (In addition, what's more exciting—six hours of programming looking at a screen with only the words `Insert Title Screen Here` running across it or with the artful title screen you labored to create?) After you have several graphics in place, you can use them to test whether your code works.

You will use 11 screens for the "Pirate Adventure" game: the title screen (which is displayed before the game starts), a screen to display a city when the player enters it, and 9 screens for the game maps.

The basic idea of this game engine is that you follow a map to sail around the Caribbean. The entire map is shown in Figure 14.1. The map will be divided into 9 pieces (9 squares forming a 3 x 3 grid). Each piece will be the size of a computer screen (800 x 600). Each of the 9 pieces will be divided into a separate bitmap (.bmp) file, with names ranging from map1.bmp to map9.bmp, shown respectively in Figures 14.2 through 14.10.

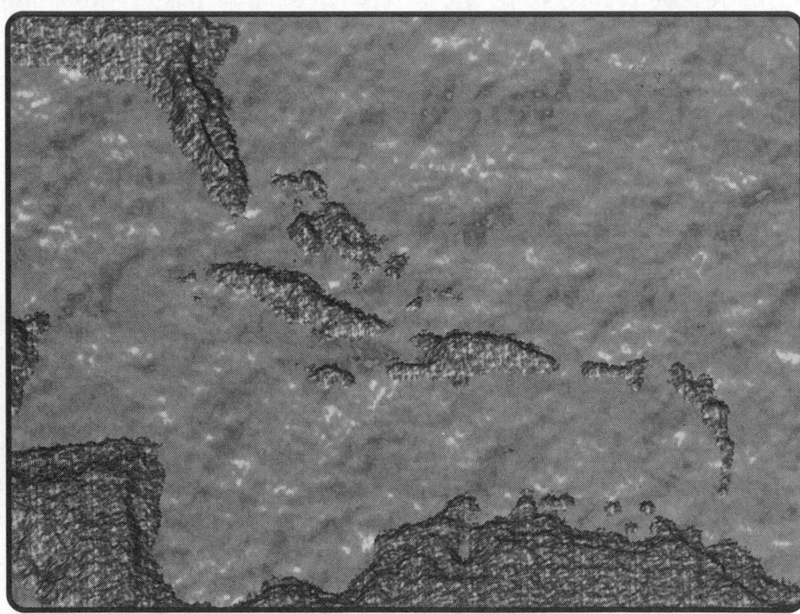

**FIGURE 14.1**

This is the entire playing area of the game. Each screen will be one-ninth the size of this map (map.bmp).

**FIGURE 14.2**

The northwest corner of the map shows the bottom of the United States, including Florida (map1.bmp).

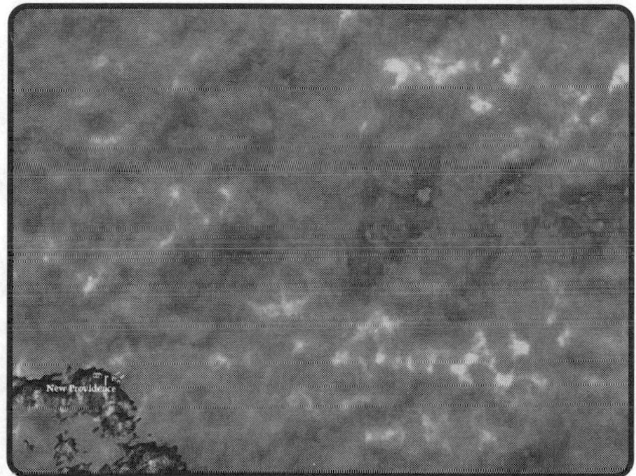


**FIGURE 14.3**

The large sea area with New Providence near the bottom is the upper-center section of the map (map2.bmp).

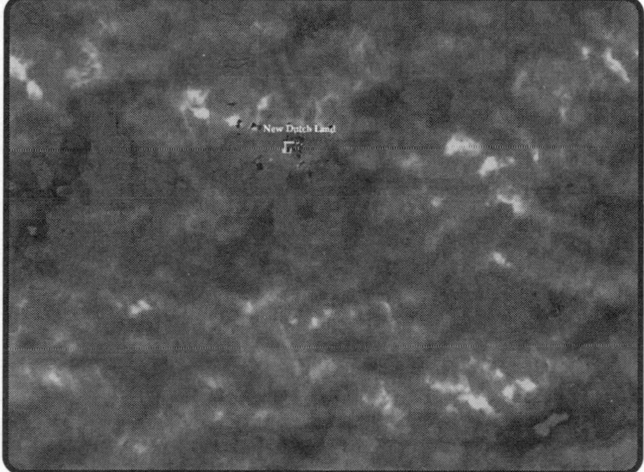


**FIGURE 14.4**

New DutchLand (a fictional city) is isolated in the middle of the upper-right section of the map (map3.bmp).

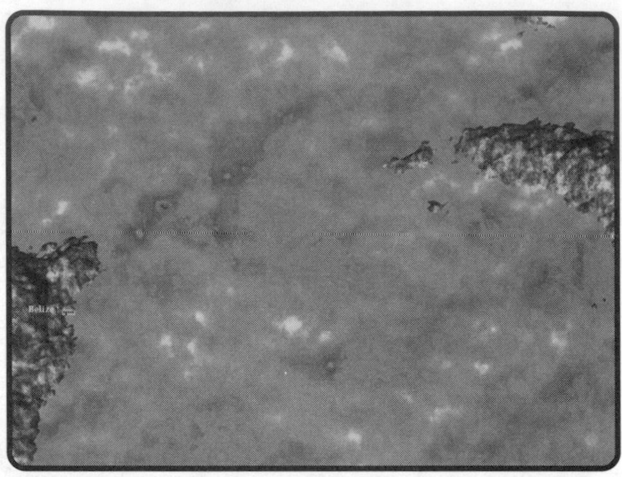


**FIGURE 14.5**

Right below map 1 comes the center-left section of the map, showing Belize (map4.bmp).

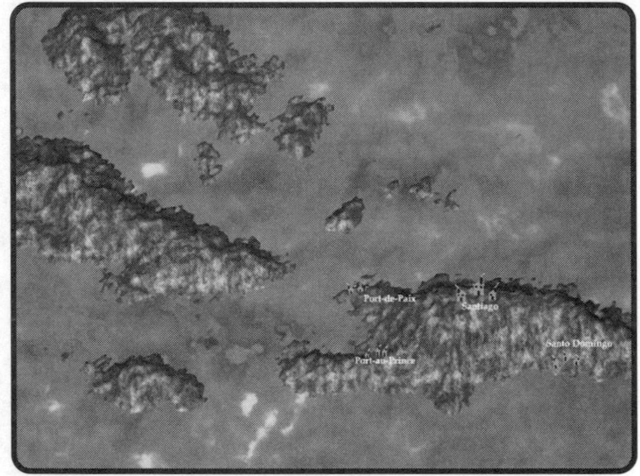


**FIGURE 14.6**

The exact center of the map shows a thriving area, with many cities (map5.bmp).

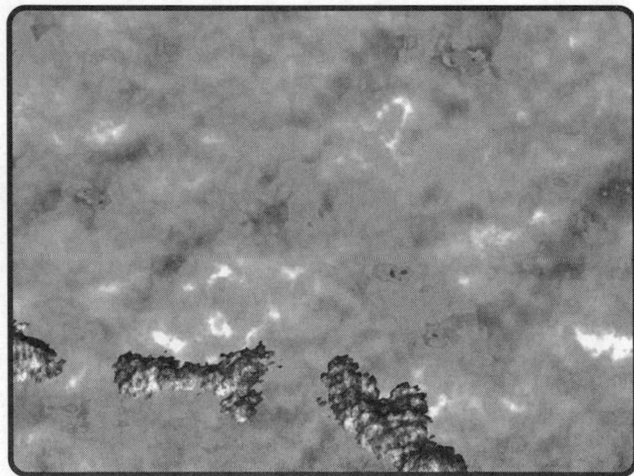

**FIGURE 14.7**

Immediately below map 3 and beside map 5 is the center-right portion of the map (map6.bmp).

FIGURE 14.8

A lot of land but few cities are on the lower-left corner of the map (map7.bmp).

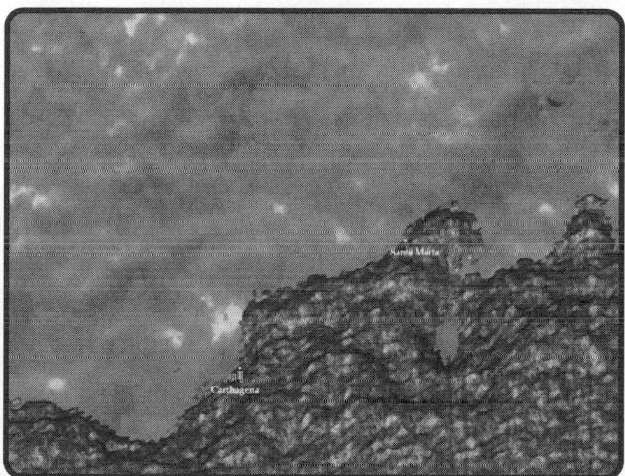


FIGURE 14.9

On the lower-center section of the map, you see Santa Maria and Carthagena (map8.bmp).

FIGURE 14.10

On the lower-right corner of the map, you see Caracas all by itself (map9.bmp).

In order to appear like a professional game, the "Pirate Adventure" needs a title screen. A title screen generally displays the title of the game (on most games, the title screen will also be where you can choose to start a new game). The title screen (Figure 14.11 shows the title screen for the "Pirate Adventure") displays for 5 seconds before the "Pirate Adventure" begins.

Finally, the city screen (see Figure 14.12) displays whenever the player enters a city. This gives some variation to the game. The player isn't always on the same screen for the entire game.

Now that you have the background on the screen images, you can turn your attention to the graphics for the ship. In this game engine, there is only one ship (the player), but you could easily reuse the graphics for the first ship and create a second one on the screen. Because the ship travels in only four directions, you need only four graphics for the ship, one image for each direction. Fortunately, all these images are small enough to fit into one image. When you need one, you just copy that part of the image.

Each picture of the ship is called a *sprite*. (See Figure 14.13 for a picture of the sprites.) Because the ship must sit seamlessly on the map screen, its background needs to be transparent. To accomplish this, you make the sprite background an odd color that will never be used anywhere else. Then you tell DirectX that you want this color to be transparent by setting the color key.

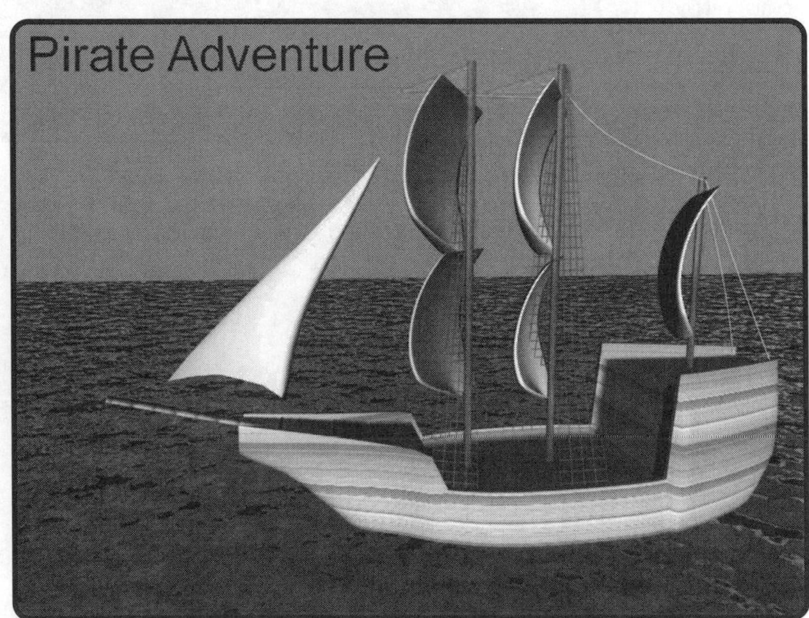


**FIGURE 14.11**

Here is the "Pirate Adventure" game's title screen in all its glory (Screen.bmp).

FIGURE 14.12
This is what the city screen looks like (cityScreen.bmp).

FIGURE 14.13
You use the ship sprites to give the ship a sense of direction (sprites.bmp).

## Programming the Game Engine

Now that you have the graphics all sorted out, it is time to start programming. You can find a listing of the complete game engine beginning in the next section, "Declaring the Globals," and ending in the section "Visiting Towns."

## Declaring the Globals

The first file is globals.h. This file contains some of the declarations of the global variables and functions (see Chapter 4, "Writing Functions," for more on global variables). The functions declared in this file are the Windows functions. The actual implementation of these functions comes later, in globals.cpp (listed after globals.h).

```
//14.1 - globals.h - Mark Lee - Premier Press

#ifndef GLOBALS_H
#define GLOBALS_H //makes sure this file is included only once

#include "Ship.h"

#include <windows.h>

#include "ddutil.h"
#include "drawing.h"
#include "Movement.h"
#include "Towns.h"

//convenient constants
#define OpeningScreen "OpeningScreen.bmp"
#define CityScreen "city.bmp"
#define OpeningTimer 1
#define MainTimer 2

//the global variables
//stores which direction the ship should move
BOOL moveUp, moveDown, moveLeft, moveRight,fire;
Ship* ship; //the player's ship
int currentMapX; //current map on a 3x3 grid (0,1,or2)
int currentMapY; //same
HBITMAP entireMap[3][3];//All of the maps (all 9)

//do the event loop from WinMain
int DoEventLoop();
//create the window
void InitApp(HINSTANCE hInst,int nCmdShow);
//process messages
```

```
LRESULT CALLBACK WndProc( HWND hWnd, UINT messg,
     WPARAM wParam, LPARAM lParam );
#endif

//14.2 - globals.cpp - Mark Lee - Premier Press
#include "globals.h"

int DoEventLoop()
//this function is the event loop from WinMain
{
     MSG msg;

     //event loop - handle all messages
     while(GetMessage(&msg, NULL, 0, 0))
     {
          TranslateMessage(&msg);
          DispatchMessage(&msg);
     }

     //standard return value
     return (msg.wParam);
}

void InitApp(HINSTANCE hInst,int nCmdShow)
//creates the window
{
     HWND           hWnd;
     WNDCLASSEX      wc;

     //fill the WNDCLASSEX structure with
     //the appropriate values
     wc.cbSize = sizeof(WNDCLASSEX);
     wc.style = NULL;
     wc.lpfnWndProc = WndProc;
     wc.cbClsExtra = 0;
     wc.cbWndExtra = 0;
     wc.hInstance = hInst;
     wc.hIcon = LoadIcon(NULL, IDI_APPLICATION);
     wc.hCursor = LoadCursor(NULL, IDC_ARROW);
     wc.hbrBackground = (HBRUSH)GetStockObject(BLACK_BRUSH);
```

```
        wc.lpszMenuName = NULL;
        wc.lpszClassName = "PiratesAdventure";
        wc.hIconSm = LoadIcon(NULL, IDI_APPLICATION);

        //register the new class
        RegisterClassEx(&wc);

        //create a window
        hWnd = CreateWindowEx(
              NULL,
              "PiratesAdventure",
              "Pirates Adventure",
              WS_POPUP,
              0,
              0,
              800,
              600,
              NULL,
              NULL,
              hInst,
              NULL
        );

        //load the maps
        LoadMaps();
}
```

As you can see, DoEventLoop executes the event-handling loop for Windows. This is the same code as shown in Chapter 12.

InitApp creates a window and displays it. The window is a full screen, completely black, and has no title bar. The LoadMaps function from Drawing.h is then called to load the map screens.

The #ifndef, #define, and #endif directives are used to ensure that globals.h is not included twice.

## Creating a Ship Class

The next file is Ship.h. This is the declaration file for the Ship class (see Chapter 5, "Fighting with OOP," for more on creating classes). The actual implementation of this class is in Ship.cpp.

```
//14.3 - Ship.h - Mark Lee - Premier Press
#ifndef SHIP_H
#define SHIP_H

#include "ddraw.h"
class Ship // the Ship class - stores the player's ship
{
      RECT position;//position on 3x3 grid (max is (2399,1799))
      LPDIRECTDRAWSURFACE7 c_pddsone; //holds the sprite bitmap
      int speed; //the speed of the ship
      int direction; //determines which sprite is used
      //stores the location of sprites on
      //the bitmap(4 directions = 4 sprites)
      RECT sprites[4];
public:
      Ship();
      void Move(int direction);//move the ship
      BOOL isCollision(int, int);//test for a collision
      void moveBack(); //move in reverse direction
      RECT GetPosition() {return position;}
      int GetDirection() {return direction;}
      void Draw();//draw the entire game screen

};
#endif
```

```
//14.4 - Ship.cpp - Mark Lee - Premier Press
#include "ddraw.h"
#include "Ship.h"
#include "globals.h"

Ship::Ship()
//construct a ship object
{
      //load the sprites onto the surface
      c_pddsone = DDLoadBitmap(g_pdd, "sprites.bmp",800,600);
      //make the sprite background transparent
      DDSetColorKey(c_pddsone,RGB(0,255,0));
      //calculate and store location of sprites
      for (int i = 0; i<4;i++)
      {
```

```
            sprites[i].top = 0;
            sprites[i].left = i*32;
            sprites[i].bottom = 31;
            sprites[i].right = i*32 + 31;
        }
        //provide a starting position,direction and speed
        position.top = 200;
        position.bottom = 231;
        position.left = 100;
        position.right = 131;
        direction = 3;
        speed = 4;
}

BOOL Ship::isCollision(int moveX, int moveY)
//test for a collision with land based on
//how much the ship will move
{
        //figure out the filename of the current map
        char* temp;
        if (currentMapX == 0 && currentMapY == 0)
            temp = "map1.bmp";
        if (currentMapX == 1 && currentMapY == 0)
            temp = "map2.bmp";
        if (currentMapX == 2 && currentMapY == 0)
            temp = "map3.bmp";
        if (currentMapX == 0 && currentMapY == 1)
            temp = "map4.bmp";
        if (currentMapX == 1 && currentMapY == 1)
            temp = "map5.bmp";
        if (currentMapX == 2 && currentMapY == 1)
            temp = "map6.bmp";
        if (currentMapX == 0 && currentMapY == 2)
            temp = "map7.bmp";
        if (currentMapX == 1 && currentMapY == 2)
            temp = "map8.bmp";
        if (currentMapX == 2 && currentMapY == 2)
            temp = "map9.bmp";
        //use landCollision to test
        return landCollision(position.left%800 + 16 +
            moveX, position.top%600 + 16 + moveY, temp);
}
```

```
void Ship::Move(int dir)
//move the ship
{
    //make this the new direction
    direction = dir;
    int moveX; //how much are we going to move?
    int moveY;
    //calculate where to move based on direction
    switch (direction)
    {
        case 0:
            moveX = speed;
            moveY = 0;
            break;
        case 1:
            moveX = 0;
            moveY = speed;
            break;
        case 2:
            moveX = -speed;
            moveY = 0;
            break;
        case 3:
            moveX = 0;
            moveY = -speed;
            break;
    }

    //if player is moving off of 3x3 map grid then don't move
    if ((position.bottom + moveY > 1799) ||
            (position.top + moveY < 0))
        moveY = 0;
    if ((position.right + moveX > 2399) ||
            (position.left + moveX < 0))
        moveX = 0;
    //if player is running into land then don't move
    if (isCollision(moveX, moveY))
    {
        moveX = 0;
        moveY = 0;
    }
```

```
        //move the ship
        position.top += moveY;
        position.bottom += moveY;
        position.left += moveX;
        position.right += moveX;

        //figure out if we changed maps
        int tempX = position.left/800;
        int tempY = position.top /600;
        //change current map if necessary
        if (tempX != currentMapX || tempY != currentMapY)
        {
                currentMapX = tempX;
                currentMapY = tempY;
        }
}

void Ship::Draw()
//draws the game screen
{
        //location is the position of screen to place the ship
        RECT location = makeRECT(position.left%800,
                position.top%600,
                position.right%800,
                position.bottom%600);
        //prepare the blitting info
        DDBLTFX ddbltfx;
        ZeroMemory(&ddbltfx,sizeof(ddbltfx));
        ddbltfx.dwSize = sizeof(ddbltfx);
        //copy the background map to the screen
        DDCopyBitmap(g_pddsback,
                entireMap[currentMapX][currentMapY],0,0,800,600);
        //write the ship on top,
        //making the sprites background transparent
        g_pddsback->Blt(&location,c_pddsone,&sprites[direction],
                DDBLT_WAIT | DDBLT_KEYSRC,&ddbltfx);
        //display the screen
        g_pddsprimary->Flip(NULL,0);
}
```

```
void Ship::moveBack()
//moves backwards - used for getting out of town's area
{
      int temp;
      if (direction == 0)
            temp = 2;
      if (direction == 1)
            temp = 3;
      if (direction == 2)
            temp = 0;
      if (direction == 3)
            temp = 1;
      this->Move(temp);
}
```

The constructor for this class loads the sprites into a surface, calculates their position on the surface, and initializes the ship to a certain position and direction.

The `isCollision` method figures out which map file the ship is on and passes this and the ship's coordinates (what they will be after moving) to the `landCollision` function, which is in Movement.h.

The `Move` method first calculates how much the ship is going to move, tests for collisions (in which case, it sets the movement to `0`), moves the ship, and calculates whether the ship is on a new map.

The `Draw` method first calculates the position of the ship on the screen (the position stored is the position on the whole 3 x 3 grid), copies the map to the back buffer, and blits the sprite to the back buffer. Then it flips the surface onto the screen.

The `moveBack` method reverses the direction of the ship and then moves it. This function is used to get out of a town's area. Otherwise, the city screen displays again and again.

## Creating the Game Chassis

The next file is Pirates.cpp. This is the main file, from which all other files are included (see Chapter 5 for more on creating a chassis for your classes). In this file, you find `WinMain` and `WndProc`.

```
//14.5 - Pirates.cpp - Mark Lee - Premier Press

#include "globals.h"
```

```
int WINAPI WinMain(/*Win32 entry-point routine */
                            HINSTANCE hInst,
                            HINSTANCE hPreInst,
                            LPSTR lpszCmdLine,
                            int nCmdShow )
{
      //call InitApp to do initialization
      InitApp(hInst, nCmdShow);
      //call DoEventLoop to handle the event loop
      return DoEventLoop();
}
/*callback procedure */
LRESULT CALLBACK WndProc( HWND hWnd, UINT messg,
                                          WPARAM wParam, LPARAM lParam )
//this function processes user input
//and the timers used to run the game
{
      static bool inCity = false; //stores if player is in a city
      switch(messg) //figure out which message is being sent
      {
            case WM_CREATE: //if the window is being created
                  //do DirectX initialization
                  InitializeDirectX(hWnd);
                  CreateTowns();//create all of the Town objects

                  //The title screen is displayed for
                  //5 seconds (5000 milliseconds)
                  //After this we enter the main part of the game
                  //Set the opening screen timer
                  SetTimer(hWnd,OpeningTimer,5000,NULL);
                  //display the opening screen
                  DisplayScreen(OpeningScreen);

                  break;//end case WM_CREATE

            //this event is used to get rid of the mouse
            case WM_SETCURSOR:
                  SetCursor(NULL);//set it to NULL
                  break;//end case WM_SETCURSOR
```

```
case WM_KEYDOWN: //if a key is pressed
     //if player is in city then
     //only the Enter key works
     if (inCity)
     {
          //if the key is Enter then
          //we exit the city screen
          if(wParam == VK_RETURN)
               inCity = false;
          break;
     }
     //handled if city screen,
     //so treat as normal game now
     switch(wParam)//figure out which key it is
     {
          case VK_UP://the up arrow
               //inform everyone else
               //that we should move up
               moveUp = true;
               break;
          case VK_DOWN://the down arrow
               moveDown = true;
               break;
          case VK_LEFT://the left arrow
               moveLeft = true;
               break;
          case VK_RIGHT://the right arrow
               moveRight = true;
               break;
          case VK_SPACE://the space bar
               //we should fire
               //note that firing has
               //not been implemented yet
               fire = true;
               break;

          case VK_ESCAPE://the Esc key
               //end the main timer
               KillTimer(hWnd,MainTimer);
               PostQuitMessage(0);//end the program
```

```
                break;
        }
        break;//end case WM_KEYDOWN

    case WM_KEYUP://if a key is released
        switch(wParam)//figure out which key
        {
            //stop moving if key is released
            case VK_UP:
                moveUp = false;
                break;
            case VK_DOWN:
                moveDown = false;
                break;
            case VK_LEFT:
                moveLeft = false;
                break;
            case VK_RIGHT:
                moveRight = false;
                break;
            case VK_SPACE:
                fire = false;
                break;
        }
        break;//end case WM_KEYUP

    case WM_TIMER://if a timer goes off
        //if player is in city then don't use the timer
        if (inCity)
            break;//exit the WM_TIMER message

        switch(wParam)//find out which timer is going off
        {
            //the timer for the opening screen
            case OpeningTimer:
                //start the main timer
                SetTimer(hWnd,MainTimer,15,NULL);
                //kill the opening screen timer
                KillTimer(hWnd,OpeningTimer);
                //draw the screen for the first time
```

```
                    Draw();
                    break;//exit case OpeningTimer

                //the timer for the main game
                case MainTimer:
                    DoMove();//move ship based on input
                    Redraw();//redraw the screen
                    //if player has entered a city
                    if(isInCity(&ship->GetPosition()))
                    {
                        //inform everyone else
                        inCity = true;
                        //display the city screen
                        DisplayScreen(CityScreen);
                        //put the player outside of city radius
                        ship->moveBack();
                    }
                    break;//end case MainTimer
            }
            break;//end case WM_TIMER

        default: //let Windows handle all other messages
            return( DefWindowProc( hWnd,
                messg, wParam, lParam ) );
    }

    return(0);//default return value
}
```

Notice that the WM_SETCURSOR method makes the mouse invisible. Two timers are used as well, one for the title screen, which is displayed for 5 seconds, and the other for the main game loop. The screen is continually redrawn at something like 20 times per second.

## Making the Ship Move

The next file is Movement.h. This file declares the movement algorithms used for getting the ship to move. The collision detection functions are also in this file. You will find the implementation of all these functions in Movement.cpp.

```
//14.6 - Movement.h - Mark Lee - Premier Press
#ifndef MOVEMENT_H
#define MOVEMENT_H

#include <fstream>
#include "globals.h"

using namespace std;

//constructs a RECT from four integers
RECT makeRECT(int x1, int y1, int x2, int y2);
//returns true if the point (x,y) is in the RECT
BOOL PointInRECT(int x, int y, RECT* rc);
//returns true if the two rect's overlap
BOOL RECTinRECT(RECT* one, RECT* two);
//returns true if the rect is touching any city
BOOL isInCity(RECT* pos);
//returns true if the point (x,y) is land
bool landCollision(int x, int y, string filename);
//Moves the ship based on input
void DoMove();
#endif
```

```
//14.7 - Movement.cpp - Mark Lee - Premier Press
#include "Movement.h"

BOOL PointInRECT(int x, int y, RECT* rc)
//returns true if the point is inside the RECT
{
      //big if statement to test
      if (x < rc->right && x > rc->left &&
            y < rc->bottom && y > rc->top)
            return true;
      //return false if not inside
      return false;
}

BOOL RECTinRECT(RECT* one, RECT* two)
//returns true if two RECTs are inside each other
{
```

```
        //tests if any of the four corners of one are inside two
        if (PointInRECT(one->left, one->top, two))
            return true;
        if (PointInRECT(one->left, one->bottom, two))
            return true;
        if (PointInRECT(one->right, one->top, two))
            return true;
        if (PointInRECT(one->right, one->bottom, two))
            return true;
        //return false if not inside
        return false;
}

BOOL isInCity(RECT* pos)
//returns true if pos is within any town boundaries
{
        for (int i = 0; i <13; i++)
            //go through each tow one by one
            //and test with RECTinRECT
            if (RECTinRECT(pos,&towns[i].position))
                return true;
        return false;
}

bool landCollision(int x, int y, string filename)
//returns true if the point at (x,y) is land
//uses filename as the name of a bitmap file to read from
{
        y = 599 - y;//switch to computer coordinates
        //if (x,y) is offscreen then no collision
        if(x < 0 || y > 599)
            return false;
        if(y < 0 || x > 799)
            return false;
        //perform file io
        ifstream file(filename.c_str(), ios::in|ios::binary);
        //start reading from the correct position
        file.seekg(3 * y * 800 + 3 * x + 54);
        //three bytes for each pixel
        //3 - Red, 2 - Green, 1 - Blue
```

```
	char array[3];
	file.read(array, 3);
	//end file io
	file.close();
	//if green is less than blue then we are in the sea
	if((int)array[1] < (int)array[0])
		return false;
	//otherwise there is a collision
	return true;

}

void DoMove()
//moves the ship based on what keys were pressed
{
	//process which direction to move based on input
	int dir = ship->GetDirection();
	if (moveUp == true)
		dir = 3;
	else if (moveDown == true)
		dir = 1;
	else if (moveLeft == true)
		dir = 2;
	else if (moveRight == true)
		dir = 0;
	else return;
	//actually move the ship
	ship->Move(dir);
}

RECT makeRECT(int x1, int y1, int x2, int y2)
//constructs a RECT from 4 integers
{
	//the theory: code it once, never have to code it again
	RECT temp;
	temp.left = x1;
	temp.top = y1;
	temp.right = x2;
	temp.bottom = y2;
	return temp;
}
```

PointInRECT returns true if the point at (x,y) is inside the RECT structure.

RECTinRECT uses PointInRECT four times to test whether any of the corners of the first RECT are inside the second RECT.

isInCity uses RECTinRECT 13 times to test whether the RECT passed to it (the position of the ship) is inside the area of a city.

landCollision opens the file (from the filename provided) as a bitmap and tests whether the point at (x,y) is more green than blue (that is, whether it is land).

doMove translates the user input into a direction to move and then tells the Ship object to move in that direction.

makeRECT is a utility function that constructs a RECT structure out of four integers.

## Drawing to the Screen

The next file is Drawing.h, which contains all the functions used for drawing to the screen. Almost all the DirectX code is in this file (see Chapter 13 for more on DirectX). You will find the implementations of these functions in Drawing.cpp.

```
//14.8 - Drawing.h - Mark Lee - Premier Press
#ifndef DRAWING_H
#define DRAWING_H

#include "ddraw.h"
#include "globals.h"

LPDIRECTDRAW7 g_pdd; //the DirectDraw object
LPDIRECTDRAWSURFACE7 g_pddsprimary; //the primary surface
LPDIRECTDRAWSURFACE7 g_pddsback; //the back buffer
LPDIRECTDRAWSURFACE7 g_pddsone; //a temporary surface
DDSURFACEDESC2 ddsd; //used to store surface descriptions
DDSCAPS2 ddsc; //stores the capabilities of a surface
//used to temporarily store the result of a function
HRESULT hRet;

//initializes all of the directX surfaces
void InitializeDirectX(HWND hWnd);
//do initial drawing of game screen
void Draw();
//load all of the maps into HBITMAPs
void LoadMaps();
```

```
//draws the game screen after the first time
void Redraw();
//displays the bitmap specified by bmp
void DisplayScreen(char* bmp);
#endif
```

```
//14.9 - Drawing.cpp - Mark Lee - Premier Press
#include "drawing.h"

void DisplayScreen(char* bmp)
//displays the specified bitmap on the screen
{
	//prepare blitting info
	DDBLTFX ddbltfx;
	ZeroMemory(&ddbltfx,sizeof(ddbltfx));
	ddbltfx.dwSize = sizeof(ddbltfx);
	//create a surface from the bitmap
	g_pddsone = DDLoadBitmap(g_pdd,bmp,800,600);
	//blt the surface to the back buffer
	g_pddsback->Blt(NULL,g_pddsone, NULL,NULL,&ddbltfx);
	//display this prepared screen
	g_pddsprimary->Flip(NULL,0);
}

void Redraw()
//function used to draw the screen after the first time
{
	ship->Draw();
}

void LoadMaps()
//create HBITMAPs from all of the map files
{
	//use Win32 LoadImage function
	entireMap[0][0] = (HBITMAP)LoadImage(NULL,
		"map1.bmp",IMAGE_BITMAP, 800,600,
		LR_LOADFROMFILE | LR_CREATEDIBSECTION);
	entireMap[1][0] = (HBITMAP)LoadImage(NULL,
		"map2.bmp",IMAGE_BITMAP, 800,600,
		LR_LOADFROMFILE | LR_CREATEDIBSECTION);
	entireMap[2][0] = (HBITMAP)LoadImage(NULL,
```

```
        "map3.bmp",IMAGE_BITMAP, 800,600,
        LR_LOADFROMFILE | LR_CREATEDIBSECTION);
    entireMap[0][1] = (HBITMAP)LoadImage(NULL,
        "map4.bmp",IMAGE_BITMAP, 800,600,
        LR_LOADFROMFILE | LR_CREATEDIBSECTION);
    entireMap[1][1] = (HBITMAP)LoadImage(NULL,
        "map5.bmp",IMAGE_BITMAP, 800,600,
        LR_LOADFROMFILE | LR_CREATEDIBSECTION);
    entireMap[2][1] = (HBITMAP)LoadImage(NULL,
        "map6.bmp",IMAGE_BITMAP, 800,600,
        LR_LOADFROMFILE | LR_CREATEDIBSECTION);
    entireMap[0][2] = (HBITMAP)LoadImage(NULL,
        "map7.bmp",IMAGE_BITMAP, 800,600,
        LR_LOADFROMFILE | LR_CREATEDIBSECTION);
    entireMap[1][2] = (HBITMAP)LoadImage(NULL,
        "map8.bmp",IMAGE_BITMAP, 800,600,
        LR_LOADFROMFILE | LR_CREATEDIBSECTION);
    entireMap[2][2] = (HBITMAP)LoadImage(NULL,
        "map9.bmp",IMAGE_BITMAP, 800,600,
        LR_LOADFROMFILE | LR_CREATEDIBSECTION);
    //first map is top left corner
    currentMapX = 0;
    currentMapY = 0;
}

void InitializeDirectX(HWND hWnd)
//performs all DirectX initialization
{
    //create the DirectDraw object
    hRet = DirectDrawCreateEx(NULL, (void**)&g_pdd,
        IID_IDirectDraw7, NULL);
    if(hRet != DD_OK)
        MessageBox(hWnd, "DirectDrawCreateEx Failed",
            "Error", NULL);
    //Set the Cooperative Level
    hRet = g_pdd->SetCooperativeLevel(hWnd,
        DDSCL_FULLSCREEN | DDSCL_EXCLUSIVE);
    if(hRet != DD_OK)
        MessageBox(hWnd, "SetCooperativeLevel Failed",
            "Error", NULL);;
```

```
    //Set the display mode: 800x600 with 16 bits per pixel
    hRet = g_pdd->SetDisplayMode(800, 600, 16,0,0);
    if(hRet != DD_OK)
        MessageBox(hWnd, "SetDisplayMode Failed",
            "Error", NULL);;

    //prepare primary surface info
    ZeroMemory(&ddsd,sizeof(ddsd));
    ddsd.dwSize = sizeof(ddsd);
    ddsd.dwFlags = DDSD_CAPS | DDSD_BACKBUFFERCOUNT;
    ddsd.dwBackBufferCount = 1;
    ddsd.ddsCaps.dwCaps = DDSCAPS_PRIMARYSURFACE |
        DDSCAPS_FLIP | DDSCAPS_COMPLEX;

    //create the surface
    hRet = g_pdd->CreateSurface(&ddsd,
        &g_pddsprimary, NULL);
    if (hRet != DD_OK)
        MessageBox(hWnd, "CreateSurface Failed",
            "Error", NULL);

    //prepare the back buffer info
    ZeroMemory(&ddsc,sizeof(ddsc));
    ddsc.dwCaps = DDSCAPS_BACKBUFFER;

    //get a pointer to the back buffer
    hRet = g_pddsprimary->GetAttachedSurface(&ddsc,
        &g_pddsback);

}

void Draw()
//initial drawing function - draws the game screen
{
    //create the ship
    ship = new Ship();
    //draw the ship on top of the map
    ship->Draw();
}
```

DisplayScreen is a function that takes the string passed to it and then creates a surface from the file specified by this string. It then blits this surface onto the back buffer and flips it onto the screen.

Redraw is used when the game screen needs to be redrawn after the first time. It simply tells the ship to draw itself.

LoadMaps uses LoadImage nine times to load all the bitmap files into HBITMAP structures. It then sets the current map as the map at the upper-left corner.

InitializeDirectX does all the DirectX initialization. It creates a primary surface and a back buffer.

You use Draw to draw the game screen for the first time. It creates a ship object and then tells it to draw itself.

## Visiting Towns

The next file is Towns.h; it contains all the functions used to handle the towns. The Town structure, which stores a single town, is also declared here (structures were introduced in Chapter 9, "Using Templates"). You will find the implementation of these functions in Towns.cpp.

```
//14.10 - Towns.h - Mark Lee - Premier Press
#ifndef TOWNS_H
#define TOWNS_H

#include <vector>
#include "Movement.h"

using namespace std;

//stores the info for a Town
struct Town
{
      LPCTSTR name;
      RECT position;
};

vector<Town> towns;//all of the towns (13 of them)

//creates all of the Town objects
void CreateTowns();
```

```
#endif

//14.11 - Towns.cpp - Mark Lee - Premier Press
#include "Towns.h"

void CreateTowns()
//initializes the towns
{
      Town* temp = new Town;//create a new Town
      towns.push_back(*temp);//add it to the vector
      towns[0].name = "New Orleans";//set the name
      //set the position
      towns[0].position = makeRECT(90,100,190,150);
      temp = new Town;
      towns.push_back(*temp);
      towns[1].name = "Tampa";
      towns[1].position = makeRECT(475,310,530,365);
      temp = new Town;
      towns.push_back(*temp);
      towns[2].name = "New Providence";
      towns[2].position = makeRECT(840,460,945,500);
      temp = new Town;
      towns.push_back(*temp);
      towns[3].name = "New Dutch Land";
      towns[3].position = makeRECT(1950,150,2020,200);
      temp = new Town;
      towns.push_back(*temp);
      towns[4].name = "Belize";
      towns[4].position = makeRECT(20,980,90,1010);
      temp = new Town;
      towns.push_back(*temp);
      towns[5].name = "Port-de-Paix";
      towns[5].position = makeRECT(1220,945,1320,990);
      temp = new Town;
      towns.push_back(*temp);
      towns[6].name = "Port-au-Prince";
      towns[6].position = makeRECT(1235,1030,1320,1070);
      temp = new Town;
      towns.push_back(*temp);
      towns[7].name = "Santiago";
```

```
    towns[7].position = makeRECT(1360,940,1435,1000);
    temp = new Town;
    towns.push_back(*temp);
    towns[8].name = "Santo Domingo";
    towns[8].position = makeRECT(1485,1030,1580,1090);
    temp = new Town;
    towns.push_back(*temp);
    towns[9].name = "Prinzapolca";
    towns[9].position = makeRECT(335,1530,460,1595);
    temp = new Town;
    towns.push_back(*temp);
    towns[10].name = "Santa Marta";
    towns[10].position = makeRECT(1285,1490,1370,1525);
    temp = new Town;
    towns.push_back(*temp);
    towns[11].name = "Carthagena";
    towns[11].position = makeRECT(1060,1660,1130,1705);
    temp = new Town;
    towns.push_back(*temp);
    towns[12].name = "Caracas";
    towns[12].position = makeRECT(1960,1510,2010,1545);
    //a total of 13 towns
}
```

Only one function is in this section. `CreateTowns` is a fairly large function that fills the `towns` vector with `Town` objects. Each town knows its own position.

## Congratulations, Reader!

You've made it. Only the best of the best make it this far. You can genuinely call yourself a programmer now. If you are still interested in learning more, we suggest that you check out other sources on topics such as Windows programming or DirectX. For a great book on Windows programming, see *Programming Windows,* Fifth Edition, by Charles Petzold (Microsoft Press). The DirectX help files that are included with the SDK are the best source for DirectX information. If you want to improve your skills with C++, investigate *The C++ Programming Language,* by Bjarne Stroustrup, the creator of C++ (Addison-Wesley). You could even explore other programming languages, such as Java or Visual Basic. The world is yours now!

## Contest

In the "Pirate Adventure" game, you barely scratched the surface of what can be done. For example, the cities don't do anything. If you improve the game and send it to us by December 31, 2001, and your game is the best one we receive, you will be the lucky recipient of a full academic version of CodeWarrior 7!

Just to get you thinking, here are some ideas on how to improve the game:

- Add clouds
- Add other ships and different kinds of ships
- Give the cities functionality
- Add the different nationalities in the Caribbean area
- Create an opening cut scene

E-mail your completed copies of the game to marklee@powersurfr.com or burn the files onto a CD-ROM and send it to us at the following address:

Dirk Henkemans
10714-126 St.
T5M 0N8
Edmonton Alberta Canada

We will post the winning game at http://plaza.powersurfr.com/FireStorm.

# APPENDIX A

# Answers to Chapter Challenges

This appendix provides the answers to the challenges that you find at the end of each chapter. As we say throughout the book, we highly recommend that you try to solve the challenges before looking at the following answers. (Note that in some cases, the answers we provide are only suggested ways to answer the questions.)

## Chapter 1 Answers

1. Create a program that displays a picture of a house that looks like the ASCII house in Figure 1.7.

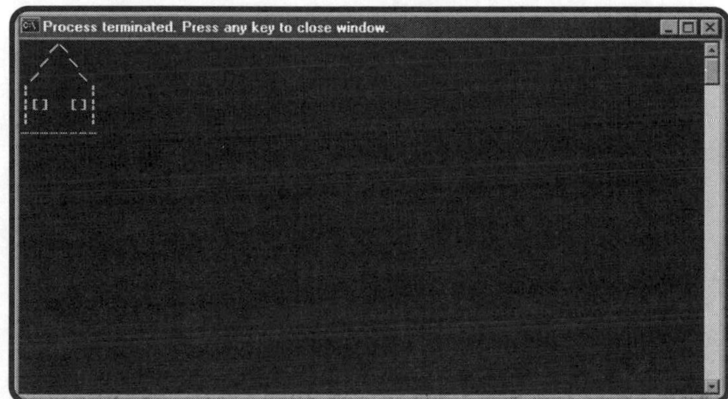


FIGURE 1.7

An ASCII House.

**Answer:**

```
//displays a house
#include <iostream>
using namespace std;

int main( void )
{
      cout << "     /\\     " << endl;
      cout << "   /    \\   " << endl;
      cout << " /        \\ " << endl;
      cout << " |        | " << endl;
      cout << " |[]    []| " << endl;
      cout << " |        | " << endl;
      cout << " -----  " << endl;

      return 0;
}
```

2. What is the output of the following program?

```
#include <iostream>
using namespace std;       //introduces namespace std
int x = 25;
string str2 = "This is a test";

int main( void )
{
      cout<<"Test"<<1<<2<<"3";
      cout<<25 %7<<endl<<str2.c_str();
      return 0;
}
```

**Answer:**

```
Test1234
This is a test
```

Remember that the `cout` statement does not automatically skip a line at the end of a line of code.

3. Write a program that asks users for their names, that greets them, and that asks them for two numbers and then provides the sum.

**Answer:**

```
#include <iostream>
using namespace std;        //introduces namespace std
string name = "";
int integer1;
int integer2;

int main( void )
{
      //asks the user for their name
      cout<< "What is your name? ";
      //the user inputs their name and
      //it's stored in the name variable
      cin>> name;
      //The program says hello and skips a line
      cout<< "Hello " << name << endl;
      cout<< "Enter the first number to add together: ";
      cin>> number1;  //the user inputs the first number
      cout<< "Enter the second number: ";
      cin>> number2;  //the user inputs the second number
      \\displays the sum of the two numbers
      cout<<"the sum is " << (number1 + number2);
      return 0;
}
```

4. What happens when you store 10.3 as a integer? What about 0.6? Can you store −101.8 as an integer?

**Answer:**

C++ will truncate (remove) the decimal, making the numbers 10, 0, and −101.

5. Write code that will multiply some number by 2 if the number is between 1 and 100 (including 1 or 100) and if it is evenly divisible by 3; otherwise, multiply by 3 if it is between 1 and 100 but not divisible by 3; finally, if it isn't between 1 and 100, multiply the number by the number modulus 100. (Hint: Use the nested `if` statement.)

**Answer:**

```
#include <iostream>
using namespace std;

int main( void )
```

```
{
        int number;

        cout << "Enter a number" ;
        cin>> number;
        if (number >= 1 && number <= 100 && (number % 3 == 0))
        {
                number = number * 2;
        }
        else if (number >= 1 && number <= 100
                && !(number % 3 == 0))
        {
                number = number * 3;
        }
        else if (!(number >= 1 && number <= 100))
        {
                number = number * number % 3;
        }

        return 0;
}
```

## Chapter 2 Answers

1. What is the correct variable type for storing the following data:

   The number of books in a bookshelf

   The cost of this book

   The number of people in the world

   The word *Hello*

   **Answer:**

   - The best approach is probably to store the number of books on a bookshelf in an unsigned integer or unsigned short because you cannot have a negative number or partial number of books on a bookshelf.
   - Store the cost of this book as a floating-point data type because a float will enable you to store both dollars and cents.
   - Store the number of people in the world as a float because the float stores numbers in scientific notation, thereby allowing very large numbers.
   - Store the word *Hello* either as a string or as an array of characters.

2. Provide meaningful variable names for the variables in the first challenge.

**Answer:**

Your variable identifiers can differ, but each express the variable's purpose. This allows other programmers, and you, to understand your code. Sample variable identifiers for Challenge 1 are `numOfBooks`, `bookCost`, `numOfPeople`, and `helloString` for each section, respectively.

3. Name two reasons to use constants rather than literals.

**Answer:**

You have to change only one value, where the constant is declared, to change the value in the whole program. Also, using constants makes your code more readable.

4. Write a program that calculates and displays the sizes of all the fundamental types.

**Answer:**

```
//displays the size of fundamental variable types
#include <iostream>
using namespace std;

int main( void )
{
      cout << "Here is the size of the"
            " fundamental variable types.";
      cout << "\nint - " << sizeof(int);
      cout << "\nshort - " << sizeof(short);
      cout << "\nfloat - " << sizeof(float);
      cout << "\ndouble - " << sizeof(double);
      cout << "\nbool - " << sizeof(bool);
      cout << "\nchar - " << sizeof(char);
      cout << "\n And that concludes the experiment :)";

      return 0;
}
```

5. Test what happens if you declare a character as unsigned. Do you get the results you expected? Formulate a reason why or why not.

**Answer:**

The results for the ASCII characters are the same whether the character is signed or unsigned. However, when you attempt to use negative values with the signed character or values above 127, the ASCII table becomes erratic because it is not standardized.

## Chapter 3 Answers

1. Write a conditional statement (an `if` statement) that will assign x/y to x if y doesn't equal 0.

**Answer:**

```
if(y != 0)
{
        x = x/y;
}
```

2. Write a `while` loop that calculates the summative of positive integers from 1 to some number *n* (if you want to check this, the formula is n (n + 1) / 2).

**Answer:**

```
int i = 0;
int sum = 0;
while(i < n)
{
      i++;
      sum += i;
}
```

3. Write a conditional statement that assigns x * y if x is even; otherwise, if x is odd and y doesn't equal 0, assign x to x / y; if neither of the preceding cases is `true`, output to the screen that y is equal to 0.

**Answer:**

```
if(x % 2 == 0)
{
        x = x * y;
}
else if((x % 2) == 1 && y != 0)
{
        x = x / y;
}
```

```
else
{
        cout << "y = 0" << endl;
}
```

## Chapter 4 Answers

1. Write a function, called `multiply`, that multiplies two numbers and returns the result.

   **Answer:**

```
long multiply(int x, int y)
{
      return  (x * y) ;
}
```

2. Change the function you wrote in Challenge 1 so that it remembers how many times you called it.

   **Answer:**

```
int multiply(int x, int y)
{
      static int staticMember;
      staticMember++;
      return  (x * y) ;
}
```

3. What is the difference between a global variable and a static variable? Which is better in which situation and why?

   **Answer:**

   Both the global and static variables exist for the entire program. The difference arises when you look at the two kinds of variable scopes. You can access the global variable from anywhere in the program, whereas you can access the static variable only in the method in which the variable is created. So, a static variable is better when you access the variable only from within the function. You, therefore, use a global variable if you must access the variable in more than one function.

4. Try rewriting "The Cave Adventure Game" so that it does not use functions (an exercise to convince you how useful functions are).

**Answer:**

You can do this; however, trying to conglomerate all your code into one function (called *spaghetti coding)* makes the code confusing. Trust us, the functions are useful!

5. If you actually made it through the last question, buy yourself a Slurpee.

**Answer:**

The five steps to getting a Slurpee are:

1. Earn $1.50.
2. Run to the nearest convenience store.
3. Remember, programmers never walk; drive to the convenience store.
4. Pay for the Slurpee.
5. Enjoy the Slurpee.

# Chapter 5 Answers

1. Create a class that can be used to represent a character in a role-playing game. Store the character's name, class, and race.

**Answer:**

```
class player
{
     string name;
     string charClass;
     string race;

     player(string lname, string lclass, string lrace);
};
//a constructor that uses an intializer list
player::player(string lname, string lclass, string lrace)
    : name(lname), charClass(lclass), race(lrace);
{
}
```

2. Explain the three main principles of OOP.

**Answer:**

The three main principles are

- **Data abstraction.** Hides and protects the data inside the object. The data must then be extracted by using a method.

- **Encapsulation.** Each task is encapsulated into a single object.
- **Polymorphism.** Each object can accomplish its task in any program it's used in. This allows for portability and reusability of code.

3. What is the difference between a class and an object?

**Answer:**

A class is like a template in that a class tells the computer how to create something. Declaring a class essentially is saying to the compiler, "Here is a new data type, and here is what it is capable of doing." A class is similar to a function that hasn't been called. An object is an instance of a class; basically, you are taking the class and creating something from it. An object consumes space in memory, but a class does not.

4. If you have a choice between declaring something public, private, global, or local without loss of functionality, which scope should you pick?

**Answer:**

Select local because it protects the data in a smaller scope more than any of the other scopes do. This follows the OOP principle of Data Abstraction.

5. What attributes present in constructors and destructors are not present in other functions?

**Answer:**

- Neither the constructor nor the destructor can return values.
- The destructor cannot have parameters.
- The destructor is the only function to start with a tilde.
- Both the constructor and destructor have the same name as the object.

## Chapter 6 Answers

1. What is the size of the string `"Hello World"`? What is the length of this array named `s`?

```
char s[] = "Hello World";
```

**Answer:**

The size of the string `"Hello World"` is 12 bytes. This is because each of the alpha characters requires 1 byte, plus one space and the terminating character at the end of the string, resulting in an array length of 12. Remember, though, that the array indexes extend only from 0 to 11.

2. List five reasons to use pointers.

**Answer:**

Possible uses include

- Pointers give you access to specific indexes in an array.
- Pointers can enable you to pass a reference to a data value, instead of passing the data itself.
- Pointers are the basis for using dynamic memory.
- Pointers are the basis for binary file access.
- They are the basis for iterators.
- Pointers are fun!

3. What are the problems with the "Tic Tac Toe" game at the end of the chapter? How can you improve the game?

**Answer:**

The interface is rather awkward. Entering a row and column number (0–2) requires knowing that the numbering starts at 0. You can improve it by labeling the rows and columns.

Also, you can add a computer opponent. The computer opponent *AI* (artificial intelligence) will have to check first to see whether it can get three Xs or Os in a row, then check to see whether the opponent can receive three in a row, and finally try to set itself up for three in a row.

4. List three reasons to use dynamic memory.

**Answer:**

- You can create an array of arbitrary length.
- Dynamic memory is more plentiful than system memory. The system memory is assigned to the program by the operating system, whereas the program "borrows" dynamic memory from big blocks of free memory.
- The program can decide when to gain or release the memory.

## Chapter 7 Answers

1. Explain why someone would want to use a namespace.

**Answer:**

You can use namespaces to divide a large scope into two smaller ones. This enables programmers using the code to avoid naming conflicts.

2. What is the advantage of an unnamed namespace over a named namespace?

   **Answer:**

   An unnamed namespace automatically has a unique identifier, whereas a named namespace could conflict with another named namespace identifier.

3. What are the two ways that you can gain explicit access to a namespace and how do they differ?

   **Answer:**

   The first way is to use the `using` declaration. The `using` declaration declares that you are going to use a particular member of a namespace's subscope. As a result, the need for explicit scope qualification is eliminated when accessing that member.

   The second way is to use the `using` directive. The `using` directive declares that you are going to use all the members of a particular namespace. The `using` directive works like the `using` declaration, except that it applies to all the members of that namespace. Once you've used the `using` directive, you no longer have to qualify any of the members of that namespace in the rest of the program.

4. Looking at the code that follows, how do you call the `breathFire()` function from each of the following places?

   a. From the global namespace

   b. From inside the `dragon` namespace

   c. From inside another namespace

```
namespace dragon
{
      void breathFire() {cout<< "The dragon breaths fire \n"; }
}
using dragon::breathFire();
```

   **Answer:**

   a. `breathFire();`

   b. `breathFire();`

   c. `breathFire();`

## Chapter 8 Answers

1. Create a weapon hierarchy, with at least four weapons being derived from a single parent class. What kind of data members should each contain? What about methods?

   **Answer:**

   A possible weapon hierarchy can use a weapon class as its base class and have specific weapons classes derive from this class. Examples include a sword, a dagger, and a bow. Each class should then have several class-specific methods that highlight the weapon's capabilities.

2. Give an example of a situation in which multiple inheritance might be useful. Is it easier to program with single inheritance than with multiple inheritance?

   **Answer:**

   Any class that needs the properties of two base classes should use multiple inheritance. For example, a `tank` class can be derived from both the `weapon` class and the `vehicle` class.

3. When would you use protected and private inheritance?

   **Answer:**

   If you are deriving from a class for the implementation rather than the interface of your class, you make the inheritance private or protected so that the implementation stays hidden.

4. Design and fully implement an abstract `Shape` class. What should be included? What should be left to the derived classes?

   **Answer:**

   Leave everything to the derived classes. The abstract class should have only an object interface. Here is an example of how a `Shape` class might look:

```
class Shape
{
      //draws the shape onto the screen.
      virtual void Draw() = 0;
};
```

## Chapter 9 Answers

1. Create a vector that stores a set of vectors that each store a set of integers.

   **Answer:**

```
typedef vector<int> Vi
vector<Vi> vvi;
```

2. Create a template class called `store` that stores an array of `T` (where `T` is the template parameter).

   **Answer:**

```
template<class T> Store
{
     T array[5];
};
```

3. Create an iterator, called `random_iterator`, that uses another iterator to iterate through a container in random order.

   **Answer:**

```
template<class Iter> class random_iterator :
public iterator<iterator_traits<Iter>::iterator_category,
iterator_traits<Iter>::value_type,
iterator_traits<Iter>::difference_type,
iterator_traits<Iter>::pointer,
iterator_traits<Iter>::reference> {

protected:
     //used to internally iterate randomly
     //with a normal iterator
     Iter current;
     int size;
public:
     //give the iterator type a standard name
     typedef Iter iterator_type;

     //default constructor
     random_iterator() : current() {srand(time(0));}
     //constructor from a normal iterator
     random_iterator(Iter x, int y) : current(x), size(y) {}
     //construct from another random_iterator
```

```
        template<class U> random_iterator
             (const random_iterator<U>& x) : current(x.base()) {}

        //return the normal iterator that this class uses
        Iter base() const {return current;}

        reference operator* () const { Iter tmp = current;
             return *--tmp;} //dereferencing
        pointer operator-> () const; //access member operator
        reference operator[] (difference_type n) const;

        random_iterator& operator++ () {return
             current[rand()%(size + 1)] } // (random)
        random_iterator& operator-- () { return
             current[rand()%(size + 1)];} // (random)

        random_iterator operator+ (difference_type n) const;
        random_iterator operator+= (difference_type n);
        random_iterator operator- (difference_type n) const;
        random_iterator operator -= (difference_type n);
};
```

4. Name three places where you can get quick information about the components of the standard library (not including this book).

   **Answer:**

   - The source files
   - http://www.cplusplus.com
   - Your compiler's help files

## Chapter 10 Answers

1. Create a program to write the following two lines of text to a file called Question1.txt:

   ```
   Programming is fun.
   I love programming.
   ```

   **Answer:**

   ```
   #include <fstream.h>

   int main () {
   ```

```
    //opens the file
    ofstream file("Question1.txt");

    //makes sure the file is open
    if (file.is_open())
    {
        //writes two lines to the file
        file << "Programming is fun.\n";
        file << "I love programming.\n";

        //closes the file
        file.close();
    }
    return 0;
}
```

2. What method can you use to test whether a file has reached its end? What method can you use to test whether a file has an error? What method can you use to test whether a file has reached its end *and* has an error?

**Answer:**

- `eof()` is used to test whether a stream has reached the end of a file.
- `fail()` and `bad()` can be used to test whether a file stream has an error.
- `good()` can be used to test both.

3. What is the result when the letter A is bit-shifted to the left three places (<<3)? What is the result when the letter A is bit-shifted to the right two places (>>2)?

**Answer:**

Without any bit shifting, A is 01000001 (or 65). When shifted left three places, A becomes 00001000, and when shifted right two places, A becomes 00010000.

4. Explain why the encryption program needs to be run a second time in order to decrypt the file placed into the program.

**Answer:**

When the program is originally encrypted, the program is simply switching the first and last 4 bits in every byte. When they are switched again, you end up with every byte returning to normal, producing the original file.

## Chapter 11 Answers

1. What does the keyword `try` do?

   **Answer:**

   Use `try` to tell the computer that a section of code might throw an exception. If you use a `try` statement, you can catch the exception.

2. What is the purpose of an exception hierarchy?

   **Answer:**

   Having numerous different exceptions can make exception handling unmanageable, but having a few generalized ones is not always optimal. With an exception hierarchy, you can choose exactly how detailed you need to make your exception catches.

3. How can you design your programs so that they will not crash?

   **Answer:**

   You will never be able to create programs that will never crash. However, designing your program carefully, using exception handling, and doing a good job with debugging will definitely help in this regard.

4. What is the definition of an exception?

   **Answer:**

   An exception is a non-routine circumstance that a section of code can't handle.

5. At what point in your program's development should you use assertions?

   **Answer:**

   You should use assertions throughout your program's development, but you should remove them when the program is released to the public.

## Chapter 12 Answers

1. Write a Windows program that displays a circle that changes to different random locations every second.

   **Answer:**

```
#include <windows.h>
#include <cstdlib>
#include <ctime>
using namespace std;
```

```
LRESULT CALLBACK WndProc(HWND hWnd, UINT nMsg, WPARAM wParam,
                                        LPARAM lParam);

int WINAPI WinMain(HINSTANCE hInst, HINSTANCE hPreInst,
                         LPSTR lpszCmdLine, int nCmdShow)
{
     HWND           hWnd;
     MSG                 msg;
     WNDCLASSEX     wc;

     //fill the WNDCLASSEX structure
     //with the appropriate values
     wc.cbSize = sizeof(WNDCLASSEX);
     wc.style = CS_HREDRAW | CS_VREDRAW;
     wc.lpfnWndProc = WndProc;
     wc.cbClsExtra = 0;
     wc.cbWndExtra = 0;
     wc.hInstance = hInst;
     wc.hIcon = LoadIcon(NULL, IDI_EXCLAMATION);
     wc.hCursor = LoadCursor(NULL, IDC_ARROW);
     wc.hbrBackground = (HBRUSH)GetStockObject(WHITE_BRUSH);
     wc.lpszMenuName = NULL;
     wc.lpszClassName = "RandomBall";
     wc.hIconSm = LoadIcon(NULL, IDI_EXCLAMATION);

     //register the new class
     RegisterClassEx(&wc);

     //create a window
     hWnd = CreateWindowEx(
          NULL,
          "RandomBall",
          "The Random Ball Program",
          WS_OVERLAPPEDWINDOW | WS_VISIBLE,
          50,
          50,
          600,
          600,
          NULL,
          NULL,
          hInst,
          NULL
```

```
	);

	//event loop - handle all messages
	while(GetMessage(&msg, NULL, 0, 0))
	{
		TranslateMessage(&msg);
		DispatchMessage(&msg);
	}

	//standard return value
	return (msg.wParam);
}

LRESULT CALLBACK WndProc(HWND hWnd, UINT nMsg, WPARAM wParam,
                                        LPARAM lParam)
{
	//static variables used to keep
	//track of the balls position
	static int oldX, oldY;

	//device context and brush used for drawing
	HDC hDC;
	HBRUSH brush;

	//find out which message is being sent
	switch(nMsg)
	{
		case WM_CREATE:
			//create the timer (1 second)
			SetTimer(hWnd, 1, 1000, NULL);
	srand(time(0));
			break;

		case WM_TIMER: //when the timer goes off (only one)
			//get the dc for drawing
			hDC = GetDC(hWnd);
			//use pure white
			brush = (HBRUSH)SelectObject(hDC,
				GetStockObject(WHITE_BRUSH));

			//fill a RECT object
			//with the appropriate values
```

```
                RECT temp;
                temp.left = rand()%600;
                temp.top = rand()%600;
                temp.right = temp.left + 30;
                temp.bottom = temp.top + 30;
                RECT temp1 = {oldX,oldY,oldX+30,oldY+30};

                //cover the old ellipse
                FillRect(hDC, &temp1, brush);
                //get ready to draw the new ellipse
                brush = (HBRUSH)SelectObject(hDC,
                     GetStockObject(GRAY_BRUSH));
                //draw it
                Ellipse(hDC, temp.left, temp.top,
                     temp.right, temp.bottom);

                //put the old brush back
                SelectObject(hDC, brush);
                //release the dc
                ReleaseDC(hWnd, hDC);
                break;
case WM_DESTROY:
                //destroy the timer
                KillTimer(hWnd, 1);
                //end the program
                PostQuitMessage(0);
                break;

           default:
                //let Windows handle every other message
                return(DefWindowProc(hWnd, nMsg,
                     wParam, lParam));
      }

      return 0;
}
```

2. Name four messages that can be sent to WndProc.

**Answer:**

WM_PAINT, WM_CREATE, WM_DESTROY, and WM_TIMER.

**3.** What are the steps for creating a window?

**Answer:**

1. Fill a WNDCLASSEX object.
2. Register the new window class.
3. Create the window.
4. Display the window.

**4.** Name five virtual key codes from memory.

**Answer:**

VK_SHIFT, VK_RETURN, VK_UP, VK_LEFT, and VK_RIGHT.

## Chapter 13 Answers

**1.** What are the two ways to load a bitmap onto the screen?

**Answer:**

You can create a temporary surface with DDLoadBitmap and then blit the temporary surface onto the other one, *or* you can create a handle to the bitmap with the LoadImage function and then copy the bitmap onto the surface with the DDCopyBitmap function.

**2.** Name the seven components of DirectX.

**Answer:**

DirectDraw, DirectSound, Direct3D, DirectInput, DirectMusic, DirectSetup, and DirectPlay.

**3.** What are the steps for creating a DirectDraw surface?

**Answer:**

1. Fill a DDSURFACEDESC2 object with the relevant information about the surface.
2. Call the method CreateSurface to create the surface.
3. Call the method GetAttachedSurface to retrieve the back buffer.

**4.** What does the primary surface represent?

**Answer:**

The primary surface represents the screen.

# Using the Octal, Hexadecimal, Binary, and Decimal Systems

To most people, the standard number system is the *decimal system* (also called *base-10*). All numbers in the decimal number system are based on exponents of 10. Each digit holds 10 possibilities (1, 2, 3, 4, 5, 6, 7, 8, 9, or 0). Based on theories of permutations, if you have two digits in the decimal system, you can have 100 different values (1 to 99 and 0). This principle is behind all numeric systems.

In the *binary number system* (also called *base-2*), if you have two binary digits, you have four possibilities, as follows (equivalent values appear in parentheses): 00 (0), 01 (1), 10 (2), and 11 (3).

The *hexadecimal number system* (also called *hex* and *base-16*) is useful in computers (and, so, to programmers). Each digit has 16 possibilities (0–9 and A–F). The decimal number system has only 10 unique digits, so to represent 16 unique digits, the first five letters of the alphabet are used. A represents 10, B represents 11, C represents 12, D represents 13, E represents 14, and F represents 15. Hex numbers are written with *0x* prefixing the number; for example, 0x3E1 is a hexadecimal number.

*Octal* is a *base-8* number system, which is also useful in computers. Each digit has eight possibilities (0–7). Octal is represented with an *x* prefixing the number—for example, x95.

## Converting to Decimal

Don't be intimidated by number systems other than the decimal system. All your old, familiar numbers are still there; other systems just represent them differently. So, how exactly do you convert a number in other systems to a number in the decimal system? It's easy. Take the first digit (the one on the far right) and multiply it by *n* (the base of the system) raised to digit number −1. That is, the value of the first digit is multiplied by n^0, the second by n^1, the third by n^2, and so on. Then you add all the resulting numbers.

As an example, convert the hexadecimal number 0x3E1. Remember that the 0x is just telling you that the numeric representation is in hexadecimal and does not actually contribute to the number. Also, remember that E is the same thing as 14 in the hexadecimal system.

1 x 16^0 = 1

E x 16^1 = 224

+3 x 16^2 = 768

Then you add them all together to get the resulting decimal number, 993.

## Converting from Decimal

The process for converting from the decimal system to a base *n* system is slightly harder. First, take a number and divide it by the base raised to the digit number. That is, the first column is 1, and the second is 2, and so on. Then subtract the remainder from the original number. To find the value of the digit in the column, divide the remainder by the base raised to the power of 1 less the digit number. Although this concept might seem confusing, it is not too difficult. For example, convert 993 back to hexadecimal:

**Column number 1:**

993 / 16^1 = 62 Remainder: 1

Hexadecimal digit = 1 / 16^0 = 1

Hexadecimal number so far: 1

993 – 1 = 992

**Column number 2:**

992 / 16^2 = 3 Remainder: 224

Hexadecimal digit = 224/16^1 = 14 (E)

Hexadecimal number so far: E1

992 – 224 = 768

**Column number 3:**

768 / 16^3 = 0 Remainder: 768

Hexadecimal digit = 768/16^2 = 3

Hexadecimal number so far: 3E1

768 – 768 = 0

You're finished! 0x3E1 is the hexadecimal number.

# Using the Standard ASCII Table

In the world of computers, every character has a corresponding number. The numbers provide a way for a computer to represent the characters in memory (because computers work only with numbers). Each character can be assigned 256 values, but only 128 of these values are standardized.

Table C.1 lists the 128 standard character values. The corresponding numeric value is listed in decimal (base 10), octal (base 8), hexadecimal (base 16), and binary (base 2). See Appendix B, "Using the Octal, Hexadecimal, Binary, and Decimal Systems," for an explanation of the different number systems. You can assign any of the numeric values to a `char`. For example, assigning `65` to a `char` is the same as assigning `'A'`.

**Table C.1 The Standard ASCII Table**

| Decimal | Octal | Hexadecimal | Binary | Value |
|---|---|---|---|---|
| 000 | 000 | 000 | 00000000 | NUL (Null character) |
| 001 | 001 | 001 | 00000001 | SOH (start of header) |
| 002 | 002 | 002 | 00000010 | STX (start of text) |
| 003 | 003 | 003 | 00000011 | ETX (end of text) |
| 004 | 004 | 004 | 00000100 | EOT (end of transmission) |
| 005 | 005 | 005 | 00000101 | ENQ (enquiry) |
| 006 | 006 | 006 | 00000110 | ACK (acknowledgment) |

## Table C.1 The Standard ASCII Table (continued)

| Decimal | Octal | Hexadecimal | Binary | Value |
|---|---|---|---|---|
| 007 | 007 | 007 | 00000111 | BEL (bell) |
| 008 | 010 | 008 | 00001000 | BS (backspace) |
| 009 | 011 | 009 | 00001001 | HT (horizontal tab) |
| 010 | 012 | 00A | 00001010 | LF (line feed) |
| 011 | 013 | 00B | 00001011 | VT (vertical tab) |
| 012 | 014 | 00C | 00001100 | FF (form feed) |
| 013 | 015 | 00D | 00001101 | CR (carriage return) |
| 014 | 016 | 00E | 00001110 | SO (serial in) (shift out) |
| 015 | 017 | 00F | 00001111 | SI (serial out) (shift out) |
| 016 | 020 | 010 | 00010000 | DLE (data link escape) |
| 017 | 021 | 011 | 00010001 | DC1 (XON) (device control 1) |
| 018 | 022 | 012 | 00010010 | DC2 (device control 2) |
| 019 | 023 | 013 | 00010011 | DC3 (XOFF) (device control 3) |
| 020 | 024 | 014 | 00010100 | DC4 (device control 4) |
| 021 | 025 | 015 | 00010101 | NAK (negative acknowledgment) |
| 022 | 026 | 016 | 00010110 | SYN (synchronous idle) |
| 023 | 027 | 017 | 00010111 | ETB (end of transmission block) |
| 024 | 030 | 018 | 00011000 | CAN (cancel) |
| 025 | 031 | 019 | 00011001 | EM (end of medium) |
| 026 | 032 | 01A | 00011010 | SUB (substitute) |
| 027 | 033 | 01B | 00011011 | ESC (escape) |
| 028 | 034 | 01C | 00011100 | FS (file separator) |
| 029 | 035 | 01D | 00011101 | GS (group separator) |
| 030 | 036 | 01E | 00011110 | RS (request to send) (record separator) |
| 031 | 037 | 01F | 00011111 | US (unit separator) |
| 032 | 040 | 020 | 00100000 | SP (space) |
| 033 | 041 | 021 | 00100001 | ! |
| 034 | 042 | 022 | 00100010 | " |
| 035 | 043 | 023 | 00100011 | # |

| Decimal | Octal | Hexadecimal | Binary | Value |
|---|---|---|---|---|
| 036 | 044 | 024 | 00100100 | $ |
| 037 | 045 | 025 | 00100101 | % |
| 038 | 046 | 026 | 00100110 | & |
| 039 | 047 | 027 | 00100111 | ' |
| 040 | 050 | 028 | 00101000 | ( |
| 041 | 051 | 029 | 00101001 | ) |
| 042 | 052 | 02A | 00101010 | * |
| 043 | 053 | 02B | 00101011 | + |
| 044 | 054 | 02C | 00101100 | , |
| 045 | 055 | 02D | 00101101 | – |
| 046 | 056 | 02E | 00101110 | . |
| 047 | 057 | 02F | 00101111 | / |
| 048 | 060 | 030 | 00110000 | 0 |
| 049 | 061 | 031 | 00110001 | 1 |
| 050 | 062 | 032 | 00110010 | 2 |
| 051 | 063 | 033 | 00110011 | 3 |
| 052 | 064 | 034 | 00110100 | 4 |
| 053 | 065 | 035 | 00110101 | 5 |
| 054 | 066 | 036 | 00110110 | 6 |
| 055 | 067 | 037 | 00110111 | 7 |
| 056 | 070 | 038 | 00111000 | 8 |
| 057 | 071 | 039 | 00111001 | 9 |
| 058 | 072 | 03A | 00111010 | : |
| 059 | 073 | 03B | 00111011 | ; |
| 060 | 074 | 03C | 00111100 | < |
| 061 | 075 | 03D | 00111101 | = |
| 062 | 076 | 03E | 00111110 | > |
| 063 | 077 | 03F | 00111111 | ? |
| 064 | 100 | 040 | 01000000 | @ |
| 065 | 101 | 041 | 01000001 | A |
| 066 | 102 | 042 | 01000010 | B |
| 067 | 103 | 043 | 01000011 | C |
| 068 | 104 | 044 | 01000100 | D |

## Table C.1 The Standard ASCII Table (continued)

| Decimal | Octal | Hexadecimal | Binary | Value |
|---|---|---|---|---|
| 069 | 105 | 045 | 01000101 | E |
| 070 | 106 | 046 | 01000110 | F |
| 071 | 107 | 047 | 01000111 | G |
| 072 | 110 | 048 | 01001000 | H |
| 073 | 111 | 049 | 01001001 | I |
| 074 | 112 | 04A | 01001010 | J |
| 075 | 113 | 04B | 01001011 | K |
| 076 | 114 | 04C | 01001100 | L |
| 077 | 115 | 04D | 01001101 | M |
| 078 | 116 | 04E | 01001110 | N |
| 079 | 117 | 04F | 01001111 | O |
| 080 | 120 | 050 | 01010000 | P |
| 081 | 121 | 051 | 01010001 | Q |
| 082 | 122 | 052 | 01010010 | R |
| 083 | 123 | 053 | 01010011 | S |
| 084 | 124 | 054 | 01010100 | T |
| 085 | 125 | 055 | 01010101 | U |
| 086 | 126 | 056 | 01010110 | V |
| 087 | 127 | 057 | 01011111 | W |
| 088 | 130 | 058 | 01011000 | X |
| 089 | 131 | 059 | 01011001 | Y |
| 090 | 132 | 05A | 01011010 | Z |
| 091 | 133 | 05B | 01011011 | [ |
| 092 | 134 | 05C | 01011100 | \ |
| 093 | 135 | 05D | 01011101 | ] |
| 094 | 136 | 05E | 01011110 | ^ |
| 095 | 137 | 05F | 01011111 | _ |
| 096 | 140 | 060 | 01100000 | ` |
| 097 | 141 | 061 | 01100001 | a |
| 098 | 142 | 062 | 01100010 | b |
| 099 | 143 | 063 | 01100011 | c |

| Decimal | Octal | Hexadecimal | Binary | Value |
|---|---|---|---|---|
| 100 | 144 | 064 | 01100100 | d |
| 101 | 145 | 065 | 01100101 | e |
| 102 | 146 | 066 | 01100110 | f |
| 103 | 147 | 067 | 01100111 | g |
| 104 | 150 | 068 | 01101000 | h |
| 105 | 151 | 069 | 01101001 | i |
| 106 | 152 | 06A | 01101010 | j |
| 107 | 153 | 06B | 01101011 | k |
| 108 | 154 | 06C | 01101100 | l |
| 109 | 155 | 06D | 01101101 | m |
| 110 | 156 | 06E | 01101110 | n |
| 111 | 157 | 06F | 01101111 | o |
| 112 | 160 | 070 | 01110000 | p |
| 113 | 161 | 071 | 01110001 | q |
| 114 | 162 | 072 | 01110010 | r |
| 115 | 163 | 073 | 01110011 | s |
| 116 | 164 | 074 | 01110100 | t |
| 117 | 165 | 075 | 01110101 | u |
| 118 | 166 | 076 | 01110110 | v |
| 119 | 167 | 077 | 01110111 | w |
| 120 | 170 | 078 | 01111000 | x |
| 121 | 171 | 079 | 01111001 | y |
| 122 | 172 | 07A | 01111010 | z |
| 123 | 173 | 07B | 01111011 | { |
| 124 | 174 | 07C | 01111100 | \| |
| 125 | 175 | 07D | 01111101 | } |
| 126 | 176 | 07E | 01111110 | ~ |
| 127 | 177 | 07F | 01111111 | DEL (delete) |

# The C++ Keywords

The C++ language has surprisingly few keywords. However, with those 70 or so keywords, you can accomplish almost anything you will need to do as a programmer. Table D.1 provides a list of all the keywords in the C++ language. Use this list as a reference or as a stepping-stone to expand your C++ vocabulary.

**Table D.1 The C++ Keywords**

| Keyword | Description |
|---|---|
| `and` | Synonymous to the && operator. |
| `and_eq` | Synonymous to the &= operator. |
| `asm` | Use to insert assembly language code into your programs. |
| `auto` | Use to ensure that a variable is stored in automatic memory. |
| `bitand` | Synonymous to the & operator. |
| `bitor` | Synonymous to the \| operator. |
| `bool` | Boolean fundamental data type. |
| `break` | Exits a `case` statement. |
| `case` | Flow control statement. |
| `catch` | Use to catch errors. |
| `char` | Character fundamental data type. |
| `class` | Abstract data type. |
| `compl` | Synonymous to the ~ operator. |

**TABLE D.1 THE C++ KEYWORDS (CONTINUED)**

| Keyword | Description |
|---|---|
| const | Use to declare a constant. |
| const_cast | Use for converting constants to non-constants. |
| continue | Jumps to the next iteration in a loop. |
| default | Use as the default case in a switch statement. |
| delete | Use to free objects from dynamic memory. |
| do | Use in the do while loop. |
| double | A more exact version of the float. |
| dynamic_cast | Determines whether an object is of a certain type. |
| else | Use after an if statement. |
| enum | Declares the enumeration fundamental data type. |
| explicit | Use to ensure that a constructor isn't implicitly invoked. |
| export | Use to make a variable accessible to another file. |
| extern | Use to import functions and classes from other files. |
| false | Represents a bit with the value 0. |
| float | A variable that holds decimal numbers. |
| for | Use in the for iterative statement. |
| friend | Use to give certain classes or functions special access to classes. |
| goto | Flow control statement. |
| if | Use in the basic if conditional statement. |
| inline | Causes a function to be placed wherever it is called, like a macro. |
| int | Declares the integer data type. |
| long | A synonym for int. |
| mutable | A specifier that says a member can be changed in a const object of the class. |
| namespace | Use to subdivide scope. |
| new | Creates a new object in dynamic memory. |
| not | Synonymous to the ! operator. |
| not_eq | Synonymous to the != operator. |
| operator | Use to overload operators. |
| or | Synonymous to the \|\| operator. |
| or_eq | Synonymous to the \|= operator. |
| private | Specifies that the following members are private in a class. |
| protected | Specifies that the following members are protected from outside access in a class. |

| Keyword | Description |
|---|---|
| `public` | Specifies that the following member of a class will be public. |
| `register` | A specifier for a variable that tells the compiler to optimize for frequent access. |
| `reinterpret_cast` | Use to explicitly cast between unrelated types. |
| `return` | Returns a value from a function. |
| `short` | An integer type variable that takes half the memory of an integer. |
| `signed` | Specifies that an integer type value can take both positive and negative values. |
| `sizeof` | Use to find the size in memory of a data type. |
| `static` | Declares that the member is static in a class. |
| `static_cast` | Use to explicitly cast between related types. |
| `struct` | Use to create a structure (similar to an object). |
| `switch` | Use in the `switch` conditional statement. |
| `template` | Use to declare templates. |
| `this` | Points to a class's own memory address. |
| `throw` | Use to throw an exception. |
| `true` | Means that a bit has the value of `1`. |
| `try` | Use to throw errors. |
| `typedef` | Defines a type alias. |
| `typeid` | Use like `sizeof` to determine the type of an expression. |
| `typename` | Use to access the members of a template parameter. |
| `union` | A type of `struct` that can store only a single member at a time. |
| `unsigned` | Specifies that an integer type variable can take only positive numbers. |
| `using` | Use to include a namespace in the global namespace. |
| `virtual` | Declares a virtual function. |
| `void` | Specifies that a function will not return anything. |
| `volatile` | A specifier that tells the compiler an object might change its value outside C++. |
| `wchar_t` | A character type that holds more than 256 possible characters. |
| `while` | Use for `while` and `do while` statements. |
| `xor` | Synonymous to the ^ operator. |
| `xor_eq` | Synonymous to the ^= operator. |

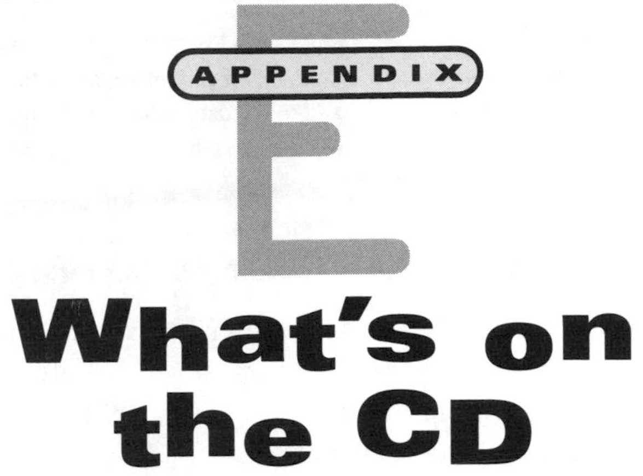


# What's on the CD

The CD that accompanies this book contains the complete DirectX 8 Software Development Kit from Microsoft. The sample files used in this book are included on the CD.

## Running the CD with Windows 95/98/2000/NT

To make the CD user-friendly and take less of your disk space, no installation is required to view the CD. This means that the only files transferred to your hard disk are the ones you choose to copy or install. You can run the CD on any operating system that can view graphical HTML pages; however, not all the programs can be installed on all operating systems.

If AutoRun is turned on, the HTML interface automatically loads into your default browser.

If AutoRun is turned off, access the CD by following these steps:

1. Insert the CD into the CD-ROM drive and close the tray.
2. Go to My Computer or Windows Explorer and double-click the CD-ROM drive.
3. Find and open the start_here.html file (this works with most HTML browsers).

**The first window you see contains the Premier Press License Agreement. Take a moment to read the agreement, and if you agree, click the I Agree button to accept the license and proceed to the user interface. If you do not agree to the terms of the license, click the I Disagree button. The CD will not load.**

## The Premier Press User Interface

The opening screen of the Premier Press user interface contains navigation buttons and a content area. The navigation buttons appear on the left side of the browser window. Navigate through the Premier Press user interface by clicking a button. Each page loads, and the content displays to the right.

For example, if you want to view the source code, click the button labeled Source Code. The new page that loads includes links to all the available source code files on the CD. Each chapter's files are compressed for easy distribution. You can uncompress the files using any unzip program. You can install WinZip from the Programs page. Alternatively, if you want to view the uncompressed files, you can navigate to the /Source Code folder on the CD. Each chapter has a separate folder.

### Resizing and Closing the User Interface

To resize the window, position the mouse over any edge or corner, click and hold the mouse, drag the edge or corner to a new position, and release the mouse when the size is acceptable.

To close and exit the user interface, select File, Exit.

# Glossary

**abstract class.** A class with a pure virtual function. You cannot create an object from an abstract class.

**access specifiers.** Specify the scope of members of a class.

**address.** A unique number that represents a memory location.

**algorithm.** The logic that accomplishes a specific task.

**allocate memory.** To declare and reserve a certain portion of memory.

**ANSI (*American National Standards Institute*).** An organization that develops standards for the computer industry.

**argument.** Data sent to a called function by a calling function.

**array.** A list that holds data with each data element referenced by its subscript.

**array, multidimensional.** An array of arrays.

**ASCII code (*American Symbolic Code for Information Interchange* code).** A code that determines a unique bit pattern for 256 characters represented by computers.

**assertion.** A statement (typically a macro) that ensures a certain condition holds true.

**automatic memory.** Memory where all local variables are stored by default.

**base class (also called *superclass* and *parent class*).** A class from which another class is derived.

**binary.** A numbering system that uses the digits 1 and 0.

**binary file.** A file, unlike text files, in which data is stored in a compressed format.

**bit.** The smallest unit of memory; typically represented by 1 or 0.

**blit (binary linear transfer).** A process in which a block of memory (usually graphics DirectX programming) moves without requiring the processor's time.

**block.** A section of C++ code offset by braces.

**boolean.** A fundamental data type that represents two possible values, true or false.

**boolean logic.** The study of the relationship between boolean data types.

**bug.** A computer error.

**byte.** A unit of memory represented by 8 bits; can store any one of 256 values.

**calling.** The act of initiating a function from another part of the program.

**calling procedure.** A function that calls another function.

**character.** A variable that can store one of 256 different characters from the ASCII character set.

**child class.** See *derived class*.

**class.** A structure that defines the characteristics of an object, including the object's data and function members.

**class hierarchy.** A tree-like structure that shows the inheritance relationship between classes.

**class template.** A class that is not specific to a certain kind of data; uses templates in order to accomplish this feat.

**code fragment.** A section of a program.

**command.** A programming language instruction.

**comment.** Informational code placed in the source code for the convenience of the programmer or someone trying to understand the code. The compiler ignores comments.

**compiler.** Converts source code to an executable format.

**compiling.** The act of sending your source code through a compiler to be converted to an executable format.

**complexity.** The measurement of an algorithm's efficiency.

**concatenation.** Merging of two or more strings.

**conditional statement.** See *control statement.*

**console application.** An application that uses a DOS-based text window rather than the Windows libraries.

**control statement.** A statement that alters the flow of a program based on a condition.

**constructor.** A function with the same name as its class. The constructor is executed every time an object derived from that class is created. Used to declare memory and assign initial properties to an object.

**C-style strings.** An array of characters terminated by 0.

**debugging.** The process of removing errors from a program.

**declare.** To inform the computer about the name and attributes of a variable, function, or class.

**decremental operators.** The -- operators used to decrease the value of a variable by one.

**derive.** To create a class from another class.

**derived class (also called a *subclass* or *child class*).** A class formed from a base class that inherits all the base class's characteristics.

**derives-from.** Another name for a type-of relationship.

**destructor.** A member function that is automatically executed when an object is deleted. The destructor has the same name as the class, preceded by a ~.

**development cycle.** The general steps taken when creating and debugging a program.

**disk memory.** The memory—made up of hard drives, CD-ROMs, floppy drives, zip drives, and so on—that stores data on a semi-permanent basis.

**DirectDraw.** The 2D graphics portion of the DirectX library.

**DirectX.** A library published by Microsoft, primarily for graphics and game interaction. DirectX enables programmers to interact directly with the end user's hardware without concern about compatibility issues.

**dynamic memory (also called the *free store* and *heap*).** A section of memory that programmers can access for new data. Allocated and deallocated with the `new` and `delete` operators.

**element.** One piece of data from an array.

**encapsulation.** A principle of OOP in which objects do one, and only one, specific task.

**escape characters.** A special set of characters used to represent other characters that cannot easily be in literal form (for example, a line break).

**exception handling.** Handling of nonroutine circumstances in a program.

**extractions.** Removal of bytes from a stream.

**extractors.** The functions that perform extractions.

**free store.** See *dynamic memory.*

**freeing memory.** The process of telling the computer that you are finished with a particular section of memory.

**function.** A section of code that performs a specific task when called.

**function declaration.** Introduces a function to a program and defines the function's return type, name, and arguments. Also called a *prototype.*

**function definition.** The implementation of code inside a function.

**function template.** A function that is not specific to any one data type. It uses a template to accomplish this.

**fundamental types.** The data types built into the C++ language.

**global.** A variable that can be accessed anywhere within a source file.

**heap.** See *dynamic memory.*

**header files.** The files you include in C++ programs that often represent the C++ standard library files.

**hexadecimal.** A base-16 numbering system that uses the numbers 0–9 and the letters A–F to create 16 unique digits.

**identifiers.** Names given to variables so that programmers can conveniently refer to the variables later in the program.

**implementation.** The definition of a function.

**incremental operators.** The ++ operator that increments a variable by one.

**index (also called a *subscript*).** A number used to access a particular element of an array.

**inheritance.** The derivation of one class from another.

**inheritance chain.** The inheritance line of a class.

**initializer list for arrays.** A list of values separated by commas; used to initialize an array.

**initializer list for objects.** A list of values after the constructor that initializes the variables of an object.

**input/output (I/O).** A term used to describe the way in which a computer communicates with the outside world. Input devices include the mouse, keyboards, joysticks, and so on. Output devices include monitors, printers, speakers, and so on.

**inserters.** The functions that perform stream insertions.

**insertions.** Place bytes into an I/O stream.

**integer.** A variable type that stores only whole numbers (can be positive, negative, and zero).

**integer wrapping.** When an integer reaches one more than its maximum value, it "wraps," thereby setting the integer to its minimum value.

**Integrated Development Environment (IDE).** A graphical interface that incorporates your compiler, file browser, settings, and source code editor.

**iterative control statements.** Control statements that allow the repetition of code based on a condition.

**jump statements.** Keywords used to jump the flow of a program from one part to another bypassing everything in between.

**kilobyte.** A unit of memory made up of 1024 bytes. One of the primary units of memory measurement.

**libraries.** Sets of compiled code that you can use in your programs.

**line break.** A meta-character that represents a new line.

**linking.** The process of checking to see whether the code works with all the files that you include in a program, not only your files, but also external libraries such as DirectX.

**literals.** A representation of actual data values in a program. Numbers are literally represented by the Arabic number system (1, 2, 3, and so on); strings are represented by letters and numbers enclosed within quotation marks.

**local.** A variable that is declared within a function. It can be accessed only within that function.

**lvalues.** Expressions that can be assigned to or located on the left side of an equal sign in an assignment statement.

**machine language.** The compiled, executable version of a program.

**macros.** Directives that enable you to assign a name to an expression or other program element.

**main function.** The first function to execute when a program begins. The most common prototype is `int main(void)`.

**manipulators.** Manipulate the data of the stream in some way. For example, a manipulator might make all characters uppercase or convert decimal numbers to hexadecimal.

**mathematical operator.** An operator that performs mathematical functions such as addition and subtraction.

**memory.** The part of the computer where data is stored and retrieved. The most common sources are hard drives, disks, and random access memory (RAM).

**meta-character**. A character that doesn't display onscreen but that is used by the computer for special formatting or to represent other characters. These characters include tabs, line breaks, and so on.

**modulus operator (%).** The remainder of x divided by y (`x % y`).

**multiple inheritance.** When a derived class has more than one base class.

**namespace.** A C++ keyword used to divide a single scope into multiple subscopes.

**nesting.** Placing `if` statements (and other control statements) inside other control statements.

**null pointer (also called *undeclared pointer*).** A pointer that stores the value of 0 and that is assumed not to be pointing to data.

**null zero.** The terminating character of a string; represented by the escape character, `\0`.

**object.** A specific instance of a class.

**object-oriented programming (OOP).** A technique of programming that activates data by creating objects that have both characteristics and code.

**operands.** Values that operators manipulate.

**operation.** A phrase containing both an operator and its operands.

**operator**. Any symbol or double symbols such as <=—and, in some cases, even words such as `sizeof()`—that cause the compiler to take an action.

**operator overloading.** Creating new uses for existing operators.

**order.** The growth pattern of an algorithm.

**order of operation.** The precedence that some operators have over others. For example, the + operator has a lower precedence than the * operator. Therefore, it is executed after the * operator unless overridden by a higher operator such as parentheses.

**order of precedence.** See *order of operation.*

**overloading.** To create more than one version of a function with the same name. The computer uses the arguments to determine which version to call.

**overriding.** When a derived class declares a method with the same name as one from its base class. The derived version is preferred when using a derived class object.

**parameter.** See *argument.*

**parent class.** See *base class.*

**pointer.** A variable that stores a memory address of another data value.

**point of instantiation.** When a class template or function template is generated from a particular set of template parameters.

**polymorphism.** A principle of OOP in which each object can be used in more than one program.

**program.** A sequence of instructions that are executed by a computer. Also, the process of entering source code into the computer to be compiled and run.

**prototype (also called a *function prototype*).** A function's representation; used so that the compiler can set up the function. The prototype contains the return type, function name, and type of variables that should be passed.

**pure virtual function.** A virtual function that is not implemented but that is used only to create abstract classes.

**quadratic.** Any equation that can be expressed in the following form:

ax^(2) + bx + c

**quotient.** The result from the division of two numbers.

**Random-Access Memory (RAM).** The memory that temporarily stores data while the computer is turned on.

**random numbers.** Numbers that appear in seemingly random order; generated from complex mathematical formulas.

**recursion.** A method of programming where a function calls itself.

**return value.** Data that is sent back from a function to the calling function; often used for returning numerical results from a function's calculations.

**scalar variables.** Variables that can hold only one piece of data as opposed to array data.

**scope.** A variable's range defined by how much of the surrounding source code can use the variable.

**scientific notation.** A succinct way to represent numbers of extreme magnitude.

**shadow.** A local variable that is declared with the same name as a global variable; the local variable takes precedence when the variable's name is used.

**single inheritance.** A derived class that has one and only one base class.

**source code.** The text representation of a program, written in a programming language such as C++.

**static memory.** The part of memory where the compiler stores static and global variables.

**static variables.** Variables that retain their values throughout the whole program but do not necessarily have global scope.

**stream object.** Acts as both a source and a destination for the input and output (I/O) of data. The stream object manipulates an ordered linear sequence of bytes.

**string.** An object type that stores a sequence of characters in a character array, terminated by a null zero.

**subclass.** See *derived class.*

**subscript.** A number that represents a single data element from an array.

**substring.** A string formed from part or all of another string.

**superclass.** See *base class.*

**surface flip.** When the graphics pointer is changed from one DirectDraw surface object to another.

**surface, DirectDraw.** A block of memory used to store images.

**switch statement.** A statement that utilizes the `switch` keyword to execute specific code based on selected cases.

**template.** A way of generalizing a class or function so that it doesn't use any particular data type.

**template parameter.** A parameter, such as a function parameter, that stores a type of data.

**test chassis.** A function that is used to test the capabilities of an object.

**text file.** A file whose data is represented by characters.

**try-block.** A section of code that attempts to catch any exceptions that are thrown.

**type-of.** A relationship between two elements where one is a category and the other is an object from that category.

**type.** A representation of data, such as an integer and a floating-point.

**type alias.** Another name for a type; often specified with the `typedef` keyword.

**undeclared pointer.** See *null pointer.*

**unsigned variable.** An integer type variable that can store only positive values.

**variable.** A named memory location where data is stored within a program.

**variable lifetime.** The amount of time that the memory used for a variable is reserved.

**variable scope.** The range of a program where a particular variable can be accessed.

**vector.** A complex data structure that is part of the standard library. It is in the `<vector>` library.

**virtual functions.** Polymorphistic functions that ensure the correct class is referenced when pointing to a virtual function.

**Win32.** A 32-bit Windows application that uses the Windows libraries rather than the 16-bit DOS system.

**Windows messages.** Messages that Windows sends to a Win32 program when events occur, such as when the user clicks a mouse button.

**wrapper class.** A class that extends the basic functionality of a primitive data type or object.

# Index

## symbols



## A

## B



## C

# D

## E



## F

## G

## K

## L



## M

## N



## O

## P

## Q



## R



## S

## T

## U



## V



## W

# License Agreement/Notice of Limited Warranty

By opening the sealed disk container in this book, you agree to the following terms and conditions. If, upon reading the following license agreement and notice of limited warranty, you cannot agree to the terms and conditions set forth, return the unused book with unopened disk to the place where you purchased it for a refund.

**License:**

The enclosed software is copyrighted by the copyright holder(s) indicated on the software disk. You are licensed to copy the software onto a single computer for use by a single concurrent user and to a backup disk. You may not reproduce, make copies, or distribute copies or rent or lease the software in whole or in part, except with written permission of the copyright holder(s). You may transfer the enclosed disk only together with this license, and only if you destroy all other copies of the software and the transferee agrees to the terms of the license. You may not decompile, reverse assemble, or reverse engineer the software.

**Notice of Limited Warranty:**

The enclosed disk is warranted by Premier Press to be free of physical defects in materials and workmanship for a period of sixty (60) days from end user's purchase of the book/disk combination. During the sixty-day term of the limited warranty, Premier Press will provide a replacement disk upon the return of a defective disk.

**Limited Liability:**

THE SOLE REMEDY FOR BREACH OF THIS LIMITED WARRANTY SHALL CONSIST ENTIRELY OF REPLACEMENT OF THE DEFECTIVE DISK. IN NO EVENT SHALL PREMIER PRESS OR THE AUTHORS BE LIABLE FOR ANY OTHER DAMAGES, INCLUDING LOSS OR CORRUPTION OF DATA, CHANGES IN THE FUNCTIONAL CHARACTERISTICS OF THE HARDWARE OR OPERATING SYSTEM, DELETERIOUS INTERACTION WITH OTHER SOFTWARE, OR ANY OTHER SPECIAL, INCIDENTAL, OR CONSEQUENTIAL DAMAGES THAT MAY ARISE, EVEN IF PREMIER PRESS AND/OR THE AUTHOR HAVE PREVIOUSLY BEEN NOTIFIED THAT THE POSSIBILITY OF SUCH DAMAGES EXISTS.

**Disclaimer of Warranties:**

PREMIER PRESS AND THE AUTHORS SPECIFICALLY DISCLAIM ANY AND ALL OTHER WARRANTIES, EITHER EXPRESS OR IMPLIED, INCLUDING WARRANTIES OF MERCHANTABILITY, SUITABILITY TO A PARTICULAR TASK OR PURPOSE, OR FREEDOM FROM ERRORS. SOME STATES DO NOT ALLOW FOR EXCLUSION OF IMPLIED WARRANTIES OR LIMITATION OF INCIDENTAL OR CONSEQUENTIAL DAMAGES, SO THESE LIMITATIONS MAY NOT APPLY TO YOU.

**Other:**

This Agreement is governed by the laws of the State of California without regard to choice of law principles. The United Convention of Contracts for the International Sale of Goods is specifically disclaimed. This Agreement constitutes the entire agreement between you and Premier Press regarding use of the software.